Interviews
with
Contemporary Writers

Interviews
with
Contemporary Writers

Second Series, 1972–1982

Edited by L. S. Dembo

THE UNIVERSITY OF WISCONSIN PRESS

Published 1983

The University of Wisconsin Press
114 North Murray Street
Madison, Wisconsin 53715

The University of Wisconsin Press, Ltd.
1 Gower Street
London WC1E 6HA, England

First printing

Printed in the United States of America

ISBN 0-299-09330-1 cloth; 0-299-09334-4 paper
LC 82-051092

Contents

Prefatory Note

When, in 1972, we published our first series of interviews from *Contemporary Literature,* we argued that this "genre" had possibilities extending far beyond the literary gossip or small talk of which many interviews seemed to consist. Ironically, we had in mind, as the example we did not want to follow, the kind of interview that regularly appeared in *The Paris Review,* the very journal that had been praised by Malcolm Cowley for not only raising the standards of, but virtually inventing, the modern interview in English. Surveying the first *Paris Review* collection (*Writers at Work*) Cowley had gone on to synthesize the material under the rubric "How Writers Write," wherein he dealt with such matters as stages in the composition of a story ("First comes the germ . . . then a period of more or less conscious meditation, then the first draft, and finally the revision") the nature of the writer's working day ("The hardest problem for any writer . . . is getting to work in the morning"), the reason a writer writes ("self-expression, self-discovery, self-aggrandizement, or the pain of not writing," and whatever new purposes develop out of his accomplished work), and so forth.

I shall not be so foolish as to argue that these concerns have no value as sources of information or entertainment. Indeed Cowley sees those who have conducted such interviews as the first really competent interviewers of literary figures: "[In the past] most of the interviewers either have had no serious interest in literature or else have been too serious about themselves. Either they have been reporters with little knowledge of the author's work and a desire to entrap him into making scandalous remarks about sex, politics, and God, or else they have been ambitious writers trying to display their own sophistication, usually at the expense of the author, and listening chiefly to their own voices." Still, if questions on the writer's "craft" represent a higher standard than the truly trivial or leading questions of the pre-*Paris Review* days, they tell us little about the details of his work and the personal, social, and philosophic contexts in which they become significant. Usually, writers talking off-the-cuff about sex, politics, and God are, it seems to me, not so much scandalous as merely banal, but writers responding ex-tempore to routine questions on their work habits, their list of greats, or their estimate of the current literary scene are no more exciting and a lot less revealing. They may or may not satisfy the curious, but they exasperate anyone with a genuine interest in the writing itself.

Accordingly, our approach demanded more from the interviewer and more from the author: from the one, a comprehensive and in-depth knowledge of the work; from the other, a willingness to discuss the writing in detail. The success of this method depended upon the interviewer's ability to establish an emotional and intellectual rapport with his subject, and correspondingly, on the subject's ability to overcome both personal and socially decreed taboos against talking about one's own work.

But if things didn't work out, that was also all right. We were not so singleminded as not to realize that the interview is an event as much as a record, and that spontaneity and personal charisma can elevate what might be no more than a record into an experience. For the interview is indeed an emotional situation, with considerable risk taken by all participants—an engagement of personalities in which a lapse of tact, knowledgeability, or attention can end in ruination. Although such moments make far more exciting reading than successful but less colorful interviews, they rarely see print, for either they reveal more than any of the participants wants revealed or else hard feelings have soured the whole enterprise. (As one can guess, I have actual episodes in mind that I'd just as soon not elaborate upon.)

The interviews published in *Contemporary Literature* over the past decade by and large follow this policy and, when they don't, they have something of their own to offer. Of the three dozen or so, about a third were conducted by members of the staff or persons to whom we could speak directly on guidelines. Most of the others were conducted by persons who, either through their own initiative or at our request familiarized themselves with the kind of interview we desired. Several unsolicited pieces were accepted on their own merits. All this represented a divergence from the first collection, which contained sixteen interviews spanning six years and for the most part conducted by only three of us working in close association. These have a unity of approach that is, in its extent, not duplicated in the present volume. (We also believed at the time that they were sufficiently unified in theme to warrant an index and a long introduction calling attention to important relationships. These have not been duplicated, either.)

But what it lacks in unity, this collection, we feel, gains in variety, scope, and sheer number of well-known authors. Whereas in the first volume, foreign writers were represented by only Per Olaf Sundman and Sara Lidman (two Swedish novelists of great appeal but virtually unread in the U. S.), Jorge Luis Borges, and the British poet, George Barker, the present one contains in-depth sessions with Swiss novelist/playwright Max Frisch, the Japanese novelist/playwright Abé Kobo (held in Abé's Tokyo studio by Nancy Hardin, who merely in gaining entrance achieved the nearly impossible); French novelists Marguerite Duras, Nathalie Sarraute (Interviewer Germaine Brée has had a longtime intimate knowledge of and association with the Parisian scene), Alain Robbe-Grillet, and Michel Butor; British writers Kingsley Amis, Charles Tomlinson, Angus Wilson, Margaret Drabble, and South African novelist Nadine Gordimer.

Beyond their appeal as individual interviews they do form a mosaic that reflects recent literary history. The French writers are all associated with, or were influenced by, the *nouveau roman,* and most of the British have ties with the Movement; American poets Blackburn, Dorn, and Duncan, with the Black Mountain School. On the other hand, we are certain that the chief value of these pieces lies finally not only in the stature of their subjects or their record of the literary trends of the recent past; it lies as well in the vitality of the writer stimulated by an informed, sympathetic interviewer to engage in substantive discussion of his work and life.

A large part of the editorial work on these interviews was done, by various members of the staff of *Contemporary Literature,* at the time of their original appearance in print. I am especially indebted to Catherine Rasmussen (managing editor between 1977 and 1982), Betsy Draine (associate editor), and Nancy Pellmann (administrative assistant).

September, 1982   L. S. Dembo
Madison, Wisconsin

Interviews
with
Contemporary Writers

An Interview with Max Frisch

*Conducted by Rolf Kieser**

Q. Mr. Frisch, you said recently that you are disillusioned with the theater.

A. It's true that I feel uneasy about the theater—my own as well as that in general. Actually, I seldom go to the theater. I don't know exactly why. As far as my own plays are concerned, I must admit that after *The Firebugs* and *Andorra,* I developed a dissatisfaction with the parable.

Let me first explain how I came to use the parable: I did not use it only because of Brecht's example—there are others, too—but rather because the parable is one of several ways to avoid the theater of imitation, since the theater of imitation is to me a total mistake. It is the kind of theater represented in plays such as those by Tennessee Williams where something is shown on stage as if it were a copy of nature. This kind of drama cultivates "illusionism" and that is certainly not the mission of the theater. We see enough of nature and life ourselves. What we want is something different. "Illusionism," by the way, is a blunder of a later period of the theater. Neither the original drama, the ancient drama, the medieval drama, nor the Shakespearean drama were imitative. In each the play did not represent reality but instead created a new kind of reality. Desiring to avoid this later tendency of the theater, I wrote, for example, the costume-play. My *Don Juan* is from the onset a play that knows it is one. Furthermore I wrote *The Great Wall of China* (incidentally, a play which I do not particularly like) which from the

---

* The interview, conducted in German, was held on April 23 and May 11, 1971, in New York City. The translation is by the interviewer.

3

beginning is a revue and does not depict reality at all. Finally, I tried
out the parable since this form does not claim to be a story about something that actually happened. Its connection with reality lies only in the
fact that the parable develops a meaning that can be applied to reality.
Therefore the parable has always and unfailingly a tendency to be
didactic. It concludes with a meaning, thus becoming a *Lehrstück*. And
so it happens that through the form as such, one assumes a didactic
attitude. This means that one delivers a message, a didactic message,
which is not necessarily intended and in which one is not interested.
The doubts I had at the time about my didactic vocation in the theater
were expressed in that abstruse subtitle *Ein Lehrstück ohne Lehre*. Let
me add just one more thing to what I said about my uneasiness in reference to the parable. Some time ago I saw a first production of *Turandot,
or the Congress of the Whitewashers* which, by the way, is not a very
accomplished play, and I saw there, too, how questionable the parable
is, by the fact that it can work in either direction. This, I feel, is also
true for the *Firebugs*. One could say that one thing is meant or another.
It can be asked why I do not spell out what is meant—is it the bourgeoisie or is it fascism? How is it based on history? Well, I have to answer
that it can refer to this or to that but it is not necessarily so. That proves
that the parable is vague.

Q.   Do you believe that all those misunderstandings in connection with
Andorra also have their origin in this ambiguity of the parable?

A.   Yes, it applies there, too. In *Andorra* the parable goes so far as to
set up antisemitism as an example only—"only," of course, being a
strange word in relation to the tragedy which in this century is historically connected with it. But it is not a play about antisemitism; the latter
is used as an exemplary motive, yet the spectator tends to focus on anti-
semitism as the topic (at least in those countries where it exists). When
the play was performed in South America, the accent was placed differently. The outcast, the scapegoat, was identified there with the leftist
minority—again, an example of how the parable can be easily applied
in different ways. That is the reason I wanted to get out of it by starting
the experiment of *Biography,* where I was most concerned about eliminating the illusion that we, as voyeurs, take part in reality. My experiences with this play—which was successful—are negative because when
the play is performed in that psychological manner (which is also part
of the play, of course), an illusion is created over and over again through
the dialogue: Now we are taking part in the real thing. Or rather, it is
not the illusion that exists as much as the embarrassing notion that the

performance forces me into entering an illusion which, of course, I cannot accept.

Q.   It is your opinion, then, that *Biography* does not reflect sufficiently the rehearsal-situation?

A.   It is too little of a rehearsal. The structure of the play, after all, was of interest to me, too. It is like a chess game played backwards. That is the reason I have chosen such a trivial, or let us say, average topic, a biography which does not interest me as such, which is average in the sense that it does not show us a criminal, for instance, neither a terribly poor person nor an important person. The plot did not interest me but the structure did. Now, while illusion is created on stage, phase after phase, the structure disappears and the plot appears. And this plot is trivial. It is unimportant whether the protagonist finally gets his Antoinette or not. That is why I was disappointed with the play. It did not turn out the way I wanted it to. The stage proved me wrong. The stage has much more of an illusionary power than I wished for. One would therefore have to continue—at this point I do not yet know how —by digressing much more radically from all, let us call it, natural content or from all styles of performance which are still relatively close to imitation. The new development of the drama clearly points away from imitation which first of all means away from literature. The theater regains a consciousness of itself by reducing itself to the play of the body, the pantomime, to different kinds of dance. The word does not matter anymore, or it matters very little. Personally, I do not deplore this development at all, although primarily it eliminates us, the authors, completely.

Q.   You are presently engaged in writing narrative prose. Do you expect to find in your prose work that which you cannot realize in the drama?

A.   The prose narrative, the novel, and the story, as we know, have for some time been in crisis. It started with the realistic novel, and we could call it the crisis of fictionality. What is our attitude toward the fictional character of a story? Homer, for example, did not have this particular problem. He was the singer who sang; that is, he told something which the reader, the receiver, the listener, knew already—namely, the saga. Still open was the manner in which it was performed, the way it was told. One knew that the war of Troy had taken place. One knew that this hero was cunning, that one was a coward. Homer did not have to introduce, but only to produce. This is one position—the delivery, the presentation of an already known topic. Then there is another narrative position, that of the evangelists, who, of course, are not generally placed in the same class with writers of literature. But let me mention them anyway. They are the witnesses who are not asked where they received all their information. Even if the individual disciple does not have the information, the collective of the disciples will, by being united through faith. If one of them has heard this or that about the Lord Jesus, it is true for the others, too.

Now we have the next step. (I have to leave out several intermediary stages, of course.) There is, for example, *Don Quixote,* the made-up novel. There the narrator does not have to, and does not want to, achieve credibility, to insist that everything really happened in such a way that a gentleman took his cardboard hat and marched off. The work is pure fantasy, pure invention. Nobody questions the position of the narrator. It works like a joke; it either convinces you or it does not. If it does convince you and if I tell you afterwards that it really happened that way, I spoil it. It becomes uninteresting. The problem of the novel, of the narration, actually began only with the realistic novel, Tolstoy's *Anna Karenina,* for example. One cannot help wondering how the narrator knows what Anna is thinking, or Vronsky, or the others. Here the narrator assumes the difficult and questionable position of omniscience. From here we see the consequences with regard to the *nouveau roman* and to that which we can call pure optical prose. None of this applies to the theater.

The problem in prose is whether to incorporate fictionality into our consciousness. I tried it and others did too. I tried it in *A Wilderness of Mirrors.* At no point is it maintained there that anything actually happened, that one actually said something, but rather that it could have happened, that one could have said something. (The key phrase is: "I imagine . . . .") Everything is elevated to the conditional mood. After completing this novel I tried to do the same on stage. I did not mean to demonstrate that the story took place in this or that manner; I wanted to show how it could have happened differently, thus fictionally. At that time I believed that the stage was the right place for such a demonstration. But something strange became evident; namely, that each time something is performed it instantly turns into the present, thus achieving a false authenticity. That is, one feels it is happening now or it happened exactly like that. This is simply a theoretical error which I tracked down to this point.

Q. Here we are approaching the problem of coincidence. Would you still maintain, as you did in the last sentence of your *Diary*, that "it is always the due which falls due"?

A. I have always been somehow concerned with coincidence and with accident, although, at the beginning, in a more religious way. Today I would regard that sentence from the *Diary* as not exactly a pun. But it appears to me a mere formulation and not entirely true since the undue also falls due. The term "probability" means that something is probable in ninety-nine out of one hundred cases. But the hundredth case is also possible. I am uneasy in regard to the dramatic theory which we have learned is caused by the fact that a story—and always a particular one—is demonstrated, narrated, played, as if it were real life. There you can make up for an action which you regret, but you cannot change it. If we had had a quarrel and I were embarrassed about the things I told you, I could apologize and try to watch my tongue next time, but I could not undo what I had done. Therefore everything that happens always assumes a meaning that I cannot accept—namely, that it had to happen. Thus dramatic theory forced me into a faith in coincidence which I do not have at all.

Q. Your friend and colleague Friedrich Dürrenmatt also discussed the playwright's problem of dealing with the element of coincidence. Although it is obviously wrong to compare the works of the two most prominent contemporary Swiss authors too closely, I wonder if there has not been something like a dialectical exchange between you and Dürrenmatt—one that becomes evident in some of your plays?

A. First let me refer to your initial remarks. There was a time, which fortunately has passed, when the two of us, for very simple reasons, were always mentioned together, like Castor and Pollux. After the war there were very few, almost no, German playwrights. Both of us are Swiss— I am somewhat older than he—and that is one more reason they linked us, not realizing how great the differences are. Our viewpoints, our kinds of talent, and the points of departure of our thinking are entirely different. Fortunately this nonsense has stopped—first because we are not alone anymore and second because we are no longer the advance guard. Therefore, everything has become less interesting. Of course, at the time of production each one of us took a friendly and critical interest in the other's work, that is quite clear. Had I had a partner like Sartre, certain elements in my work would have responded to the fact; had I had a partner like Montherlant the answer again would have been different. After all, one does not work in a vacuum. I do not believe, however, that there was a real dialectical exchange, simply because we are unintelligible to each other even though we are good colleagues. I frankly do not believe that a study about our mutual influence would yield more than a trifle.

Q. A passage from your *Count Öderland* comes to my mind and a parallel passage from Dürrenmatt's *Marriage of Mississippi*. Why this sudden appearance of the two counts at almost the same time— Überlohe and Öderland . . . ?

A. Yes, and there is also the public prosecutor, isn't there? Well, let me tell you how it happened. When I told Dürrenmatt what I was doing and he told me about his project, we both burst into laughter because of our "independence." "So you are having an affair with a public prosecutor, too!" each of us said. But each found his own public prosecutor by following a completely different path. In my case the prosecutor is obviously the representative of a social order, of the bourgeois middle-class order; in his case the prosecutor is the representative of human justice in contrast to the absurd divine justice. For Dürrenmatt, it is the prosecutor himself who is an assassin, since human justice, according to his religious background, is not possible.

Q. Let me return to what you said before about your prose work. You are about to publish a new diary. When Horst Bienek asked you some years ago why you were writing your novels in the form of diaries, you answered almost grumpily by using the parable of the pointed nose. . . .

A. One cannot do it differently. . . .

Q. Do you see in the diary—I dare to go back to this theme once more—the chance of a parallel connection or combination of fiction and of experienced reality? Is this the reason you began to work on a new diary?

A. That is a possible explanation. *De facto,* it is the way you suggest. After having written my first plays as a student, and then later on when I got into the more serious period of writing, there were diary items which I do not want to mention at this point. The two novels *Stiller* and *Homo Faber* clearly have a notebook structure, although there are different motivations for it. Stiller, as you know, has to write a diary in order to please his attorney. He is involved in a struggle. The other one, threatened by death, wishes to call himself to account: this results in another notebook. Then there was the actual *Diary,* and there is this new one right now. It may indeed have something to do with the fact that I wish to confront what is fictional, like the narration or the drama, with—as far as it is comprehensible at all—the obvious, let us call it the *de facto,* reality. In my first *Diary* there were fictional beginnings, sketches, incorporated into a calendar: '46, '47, I saw this, I experienced that. There will be a similar structure in my new diary; at least it looks that way for the time being. (I have worked on it for six years now and I intend to finish it shortly.) It consists of mere reports—for example, "journey to Russia" or "meeting people." And there is the other branch containing the reflections whose present appearance is a mystery, but there they are. Perhaps there is a subconscious connection that appears in fictional modes of which one cannot figure out the connection with reality. But they can be connected, and it is a matter of research. Yes, it is true, the diary has something to do with the problem of our consciousness with regard to fiction. First I have a forefront reality. Let us assume I described how I drove with you through Brooklyn and Queens today (don't worry, I won't) and I indicated the exact date and what I had seen in the manner of a report. Then suppose I wrote a reflection or a fictional story. The fiction would then be much more aware of its own fictionality and would therefore be much purer than one I simply invented. For example, I would never again—actually, I never did it before . . . oh yes, on second thought, I did it in *Stiller*—I would never again mix with fiction things I could say nonfictionally, too. Our problem is how to deal with our consciousness, in that we tell things that did not happen or of which we could not possibly know. We can do that, we must do that, in order to create an image of our experiences. But we should know exactly, or rather, we want to know, whether *this* has been invented or *that* has been seen. In the diary this conflict always becomes evident. But I would like to get out of it again after the past six years. Frankly, I'm not very sure what I'll do next. All I know is that I would like to spend some time again with pure fiction, either with drama or prose.

Q.   How come you haven't yet tried to express yourself in poetry?

A.   Well, I did a very long time ago. I simply cannot come to grips with it . . . no talent for poetry. Or, if I ever tried it, as a twenty-year-old, for instance, it was nothing but a copy of other poems. I shall never try again; that's certain.

Q.   "Narratability" seems to have become one of the central problems of contemporary literature. Such writers as Bichsel, Wondratschek, and Handke try different approaches. You already talked about the position of the narrator. How would you describe your attitude towards language as a medium?

A. You mentioned Handke. In his hitherto existing work you do not find descriptive literature anymore. The question is whether literature still has the same obligation it undoubtedly had at an earlier age— namely, to give information about conditions. Today we have different sources of information; we have documents, more than any previous epoch ever had; we have tapes; we preserve everything on film so that literature simply does not have this compulsion to inform anymore. Thus it has become free to do something else, to become a linguistic work of art that goes beyond information and establishes a counter-reality.

Q. Fiction and nonfiction blend in certain works of literature. There is the still prevailing discussion about documentary literature. It looks as if the document in contemporary German literature is used in many different ways. I am thinking of such playwrights as Weiss, Hochhuth, Kipphardt, and Walser, and of the novelist Kluge. Can this kind of literature in which the author relinquishes his own language still be called real literature?

A. Actually, I do not know myself what literature is and what it is supposed to be. After all, our problem of fictionality relates to our doubts about factuality. I can proceed in a documentary manner by stating precisely, this happened at exactly that time; I was then in Washington, taking part in that particular rally; there were two thousand demonstrators or two hundred thousand or approximately three hundred thousand. . . . All this looks like fact. But even if we knew exactly how many people were there (which nobody does), such a figure would mean nothing. For my novel *A Wilderness of Mirrors* I had the theory that experience was a sudden idea, not a result of stories. Quite the contrary. Experience *is* a sudden idea, but this idea cannot be tolerated unless it is illustrated by stories. These stories can be purely fictional, but they can also include documentary material functioning as interpretation. The facts as such never declare themselves. We always manipulate them, and it is impossible to cover all of them. A computer could do it but in that case nothing would be expressed anymore. The selection of facts already means interpretation, representing an intent, and it is therefore not so important whether the material is fictional or factual.

Concerning the authors you mentioned, I have a high esteem for Peter Weiss as a prose writer and as the author of *Marat/Sade*. His later plays such as *The Investigation* and *The Bogy* appear nonsensical to me since there on stage the document loses exactly the element which makes a document interesting: authenticity. If someone like you or me stands there and speaks the authentic sentences of Kaduk, the concentration camp warder, the authenticity is lessened by the fact that a play is being performed. That which a play like *The Investigation* communicates and evokes I can find in pure documentation, too; and, in my opinion, it is much stronger at that—that is, more precise. In this instance I do not know whether it is literature or not, but in any case, it makes no sense.

Q. In your play *Biography* you use a technique of projecting world news above the plot of the drama. Is this meant as confrontation of facts and fiction?

A. There is another reason for that. There I use world history like a calendar, as a kind of optical clock, so that we know something happened at a certain time—like the fall of Khrushchev. I used this calendar because the play takes place in a private world and because we should not get deeply involved in the private life of this particular man; actually, we cannot get involved at all. But we do know: "Ah! This was before the Hungarian uprising." Those are the collectively obliging dates, so to speak, as in contrast to the particular date on which the protagonist became acquainted with the lady, Antoinette—a date that is of no concern to us. Thus I used this element simply as a screen, as a calendar. To be accurate, I should add that I also used the device to play off the limited relevance of a private life against the events of our time. I did so in order to demonstrate how little those things which happen to us have to do with real events. I do not suggest thereby that my problems or yours are therefore eliminated; they must be dealt with even though they are of no concern to the world.

Q. In *Biography* you use world events like the pages of a calendar or like the seconds of a relentlessly ticking clock. In your diaries and in some of the novels, we find the calendar being used as a framework of time within which events and experiences take place. Calendar, clock— are these your favorite metaphors of time?

A. What has interested me from the beginning are the two kinds of time. There is first chronology, watch-time, the date of yesterday, today, this morning, this afternoon, tonight; the other is time as the experience of something which is transitory, and the two of them do not go together. As far as experiences are concerned, it is possible that an experience you had last night—which you can localize temporarily—does not interest you at all, but at the same time by association you remember an experience of your school days or a war-time event. This is as present as the fact that I was here or there last night. We experience according to the rules of "experience-time." Chronological time is merely an auxiliary construction which seems objectively correct and which has always been a formidable obstacle for fiction. Musil, in his *Man Without Qualities,* writes about this, jeering at our attempt to look for a sequential order so that we can reach a logical order or an order in the sequence of our experiences. Therefore, we are trying to create a simultaneity of experienced events in fiction even when we date them by stating that eighty years ago the situation was such and such. It means that something I remember, as reminiscence, becomes present. I experience, in the present, that spring is here again. It is a transitional experience. Winter has disappeared and there will be another spring, etc. Fiction, of course, deals primarily with experience-time. Chronological time, or (shall we call it) historical time, is secondary. This is the reason we become bored whenever we run into a story which is based on the chronological time structure. The narrator, with a certain naive cunning, makes us believe, as others did in earlier times, that he is unable to tell us what will happen afterwards. He crawls along as slowly as a snail, just up to a certain point but not beyond. As you know, this scheme was already violated by such writers as Kleist. Just think of the Kleist novella which anticipates the end. In *The Marquise of O.,* we already know at the beginning what has happened. We are in fact eliminating the chronological sequence, and only afterwards do we return to it.

Q.   To what extent does the world of experience of your home country, Switzerland, affect your literary work?

A.   Well, one did not simply drop from heaven. One was born. It was in that country I had my experiences—school experiences as a child, and then everything else. I have to work with these experiences, and I cannot simply exchange them for others, even if I wanted to. For example, as far as the United States is concerned, a country which interests me very much, I have to admit that there are things, a great many things in fact, about which I cannot write at all. I did not go to school here; I have never been poor here; I did not experience my puberty here. To be sure, I can see all these things, but particularly as a narrative author—much less as a dramatist or as a lyricist—one is bound by one's material experiences. It so happens that I had them in Switzerland and this results in a bond against which I may protest but which no protest can dissolve.

Q. In your *Diary*, after having met Brecht who let you proofread his *Little Organon for the Theatre*, you were asking yourself whether it was possible to adopt the concept of alienation for prose fiction, too. Did you ever consciously try to apply the technique of alienation to your own prose or was your question merely rhetorical?

A. It was actually a belated question which had already been answered for a long time. Of course, alienation exists in prose fiction. I myself tried it, too, in *A Wilderness of Mirrors* and in some of the narrative sketches of my new *Diary II*. The question was then naive because of my lack of knowledge of contemporary literature. I am, of course, not the only one who has tried it. Almost everyone has made a similar attempt. It is actually only the realistic novel which does not know alienation. But even in the Kafka novel (if it can be placed in a special category), this technique becomes evident. What Kafka presents is a description that is completely alienated by language just as a play is "alienated" on stage by the actor.

Q. Let me ask you a question concerning your treatment of language. Your early prose seems to be under the influence of Albin Zollinger in that your language was then almost lyrical. This changed considerably after *Bin, or the Voyage to Peking* in which the emotional element is still strongly emphasized. Later on your prose becomes increasingly sober and matter-of-fact. Nothing but a plain statement without any lyrical trimming is attempted. Can you explain this change?

A. It is difficult to explain. What I dislike now in my early works, which were in fact written under the influence of Albin Zollinger, is the exhibition of feelings, the use of the so-called poetical metaphor. Feeling is offered directly. You are certainly right if you say that my later work is more sober. Yet it is not true that emotions are completely absent. They—consciously—flee less and less often into metaphors. On the other hand, the language material is arranged, combined, composed to a collage in such a way that the emotional qualities appear between the statements without being spelled out or talked to death. I consider this a more poetical form than the first one. It expresses the same radical doubt of the metaphor which has befallen the new literature, and rightfully so. The metaphor compares something inaccurate with something even more inaccurate. In the negative case the result is nothing more than a slightly bombastic elevation. There is of course a metaphor in every word or in almost every word, whereupon we would have to single out words which we still experience as metaphors. The word "understand," for instance, is such a metaphor, but we do not experience it as a metaphor anymore. "To veil" is undoubtedly a metaphor, but it has become a concept. The language of sociology uses this word without understanding it as a metaphor. We cannot operate without these metaphorical remnants. What we should avoid, however, because they are simply meaningless, are cheap metaphors like "the spring of time," "the stream of time." "Stream" and "time" have something very superficial in common whereas there are many aspects they do not have in common. The result is pseudo-poetical. Sobriety, on the other hand, does not necessarily mean that there is no emotional impetus behind it. But this takes place in such a way that the feeling is not babbled out but created through language material. There are many things which cannot be spelled out anymore.

In Handke's case there is a funny example, by the way. (I do not suggest that we became aware of this problem only through him. But it is clear that it will be intensified in the next generation and in the generation after.) Well, Handke at one time in an essay against the metaphor used the term "stillborn thoughts" which of course is an absolute metaphor. Thought is compared with a child, since only a child can be stillborn. Perhaps we shall return to the metaphor one day. But the present trend—prevailing for fifty years—is iconoclastic in that false pictures and those which convince too easily and for the wrong reasons are being removed. New metaphors originate in front of the naked wall. If you look at many of today's metaphors, you will realize that they do not relate to items from our own world of experience but from the world of our grandfathers or great-grandfathers. They do not provide a bridge. For instance, if I explained to you how I feel in the subway of New York by saying—pardon the idiotic example—that it feels like riding on a heavy old horse that has not been watered for a long time. . . . Neither of us rode such a horse but both of us travelled in the subway. Thus I am comparing something close with something far off. This is sheer heraldry. Or I can compare something with a snake. Only very few of us have had experiences with snakes. This worked as long as practical knowledge was involved, so that something strange could be made clear by a partial congruity with something well-known. Because metaphors have fallen and have become poetry, they are as lifeless as objects in a museum and I am making a comparison with elements they do not include. It is as if I were to compare something with the way you feel when wearing a medieval knight's armor. Where do you get this feeling? You get it from literature. Therefore, after the disposal of all this trash, there will be new metaphors which will have the power of explanation since they derive from a new range of experience.

Q. Speaking of a new range of experience, what exactly is the new which will replace the old and which will no longer originate from literary experience?

A. This question is difficult to answer—not because it is an impossible question, but let us take for example some writers who grew up in Latin America, in a very unliterary civilization, and who now begin to write. They have, of course, a much smaller literary burden to carry than most of us, whether we are students of literature or not. In the occidental countries, we have an already established literature, a literature which has been overrun by time. And we all joined a tank battle in a knight's armor.

Q. In some of your remarks about America you express your admiration for the unreflected manner of description in American literature. Would you rate American literature *in toto*?

A. Early American literature, in any case. I have to admit that I am no great connoisseur of it. But early American literature of course was truly epical because it still had to describe the country, a *terra incognita*; the story had to be told for the first time. But if you take, for instance, the work of Barthelme, there everything is already so late and sophisticated, that this dictum does not apply anymore. Nowadays it would apply rather to the Latin American countries looking for self-understanding in literature by simply describing their own way of life.

Q. Is there any opportunity for the European author to start all over again despite his being burdened with the occidental tradition and consciousness?

A. We cannot forget it, but we also do not want to forget it. There are the possibilities of a late literature, of a strong tradition, of a struggle with tradition. We cannot possibly play children anymore. But there is a great opportunity. If one is burdened with tradition one has to shake off much of what has become lifeless, as I tried to explain when we were talking about metaphor.

Q. How can the modern intellectual—who is incidentally the central figure in most of your plays and novels—ever escape his consciousness of being embedded in a powerful tradition? In your latest novel and in your latest play a strong element of playfulness is apparent. Do you suggest the game—be it an artistic game or a game of chess—as a possible escape?

A. Game is no escape. Art as such is game. The question is, what is meant by game? Game is what we can do without any compulsion, out of sheer pleasure. Game means that we can repeat something we cannot do in real life. Game also means that we do not necessarily have to serve a direct necessity of life. If you start a fire so that you do not freeze, it can easily turn into a game. You can start another fire to keep you warm, but you can do it differently; you can play with it. Game is an exalted kind of existence, though not necessarily the easiest kind. From this point of view even that absurd saying by Schiller can perhaps be interpreted: "Ernst ist das Leben, heiter die Kunst." But this is very difficult. It is *homo ludens* facing *homo faber.* And somewhere in between there is the still unknown position of *homo sapiens.* But that is a different story.

An Interview with Paul Blackburn

*Conducted by L. S. Dembo**

Q. I notice that the epigraph to one of your volumes is taken from Aristotle, a passage from *The Metaphysics,* in which the eye is considered one of the most important senses for obtaining a knowledge of things. Many of your poems seem to demonstrate this view. They seem to delimit a world in which sharp observation rather than judgment, sentiment, or introspection is paramount. Would you agree that you are carrying on a tradition established by poets like William Carlos Williams and Louis Zukofsky?

A. That's fair. As a matter of fact, I ran across the quote not in Aristotle but in that big book of Louis', *Bottom: On Shakespeare.* I had those lines hanging on my wall for years.

Q. How did you come across Zukofsky's work?

A. Well, that's a long history. I was corresponding with Pound when I was going to college here [Wisconsin] and Pound was then in the nut house in Washington. I hitchhiked down to Washington from New York to visit him a few times. I'd write long letters and he'd write short ones. We talked about everything, but I never showed him anything and I never told him I was a writer. Well, that doesn't tell you about Zukofsky. I had a poem at that point that I was pretty disgusted with; it was my first attempt at a long piece of work. Since I was so much into Pound, I was very concerned about how to sustain a poem over a page long. This was something I just did not know how to do and I really worked at it. I started this poem in New York during the summer. I'd done

---

* The interview took place in Madison, May 25, 1971. Mr. Blackburn died of cancer on September 13, 1971.

twenty-one versions of the damn thing and it was finished. I mean it was finished; you couldn't change anything in it. It was perfect and it was dead. I was disgusted with it. I submitted it to the campus literary magazine and they must have considered it a big bore. They didn't understand it; they didn't like it, and I figured that was all right. The same spring, I got a letter from James Laughlin at New Directions saying that he had a note from Pound in St. Elizabeth's saying that I wanted to contribute something to his *New Directions Annual.*

Q. Pound was still going strong. . . .

A. Oh, Pound was fantastic. I mean because of Pound, I was in touch with Creeley, I was in touch with Olson, I was in touch with Cid Corman. My correspondence, which unfortunately all has been lost . . . my correspondence from those years, in light of subsequent events, would have been fantastic. None of us knew each other and we were all writing each other letters, and all of this comes through that little center down there in St. Elizabeth's mental hospital in Washington, D. C. You know, "Write Creeley, chicken farmer up in New Hampshire. . . ." I didn't actually meet Creeley until almost two years later. That was before the beginning of *Origin.*

Q. That's before 1952 then?

A. Sure, that was '49 or '50. I graduated in '50 or so.

Q. How did Pound know that you were writing?

A. I think he just assumed that because I never mentioned that I wrote or ever showed him anything, I must really be good. I would never have recommended anybody whose work I had never seen. Of course, this happened at a time when I had made up my mind that . . . I must have been twenty-four; I was quite late as a graduate . . . I had made up my mind that I wouldn't publish anything until I was thirty. I felt that maybe by that time I'd know what I was doing. Anyway, I sent the poem to Laughlin and he published it. That made me feel pretty good— embarrassed, but excited.

Q. Where does Zukofsky fit into all of this?

A. Well, you see here is where the whole cycle starts: from Pound to Creeley to Corman to Olson. Into that comes a young man from North Carolina, who is still in the army over in Germany, named Jonathan Williams. I was in New York; Creeley went to the south of France and lived in a small town in which someone named Denise Levertov also happened to be living. It was all accidents. Just sheer, outright, damned accidents. Creeley passed through New York and spent a week with me in preparing passage for his whole family to Europe. I don't think he slept all week. I was working in a print shop down below Canal Street; I was foreman on the night shift. Creeley stayed in my apartment; I would come home at one-thirty or two o'clock in the morning and he'd be up reading. Of course, that's still my day, so we'd sit up and talk the rest of the night. I'd go to bed around 8:00 a.m. after having had supper and Bob would continue reading; I would wake up and he'd still be reading. I think he must have read the whole *Cantos* that week; I don't know. Finally, Ann and the kids arrived and I got them all on the boat, waved, kissed everybody goodbye, and didn't see them for two years.

Q.   Had Olson put in an appearance this early?

A.   Olson was still up in Gloucester. It was either Gloucester or Black Mountain. As a matter of fact, Olson wanted Creeley to come back from Majorca and go to work at Black Mountain. While Creeley was still refusing to come back (for which I didn't blame him), I was also interviewed for a position down there. But then, I guess, Creeley finally decided to come, so that was OK too. I mean I already had a job.

Q.   You didn't get down there at all then?

A.   No, I was never at Black Mountain until ten years after it closed— sightseeing, but that was all. The point is that out of Creeley's European contacts, he ended up somehow with Jonathan Williams. Now whether Jonathan got in touch with him or there had been correspondence before, I have no idea. I ended up as the first distributor of Jargon Books in New York City. As you know, I was the New York part of this poetry conspiracy. We didn't realize we were building a mafia. Well, anyway, Jonathan somehow fell into Zukofsky, and like nobody had seen Zukofsky since the 1930s. That 1931 issue of *Poetry,* with the objectivist poets in it—well, all of a sudden people were talking about Zukofsky. So everyone starts digging around to find out about him and it turns out that he'd been living over in Brooklyn all this time, quietly teaching at Brooklyn Polytech. It was the same with Basil Bunting. Who in the hell had heard of Bunting? I had. How did I hear of Bunting? Pound. And not only that, some kook, one of Pound's political nuts somewhere in Texas whom I'd also been in correspondence with, had pirated an edition of Bunting in 1949.

Q. Did you actually get in touch with Bunting?

A.   No, no. Strangely enough, the people who'd stayed in contact all those years were Bunting and Zukofsky. They had been corresponding all those years, and, I guess, Zukofsky had also been in touch with Pound. They had had that thing going since the twenties. That whole crew was working together, and somehow the whole circle we were building was intersecting at all different points.

Q. But this was not a matter of personality; it was a matter of influence, of poetry and poetics.

A.   Sure. These people come into your life when you're twenty-two, twenty-three, twenty-four, twenty-five years old. Williams lived right across the damn river. For some reason, almost by the closeness of it, I had never got in contact with him. I had always felt it would have been an imposition. He had his own thing there. It was not a scene; he was a doctor and he had work to do. I met him a few times but years later.

Q. What about that poem in *The Cities,* "Phone Call to Rutherford"? Did you actually call him up?

A.   Oh, sure. By that time, I'd been over and had met him. That was when he was very old. Floss was a lot tougher than he was about visitors, in that sense. She wanted him to have more contact. There were a lot of poets in the city at the time and I figured, what the hell, two or three of us could go out at a time, just once a week. We'd figure out the day with Flossie so that he would have some sense of continuity, a constant flow of visitors. It was at that point I wrote the poem about calling him up. He died the next spring.

Q. Where do people like Ed Dorn come into the picture?

A.   Ed was a student at Black Mountain. So was Joel Oppenheimer. Duncan was a teacher there, although he's from the west coast.

Q. Let me ask you a little about your poetry. Actually, the world you depict appears to be even more sensationalistic than either Williams' or Zukofsky's. For example, you wrote in "Song of the Wires," "There is always something/to touch or feel or smell or see."[1] Do you agree with this?

---

[1] *The Cities* (New York: Grove Press, 1967), p. 64. Subsequent references to this edition will be noted parenthetically in the text.

A.   Yes, I'm very much there. That poem's about riding trains in Spain.

Q.   Would you agree that you put an even greater emphasis on the sensual than Williams and Zukofsky?
A.   I wouldn't say so. Take a couple of Williams' poems, like the one about the woman on the street eating plums. She's got half of this plum in her hand and it tastes good to her. It tastes good to her. It tastes good to her. Don't talk to me about Williams' not being sensual.

Q.   Oh he's sensual, all right. But look at Blackburn's poems—the description of love, for example. Love seems to be reduced to that of animal passion. In "Poor Dog," for instance, the speaker ostensibly identifies himself with a cat in heat—"looking/out of our minds/down to the street with glazed eyes" (p. 73).
A.   I've lived with cats for years and I appreciate them. The same goes for women.

Q.   It's a cat's appreciation of women.
A.   Well, in a way I have an appreciation of cat-like women. There's been a cat-like sense about all of my women.

Q.   There's a cat-like sense about you, too. The speaker of your poems is kind of a cat-like personality, isn't he?
A.   Untrustworthy, independent.

Q.   That isn't what I meant. But what about the poem, "Purse Seine"?
A.   Well, that was the beginning of a very serious relationship. I was between marriages and was really afraid of getting trapped, yet knowing that I had to give myself to her. That's what that poem was about.

Q.   The description of love in this poem seems different from that in the other poems. You write a poem like "Love Song" which gives a physical kind of description; this poem does too, but it also seems to take on a kind of mythical cast:

> here on this bed
> enact the tides, the swells, your hips rising toward me,
> waves break over the shoals, the
> sea bird hits the mast in the dark and falls
> with a cry to the deck and flutters off[2]

---

[2] *The Nets* (New York: Trobar, 1961), p. [25].

This seems like more than a sensual experience.

A. Well, I don't know what happens. One either has good luck or bad luck with such poems, I guess. I think this has pretty good luck in it. It seems to work, and you come to a point where . . . it's almost like fighting one's way through, and none of the resistances are explicit in the poem. But there are lots of images of resistance in there. I've had a bad experience in love and had one marriage rocked on me and I'm afraid to get into another thing. I don't trust myself. I don't trust her or the incredible attraction that there is literally, physically, between two people, but finally you give yourself to it in a way that you want to, as fully as you can. It's almost picky in that way . . . it's almost picking at it and working the whole image of getting trapped in that net.

Q. That's the bird hitting the mast?

A. Well, you can read that image in two ways. The previous marriage breaking up or approaching disaster, or even the impact of literal violence that is also in love. It falls with a cry to the deck and flutters off.

Q. Do you feel that any love relationship is a trap?

A. I feel that less now. My own life has changed sufficiently that I'm in a much more open set of possibilities. But it's a limitation, especially for a young man. Any love has got to limit you; any set of things in life you commit yourself to has got to limit you. You free yourself through entrapment, in a way; you just have to choose your traps right.

Q. Do you find freedom on the deck of a ferry boat?

A. You mean in the poem, "The Net of Moon"? No, that again is nailing it down, nailing down the choices:

> Impact of these splendid
>   things
> upon the appropriate sense
> How refuse to meddle with it, throw it away, play
> to hide our passion in the dance of that moon
>   upon the small waves, how come to it hugely
>   erected and keep, we tell ourselves, a just balance be-
> tween the emotion and the motion of wave on the bay, the
> leap of the dolphin in our dreams, accompanying us home?

Hello moon.

From the *Mary Murray*'s upper deck
the wind is stiff in our faces
                    Another spring as warm
                    10 days earlier
                    the moon is still out
another year falling across its face so slowly, so flatly the motion of wave as I do
fall back astonished, take my glasses off, the shore lights
so close,
fuzz to myopic eyes sting in wind, the
tide is full, he said, the moon lies fair upon the straits.
Let me tell you, let me tell
you straight, strait and very narrow indeed, encloses

Lights white
or red mark the
bell buoy's
clang against the dark bay
over it, over . it . The tail
of a Brooklyn ferry disappears behind
an anchored tanker, fail,
I fail to see and put glasses back on,
I fail
to .

Laughter along the lift of deck,
lovers stand at the rail, close on
From the rail we see
fire-glow from the interior of the
island, smoke-smell drifts out
across the lower
                    bay,

to us, ten days later, a year gone,
          burnt across a bright face
that looks like it's been chewed on,
                    but will not die .

The quarter-moon glints on the water
          nailed, nailed on the sky

Goodbye moon . (pp. 155-56)[3]

---

[3] Reprinted by permission of Grove Press, Inc. Copyright © 1967 by Paul
Blackburn.

The sense of limitation closes in again and you regret something that did not work out but has changed. That year was a particularly bad year in that sense or a good year in another sense. I mean your images come to you from around you. That's my second wife with me on the deck of that ferry boat.

Q. Would you see love more a matter of passion than salvation?

A. Well, certainly passion has a great deal to do with it. You see, I can't pick it apart that way. Your body is reacting with another person's body. I mean that's got to be really there, a real exchange of cells, of feelings, of warmth.

Q. Let me ask you about "Brooklyn Narcissus." The more the poet describes cities, the more one senses his isolation. He seems to confirm his loneliness even in the ale house or the Bakery Restaurant. Especially in the Bakery poems, he seems to be overhearing rather than really participating in the conversation. And in "Sun Flower Rock," after describing the eviction of a derelict old man, he explicitly reveals that his own condition is little different: "Soon we step into ourselves, stop to buy/a half pint at the corner for the cold night."[4]

A. Again that's place. It's the geography literally of the city. And geography doesn't isolate you in that sense; it sets up the lines and the directions—the streets with their grid, as they very often are in New York. But they are very much in on you wherever you are—if you're sitting on Twenty-fourth Street and Third Avenue or if you're sitting on Seventh Street opposite Hall Place.

Q. I never quite understood this business of geography that seems so important in Black Mountain writing. Does geography actually get substituted for human relations?

A. No, it just keeps the mind clear, gives it certain tracks to run on. I mean geography in the quite literal sense. This afternoon, I took the scenic route to Madison. The contours of the land are really lovely— the valleys, the hills, and the whole nice roll of this part of the country; the glacier mounds are beautiful at this time of the year. I had a better time than I would have just coming in nice and fast. So it took an extra ten minutes. It keeps your head clear. It gives you something to look at, to think about.

---

[4] *In, On, or About the Premises* (London: Cape Goliard, 1968), n.p.

Q. But you're not really in a world of men, a world of people, anymore. You're in a world of nature, aren't you?

A. Geography is the human world, animal world. Why are the mountains of Spain stripped, timbered off before the Romans? The major railroads in this country, the transcontinental railroads were all once buffalo trails. . . . We're all a part of what our landscape is. If it amounts to looking out the window and seeing a wall ten feet away, that's it; it's what you've got.

Q. Does geometry enter into this? You've got a poem about a girl walking along a "hypotenuse" to cross a square.

A. That's working the city, where things are not necessarily grid. It just so happens I like squares and there are fewer of them in American cities than in Europe. America on the whole is less graceful; our constructs are much too often ugly.

Q. What about Manhattan?

A. Well, when they finish the town, I'll let you know.

Q. That'll be never!

A. That's right! The sense of Manhattan's changed very much in the last twenty years. Look at the place from Brooklyn Heights and it's a tower of glass, man; it's light. It floats. You get that old sense . . . from water, you know, from really seeing it from there, where you can see the bay. You can see out to the island and sense that this boat is floating and it's light now. It used to be heavy. It used to be stone. And now it's not; it's changed.

Q. But you still feel at home there.

A. Definitely. You have tracks inside a city. You build from wherever your center is. Wherever you sit your ass, wherever you put your drink, the place you eat in or a house or an apartment, you build your tracks from here to there. If you're going shopping, you find your stores; you usually even go to those stores a certain way. You follow certain tracks through the city. You might even work it into a sense of birth. Constantly, you're moving toward something, but you always return to wherever your womb is, whether it's McSorley's bar or you know. Just put me on Second Avenue; I can hang on. I'm driving down this ugly street again and like I know where I am. I know where the parking places are, if there are any, or what streets they're likely to be on. And it's get out of the car and get into a subway and go where you're going—that's much more sensible. But you immediately move into a whole new set of grooves, your head turned around, and you're moving places. You have friends here. It's easier to walk over to Carmine Street or to Van Dam Street than it is to take any kind of transportation whatsoever from the Lower East Side. You have a fifteen or twenty-minute walk, but it's much simpler than taking any transportation. And not only that, you can vary your routes. There are all sorts of channels inside a city, ways of doing things, going places. . . .

Q.   It must give you a sense of order and harmony.

A.   No, it's somebody else's system. You use this whole complex of systems, somehow to satisfy your own sense of moving from here to there. I don't build roads, man; I didn't lay out the city. But I can walk all over Central Park practically in the dark. South of Eighty-first Street now, I can walk almost any place and know where I am. I'm completely located in this wild little park.

Q.   Is that what you meant when you said of *The Cities*, "Finally it is a construct, out of my own isolations, eyes, ears, nose and breath, my recognitions of those constructs not my own that I can live in" (p. 11).

A.   That's right. In Barcelona, my God, the tracks I've got in Barcelona. I could spend a week getting drunk with you there and never go out of a thirty-block area, and you'd be completely lost. I know every goddamn little alley in that section.

Q.   Do you build these groove channels into the poetry?

A.   That's a good question. I don't know what builds which. I think that's a good point, but it works both ways. The geography works in the rhythms. It's also visual. For instance, a poem in the *Nets* book has got to be read from the bottom to the top. That is a picture of Bañalbufar and the terraces from the sea up to the top of the mountain. That's the way that the town runs, you know, the way I laid my lines out, from the bottom reading up.

Q.   What about the emphatic voice pauses when you read the poems aloud?

A.   I want other people to be able to read the poems with as much of the emphasis of my own voice as possible, and to do that you have to control the poem typographically on the page. You can control your rhythms visually in many ways; you can lay them out on a page in any way that is comprehensible to the reader—what the pauses are, where they fall, how long they are.

Q. That is something Olson is very much interested in—speech rhythms. Duncan and Creeley read their poetry in that emphatic, breathless way.

A. Duncan is very musical. He dances when he reads, whereas Creeley hunches down in his chair and bends over the book as though the whole dance were taking place in his head. His breaks are so precise.

Q. One more question. Why is the secret to *The Cities* scissors, paper, and rock?

A. I had to put that book together somehow. I wrote basically three kinds of poems in different proportions. Rock, say, is the concrete. The center of the poem is the object in Williams' sense, a person or a thing. It has as much sense as words can bring to it. That's the rock. Paper is where the form is basically an idea, even if the idea is never mentioned. And scissors, what do they remind you of? That's love poems, man. It's the legs opening and closing. The thing was to set up the volume in terms of a rhythm, so that the reader didn't get bored with too many of one kind of poem all in a row. My intention was not to put all the idea poems together and all the love poems together and all the hard object things together, but to keep a rhythm going among them that would be a kind of ground base. In other words, you can read that book from beginning to end and not get bored at any point with any particular kind of poem. There's always something new coming up. They aren't all alternated; sometimes you'll get two or three love poems in a row. But then something else will strike in, a very different kind of poem. Keep a rhythm among those three and you've got the secret of that book.

An Interview with Marguerite Duras

*Conducted by Germaine Brée**

An interview with Marguerite Duras is a memorable event. This one took place last fall in her apartment on the Left Bank; a mutual friend Jean-Louis Jacquet was the second interlocutor. (His questions are marked *Q.**) Small, dark, sturdy, warm, and forthrightly brusque in manner, Marguerite Duras is always unpredictable. People walked in and out; the telephone rang; interrupted, the conversation rebounded in unexpected directions. Duras' writing too has steadily developed in unpredictable ways. On the table lay the manuscript of the strange "text" she mentions, now published under the title *L'Amour*. And love—indeed, the need, possibility, and impossibility of love—is the theme underlying all her strangely haunting work. With thirty years of fiction writing behind her, constantly remolding the forms she works with, Duras cannot now be classified under any label. Since 1959, when she wrote the script for Alain Resnais' *Hiroshima mon amour*, with characteristic passion she has become involved with the cinema. Theater has never caught her imagination in the same way, in spite of the success in 1960 of *Des journées entières dans les arbres*, with Madeleine Renaud in the lead part.

Born in Indochina, where she lived some eighteen years and began to write, Marguerite Duras has always been an outspoken anticolonialist, and for some years a militant communist whose break with the Party finds its expression in the strangely haunting *Abahn, Sabana, David* which she discusses in the interview. Generous, she is always to be found among France's leftist intellectuals; but she does not intellectualize a position which she feels, lives, and expresses through the situations, characters, and dialogues in her writing. Whether fiction, drama, or film her work is impressive in its uniqueness and scope .

---

*The interview, conducted in French, was translated by Cyril Doherty.

28

Q. I should like, first of all, to ask you whether all your works have appeared in English. In the last twenty years or so you have written about fifteen works that can be called novels or stories, about ten plays that, I believe, have all been performed in France. About how many of all these works have appeared in England or in English?

A. All of them, I think.

Q. So, your English readers can see your work as a whole. In your opinion, is there an organic link from one work to another?

A. I don't think there is a "current" that one could trace. Perhaps that's not the right word to describe some kind of underlying meaning. At any rate, it doesn't matter. I think that there are different periods.

Q. Different developments?

A. Yes.

Q. That are quite distinct?

A. Yes. For example, *Moderato cantabile* constitutes a break.

Q. I noticed that the term "novel" has disappeared from your works. The last one to be so termed was *Le Vice-Consul.*

A. I hadn't noticed that myself. But that's fine.

Q. I had wondered whether or not your dropping the term was intentional and whether you meant to make a distinction concerning your present works with regard to the novel form.

A. I dropped the word "novel" for the last two deliberately. It seemed to me that they weren't exactly novels, given the way in which the term is used in present-day productions.

Q. Nevertheless, they are stories?

A. It's just something I happen to do easily. They are closer to *récits* than to novels, it seems to me.

Q. Nevertheless, your *récits* tell a story. Could you tell us what a story is for you?

A. You mean a story with a beginning, a development, and an end?

Q. Something happens in all these novels. I was going to ask you the question with respect to the last two. What really happens?

A. Yes, but in the two books *Détruire* and *Abahn, Sabana, David* the substance of the novel, in the Balzacian sense of the word, is extremely reduced and almost skimpy at the start. Only a few colors are given; the place is not named but only described. Therefore, it seems to me that because of the sparseness of the setting, these tales break with the traditional novel. It is specifically in the effort that the reader must make, with the little that is given him, that the break with the usual type of novel occurs. I have always been struck by the richness of the novels I read in comparison with mine.

Q. One of your concerns seems to be to choose a subject matter which is, as you say, meager, but which is nonetheless rich in its power of suggestion. In other words, as soon as one begins to read, from the very first word, one is gripped by the scenario, the setting. But why do you go to such lengths to strip the novel of its substance since evidently in works like *Un Barrage contre le Pacifique* you were closer to the traditional novel?

A. Yes, indeed I was. *Le Marin de Gibraltar,* in fact all the novels right up to *Moderato cantabile,* were much more prolific. Since *Moderato,* I have tried to work with what novelists have usually neglected.

Q. That is?

A. The positive effect, or the results. Take anything at all, a family scene, an unusual incident, a storm, a discussion, a love affair, and so on. What interests me is the area which these things perturb and which is as yet unknown to me. What I have already explored in my first books no longer interests me at all.

Q. In that sense, then, there is a link between your first works and those which follow even if it's only by the elimination of what you have already explored.

A. From that point of view, yes. One could say that *Détruire dit-elle* was written over and against *Les Petits Chevaux de Tarquinia.*

Q. How do you mean?

A. Because *Détruire* works in depth what *Les Petits Chevaux* merely outlined. In the background of *Les Petits Chevaux* there is already something of *Détruire dit-elle* which I had totally overlooked.

Q.   *Les Petits Chevaux* goes back quite a way. Between them and *Détruire* there are several novels, aren't there?

A.   There certainly are. People generally like them, but as far as I'm concerned, I no longer care for them.

Q.   Are you removed from all of your past novels, in that sense, or are there some which stay very much with you?

A.   Some still remain very close to me; for example, *Le Ravissement de Lol V. Stein.*

Q.   That's an extraordinary book and I want to talk about it in a moment. At least it is one of your most mysterious.

A.   And *Le Vice-Consul* . . .

Q.   Also is exceedingly mysterious. The extraordinary character, the atmosphere . . . they seem to be quite close to you?

A.   Very close, and, indeed, totally present to me. *Détruire* and even *Abahn, Sabana, David.*

Q.   Those are both very strange too. Perhaps we could discuss them in turn. But first I should like to ask you a few more general questions. You and Beckett are perhaps the only renowned novelists of the fifties not to formulate a theory of the novel, about the art of writing and the task of the writer.

A.   There are also Genet and Des Forêts. We are classified as the "outsiders" of the novel in this sense because we have no theory of the novel.

Q.   Did you begin to write when you were in Indochina or when you were in France?

A.   I always wrote.

Q.   Always? Even as a child?

A.   Yes. From the age of twelve.

Q.   What did you write about?

A.   About discoveries, as everyone else does.

Q.   What got you started?

A.   I don't know.

Q.   Might it have been loneliness?

A.   I was living at an outpost way out in the country in Indochina.

Q.   Would that be reflected in *Un Barrage contre le Pacifique?*

A.   *Barrage* is entirely autobiographical. I was living far away from Saigon in the country with my mother, who was a widow with three children, and practically all I read were my school books.

Q.   And you began by writing about . . .

A.   About winter. I remember a poem about winter. I had never seen a winter.

Q.   Your writing them led to the imaginary. It seems that in all your novels you start with something quite banal which then becomes highly imaginative, then develops almost beyond the imaginable, in short, reaches the level of mystery.

A.   Perhaps, but I don't feel it that way.

Q.   You don't feel the story as . . .

A.   Not as imaginary. It is as if I had been afflicted with a disease of the eyes, with a deformation of sight which is almost total, so that I recognize reality only in its simplest terms, almost to the point of naiveté.

Q.   And this you discover as the story develops?

A.   Yes.

Q.   Do you have any sense beforehand of how the story will go?

A.   It's as though it were there, beforehand. I know only that it has always been there and that it is there for everyone to see. One has only to make an effort to discern it and I make the effort.

Q. At any rate, I've always had the impression of an extraordinary change in dimension from daily routines to the perception of some fantastic quality in the characters.

A. You have?

Q. Yes. Two of your novels are permeated by the atmosphere of Indochina: in a direct way, *Un Barrage contre le Pacifique,* which is a very beautiful novel, and, in an indirect way, *Le Vice-Consul* which, for me, is a work full of unusual poetry. It's one of those works that continue to be haunting.

A. I prefer *Le Vice-Consul* to *Lol V. Stein. Lol V. Stein,* from the point of view of madness, is almost a regionalist novel. It's a domain of madness in which a person is involved, whereas it seems to me that *Le Vice-Consul* is no longer regionalist in that sense. Madness is what the Vice-Consul is submerged in. This anguish is an anguish of interest to everyone. Do you find this to be the case?

Q. The book fascinates me but I don't know whether I fully understand the Vice-Consul's dilemma. I realize that the man is haunted, who shoots . . .

A. Who shoots into suffering itself. It isn't only at suffering that he shoots. He shoots at the whole world; at least I think that's what he does.

Q. This raises the issue of destruction and revolt, which has so important a role in your work.

A. It has become an overriding concern since *Lol V. Stein.*

*Q.** To return to what you were saying earlier, you mentioned that you try to get close to reality in its most naive terms and I notice that in ordinary conversation the same thing happens. The simpler the thing is, the more impressive it becomes. You are the only person I know who can say, "I am going to eat," and it means something terrifying, almost stupendous. The more you simplify the expression, the greater its content of mystery.

A. That's well observed.

*Q.** One notices it, but one can't. . . .

A. I feel that way.

Q. What are you working on now?

A. Just a text. It can't be called anything else. And in a very mathematical way, a little like *Abahn*. One could say that the text is pure imbecility. I have ceased to understand what I am writing. When a certain music is present, I know that the text is progressing. When the music stops, I stop. When it begins again, I begin again.

Q. Music is often present in your novels. For instance, there is the song of the beggar girl that recurs throughout *Le Vice-Consul*.

A. That song is part of the major musical theme that reappears in the main story, the one that is more fully embodied than that of the beggar girl. Let me just say that the girl's life is beyond the story's limits. It is the terrain upon which the story of the Vice-Consul is built and without the girl, nothing is left. When the Vice-Consul shoots, it is in order to destroy suffering. He does what Breton once advised: at twenty, there is only one way out, to go into the street and shoot at random into the crowd. If the Vice-Consul can say that or do it, it is because the girl exists.

Q. The girl lives wretchedness and her song is woven into everything.

A. Yes, that's it.

Q. Could you talk about the theme of destruction? In *Le Vice-Consul* as you just said, destruction is meant as a revolt against suffering. Wasn't this revolt already present in *Un Barrage contre le Pacifique?* In your description of the little Indochinese children, it was very apparent.

A. Yes, quite concretely.

Q. And in *Détruire dit-elle*, for instance, what kind of destruction would you say is at work?

A. In the first place that of the writer, I believe.

Q. Writers often appear in novels today, but there are very few in yours. In *Détruire*, there is Stein; Max Thor isn't a writer, or, is he a potential writer?

A. He is connected with writing. He is a teacher. I don't see how one cannot be a writer (I mean in the broad sense of the term). I know all kinds of people who don't write and who are writers. By that I mean that the world passes to us by way of them. They hand it on; they don't just endure it. There are many people who write and who are much farther from being writers than people who don't. One can write very well without the blank page.

Q.   But just the same, the writer must use words or do you think that emotion and perception alone count?

A.   You have to use words in order to break them; you have to take that step. I feel that I am writing all the time. Obviously, you will say that I feel some lack. I try not to write; formerly, I wrote a good deal and now I try to write less. When I don't write for awhile, I feel a lack, the lack quite simply of the table, of the position that I'm in at this moment. I have the feeling that I never stop, but I know lots of people who don't stop either.

Q.   Even those who don't write?

A.   Yes.

Q.   Is it an impulse to write that you feel or a compelling kind of perception?

A.   A certain silence, perhaps, a certain way of seeing things.

Q.   But what starts you on a book?

A.   That is an area which is very obscure.

Q.   But does something orient you toward specific moods that make it possible for you to begin your stories?

A.   Sometimes nothing at all, sometimes a mere detail. For example, in *L'Après-Midi de Monsieur Andesmas,* it was a terrace in the forest. I saw that house. In fact, I had been taken to visit it some time before. Years went by, perhaps two years, before I wrote the novel. The terrace stayed there for a long time and then people began to appear on it. Then they began to speak to each other and that is how the book was born. Very often it's a matter of a clear-cut detail.

Q.   And at present what is the detail?

A.   Now, it's the beach at Trouville at ebb tide.

Q.   We were talking about destruction and you said that that is your only theme now. What kind of destruction is taking place in *Détruire dit-elle?*

A.   The destruction of the thing that conceals what I describe. I mean I try to be as sincere as possible. It's as if literature up to this point had masked things. For example, take a novel of the nineteenth century, any one at all. Marie-Louise was faithful to her husband; she felt a love for him that was deep and loyal. That has no meaning whatsoever. It doesn't exist.

*Q.**   Or it no longer exists.

A.   It doesn't exist. What does a faithful love mean? Love is a thing that must be brought to life each day. One generalizes the word "love" to the point—how shall I put it—where it becomes a substantive. What is a general term? To go from love to a particular love, do you see what I mean, is an abstract and artificial step.

Q.   Love is the theme, or one of the main themes in *Détruire. . . .*

A.   Well, *Détruire* describes a woman at a particular moment with a man, a moment that is fleeting—you get the color and meaning of love infinitely better in what she says than if you read that her love was faithful and deep. One must always go back to the world of the senses in order to destroy the strait jacket of style. And that means back to touch and sight; begin to touch and to see . . . yes. In *Détruire,* there is a theme of love along with a theme of destruction. There is a presence, a search for love or a presence of love. But love is never defined, never. No generalization is made about it. The lover touches, is touched; he sees and looks. You can't define that love or classify it.

Q.   But what draws these characters to Elizabeth Alione? Why do they seek her out later? Why do they pursue her?

A.   Because she is the object to be destroyed.

Q.   But why?

A.   Because she is completely self-deceived. She is married. She has a child. Don't you see in it the story of guilt? She was expecting a baby; she loved the doctor who looked after her. The child dies, and so she is guilty. All that must be destroyed. But how? Not by an active or traditional militancy. She is to be destroyed by what could perhaps pretentiously be called a "maieutic"; it is Alissa who approaches Elizabeth, asks her questions about herself, and thus forces her to destroy herself. Elizabeth answers the younger woman's questions and, to the extent that she replies, purifies herself.

Q.   She could then make herself over?

A.   Certainly. Like everyone else.

Q.   Is that destruction? It's a destruction based on fellow feeling.

A.   Yes; the meaning of *Détruire* is of general or universal import.

Q.   You said a moment ago that the book involved the destruction of the writer?

A.   By that very fact and simultaneously. In other words Elizabeth would appear quite differently if the writing had been cast in a traditional form. She would be described. She'd emerge in some place at a given moment. She would then be shown somewhere else. And her destruction would take place elsewhere again. In my book everything takes place at the same time. She is seen at the beginning of her destruction. And it is her destruction only that shows up what she was. You don't have to go into her bedroom or observe her adultery. She is there in front of us and she speaks. She answers. That is perhaps what is so strange.

Q.*   But it's almost the opposite of destruction.

A.   You haven't read *Détruire*?

Q.*   No, I haven't.

Q.   It's an extraordinary book. Among other things, it's about a woman who sleeps. The theme of madness too often recurs in your novels, for example in *L'Amante Anglaise;* but there is also the theme of sleep. People sleep and are awakened either by a question or by someone's arrival.

A.   Yes, I believe that anyone can awaken at a single sentence.

Q.   And that most of the time they sleep?

A.   Yes. Elizabeth is asleep, just as literature is asleep—in the same way. She is enmeshed in a mechanism that goes back to the nineteenth century and she never gets out.

Q. Insofar as she is a character in a novel. . . .

A. Yes. It's the said and the saying, that which signifies and what is signified at the same time—to put it in terms of the critics today . . . but I don't want to get caught up in their jargon. That's the way they think. . . . The said and the saying are one. The destruction of the thing to be destroyed and the thing itself which is destroyed are one.

Q. Hence the title, *To Destroy, She Says,* in Alissa's words.

A. Yes, and hers is a kind of thought which is thinking itself; in the realm of thought, Elizabeth is innocent.

Q. There is an amazing elimination of the cerebral in this strange distillation of thought.

A. Yes.

Q. *Abahn, Sabana, David* is a book which seems to me quite different.

A. More so the film than the book.

Q. Would you talk about the film and what drew you to the medium? The book itself is so unusual; it's hard even to speak about technique. You said that each story takes its own path and that's true, but there is the editing, the lighting, and the amazing sets with, for example, the recurrent noise of tennis balls or of barking dogs. Sounds of this sort seem to provide rhythms which give one a feeling of surrounding space.

A. They destroy. The dog destroys the silence. The tennis balls break the silence as they do in *Le Vice-Consul.* It's like a stone thrown into water. Everything must be begun over again.

Q. Everything must be begun again?

A. Always.

*Q.** Does that include a break with the self? I understood that you said Stein, for example, was a "mutant"; if there was a break with what came before, it was a break with egocentrism, with the very sense of self. There is the purification of a being who senses that he can become fully human only by destroying himself and that means destroying his egocentricity. You did use the term "mutant" with tremendous force.

A. I don't know whether the idea was mine, but someone asked me "Who is Stein?" (people are always asking me that question), and someone answered, "He's a mutant"; that is to say, a man who comes from the other side of the world, from the future rather than from the past, you see?

*Q.** Quite. Your recent books are turned more toward the future than the early ones. The others were full of the poisons of the past.

A. No, no. In the movie *Abahn*, for example, someone suddenly asks, "What time is it?" and someone else answers, "The future." But we felt very definitely that we were in the future in 1971, that we had set foot in the future. We aren't completely there, it's true.

Q. Hence our sense of uneasiness?

A. We are uneasy. We don't want to believe it, but we are in the future and we deny it. It's the fissure that always exists, shall we say, between the era in which we are in fact and the era in which we should like to be that I call the future.

Q. And is Stein already living completely in the future?

A. Yes, because if Stein were out in the streets right now, if he lived in Paris, he would be put into jail or a mental institution.

Q. What kind of behavior would destroy our uneasiness?

A. A modern behavior. I can't say it any better. When speaking of Thor, Stein says: "How he loves you; how he wants you." He says it as if he were saying it of himself: "How I love you; how I want you!" The movement of Stein towards the other, or shall we say towards otherness, has the same scope as the movement of Stein towards himself. The division no longer exists.

Q. It, then, destroys the egocentrism which has been so characteristic of our way of viewing the world since at least the time of the romantics?

A. Yes and it's a very impoverished way of viewing things.

Q. *Abahn, Sabana, David* takes place in a kind of future. What is the significance of the blind character who is almost petrified in cement?

A. David or the Jew?

Q. David.

A. His life, which had been entirely political before then, becomes entirely modern.

Q. Before *Abahn* the only directly political situation you considered appears in one of your plays, *Un Homme est venu me voir.*

A. It refers to the political thought of Moscow.

Q. Yes, that's it. And, moreover, it has extracts from newspapers about the condition of workers.

A. Yes. I tried to . . . how shall I put it . . . to situate the book in a certain well-defined era, but politically defined, starting with very concrete items, like salaries, trade unionism, and especially adherence to a Communist Party which is bureaucratic and Stalinist.

Q. With Gringo . . . and also Grinsky.

A. Yes, Gringo becomes Grinsky in the film.

Q. "Grinsky" sounds Russian; "Gringo" seems English.

A. There was Gringo-Grinsky; do you see what I'm driving at?

Q. I think so. Gringo could be the American facet of Grinsky.

A. Gringo is American and Grinsky is Russian. Political life today is what might be called the night of the East and the night of the West.

Q. In *Abahn* isn't the allusion rather to the Russia of Stalin? Grinsky is the leader, at any rate. And is David's adventure his awakening, his escape from Grinsky?

A. Yes, David has been in chains; he is in danger of death. He has been taken over by the Communist Party—drafted and pushed into all kinds of labor and managerial tasks. With the arrival of the Jew, that is to say, of refusal—this Jew embodying refusal for me—comes his freedom. David takes up again what I call the "savage" path.

Q. Thence the forest and the dogs?

A. The dogs, the hunting—an age-old activity of man and one which has never undergone the slightest change, the least modification, and is not a cultural activity. Nowadays politics is a cultural activity which has become totally degraded; *Abahn* takes a positive stand against that activity in hatred of it and against the Communist Party.

Q.   It is strange that at the end the threat to David appears illusory. Since the door is open for him, there is no need to force it.

A.   One can push it.

Q.   Grinsky's threats seem no longer to have any interest at that point.

A.   No, but what is truly at stake is not the Jew; it is David. It is the proletariat.

Q.   And the Jew you say is the power of negation. His role is to furnish the evidence but not to liberate the proletariat?

A.   Yes. The Jews represent the space offered to David wherein he may know himself. The Jews are simply there in a physical sense.

Q.   There are two of them, however.

A.   In the film there are three.

Q.   And they all have the same name?

A.   Yes. There are three . . . they are Jews. It's like a wall of Jews. A silent wall of refusal. Then the woman, Sabana, comes to ask the Jews questions. She always breaks in upon their private space; she wrenches words out of them. They speak only to ask questions, whereas the classical militant, in the classical acceptance of the term, seizes the truth, digests it, and gives it to the new recruit. And what do you do when given digested food? You vomit it. And so classical militancy is a product of culture. People denounce formal university lectures, and the traditional militants, the secretaries of the communist cells, are no better than the professors. And from that point of view, I should describe American militancy, silent and physical, as a model. There is no doubt at all that it is the young people, the American young men and women, who are not at all brainwashed, who have no political ideology, who caused the number of Americans against the war in Vietnam to rise from thirty to seventy percent. Well, even with the loquacious militants of the Party in France, we never managed to get a result of that kind, either during the war in Indochina or during the one in Algeria.

Q.   Even during the Algerian war?

A. No, absolutely not. I know what I'm talking about. I was a member of the Communist Party. I was forced out of it. So, one can say generally speaking, you see, that their way of smothering reality (I don't like the word "reality," let's say "the real")—the throat-cutting, the smothering of the real by words, by the unilateral words of the militant, of the writer, of politics—that is what must be shattered, that is what must be destroyed.

Q. It's paradoxical to put the problem in these terms, since you yourself are a writer. The world must pass through you and yet it must be shattered?

A. Absolutely. I can't read a book; in fact, I can't read at all.

Q. David, then, is to be set free for what you call "savage activity" in the forest?

A. Yes.

Q. But there are dogs in that forest—not police dogs, but hunting dogs.

A. That's it, and both of them are invented by Grinsky.

Q. Invented?

A. They are invented, but they are real for David. Grinsky invented them for David but David recreated them in their entirety, and he believes in them absolutely. He dies because of them.

Q. And David would have killed the Jew in order to possess these purely imaginary dogs because after all, he did come to kill the Jew?

A. No. He came to wait.

Q. For the killing?

A. He came to wait for Grinsky—that is, he still believed that Grinsky was going to come in order to kill. He didn't believe that he had been singled out by Grinsky. Furthermore, he is not angry at Grinsky. After all, Grinsky is the father figure. It comes to the same thing.

Q. He stands for authority. And the second woman, Jeanne . . . ?

A. One can say that Jeanne, who works inside the Party, is liberal democracy, which is the worst form of hypocrisy and soon will be extinct.

Q. *Abahn* then is completely political.

A. It's a political book and that defines its limits. That is why it doesn't go so far as *Détruire,* but the film got away from the political matrix.

Q. How do you move from your texts to films?

A. As far as *Détruire dit-elle* is concerned, the film is fairly faithful to the book, but for *Abahn, Sabana, David,* for instance, the Jew who is the principal concern, the single Jew, remains silent in the movie. I gave him over to madness. Poetry has its madmen, painting has it madmen, music too. And revolution has its madmen. The Jew is a madman of the revolution.

Q. You mean the Jew who in the book lives in the house to which David comes.

A. Yes. And two other Jews come to save him. It's the first one, who is present when the others arrive, who is mad. He is completely "unsalvageable" from the point of view of politics. This means that no leftist party, no party which is termed revolutionary, would be concerned with this man. They would leave him in his corner, of no possible use, an unredeemable element and thus fit to be thrown into the garbage. In the film the Jews put themselves out and risk their lives in order to save him. Obviously, we are in an upside-down world. And at that point, there is an indication of a way . . . which would be the freeing from prejudices which hold that a man be defined by his efficiency, by his efficacity, by his rationality. A madman is as useful as another man.

Q. Then is it the destruction of the rational, of dogma, of the a priori answer that you are talking about?

A. Yes, that's it.

Q. In the book, when Jeanne goes away, you say that the Jew has also left to follow her. Is this because of what occurs in her mind?

A. Yes, that's it; it's the movement into the other.

Q.   In other words, he moved into her concern.

A.   Once David has saved himself, the Jew leaves again. He is in constant movement—this I can say for the justification of the Jews. As Blanchot[1] said, "Abraham was, above all, a man who left." The Jews are the first to have broken the equation: unity equals identity with the state. The Jews are the first to have left the state. The Diaspora is a refusal of the state. So, you see, for me Judaism is the phenomenon of unconditional refusal. But besides Jews, all the hippies, all the young people, poetry, lovers. . . .

Q.   They are all "German Jews."[2]

*Q.**   It is also a refusal which is refused.

A.   It's a refused refusal.

*Q.**   As much by others.

Q.   There is a kind of suggestion of the wandering Jew at the end, because he starts off again as if now it were Jeanne who had taken up the question; at least, he assimilates himself to her at the end.

A.   Completely.

Q.   With the result that one gets the impression that Jeanne is now going to live her own Odyssey, whatever it may be, whereas evidently Sabana returns to the forest; she says, "I am with the Jew. . . ."

A.   But in the movie, he stays in the room and begins to speak, using a dozen words in a kind of incantation. Sabana says that she no longer knows anything and reinvents the forest. She says, "People go by, there are the leaves of the trees, no colors, David is not there yet" and so on, and the talk about the trees, the soles of shoes, the forest is all interior.

Q.   And David is saved. Is he no longer blind or is he still blind?

A.   He is almost always blind. He says, "I don't know how to kill you." (Did he say that in the book? . . . yes, I think so.) "I don't know, I don't know even where the heart is," he says and goes away.

---

[1] Maurice Blanchot, a novelist and critic, whose work since the forties has rested on an exploration of the nature of language and literary expression.

[2] An allusion to one of the student slogans in 1968: "We are all German Jews."

Q. I don't think he says that in the book. It must be in the movie version.

A. It's in the movie. There he goes off and returns to his true homeland, which is sleep.

Q. In the book David goes into the forest; he wants to live with Sabana, but he hasn't yet tried to live. I don't think he says . . .

A. "I don't know how to kill you."

Q. I don't think he says that. "David takes a step through the door; he stops. He says slowly and clearly, 'I didn't kill the Jew.' "

A. That's accurate. It amounts to the same thing.

Q. "You saw through the window that the Jew is alive. . . ."

A. He says that to Grinsky.

Q. Yes, and then at this moment the Jew's voice is heard as he says, "We shall go by the ponds, we shall head north," that is, he opens the road to David, through the forest to an open world. Where do you go from here?

A. Well, I'm writing a kind of sequel to *Lol V. Stein.*

Q. That's interesting because there seems to be a movement back and forth. You spoke of *Les Petits Chevaux de Tarquinia* and how you had felt you must write something that went beyond it, and now you are doing the same thing with this new book and *Lol V. Stein.*

A. Yes. I reread *Lol V. Stein.* I wanted to make a movie out of it, but now I'm not so sure.

Q. Why not?

A. Because rereading the novel made me pursue things farther and then I saw that it entailed something beyond the book. It's with what wasn't said that I am going to write the new book.

Q. How do you come up with the names you use? They are brilliant— Lol V. Stein and the other characters who are born with full-blown names. They aren't called simply "Jeanne," except, of course, in *Abahn,* and she enters last. Characters are often introduced by their complete names and that gives them an unusual presence. The names have a kind of power which compels attention. They surge up, perhaps.

A. I can't tell you how they come about.

Q. But did you have to search for the names?

A. As soon as one says "Stein" in *Détruire,* the woman changes, as if the word had an effect on her. And it does have an effect on her. Then she repeats it mechanically in a sort of bewilderment and she changes accordingly as she repeats it. In the movement of writing, place names often turn into the names of people. S. Tahla comes to life in *Lol V. Stein;* it becomes a man.

Q. That suggests what we might call the musical pattern of your texts, which the repetitions of the name serve to punctuate; it's almost like the tennis balls that come back again. The name comes back with all its force, in its concreteness, and the characters are never confused. One always knows who is speaking; yet you don't say "Max speaks" but "he speaks."

A. It has to be clear.

Q. It's perfectly clear.

A. It scares me a good deal. It's clarity that does it. It isn't the darkness; rather, it's the light. It's the light which is frightening.

Q. In what way?

A. I mean that the very distinct voices . . . that the voices be distinct. This troubles me much more than if they were confused, do you see?

Q. Yes. There are instances in many novels which are now appearing in which the "I's" are confused on purpose.

A. Yes, but that leads to confusion.

Q. In other works one is never sure, but in yours that is not so. It is always very clear. We know who is speaking, and that gives a tremendous force to the dialogue and to the presence of the characters. They are present and never described—or at least rarely so.

A. The eyes, the color of the eyes.

Q. Yes, the eyes.

A. The voice.

Q. And not right away. Generally, it is very uncertain; sometimes a characteristic appears, but just the same, they are present, like a mask which appears. It's an odd thing. Have you ever felt that?

Q.* Oh, yes. You feel that right away.

Q. You feel that you are in a human presence, in the presence of people, of persons. . . .

Q.* But you hear the voices. It's true. You love; you have a knowledge that is tonal, that involves tonality. From all that has just been said, in everything you do, there are myths. The forest, the departure, people leave, this is said. . . .

A. Everyone leaves. That's true. *Un Barrage.* . . .

Q. As you say, there is already a kind of music. And then people leave, but one feels there is a hidden meaning in it all.

Q. Perhaps one senses you reach depths common to us all.

Q.* One gets the impression that in your world the best way to be there is to say "I am leaving." When someone says, "I am leaving," you are sure that he is present. I'm simplifying. . . .

A. But in fact every presence is a quite relative thing, don't you think? Jean's[3] presence, for example, is always very relative.

Q.* Yes, he is elsewhere. You never know. In fact, what constitutes his presence is that you know that he is elsewhere. That's what makes his presence. . . .

A. He is clearly elsewhere. But apropos of *Détruire,* people have asked me what it's about. There is a conversation between Michel Foucault and Philippe Sollers[4] about the book. I didn't take part in it. Then, finally, I believe it was Foucault who asked me my opinion and I answered that I had only one thing to say, "an area from which sleep

---

[3] Jean Lagrollet, a novelist and friend.

[4] Michel Foucault, author of *Histoire de la folie* (*Madness and Civilization*) and *Les Mots et les choses* (*The Order of Things*); Philippe Sollers, dominant figure of the revolutionary review *Tel Quel* (founded in 1960) and an exponent and practitioner of "textual writing," based on linguistic theory.

had disappeared," do you see? *Détruire* is an area from which sleep has disappeared. As a consequence, dreams have disappeared, dreams that compensate. . . .

Q. Therefore, the characters are living lucidity.

A. Yes.

Q. And so what must be destroyed are all the dissimulations and all the compensations?

A. Yes. But it's that lucidity that scares me. I was afraid when I wrote *Détruire dit-elle.*

Q. I should like to ask you one final question, perhaps a banal one. In your opinion what are the responsibilities of the writer? As a contemporary writer, do you recognize any responsibility or do you champion a total freedom?

A. I have held two very different opinions on that score. For a long time, I held for the absolute noncommitment of the writer; now I hold that it is madness and a lie to say that the writer is not committed. A writer commits himself from the very moment he picks up the pen. Revolutionary demands and literary demands are one and the same.

Q. One doesn't destroy the other?

A. They blend. If there is a divorce between the two, there is no longer any composition. There is an absurd mechanical activity which isn't based on anything.

Q. You don't share Sartre's belief in an opposition?

A. Sartre still retains the old sense of guilt. I don't feel that old guilt of the writer at all. To feel it at one level is to feel it at the other. For me, the true intellectual isn't the man of culture; it's the worker. I think that intellectuality in all its rigorous demands has gone down into the proletariat.

Q. And have you discussed your writing with the workers?

A. I know several of them, and, good heavens, I never change my way of speaking to talk with them, never. I have seen some of them really caught up with my film, for instance. I was very happy, indeed.

Q.   Which film? *Détruire dit-elle?*

A.   *Abahn, Sabana, David,* which was against the Communist Party.

Q.   And they understood it?

A.   Thoroughly. They were filled with joy; they said they were very happy, almost ecstatic.

Q.   That is surprising because many readers found *Abahn, Sabana, David* difficult. Perhaps the movie has an immediate impact.

A.   But I was told that one critic said that it would be difficult for me to be much clearer.

An Interview with Nathalie Sarraute

*Conducted by Germaine Brée**

Nathalie Sarraute has become a well-known figure on American campuses, and students often make their way to her quiet, handsome apartment in the sixteenth *arrondissement* of Paris. Intensely sympathetic, she was immediately and totally responsive to her interlocutor. Her whole personality seemed to radiate from dark yet luminous eyes, which reflected a flood of feeling from amusement to deep concentration, as the conversation fluctuated. One could sense throughout an acute mind with an implacable power of observation.

Sarraute was destined to explore what she called *tropismes*, the ever-shifting intersubjective flow of emotions with its polarizations and eddies that exists barely discerned beneath the surface of our lives but accompanies our daily contacts with one another. The problem she faced as a writer was to transpose into words, without intellectualizing or explicating, the shared and elusive substratum of human contact expressed in what she calls "subconversations." She is a conscious and subtle craftsman, who has an uncanny sense of the ridiculousness and pathos of the many dramas played out in human affairs each day at each instant. Bewilderment is likely to overtake the reader unaccustomed to a nonoriented, transparent discourse that moves from character to character and through many levels of consciousness without relying on outer props or devices. Of the new novelists, Nathalie Sarraute has certainly been the most steadfast and coherent in her exploration of a carefully defined domain. Her later works besides are, obliquely, both pertinent and highly amusing satires of the "cultured" Paris set—critics, writers, hangers-

---

* The Sarraute interview was held in Paris in January, 1972. The interview, conducted in French, was translated by Cyril Doherty.

Q. Could you tell us when and how you began to write?

A. Well, I always wanted to write, ever since I was small. Perhaps it was because I spent my early childhood in a literary milieu; perhaps it was because my mother and her second husband, my stepfather, were writers that I didn't dare write for awhile. I liked to do the assignments in French literature at the Sorbonne, and later on I had the impression that I had no substance of my own. It was a time when the novel seemed to be dead—at least the traditional novel. Max Jacob and Valéry were both saying so. As for me, after reading Proust and Joyce, which I did between 1922 and 1924, and then reading Virginia Woolf, I felt that it was no longer possible to write as people had done previously and so, since I couldn't find anything to write about, I didn't write. The first things which I did write were wholly spontaneous. This was between 1932 and 1933 and consisted of fragments which haven't ever been changed and which still remain in the little collection of *Tropismes*. I wrote these almost unconsciously just as one writes a first poem.

Q. You call them "fragments," but they are quite perfect in a way and full of humor and a kind of human understanding. You are quite objective and yet one feels that you are not removed from your work. You describe reactions . . . you see them very clearly, but you do not arrogate to yourself the right to judge.

A. Yes, any such superiority seems to me absolutely inconceivable. I think that at a certain depth everyone has much the same interior movements and the same reactions, and it is not possible to show them if one has not experienced them oneself somehow, even with respect to things other than what one is writing about.

Q. So, after this first work, what really started you on your career as a novelist? I believe that you are about to publish a novel right now, your sixth or maybe your seventh. . . .

A. It's the seventh, if you count *Tropismes* as a novel, which it really isn't. It is, rather, a collection of short texts, but because it doesn't have the slightest plot, people have considered it as my only real novel from the point of view of the *nouveau roman*. I don't totally agree with that judgment because there is no link whatsoever between the fragments and I had no thought of making them into a novel at all. But in my new novel, *Vous les entendez,* I wanted to show a kind of interaction between consciousnesses which are extremely close to one another to the extent that they almost fuse and communicate by a kind of continuous osmosis. It is about a father and a group of young people who are his children but who are not differentiated. What each one feels and attributes to another becomes blurred in a sort of kaleidoscopic conflict in which each becomes any one of the others at any given moment.

I was interested in creating the constant motion, the actual physical motion, involved in the novel's action, since the father goes up and down the stairs to talk, to knock at the door of the children, who are laughing on the floor above him. Everything pivots around a work of pre-Columbian art and the father's and the young people's attitudes to it. By extension, it concerns all art in general, so that there's conflict involving aesthetic feeling, aesthetic joy, fatherly love, and the threat which hangs over art in general, in the father's eyes, because of the scorn shown by the new generation.

After the young people have politely looked at the sculpture, which fascinates the adults, they go upstairs and laugh and laugh endlessly. "One hears them." The father raises his head, listens to them, and becomes exasperated. He ascribes all kinds of meanings to the laughter; he reads all sorts of movements into it.

Q.   Which the laughter may not imply?

A.   Which it may or may not imply.

Q.   Since it may imply them, you are purposely being ambiguous?

A.   Yes.

Q.   You let the reader work out for himself what the meaning might be. What is the connection between this novel and the one which preceded it, *Entre la vie et la mort*?

A.   Since the publication of *Les Fruits d'or,* I have been preoccupied mainly with the relationship between the work of art, the environment into which it falls, and its fate in general. *Entre la vie et la mort* is concerned more with the author, the one who creates the work. Then in *Vous les entendez,* I take up again what seems essential, an attitude with respect to a work of art, namely, the aesthetic sense. After I had finished writing the book, I ran across an article in *L'Express,* I believe, or in *L'Observateur* which stated that Mao Tse-tung had said, "Art is the consolation of the gentleman," and I said to myself, "My two old men are like that," and that is how the young people see them . . . the two old men who sit there in ecstasy before the sculpture of a stone animal.

Q. What is your point of view about this situation?

A. I don't really have one. I pass from one side to the other.

Q. When you published *L'Ere du soupçon* in 1956, a book which really counted in the new self-awareness of the novelist, you had behind you *Tropismes, Le Portrait d'un inconnu,* and *Martereau.* Could you explain the relationship that existed between your practice of the novel and your reflections on it?

A. When I wrote *Tropismes,* I was convinced that it was absolutely impossible to continue writing novels with characters and a plot; I thought I would be able to keep on indefinitely choosing movements that just barely depended on a support that itself was almost invisible and very light, a character who is a sort of shadow, but in whom what counts would be this movement, the tropism, as it was developing. Even before this book was published in 1939, I had already begun trying to find developing tropisms like the first ones, fastened to nothing and hanging in the air all by themselves, and it was extremely difficult to do. Max Jacob had written me that it was like fishing in an enormous bowl. I stayed for days on end with the line cast and there were no bites. I told myself that perhaps it would be interesting to show someone who seeks out these tropisms through two semblances, characters externally resembling traditional ones, like the miser and the old maid in *Le Portrait d'un inconnu.* Thus I would have a richer matter that would radiate from the same center instead of my having to look here and there for disjointed fragments with which to work. And afterwards, a character right out of the traditional novel was to appear and put a stop to all that; he was to destroy all the movements, and everything would fall back again into the norm, into the classical novel. Then, when I wrote *Martereau,* I knew it was going to be the continuation of *Le Portrait d'un inconnu;* that meant a character who has a name, a profession, an external appearance, and whose dialogues with others are written in the wholly traditional form which one uses to describe attitudes—that character would be called Martereau. He would have the reassuring appearance of a character such as we are accustomed to see but this time he would be less strong than the others and, instead of destroying them and bringing the tropisms to a halt, he, in turn, would fall to pieces by coming into contact with the others.

During that time, I lived in almost complete solitude from a literary point of view, and I thought that it would be interesting to find out why these novels didn't awaken even a slight echo since no editor had accepted *Le Portrait d'un inconnu* even with a preface by Sartre. With a good deal of difficulty, one was found who sold the novel for the price of the paper. After getting rid of 400 copies, I didn't have a cent, and I said to myself, "Why do I feel that I'm going in the right direction and that it is not possible to give in and write in the traditional manner?" Because I should tell you that when I tried to write the ending of *Le Portrait d'un inconnu,* the last scenes in which Dumontet, the character who was so conspicuous and visible, is so active, I found that it was very enjoyable and amusing to do, that it didn't bother me in the least, and that I could have continued for pages describing characters like that and plots of every sort which I could have invented very easily. I wondered why I didn't do it. The truth of the matter is that I felt that something was wrong. As a result in 1947, I wrote my first article, which had as its purpose the defense of psychology. People misunderstood me. I had not wanted to defend traditional psychology, the usual analysis of feelings, but I wanted rather to state that there was a kind of psychology in movement, an inner world in movement, which should be brought to light—that people were wrong always to oppose Dostoevsky to Kafka because Kafka himself certainly had not been able to do without the inner world of the psyche.

Q.   People thought you had said exactly the opposite.

A.   They misinterpreted the essay; given all that I owed to Proust, Joyce, and Virginia Woolf, who had already expressed very interesting ideas on the need to reform the novel, it was unthinkable that I should begin to say that these people were obsolete. I had spoken but I was probably so sure I would be understood that I wasn't clear enough. I said "some of us" but I was thinking about other writers (and not about myself), people who considered those writers as decrepit monuments for school children. And people took me to task violently and would have been right had it been true, for I would have shown extraordinary ingratitude.

Q.   Sometimes it is dangerous to be ironic.

A.   Yes. I was also berated for something else, for having advocated a return to the analysis of feeling. I would like to insist that this was not my concern; nevertheless, I felt that the complete absence of an inner core led to a kind of sclerosis or void. I couldn't conceive of literature without the existence of that inner core. Afterwards in 1950, I wrote the second article of *L'Ere du soupçon,* the one which gave its title to the book, in order to show to what extent today's writer, in trying to set limits, creates various kinds of totally academic *trompe l'oeil,* and that today the character in a novel conceived by an author trying to imitate Tolstoy or Balzac could not, as I saw it, produce anything interesting. These essays came out in *Les Temps modernes,* but they didn't create the slightest stir. People asked me what I was talking about. The word "traditional" didn't mean anything to anybody. There was the novel, that's all. By dealing with *sur*-[exterior] and "subconversations," I had also tried to consider a new way of looking at dialogue. It all fell on deaf ears. It was only when the essays were reissued in book form in 1956, when probably, the situation having changed, the time was ripe, that it interested the critics and the readers much more than my other books, which had hardly been of interest to anyone. *L'Ere du soupçon* received rather wide acclaim.

It was at that moment that it attracted the attention of Alain Robbe-Grillet, who had himself written novels in an entirely different vein. He thought it would be interesting for us to form a group and to create something which has since been called *nouveau roman* by the critics. I believe it was Emile Henriot who used this expression when *Tropismes,* reedited by the Editions de Minuit, appeared or, rather, reappeared at the same time as *La Jalousie.* After that Michel Butor, who had published *L'Emploi du temps* and *Passage de Milan* with the Editions de Minuit, joined our group and so a connection was established between people who had practically nothing in common except the desire to change the forms of the novel—such changes had already been made in music and painting. Each of us had his own style and we didn't work at all in the same area.

Q.   It seems in fact that you went off in quite different directions.

A.   One could say that Robbe-Grillet and I are almost at opposite poles.

Q.   Furthermore, Butor is far more abstract.

A.   He is extremely far from both of us.

Q.   After *Le Planétarium,* do you think there was a shift in your concerns? By that I mean more specifically towards the life of the author, his relationships with others, with himself, with his work?

A.   Certainly. The idea came to me when I was writing *Le Plané-tarium*; I had just completed a passage about Germaine Lemaire, the writer, and I thought that it would be very interesting to do something about the literary text itself. I thought of *Les Fruits d'or*. It would be interesting to take a book, which would become the true hero of the novel, and follow its destiny as it rises and falls and especially to examine the tropisms which its publication generates around it. And then afterwards I thought that it would be interesting to concentrate on the writer as such, not on *a* writer. I did not portray an individual writer and anyone can see that the attitudes I described could hardly belong to the same person.

Q.   This was for *Entre la vie et la mort*?

A.   Yes.

Q.   It is a novel which moved me and made me laugh, too. I must confess that I laughed out loud when I read it and that happens rather infrequently, I think.

A.   I'm delighted at that because I like humor in general, and I was surprised to see that the English, for instance, thought that there was no humor in my books—they have such a sense of humor, so I won-dered how they could consider *Martereau* and *Le Planétarium* as humorless.

Q.   They may have read your novels too earnestly, without sufficient perspective perhaps, to see that they are extremely funny in a subtle way. But *Martereau* and *Le Planétarium* are very amusing just the same. And it seems to me that in *Entre la vie et la mort* you settle the score with the critics. It is unusually entertaining because it subtly attacks all the myths that grow up around the writer.

A.   I hoped it would. Some things, for example, have always exas-perated me. When something is unsuccessful and somebody tells the author so, the author invariably answers, "I did that on purpose." I wrote a whole passage about that reply, but it left people indifferent and they continued to say, "That bit is dull because I made it so on purpose."

Q.   I am convinced that you do it on purpose.

A.   Yes. But I don't think that books influence life. Life goes on and books do not change people's attitudes.

Q.   Perhaps not right away, but don't you think that in the long run they make people more sensitive to certain issues?

A.   I don't know.

Q.   It seems to me that they could make people sensitive, for example, to a certain "tropism" which they had not seen for what it was until then. It seems to me that your books have done that at any rate. I was saying a moment ago that I found *Entre la vie et la mort* moving because I thought it also described a drama, the drama of the struggling writer.

A.   Certainly. I had wanted to show the terrible kind of ambiguity in which he works. He is constantly tossed back and forth between the need for total solitude and the need for a certain amount of understanding on the part of others, of approbation, because in order to live a book needs a reader. A writer also suffers because the materials with which he would like to work have already been, and are all the time being, covered over with clichés, a certain varnish he has to scrape away to uncover something which, at first glance, seems ugly and even repulsive.

Q.   It seemed to me that in this book there are some moments which are quite dramatic whose intensity is conveyed by a lyricism in the imagery. The richness of the imagery is sometimes ironic with respect to the consciousness of the writer. In any case, one sees a certain mystery taking shape; for example, you say there is a moment when your writer moves into the virtual, where, all at once, his work begins to grow and take on a kind of life of its own. Doubt then besets him.

A.   Yes, yes, indeed.

Q.   Is he deluded or is the work really alive?

A.   It is very hard to say. This is what makes writing almost agonizing. The more you polish the form and perfect it, the more it hardens, becomes frozen, and dies, so that you can count on no gain from the work you have done. It is often almost dangerous to polish the writing and the form too much. It often happens—precisely when the polishing has been intense and the form has taken on an aspect of great beauty which delights the writer when he first reads it—that when he comes back to it a few days later he sees that it is a corpse, entirely dead and meaningless. The reason is that, having lost all contact with his initial feeling, he has been carried away by the charm of language as such. Language has taken over and has necessarily sought harmony and an extremely dangerous aesthetic form; the surge, the aggressive force, and the expectation of something which is about to be born have all been lost.

Q. Is that what you were saying a moment ago when you spoke of a sort of dual personality in the writer?

A. Exactly. I think that each writer, each artist in general . . . this is equally true of painters . . . has a kind of double, who, from time to time as he works, stands back and looks at his painting or rereads his text. He is both himself and someone else. He often becomes a completely merciless judge. And it is he who suddenly sees that that wasn't what he wanted and that the work is dead.

Q. Yet there seem to be times in the novel when perhaps the writer himself is mistaken.

A. There are times when he can be mistaken, but when it comes to the work, it is almost imperative that he have faith in his judgment since he is the only judge.

Q. In this development of a kind of judgment on the technique itself which is used, do you have a point of view? In a word, are your techniques conscious or do they develop as your novel grows?

A. They are unconscious. For instance, I noticed in my last book— and realized it only a long time after I had begun the book—that I was no longer separating dialogue from "subconversation." That came about quite naturally. I even thought that maybe I ought to have put in quotation marks, all the same, so as to show that the conversation starts right there. Then I thought it didn't really matter. When I wrote *Le Portrait d'un inconnu,* I hadn't even realized that it was impossible for me to give the characters names. With the exception of Dumontet, there was "he," "she," "the old man," "the daughter"; and when I was correcting the proofs, I said to myself occasionally, "Just the same, I ought to give some indication here. . . ." I don't like obscurity for its own sake. I even considered putting a name in, but I saw that it was impossible. It ruined everything because as soon as I gave a name,

"Jeanne said," for instance, I found myself standing at a distance . . .
I was no longer at the center. There, there are no names; there is
nothing. There's a kind of anonymous substance that functions on its
own. It's worked that way every time. Here, for example, there are
chapters in which everything takes place purely in the realm of the
imagination. These chapters happened that way without my realizing
it. I kept going exactly as if I were always in the realm of the real,
although I had moved out of it quite spontaneously. Sometimes I say
to myself beforehand, "I ought to do some particular thing here," but
it is always to give more life to the initial sensation.

Q.   And now that a new novel is about to come out, will another one
follow or are you going to turn to the theater?

A.   At present, I am finishing a play for the Stuttgart radio. It's a
very funny play. It comes from the same source as *Vous les entendez*
and will be called *C'est beau*. I've got about two-thirds of it done. And
then, after that, I shall have to think about a book again.

Q.   A novel?

A.   I have lots of ideas about it but still. . . .

Q.   How about your two earlier plays which are also very funny?

A.   There are really three, *Le Silence, Le Mensonge,* and *Isma*. The
last one was only given over the radio but it will be produced on stage
with my next play.

Q.   Do your characters first come to you as voices when you start
writing a play?

A.   Exactly—as voices. I don't visualize any characters. And when
Barrault wanted to stage *Le Silence* and *Le Mensonge,* he asked me
how old the characters were and who they were. It was almost by accident that I wrote "man" or "woman." In truth I could have switched
those designations or put them in the plural. I don't see them and I
don't visualize the stage either. I don't see any exterior action. I just
hear voices and rhythms.

An Interview with Stanley Kunitz

Conducted by Cynthia Davis *

Q. Mr. Kunitz, you said once to a group of students studying your poetry that no one has the "right answers" in interpretation, and that after it's published the poem belongs as much to them as to you. Are you generally reluctant to explain your poems?

A. I often don't really know what a poem means, in rational terms. There are so many currents that flow into the poem, of which the poet himself can't be totally aware. Years after you have written a poem, you come back to it and find something you didn't know was there. Sometimes, I grant, a poet can be helpful about a specific image or an obscure portion of his poem.

Q. Do you think it's helpful to talk about the circumstances that led to your writing a poem?

A. If they can be recalled, they may, in some cases, prove illuminating. But, as a general rule, the poem ought to have released itself from the circumstances of its origin.

Q. Is that related to the idea of myth—poetry as myth?

A. Yes, it's that, but it's also related to my feeling that the poem has to be found beyond the day, that it requires a plunge into the well of one's being, where all one's key images lie. The occasion for a poem,

---
* The interview was conducted on March 9, 1972, at Mr. Kunitz's home in New York. Mr. Kunitz kindly consented to read and edit the interview. Poems quoted are identified by page number with the following abbreviations: *IT—Intellectual Things* (New York: Doubleday, 1930); *PW—Passport to the War* (New York: Henry Holt, 1944); *SP—Selected Poems 1928–1958* (Boston: Little, Brown, 1958); *TT—The Testing-Tree* (Boston: Little, Brown, 1971).

which may have been something quite casual, is not the true source of the poem—it has only helped to trigger the right nerves.

Q.   When I asked about myth, I was thinking of the idea that I find in the poems of "The Coat without a Seam" especially, the idea that myth is something constant that can be expressed in many different kinds of circumstances, but that goes beyond circumstances—even beyond the individual. So a great poem speaks to everyone because all share a common condition.

A.   Jung spoke of archetypal images that go beyond the individual persona and that pertain to the collective history of the race.

Q.   Is that a reason for your use of dream and hallucination in the poetry—to reach that archetypal material?

A.   I think of dream as an actual visitation into that world, as a clue to secrets of which one is only faintly aware in ordinary consciousness.

Q.   But you wouldn't agree with the "psychic automatism" of the surrealists?

A.   No. Because I think a poem is a combination of unconscious and conscious factors. One is trying to reach a level of transcendence; at the same time, one has to keep a grip on language, not to let it run away with itself. Automatic writing is such a bore!

Q.   Is your use of metaphysical techniques—exploiting the metaphor in extended conceits—one of the ways of exercising that conscious control over language, giving form to the raw materials of the unconscious mind?

A.   The image leads you out of yourself into a world of relatives. The beautiful risk to take is to extend the image as far as you can go, until it turns in upon itself. The danger is in jumping off into absurdity, but that's part of the risk.

Q.   Perhaps we can consider some of these questions by talking about changes in your development. You eliminated almost half of the poems in *Intellectual Things* (1930) in later volumes. Was that because they were technically unsuccessful, or because you no longer agreed with the ideas you expressed in them?

A.   My main feeling was that they were immature. Maybe I felt a little embarrassed reading them, so I thought it would be better to drop them, that's all.

Q. I felt that many of the poems in that book placed much greater emphasis on the power of the intellect than later poems. I'm thinking of poems like "Mens Creatrix" (*IT*, p. 16), in which you seem to talk about the superiority of the intellect over the emotions. I wondered if perhaps one of the reasons for elimination of such poems was that you had changed your emphasis.

A. I doubt it. Certainly when I was writing the poems in *Intellectual Things*, I meant to demonstrate, if I could, not that the poem was a cerebral exercise, but the contrary, that the intellect and the passions were inseparable—which is the whole point of the Blake epigraph to the book, "The tear is an intellectual thing."

Q. Then why the poems in which you talk about putting away passion, or subduing it by intellectual power?

A. It's not a question of putting it away or rising above it. Remember, I'm thinking back a good many years, so that I wouldn't swear to this—but my recollection is that my characteristic figure at this stage, in speaking of mind and heart, was of each devouring and being devoured by the other, an act of mutual ingestion. In "Beyond Reason" (*IT*, p. 62) I spoke of taming the passions "with the sections of my mind"—as though it were a sort of dog food—but then I wanted to "teach my mind to love its thoughtless crack."

Q. One of the poems that impressed me on this theme was "Motion of Wish" (*IT*, p. 52).

A. I'll take a look at it and see whether you're right or not. . . . Yes, I think the lines you were thinking of were ". . . wish may find / Mastery only in the mind." This poem I haven't looked at in so long, but as I read it now, I see these lines as the key to understanding of the poem: ". . . mariners eat / One lotus-moment to forget / All other moments, and their eyes / Fasten on impossible surprise." And then the end: "A man may journey to the sun, / But his one true love and companion / Sleeps curled in his thoughtful womb. / Here will the lone life-traveler come / To find himself infallibly home." But you have to consider here that the mind is the eater of the passions, and the passions rest in that mind, so that what one is asserting is a sense of the unity of all experience, not a separation.

Q. And the mind contains that sense of unity.

A. Yes. The mind stands for the whole experiential and existential process. I think that the confusion here is to think that when I talk of mind in this volume, that I'm talking about brain. I'm not talking about brain; I'm talking about the whole process of existence.

Q. What about poems like "Very Tree" (*IT*, p. 21), where it seems that what you're saying is that you perceive the essence of the tree—its treeness—and discard its particulars? That the particulars are not important?

A. One of my great influences was Plato, and I was very deep in Platonic lore, especially at this period of my first work. The theme is the idea of tree, treeness, as opposed to the shadow of the idea.

Q. But you're not really suggesting that particulars of experience are unimportant?

A. You arrive at universals through the perception—the clear perception—of what Blake called "Minute Particulars."

Q. These earlier poems are much more abstract than your later work, aren't they?

A. I suppose so. That may have been the Platonic influence, as much as anything else that I can think of.

Q. Did you become dissatisfied with that kind of approach?

A. As I became more of a political being, I wanted to fasten my poems to the reality of the day. I turned away from poems that began with the grandeur of generality. I wanted to find the general through breaking the kernel of particulars.

Q. Is this why, in *Passport to the War* (1944), you make so many references to contemporary events? As concretions for your general themes?

A. Don't you think that that is possibly simply the result of maturing a bit and having more experience of the world? At the time of writing *Intellectual Things*, I was in my early twenties and was an innocent in so many ways. I had developed intellectually more than I had emotionally or experientially.

Q. This volume, especially the war poetry, seems very different even from your later poetry.

A. It was my darkest time.

Q. Do you still have the same feelings about the conditions of the modern world and what it does to man?

A. I've never stopped being a dissenter. I have no use for a superior technology that breeds hatred, injustice, inequality, and war.

Q. What do you think the poet's position should be in relationship to that kind of society?

A. Number one, he must not become a subscribing member of it. Since the beginning of the Industrial Revolution, the poet has been the prophetic voice of a counterculture. Poetry today speaks more directly to the young than ever before because they recognize its adversary position.

Q. Then you think it's more difficult to be a poet now than it was before the nineteenth century?

A. The poet before the Industrial Revolution could identify himself with State or Church, but he certainly has not been able to do so since. That's why he is a creature apart.

Q. You often talk about guilt in *Passport to the War.* Sometimes it's played upon by society, but sometimes you seem to say that everyone carries a load of guilt around with him. What is this guilt caused by and directed at?

A. When I speak of "The Guilty Man" (*PW*, p. 27), I don't mean someone who has sinned more than anybody else. I mean the person who, simply by virtue of being mortal, is in a way condemned; he's mortal and he's fallible, and his life is inevitably a series of errors and consequences. Since he cannot really see the true path—it is not given to him to see it, except in moments of revelation—he is denied the rapture of innocence.

Q. Like Original Sin?

A. Without the theological furniture.

Q. Is this related to the existentialist idea of the fear of freedom?

A. I was making noises like an existentialist before I knew what it was to be one. I keep on trying to record my sense of being alive, which means in practice my sense, from moment to moment, of living and dying at once, a condition of perpetual crisis.

Q. In particular, when I read "The Fitting of the Mask" (*PW*, p. 28), I thought of Sartre's "bad faith": the attempt to conceal one's own being from oneself.

A. If we did not wear masks, we should be frightened of mirrors.

Q. You say in "Night Letter" (*PW*, p. 9) that you "believe in love" as the salvation from this fear of one's own being and from the evils of modern society. Are you speaking primarily of love for mankind or personal love?

A. Abstract love is not love at all. One expresses love in relation to another—that's the germinal node. I don't really care much for people who are always talking about love for mankind and hate their neighbors.

Q. The treatment of the love theme is another difference I found between the first volume and later ones. In *Intellectual Things*, the love poetry is often about relationships that fail; it isn't until the later poetry that you really celebrate fulfilling relationships.

A. That's more or less to be expected. After all, the disasters of early love are legendary and part of one's education. For that reason, among others, poets in their youth tend to be melancholy. "When I was young," said Yeats, "my Muse was old; now that I am old, my Muse is young."

Q. It wasn't, then, that you had a more pessimistic conception of the relationship?

A. I've always been an optimist about love. Three marriages are the proof.

Q. I'd like to talk a little about *Selected Poems*. Perhaps we could begin with a poem that seems central to that volume, "The Approach to Thebes" (*SP*, p. 31). That poem ends with these lines: ". . . I met a lovely monster, / And the story's this: I made the monster me." Is this just acceptance of one's fate?

A. More than that. . . . I have a theory about monsters. I remember, a few years ago, telling Mark Rothko, who was a dear friend of mine, that every genius is a monster. Mark thought about that for some time, and then, with the typical vanity of an artist, said, "You mean I'm a monster?" I replied, "Well, I'm not talking about anybody in this room." But of course I was. The adversary artist in our time pays a price, in human terms, for his excess of ego and sensibility. He has had to sacrifice too much; he is poisoned by ambition; and he carries too big a load of griefs and shames—that's the hunch on his back. You're not likely to find him open, generous, or joyous. Rothko, incidentally, killed himself by slashing his wrists not long after our discussion. I have a poem about him, entitled "The Artist," in *The Testing-Tree.*

Q. And the burden of monsterdom is placed on mythic heroes, too?

A. Yes.

Q. There's one mythic hero that you seem to consider more than others, and that's Christ. Why is the Christian myth more important in your poetry than other myths?

A. Because it shakes me more. It is the supreme drama of guilt and redemption. I have no religion—perhaps that is why I think so much about God.

Q. When you speak of myth in poetry, you mean a re-creation of the human drama embodied in religious myths such as this?

A. Poetic myth is nourished by all the great traditions.

Q. Then you are saying that all myths attempt to do the same thing, to tell the same story.

A. All myths are the same myth; all metaphors are the same metaphor. When you touch the web of creation at any point, the whole web shudders.

Q. And poetry has the same function as myth?

A. Metaphorically.

Q. You draw many parallels between the poet and the mythic hero. Do you, like so many poets, see the poet as supreme example of affirmative action, of what a man can be?

A.   As I said a while back, he can be a monster. But ideally he is the last representative free man, in that he is beholden to nobody but himself and his own vision of truth. Almost anybody else you can think of is beholden to others: the pastor to his congregation, the politician to the public, the actor to his audience. But the poet, since he is not a commodity, is more blessed than others—he can strive toward the absolute purity of his art.

Q.   Aren't you beholden to your publisher and your readers, at least in some measure financially?

A.   No, I don't think so. One manages to survive. If I felt for a moment that I had to write lies in order to publish, I would stop publishing. It wouldn't matter that much. I could still go on writing.

Q.   You're especially concerned with the question of what it is to be a poet in "The Coat without a Seam," and nearly all of the poems in that section are new in *Selected Poems.* Why is it that you became more concerned with poems about poetry in that volume?

A.   I'm not sure that I did. Periodically one tries to redefine and reassert one's vocation—not always in obvious terms. Wallace Stevens made a career out of doing precisely that. "Poetry," he wrote, "is the subject of the poem." As you rightly perceived, I keep trying to relate poetic function with mythic or heroic destiny.

Q.   You note that relationship in other sections, too, in poems like "Green Ways" (*SP*, p. 5).

A.   I wonder whether you caught the logic of the various sections in the *Selected Poems.* They were meant to indicate my primary thematic concerns.

Q.   Perhaps you would talk about a couple of those sections; for example, "The Terrible Threshold."

A.   That title—"The Terrible Threshold"—comes, of course, from one of the poems, "Open the Gates" (*SP*, p. 41), where the poet sees "The end and the beginning in each other's arms." I think of the poems in this section as visionary experiences, culminating in a moment of illumination.

Q.   In speaking to a group of students studying "Prophecy on Lethe" (*SP*, p. 61), you said that that moment was one of fleeting awareness, and that you couldn't state what that awareness was of. If you can't state what you see in that moment of epiphany. . . .

A.   I don't have to state it. The awareness is in the poem, not in my memory of it. Come to think of it, I don't even remember what the last lines were!

Q.   "With your strange brain blooming as it lies / Abandoned to the bipeds on the beach; / Your jelly-mouth and, crushed, your polyp eyes."

A.   I see all those death images piled up on that shore. The key word, the transcendental word, for me is "blooming."

Q.   There's a movement there toward a sense of identity, isn't there? First an anonymous figure floating on the stream, and at the end you speak directly to the "you."

A.   Death-in-Life. Life-in-Death. The glory of the senses. . . .

Q.   This is what I was trying to get at: I saw the poem as, at least partially, a myth of the birth of consciousness, moving from a Being-in-Itself state—unconscious and no perception—to that sense of identity that you have because you're conscious. And of course, a sharper awareness of your own sensuous perceptions. I don't know whether that would be valid or not.

A.   Thanks—I'll buy it. It just occurs to me that there's a comparable evolution in my later poem, "Green Ways." I hadn't seen the affinity before.

Q.   And part of the point of "Green Ways" is that it is the duty of the conscious being to accept his consciousness, isn't it?

A.   More than that, he must affirm his vegetable and mineral existence, as well as his animal self.

Q.   Not discarding them with consciousness, then.

A.   Accepting them, in the fullness of the life-process.

Q.   Could you talk a little about "The Serpent's Word" section also?

A.   Those are love poems, or deal with the love experience. The phrase is always the key to the section that it heads; here it's from the line: "Who taught me the serpent's word, but yet the word." Which takes us back to the Garden of Eden.

Q. In "The Dark and the Fair" (*SP*, p. 33), the source of that line, there's a Fair Lady and another Dark Lady, and the Dark Lady replaces the Fair. The Dark Lady is from the past; is she symbolic of the Fall?

A. She's Lilith, in the poem.

Q. There is another poem in "The Serpent's Word" that I find more difficult than most, "As Flowers Are" (*SP*, p. 10).

A. That poem records the changes in a field through the seasons. And at the same time, it offers by implication a metaphor of the aspects of love. From week to week each species of flower, each hue, struggles to gain possession of the field.

Q. Is that the "war" of the flowers?

A. Yes. The yellows and whites of spring yield to the hot tones of summer, a riot of colors. The chill nights bring the lavenders in; and, with the first frost, the whole field turns bronze. It's a parable, I suppose.

Q. I think I see it now.

A. It's not so difficult, if you listen to the music.

Q. You've said that in an open society, poetry tends to become hermetic, more difficult, and very private. Do you think this is true of your own poetry?

A. The important question is, do I still think we live in an open society. Certainly America seems to me less open than it was. And certainly my work has undergone a sea-change. Robert Lowell wrote something to the effect that I've broken with my "passionately gnarled" earlier style and am writing in a language that "even cats and dogs can understand." Perhaps in my age I've managed to untie some of the knots of my youth. I want to say what I have to say without fuss. I want to strip everything down to essentials.

Q. You talked about some of these ideas in *Passport to the War*, and that volume also had a more open style than the first one.

A. Poets are always wanting to change their lives and their styles. Of the two, it's easier to change the life.

Q. In that last volume, *The Testing-Tree* (1971), you included several of your translations of other authors. Why did you pick those particular ones?

A. Obviously because I liked them as poems. And because they seemed to have an affinity with my own work. For example, I've been working on the poems of Anna Akhmatova for several years—they make up my next book. I've been so absorbed in her verse that it would be surprising if I hadn't been affected by it. Incidentally, I tend to think of a book as a composition, a joining of parts into an architectural whole, not just a throwing-together of the poems as written. A book ought to have an interior logic: these few translations seemed to me to fit into the logic of this particular book. I deliberately excluded scores of others.

Q. Are they fairly strict translations?

A. Close, but not slavishly close. Translating poetry is an exercise in paradox. "Be true to me!" says the poem to its translator. And in the next breath, "Transform me, make me new!" If you follow the original, word for word, and lose the poetry—as you must, if you insist on a literal rendering—your translation is a dud. But if you find the poetry in a free act of the imagination, it's a lie. I'm reminded of the citizen in Kafka's aphorism who's fettered to two chains, one attached to earth, the other to heaven. No matter which way he heads, the opposite chain pulls him back with a jolt. That's pretty much the condition of the translator.

Q. Do you read the originals yourself?

A. My knowledge of Russian is rudimentary. Though my parents came from Russia, I am not a Russian linguist or scholar. So I nearly always translate with somebody whom I can depend on for roots and connotations and allusions. Max Hayward helped me with Akhmatova, as he did before with Voznesensky.

Q. Did you do many translations earlier?

A. A few . . . from French, Spanish, and Italian. I included one of my Baudelaire translations in *Selected Poems*. He was important to me.

Q. You spoke of the "internal logic" of a volume of poetry. Does *The Testing-Tree* have a definite logic for its sections, as *Selected Poems* does?

A. A logic, but less definite, perhaps. I shuffled those poems all around. The first section is the overture, anticipating the main themes. Section two is dominated by poems of place; three, political; four deals with the role and character of the artist.

Q. The title poem seems most like your earlier poems in theme.

A. Not in form, certainly. But that and "King of the River" go back to the mythic.

Q. Were they written earlier?

A. No. Quite late.

Q. Would you say, then, that your themes are the same, that you're just expressing them in a different way?

A. A man's preoccupations and themes aren't likely to change. What changes is the extent to which he can put the full diversity of his moods and interests and information into his poems. Formal verse is a highly selective medium. A high style wants to be fed exclusively on high sentiments. Given the kind of person I am, I came to see the need for a middle style—for a low style, even, though that may be outside my range.

Q. I was interested in Robert Lowell's review of *The Testing-Tree* because I thought that he was saying, among other things, that the new poetry was more like his, more like confessional poetry.

A. I've always been an intensely subjective poet. There's never been any shift from that.

Q. The sort of open description of autobiographical detail that appears in your last volume is generally considered confessional poetry.

A. Confession is a private matter. Most so-called confessional poetry strikes me as raw and embarrassing—bad art.

Q. Do you think you've been influenced by any of the confessional poets? Lowell and Roethke?

A. In the first place, you musn't call Roethke a confessional poet.

He would have vomited at the thought. We were friends for thirty years, till his death, swapping manuscripts and criticism. My friendship with Lowell dates from the publication of my *Selected Poems* in 1958. *Intellectual Things* had brought Roethke and me together—he was still unpublished. But these are more than literary friendships. In these long and deep associations it's idle to discuss who influences whom. Friendship is a sustained act of reciprocity. We have all been touched by our interchange. Vulnerable human beings affect each other; that's all there is to it.

Q. You wouldn't then put yourself in any group?

A. Now or at any stage, I can't imagine to what group I could possibly be attached. A one-to-one relationship is the limit of my herd instinct.

Q. What earlier poets would you say influenced you greatly?

A. Donne and Herbert and Blake were my first major influences— Donne and Herbert stylistically, Blake prophetically. I must have learned something, too, from Wordsworth's "Prelude" and his "Intimations of Immortality." For awhile I steeped myself in Keats and Tennyson. After that, almost nobody until Hopkins overwhelmed me during my college years. And Yeats, of course, whom I consider to be the great master of the poem in English in this century. I suppose Eliot to a degree, though I opposed him, quarreling with his ideas, his criticism, and what I thought of as his poverty of sympathy. His theory of the depersonalization of poetry struck me as false and destructive. My work didn't fit into that picture of his at all. Both Roethke and I felt from the beginning that the Eliot school was our principal adversary. We fought for a more passionate art. Nevertheless I was so aware of his existence that even in a negative way I was influenced by him. So was Roethke. That Eliot rhythm had an hypnotic effect.

Q. I'd like to go back for a moment to the question we discussed earlier, your differences from confessional poets. Your latest volume is certainly more directly autobiographical than the others. Rosenthal justifies the use of autobiographical material in confessional poetry by the poet's assumption that the literal self is important and that it becomes symbolic of the world—what happens to the self is what the modern world does to man. How does your idea of poetry differ from that?

A. I phrase it differently. I say that the effort is to convert one's life into legend, which isn't quite the same thing. Secrets are part of the legend. My emphasis isn't on spilling everything. It's on the act of transformation, the ritual sense, the perception of a destiny.

Q.   Is it possible to see these mythic connections even if you're not a poet?

A.   I'm not contending that the poet is set apart from others. On the contrary, he is more like others than anybody else—that's his nature. It's what Keats meant by negative capability, the predisposition to flow into everyone and everything. A poetry of self-indulgence and self-advertisement is produced by the egotistical sublime—Keats's phrase again—and is simply ugly. God knows a poet needs ego, but it has to be consumed in the fire of the poetic action.

Q.   Then your view is almost the reverse of the confessional one; you begin with a general idea of the human condition.

A.   The only reason you write about yourself is that this is what you know best. What else has half as much reality for you? Even so, certain details of your life can be clouded by pain, or fear, or shame, or other complications, that induce you to lie, to disguise the truth about yourself. But the truth about yourself is no more important than the truth about anybody else. And if you knew anybody else as well as you know yourself, you would write about that other.

An Interview with James Dickey

*Conducted by David L. Arnett**

Q. Could you give some background on the writing of *Deliverance*?

A. Well, it would begin with the time I lived in Atlanta. I worked in the advertising business, and fell in with a remarkable group of men—Lewis King and Al Braselton, to whom I have dedicated the book. Lewis King especially was a fascinating character to me. He is kind of similar to the Lewis Medlock of the novel, but also in some ways very dissimilar. But what fascinated me about Lewis King is what fascinated Ed Gentry about Lewis Medlock. He's the only man with the private means to do what he wanted with his one human life and also the ambition and the willpower to realize it.

So, Lewis King, and I, and Al Braselton, who worked with me in the advertising business, used to go on these long canoe trips through north Georgia. North Georgia is largely untouched, and people are moving out of it now. There are some places that Lewis King and I have been—say in the Chattahoochee National Forest, up in the north central part of the state on the Tennessee border—that I would guarantee nobody has ever been to before. No Indian has ever seen some of those places. And it struck me that with the automobile there is this strange kind of schizophrenic or dual existence possible, where you are in a white shirt and a tie in an office one day, and then late that afternoon you can be in a canoe in an almost untouched kind of a wilderness. And it seemed to me that a kind of balance of values would be possible to show in a novel, where fellows who were decent suburban householders and commuter businessmen during the week would then be out in a totally different situation or in, as the hippies say, a differ-

* The interview, edited for concision, was conducted on March 26, 1972, at Mr. Dickey's home in Columbia, South Carolina.

ent "bag" in just a few hours—you know, where they would be up against a situation of primitive survival that nothing in their upbringing or their contemporary, quotidian situation could ever have prepared them for.

It seemed to me that in a situation of this sort, which really just does come down to gut survival, characteristics in these people over whom the veneer of civilization has placed a kind of patina would then link up with the age-old preoccupation of men to preserve themselves—that they would feel that linkup with human necessity situations that goes all the way back to the caves. And Ed Gentry, the guy who is a decent fellow and an art director and so on, sees what the situation is after Lewis, the guy who rather self-consciously trains for a situation like this, [is injured]. Ed Gentry, because of the circumstances, is thrown into the situation where he's got to be the deliverer. Either he does what he has to do—involving killing somebody—or they all die, including himself. And I would like the reader—or the viewer of the movie, as the chance may be—to sort of get the idea that this guy who sat in an art direction chair for years and has never suspected that he had any such qualities as these at all, is really kind of naturally good at this.

Q. I have read that the idea first occurred to you in 1962 in Positano, Italy.

A. Yes, that's true. After one of those big Italian meals, I was lying in bed in the full southern Italian sunlight, which is really tremendously pleasant, and it occurred to me that some events that I had undergone, or lived through, I guess you could say, plus some things that I had heard about and some things that I could invent, would go together into a kind of unified or coherent story. I had never written any stories or novels or anything like that before, but it occurred to me that it might just work out fine. So I got up from bed, reluctantly, because I was so sleepy, and I made a few notes—I'd say half a page in longhand—and went back to sleep contented. And that was the beginning. I mean I knew the whole story in five minutes. The whole thing! And where it would take place and who the people would be. And the general outline of the action I knew in five minutes or less, or maybe even one minute. But I didn't know *how* the people would be.

The hardest character for me to fix—or to find out about, or to make like I thought he should be for the novel—was Lewis. I knew how Ed would be; I knew how Bobby would be—we've all seen many of them. And I knew how Drew would be—I mean, he's the guy next door to you cutting the lawn. But I didn't know how Lewis with his strange, enigmatic personality. . . . Is he a phony? Or is it all just a put-on with him? Or is he a paranoid? Or what is he? You should think maybe one or the other. But the thing about Lewis is that he does what he says he can do! If he says he can put up 180 pounds in a military press, he can take you right out there and show you that he can do it. If he says he can shoot 180, 190, 200, or 220 on an archery field range, he can demonstrate that he can do it.

Lewis doesn't claim to be able to do anything that he can't do. And this, coupled with the fact that I gave him a tremendously impressive middle-aged body, would—I thought then, and I still do—would be so impressive to these guys that they would take his advice on anything, including questions of morality. Whether or not to bury the guy that Lewis has shot, for example, or to make a clean breast of it and stay within the law. He says, "No, no, we're not going to do that, we're going to go outside the law. We're the law!" And Lewis is the college athlete who still can outdo almost any college athlete at the age of thirty-eight. You see, he intellectualizes about it, which gives him even more authority. And then he says somewhere in *Deliverance* that the body is the one thing that can't be faked—it's either there, or it's not! And his is.

Q.   Did you write continually and revise for eight years or were there certain bursts?

A.   Oh, no! That eight years business that I see quoted around everywhere is very, very misleading, because I conceived of the idea in '62 and messed around with it a bit for several years without any great results, but I also wrote during that time six other books. It was definitely low on the priority list. My main interest was poetry then and still is. I have no desire whatever to be a best-selling novelist who has to have a best seller every four years. That doesn't interest me at all. *Deliverance* was just something I messed around with, and I talked it over a lot with my oldest son and also with Lewis and Al back in Atlanta to try to figure out what might be done with it. But I had no real notion of finishing it—oh, maybe in years and years. Twenty years later I might have finished it, if I got around to it.

But then an editor from Houghton Mifflin got wind of it. They sent someone out to Portland, Oregon, where I was living at the time, who read my 90-page draft and bought the novel on the spot. So then I had to finish it, because I had taken the dollar off the drumhead. I didn't have a deadline or anything, but the fact that my novelistic abilities would cause these editors to get into a flutter and send a guy all the way from Boston impressed me with the fact that it might actually be possible to write it instead of just fooling around. But I didn't really get to work well on the novel until I got down to South Carolina three or four years ago, although, by that time everything was in place, and all I had to do was fill in the details—put the meat on the bones, flesh out the skeleton—and it was there.

Then I began the eternal struggle with style. It was originally written in a far more introverted kind of James Agee or John Updike style, but it dawned on me very slowly—something that I should have seen much, much earlier—the notion that the main thing that the story itself had going for it was the narrative thrust, and you don't want to impede the progress of that with a lot of golden saxophone prose, so I stripped the style down and made it like essentially it came out to be in the end product. When I had that solved, when I had a consistent style and a consistent way of seeing the world for the narrator, Ed Gentry, then with the other stuff that I had accumulated over the years, it almost wrote itself.

Q. Did the writing of the novel stimulate the writing of poetry at the time?

A. No, I have a great ambition to write on a schedule and do things on a schedule—do this so much of the day, play the guitar so much of the day. If I could work out a way where I could play the guitar for three hours, I would really be happy with myself. I write for maybe six or seven. I like to do something physical. I'd like to be able to write for maybe four or five hours a day, play the guitar for three, shoot a hundred arrows a day, do a certain amount of weight lifting three times a week, and run a lot. Around the lake here where I live it's 3.7 miles, and if I go around that once a day, that would get me physically where I would much rather be than where I actually am. But then there's family life, there's this enormous correspondence, there's the endless in-fighting of movie-making, which I hope to hell to be out of after the film version of *Deliverance* is released. And there's teaching, of course, and the preparation of trying to make the courses interesting and doing them a different way every time, because I like to be in a course, in lectures, in the sense that I myself enjoy listening to what I'm talking about. . . .

Q. The transformation in Ed Gentry is prefigured, I think, by the description of the linden moth early in the novel.

A. I don't know what that symbolism means, if there is any. It's just the linden moth, this thing, this little larva hanging down on threads, is an extraordinary thing to see. It's an extraordinary visual image. And I just thought it would give Lewis a chance to talk a little more, to talk about that, to show his expertise about the woods and also to have some kind of prefiguration of death and execution. That's really all I thought about.

Q. Yet, also, there is the uncollected poem "For the Linden Moth," in which the moths are described as "Struggling to change in midair,/ On their monofilament threads,/ To their other and better selves."[1] And that certainly parallels Ed Gentry's struggle, I think, in the tree.

A. Who wrote that?

Q. You.

A. That's damn good! Why didn't I ever collect that one! Well, that's right, I agree. I love to agree with critics—especially when they're this perceptive. But, believe me, much writing is subliminal or unconscious. That's exactly the same scene—the scene of the linden moth struggling to change.

Q. We're also told in the poem that "They struggle, contending with/ Themselves, and sentenced justly/ To writhe until glorified." Resurrection is also mentioned in that poem. So, I think the same is true of Ed Gentry. Several of your poems, including "Sleeping Out at Easter," "The Lifeguard," "A Folk Singer of the Thirties," and "The First Morning of Cancer," describe the transformation of men into Christ figures.

A. "The First Morning of Cancer" was an ambitious and kind of pretentious poem that I wrote when I really didn't know what I was doing. I'm glad I wrote it. And that poem brought about—in New Orleans, by damn! You see how everything comes together? The first mention that I ever had in print was by a man in *The New Orleans Poetry Journal*—named Ashman, I think.

Q. You mention that in *Self-Interviews*.[2]

A. Did I? And he says, "This is very imaginative, but we think no poet has the right to be as obscure as James Dickey." I had no idea

---

[1] *Quarterly Review of Literature*, 13 (Winter-Spring 1964), 38–40.
[2] (Garden City, New York: Doubleday, 1970), pp. 46–47.

I was obscure, but I was glad to find it out. But, yes, I think that we all yearn to be something other than what we are. I'm really very dissatisfied with what I am. This is the whole secret of Lewis, because he despises himself. Lewis is no more or less than an intellectual and physical counterpart of Charles Atlas, who was once a skinny, 97-pound weakling, but now can be proud of himself, because he's put all this time in on his body. He is a victim of a crushing inferiority complex, so that he spends enormous amounts of time on himself, making himself impressive intellectually—physically first, and then hopefully intellectually—with all his theories and mystiques, so that he can make other people feel inferior. And Ed is sort of taken in, and this is why Lewis browbeats Bobby—this fat, out-of-shape businessman—all the time. That's much more prevalent in the movie than it is in the novel.

We see a little bit of this when they are driving. Lewis and Ed are in the car with the canoe on top, and Lewis says, "Hey, can that fat friend of yours handle himself?" "What do you mean, Lewis?" "Can he handle himself in a canoe, Ed, is what I'm talkin' about?" Lewis is always a little bit impatient—you know, always forcing you a little bit. Ed's used to it, he likes him, he's fascinated by him, but he's not taken in more than, say, about halfway by Lewis. He says, "Well, Lewis, I don't know whether he can or not. I've never seen him in a canoe. But he's very well thought of in his profession." And Lewis says, "What is his profession?" And Ed says, "Insurance." And Lewis says, "Shit! I've never been insured in my life. I don't believe in it! If you're insured, Ed, there's no risk."

The trouble with Lewis, which I did mean to show, is that he is almost totally without humor. He's so serious about these things and about this self-image of his. But at the end that breaks down some, and he becomes more fully human, as when he's lying on the bottom of the canoe with his leg broken, and Ed is trying desperately to figure out what they're going to tell people when they get back to civilization. And Lewis says to him, "You've got it figured, Ed. You're doin' it better than I could do." And there's a scene in the movie where they're desperately trying to get the change in story over to Lewis, who's lying in the hospital with his leg in traction and that sort of thing, and Lewis says, "I gotcha! I don't remember a thing!"

Q. Ed Gentry hangs from a tree with a wound in his palm, and as he destroys evil in the person of the mountaineer, he receives another wound in the side. Now, are these conscious Christ symbols equating

Gentry's better soul with the divine—Christ being the supreme example of the divine existing within the human?

A. No, if those things have any relationship to the Christ business, and again it comes as a complete surprise to me, it's through, I suppose, what Jung calls the "collective unconscious," because it surely was not conscious at all. What I thought about when I wrote those sequences in the novel was that when he's in the river and he's desperately trying to hold on to the bow and slide over the rocks without bashing his brains out, it seemed to me that his relationship to the arrows would be something dangerous to himself. And it seemed to be this business of grabbing for the bow and catching the arrowheads—these razor-sharp arrowheads—and cutting his hands on them would be a very good way to deal with this business of physicality in chaos—hurled and thrown around in the river. The real precedent for that—and I don't mean to be pretentious at all—was Milton's voyage of Satan through Chaos, which is the best thing in *Paradise Lost*. That's wonderful action writing. I've never read better anywhere. You wouldn't think that of Milton, whom you generally think of as being kind of inert. But that journey. . . .

Q. Satan spreading his wings and sailing across. . . .

A. Well, no, and he goes through Chaos, in which there's nothing to grab hold of, and things sink away under him, and he flounders and just tries to make it any way he can. That was what I was thinking about then. But the wound in the side I got more or less from the Council of Archery hunting accidents—about people falling on their arrows and what that would feel like and what would it do to you to see an arrow come through your own flesh and that sort of thing.

See, these men—especially Lewis, and Ed who follows his example—they've taken the toys of civilization to play at the wilderness. Especially Lewis. He thinks there's some kind of metaphysical value at playing at being a survivalist, and he's an impressive guy in some ways—especially physically—and mysterious. And fellows who work in offices and live in the suburbs at that age—say around thirty-seven or thirty-eight—begin to feel like they've missed the whole thing. Something has happened; their lives have gone by. And here's Lewis; he's got deathly notions about what life is about. He can do something about it, and he *will* do it, and he *does* do it. Well, why not? If this guy thinks that there's something for us up there in those woods, damn! we ought to go. What else have we got? And it might be fun, too. We'll take some whiskey, and they're going to destroy the wilderness, anyway. The river is going to be dammed up. Why don't we have a little contact with the primitive? And that's essentially the motivation for the trip. Lewis has his own private demons that make him do it, and they go with him.

Q. Can you detail the relationship of "On the Coosawattee" with *Deliverance*? For example, the first part was published in *The New Yorker* in 1962—"By Canoe Through the Fir Forest." Were all three parts written separately? And were they written before the novel itself?

A. Oh, yes. Much, much before. Actually, they were written when I was in the advertising business in Atlanta and had just come back from the trip. That was an horrendous trip! I mean, that trip down the Coosawattee through the fir forest and those other places was the grimmest physical experience I'd had since I was in the service. Lewis King has the same characteristic as Lewis Medlock—that is, he thinks he's equal to anything, and he thinks you ought to be equal to anything if you go with him. So, he plunges himself and the other people with him into situations where he doesn't know what the outcome is going to be. It was one of those trips!

Actually, the Cahullawassee, the river in the novel, is a composite of several different rivers that we've been down and were lucky to escape from. The Coosawattee—that was the one that the chicken heads were on, and that was the one that we ran up on the terrifying characters. They were not like the ones in the book. And then the cliffs—the gorge—was on another river, and the cows, the cattle and things that they see finally when they're coming down to civilization again, were on another one. It's really kind of a composite river, but it's mainly the one where the actual film was made. It was mainly the Chatuga River. That's the one where all the bad rapids are—the one that's so dangerous.

Q. About the poultry incident in "On the Coosawattee" and also in *Deliverance*. Were the poetic and fictional treatments written separately? Or does one depend upon the other?

A. The novel depends on the poem, and they both depend on the incident. That was one of the most memorably disgusting things that I've ever seen. I think that is in Ellijay, Georgia. Either that, or it's north. I don't remember whether we put in at Ellijay or whether we got out at Ellijay. Ellijay, Georgia, is really the model for Aintry in the novel. We went down there—and it's just like in the poem and the novel. We said, "There's something wrong here." And then we saw all these feathers and things and chicken heads. I changed that in the novel to make it show just one chicken head, because I thought the focus would be better if we just showed one—lots of feathers and one head.

Q.   When you wrote the fictional treatment, did you have the poem in front of you?

A.   No, no, I just recalled the incident. I remembered using it, but I used it in the novel in a different way for a different purpose. What this business of going down past the chicken heads and so on is supposed to serve in the novel is a kind of a symbolical way—I suppose you could say, I hope without being too pretentious—of showing them leaving the detritus of civilization behind and getting back into the primitive through that. It's like when they have all the junk at the side of the river, and there's this electric blue plastic jug—or whatever it is—and Ed is kind of offended by it, and Drew says, "That's plastic. It doesn't go back to its elements." Ed says, "As though that were all right." [Laughter] He's like the rest of us; he's kind of vaguely disquieted by this.

Q.   Are you implying also that man should go back to his elements? Did you have that in mind?

A.   Yes, I suppose. I wouldn't deny it.

Q.   I had thought of the chicken head as a death symbol.

A.   That, too.

Q.   Very much like the pig's head in *Lord of the Flies.*

A.   *Deliverance* is a way better novel than *Lord of the Flies*, if I do say so. *Lord of the Flies* is too contrived. This could happen. I'll tell you a funny story about *Deliverance.* When we first started getting ready to publish it, the editor-in-chief at Houghton Mifflin was a fellow named Paul Brooks. And we sat around talking about it before we signed the contracts, and then we signed all the contracts. My agent was there, stuffing the contract into his pocket and all that, and everybody heaved a great sigh of relief.

After all this was done, somebody brought in a bottle of whiskey, and we all had a drink. And Paul Brooks, who fancied himself as something of an outdoorsman and a conservationist, said, "Well, Jim, everybody here likes the book, and we think we're going to have a big success with it, but some of us frankly were a little bit worried to the effect that it might possibly be true—an eyewitness account of something you participated in." I said, "Well, yeah, some of it is true. Yeah." He said, "Were you ever in any situation where somebody was killed like that? Or two people or three people were killed?" I said, "Oh, no, certainly not. I just made that up—of course I did." Everybody again heaved a great sigh of relief, and my agent stuffed the contract deeper in his pocket, and everybody had another drink.

So Brooks said, "I'd like to see some of the southern Appalachian Mountain river country. Suppose I came down next August, and you and I got a canoe. You could take me up there and show it to me." I said, "Yeah, Paul, I'd be very happy to, if you like. Come down next August. Just let me know when you're coming, and I'll get a canoe, and I can show you where everything happened." [Laughter] My agent stuffed the contract deeper into his pocket.

Q. You mention the Osiris myth in *Self-Interviews.*[3] Were you referring to that myth in Drew's body floating down the river, foreshadowing the rebirth and regeneration of Ed Gentry?

A. Well, in a way. If there's any literary or mythological precedent for *Deliverance*, it comes from a review I read in the *Kenyon Review* in the summer '49 issue, when I was a senior in college. It was an enormously impressive thing to me, and it's been in my mind ever since. It's a review by Stanley Edgar Hyman on a number of books on myths and rituals, and he quotes Van Gennep's "rites de passage" and cites "a separation from the world, a penetration to some source of power, and a life-enhancing return."[4] If there's any literary precedent to *Deliverance*, it's that passage as I encountered it quoted by Hyman, referring to Van Gennep's concept of the "rites de passage."

Q. Many of your poems, particularly those dealing directly with death, contain images of water directly overhead—"The Movement of Fish," "Winter Trout," "The Driver"—and sometimes of water rising. "The Dream Flood" is an example,[5] and, of course, in *Deliverance* the water rises to form a lake, and everything is hidden beneath

[3] *Self-Interviews*, p. 90.

[4] "Myth, Ritual, and Nonsense," *Kenyon Review*, 11 (Summer 1949), 455.

[5] *Drowning with Others* (Middletown, Conn.: Wesleyan Univ. Press, 1962), pp. 68–69.

the surface. Traditionally, water has signified both death and rebirth, but why does it have such great meaning for you?

A. I don't know, except to say that I just like it. As I said somewhere in *Self-Interviews*, I think a river is the most beautiful thing in the world. Any river, even polluted, is beautiful. I feel very much like Heraclitus does about rivers and like Hermann Hesse did in *Siddhartha*, where the guy learns about the secret of everything by sitting and watching a river. That does it for me! Rivers always did it for me. Much more than oceans, although I like them, too, or lakes, which I like in their way, too. I'm so glad—if I never write another novel, and *Deliverance* turns out to be the only one—I'm so glad that I wrote about rivers.

Q. Is "The Driver" based on personal experience?

A. Yes, pretty much. On one of the invasion beaches at Okinawa there was a lot of old, rusted equipment sitting around under water— amtracks and so on. The water is very clear. It's a very beautiful sea around Okinawa. And I remember going down there and getting into the driver's seat, just to see what it would be like.

Q. There's another uncollected poem that I'd like to question you about, entitled "A Beginning Poet, Aged Sixty-Five."[6] Now that poem is equated in the Glancy bibliography with "To Landrum Guy," but it's entirely different.[7]

A. It is different, and I've done that more than once. I don't even have a copy of the one that was published in the *Quarterly Review*. I don't remember what it was like.

Q. It seems to be a compendium of your most familiar themes and images. Everything seems to be collected in this one poem.

A. It's funny. I like to think of beginnings and rebeginnings, but all of it's in the question of approach and the question of form that the poem takes in which you talk about these things. And in this case, as you very rightly observe, there are two completely different approaches and ways of talking about the same guy and the same situation. I don't really know. The perspective of time has made it so that I don't even remember what the differences are. I know that one was collected

6 *Quarterly Review of Literature*, 9 (Winter 1958), 272–73.
7 Eileen K. Glancy, "James Dickey: A Bibliography," *Twentieth Century Literature*, 15 (April 1969), 46.

when Richard Wilbur was my editor and told me to do the one that I did rather than the other one, so I did that one. But I often write poems on the same theme. I feel like I didn't get out of it the first time. I had the wrong approach, and there's nothing says I can't go around and try again. It's like when the tower waves you off on a landing, you go around the pattern and come back again. You try it another way. Any subject has an infinitude of possibilities, and if I'm not satisfied with the way I did the first time, I just take the whole thing and start in from another angle.

Q.   The epigraph to *Deliverance* is derived from Obadiah. How about the title?

A.   Well, you pointed out to me—I'm very grateful to you—that the word "deliverance" is used in Obadiah. But I was so struck with that part of Obadiah having to do with the climb up the cliff and lying in the cleft of the rocks and all of that sort of thing. It just fascinated me. I didn't want to read any more. I just wanted *that*. But the original title of the novel was *The Deliverer*, and it's from the biblical quote. I don't know exactly where it occurs, but it's the quote "Who shall deliver me from the body of this death?" It was originally on the basis of that quotation called *The Deliverer*, but then I also remembered that the word "deliverance" and "the day of deliverance" and phrases of that sort are relatively frequent in the Bible. And I've always liked one word titles, and *The Deliverer* did not seem to me to be as dramatic as *Deliverance*, so I just changed it.

Q.   You've written several poems including serpents, and in *Deliverance* there are several serpents. One is in the trees and almost falls in Bobby's. . . .

A.   Lewis says it does. He says, "Did you see that big snake back there? You went right under him." Well, you don't know whether it was ever there or not. I think he was, but you don't know.

Q.   Just before the canoe goes into shore, also.

A.   Yes, and he sees one. That's in the film. There's a nice thing with a snake swimming in the water.

Q.   Is that symbolic?

A.   Snakes, snakes—I like to write about animals, and snakes seem to me to be kind of the ultimate other. A bird is even more close to a human being—something with a power like that—than a snake. It's no wonder that we make the snake the personification of evil, because he *is* so much the other, and that coupled with the fact that some of them are poisonous is enough to make them the real nightmare creatures that we somehow or other have got to come to terms with.

Q. Sharks seem to hold the same fascination for you.

A. Sharks as well, because they're primitive—they're perfect. Snakes are perfect. There are fossil snakes that are exactly like the snakes we have now. The same is true with sharks. The shark has never even developed a skeleton. Because he worked so well like he was, there was no need to evolve. And those kind of perfect forms in nature are really very fascinating to me. They seem to me to demonstrate something important. You know, men were weak little creatures. That's the reason they developed one part of themselves—the head, the brain, and so on—which enabled them to do what they've done and eventually probably destroy the whole goddamn planet. But sharks didn't, and snakes didn't—very, very low mentality. But they get along fine, if men would just leave them alone.

Q. You mention in *Sorties*—this is a direct quotation: "The phantom women of the mind—I speak from a man's standpoint only—are a great deal more important than any real woman could ever possibly be. They represent the Ideal, and as such are indestructible. It is quite arguable that poor mortal perishable women are as dust before these powerful and sensual creatures of the depths of one's being."[8] Coupled with this, we often find in your poetry a search for the Ideal—a search for the ideal woman, a search for the ideal self—and this seems to point to Shelley.

A. Maybe it does, but it points way back beyond Shelley to Shelley's own master—Plato. I guess essentially I'm a Platonist, rather than an Aristotelian. Yes, sure, I think we're more or less lost without impossible ideals. Like in the novel there can be an enormous dramatic conflict and play between, say, a character who conceives of things in this kind of idealistic or eternal way and what he must settle for in the mundane human world. The Greek tragedies really are largely based on this idea, and so is a great deal of Shakespeare—people who will not bend, Coriolanus for one, who have that flaw of expecting too

---

[8] (Garden City, New York: Doubleday, 1971), p. 4.

much and not being able to function when that condition cannot be fulfilled.

You can take a more modern instance—*All the King's Men* by Robert Penn Warren, where the guy is anything but an idealist—the politician, Willie Stark. But he is given this power, and he begins to conceive that he can be, with all the state power, a force for good. He can build hospitals, highways, and bridges and do something about the plight of the poor people. And he really can. But in order to get the money and to do these things, he's got to compromise with these other forces, which are not good, and it's this business of effecting good ends by bad means that makes up the dramatic conflict of the book. And I think it's really insolvable. I mean, should he bribe this guy, or should he make a deal with this other political faction in order to get these funds to build this hospital? Which is fascinating—which is really the way things are done.

Q.   Do you think of Robert Penn Warren as one of your teachers?

A.   I wish he had been, but he's only a teacher to me through my reading of his works for a number of years and then very lately—the last five or six years—knowing him and corresponding with him. But in my formative stage as a writer, Robert Penn Warren was known to me only through his works. *All the King's Men* came out when I was in college, and I read the poems because I went to Vanderbilt, which was his old school, and he was talked about; and Donald Davidson was my teacher, who was his teacher.

Q.   You mention in *Self-Interviews* three of the writers that you consider to be your teachers—of a sort—or certainly whom you admire— Malcolm Lowry, James Agee, and John Keats.[9] Would you add anyone to that?

A.   Well, no. I suppose I could, but those are the ones that I like maybe more for their attitude toward experience—which seems to me to be an extremely creative way to take the act of living—than for what they actually wrote, although I like very much what they wrote. In the case of Keats, for example, I like *him*, John Keats, and what I know about him and what's been recorded about him a great deal more than what he wrote, although I like what he wrote. The same to a lesser extent is true of Malcolm Lowry. I like the way he experienced existence and the terms on which he took existence more than

---

[9] *Self-Interviews*, pp. 74–75.

what he wrote, although I like what he wrote more than I like what Keats wrote. James Agee is exactly the opposite. He is a born, sovereign prince of the English language. He was self-destructive, say like Dylan Thomas was or Theodore Roethke, too, and many another. But James Agee—what little there is of him—is of an order of genius far beyond Malcolm Lowry, or John Keats either, as irreverent as that may seem. But Agee's style—and that really hyperintense kind of verbalization that he has—is not right for me.

What I like about Agee more than anything else is his ability to place an unusual word in a sentence. Just to take an example, not from the prose works or the poetry either, but from directions in a screenplay for *The African Queen.* You know when they're mired up in the weeds, and he has to go to clear the propeller, and he comes up with leeches all over him, and then they're just exhausted, and they're lying there on the floorboards of the boat, and the directions are: Camera pulls back and shows panoramic view of boat and the weeds and so on. And then he says: "And then there is a vague splintering of rain." It's just that "splintering of rain." Now, my God, who would have thought of that? That's just absolutely wonderful—at least to me it is. That's why I admire him so much. And he doesn't do it as a kind of a gimmick—that's just the way he sees the rain. Or hears it—maybe both.

Q. You've mentioned several times that you're about to move into a new area of poetry—or at least a different area from what you have been working with before. Can you clarify that?

A. I'm just feeling it out. I get a glimpse of it now and then, but whether the promised land is there or not, I don't know. But if I can't find it, I'll try to invent it.

An Interview with Margaret Drabble

Conducted by Nancy S. Hardin

American readers might well ask, who is Margaret Drabble? This is a question that, I believe, will not be posed much longer, for Margaret Drabble is a strikingly interesting and productive young British novelist. The interview that follows took place in her home in Hampstead Heath, a street away from Keats's house, in the morning and evening of October 11, 1972. Drabble is a warm and friendly person with an intense quality that finds expression both in her demeanor and her works. It seems appropriate that her concern is frequently, among other things, with "the holiness of the heart's affections," for there is a kinship between her and the early nineteenth-century romantic writers who tended to give primacy to emotion over reason and who honestly trusted their inner perceptions. She is equally in tune with those later nineteenth-century novelists whose world involves predestined paths and fate. Yet, she is also very much of her own time, and her characters and their self-confrontations are burdened with choices relevant to the 1960s and 1970s.

Drabble writes novels, articles, TV plays, critical biographies; pursues an academic career; mothers three young children. When she finished her degree at Cambridge in 1960 she wanted to go on the stage, but her marriage to Clive Swift of the Royal Shakespeare Company and her pregnancies curtailed her theatrical ambitions. Instead, she turned to the writing of novels, critically appraising her own creative productivity against that of Keats: "I've always felt that one should try to keep up with those who have produced young." Her list of novels, all first published in London by Weidenfeld and Nicolson, is already lengthy: *A Summer Bird-Cage* (1963), *The Garrick Year* (1964), *The Millstone* (1965), *Jerusalem the Golden* (1967), *The Waterfall* (1969), and *The Needle's Eye* (1972). In addition, she has published a critical book, *Wordsworth*, and has almost finished a study of Arnold Bennett.*

Drabble's novels are studies of human nature with the emphasis on feminine nature. That is not to say she is a feminist writer; she is too private a person and is not one who fits well into organizations or women's liberation groups. The most she does on this score is to "give the odd lecture on the status of women, if I'm invited to do so. I've got a literary lecture called 'Feminism in the Novel' which I deliver when I think people need it, or when they request it. If they say, come and talk about feminism, I talk about literary women—Mrs. Aphra Behn, Charlotte Brontë, Virginia Woolf, Doris Lessing, and people like that." In her novels, however, Drabble shatters various female stereotypes and for the most part emphasizes women's competence and independence.

The Drabble women are notable for their resiliency and endurance; frequently they know what it is that they do not want, while they struggle to learn what it is they seek and who it is they are. They posit themselves in the world of professions, of marriage, or of making it on their own and more often than not come to recognize themselves through their lovers, husbands, or children. In addition, they see men in a fair and open-minded manner. There is little if any doubt that Drabble's characters are personalities of inner strength; indeed, she emphasizes that "the human mind is not a delicate plant . . . " (*Bird-Cage*, p. 158). Sometimes it is a matter of stressing the truth of self-knowledge, of accepting what is already known intuitively. For these women "the taste for half-knowledge" (*Millstone*, p. 199) is no longer adequate. Yet, this quest for self-knowledge is not tediously moralistic, nor dully serious and heavy, for each possesses a gentle tragicomic sense of humor, an awareness of the absurdity of self in the world.

---

* American paperback editions published to date are *The Millstone*, entitled *Thank You All Very Much* (New York: Signet, 1969); *The Waterfall* (New York: Signet, 1972); *Wordsworth* (New York: Arco Literary Critiques, 1959). Alfred Knopf published the American hardcover edition of *The Needle's Eye* in 1972. Parenthetical page references in the text, preceded by abbreviated titles, are to the Weidenfeld editions, except for the Knopf edition of *The Needle's Eye* and the Arco edition of *Wordsworth*.

Futhermore, Drabble's women are a convincing mixture of op-posites and are all the more human for being so. Their morality is congruent with "a whole host of other unlikely irreconcilable proposi-tions . . . " (*Waterfall*, p. 53). Drabble herself comments: "What I can't stand about some novelists is the way they seem to imply that there's a fixed and finished truth that their characters reach at the end of the book. There's no end to learning. You're bound to learn more. What you know at each point of your life is relevant to you then, yet isn't quite enough, because you've got to go on learning."

Drabble thus portrays complex and shifting solutions, whereby her characters come to ascertain the life style most appropriate for them. As such the reality of their experiences encourages the reader to examine, to embrace, and to trust what might often seem to be her own "contradictory hallucinatory lights" (*Waterfall*, p. 53). From this knowledge can come a sense of the daily world as rich and various. (NSH)

Q. Not only have you published six novels in nine years as well as a book on Wordsworth and a variety of articles, but you also have three children. Where do you find all the energy?

A. Well, I honestly don't know. At times I don't think I manage it at all. I think I'm going quite frantic. I suppose by cutting out a lot of things that other people find necessary, like social life. I do love it but I find I can't take it—at the moment. My idea of happiness is going to bed at nine o'clock in the evening. I used to write during the evening when the children were little, but now I work during the day. I lecture one day a week—all day long—at Morley College. I love doing it but it's really exhausting. I get home at five o'clock and there are the chil-dren waiting to talk to me, the person who collects them from school also waiting to talk to me. I just feel I can't say another word. I write during the mornings I suppose, mostly. I can't do more than three or four hours at a stretch. I've got an office where I work. If I work at home, the telephone goes. So I go out. My ideal working week would be to teach one day and then write on the other mornings, doing my reading in the afternoons, but of course it never works out like that. There are always some interruptions. I actually compose very easily. I don't sweat over the sentences at all; they just pour out.

Q. You must manage somehow to be very much in tune with the sources of your own energy. I am reminded of a passage where Sarah Bennett raises the question of energy: "And where does one get the energy for this sort of existence? The only way to be recharged is to be put in touch with external rhythms. Otherwise one will run down from exhaustion . . . " (*Bird-Cage*, p. 74). Is that true for you? What would you say are your external rhythms?

A. Yes, very much so. External rhythms. The lives of the children I find very reassuring. Although they're exhausting, they give me a regularity. I've become very regular in my habits. I get up at exactly the same time everyday and I do my shopping on the same day of the week. There is a kind of rhythm from this. It's not exactly a natural, perhaps it is, a natural rhythm of life. I used to find this repulsive as a young woman, but now I find it extremely satisfying. I love opening the blinds in the morning and I love getting the milk in.

Q. Some of your characters seem to feel the same way. Doesn't Rose Vassiliou respond "to such ordinary signals in the world. Cut prices and sunshine and babies in prams and talking in the shops . . ." (*Needle's Eye*, p. 99)?

A. This is something I have grown into. I certainly used not to be like that. I used to be much wilder. Perhaps it's a question of the amount of energy you've got and needing to prop it up in some way.

Q. Will you tell me a bit of background about your life?

A. Well, I was born in Sheffield in the North of England. My father was a barrister and is now a county court judge. This gives everyone the impression that we were a frightfully grand family. However, this wasn't at all so because both my parents were the first of their families ever to go to a university. They were very much a new generation. I suppose they were, both of them, fairly intellectual. They encouraged us to read. I was the second of three girls and there was a little brother, some years later. So there were four of us altogether. I went to a very old Quaker girls' boarding school, the Mount School, York. Then I went on to the university to read English and I enjoyed it so much that I really think it took me a long time to get over it.

Q. Are you a Quaker? Or do you ascribe to any particular religious faith?

A. No, I'm not. I wonder if I'll ever go back to it. I used to go to the

Anglican church. My father took us. My mother is an atheist and has often described the experience of religious conversion that came to her. She had been brought up in the hell-and-brimstone school. Then one day, while she was reading George Bernard Shaw, the light of God struck and said there was no God. And the relief—she's never got over it. There was no God to punish her; he wasn't there. One could say that that was a revelation from God saying not to worry about him because it was going to drive her mad if she did.

Q. What about your husband—you met him when you were in Cambridge, didn't you?

A. I was at Cambridge, yes. I don't know why one gets married. I was completely enchanted by his whole family life, which was so unlike my own. And in a way I'm still enchanted by them. I find it a terrible trial, but at the same time I can't get away from it since he left. We separated about a year ago and I see more of them since than ever before.

Q. That makes me think of Jane Gray of *The Waterfall* who strengthens the bonds with her in-laws after the dissolution of her marriage.

A. Jane gets fond of her in-laws. My in-laws are so much more likeable than hers. They really are delightful, but it's a funny business. I haven't written a novel since Clive and I separated and I'm very interested to see what comes out next. I wrote the whole of *The Needle's Eye* while we were still together. And I might not have made it end like I did if we had separated first. I might have allowed her her freedom. I wonder. I got married almost immediately after leaving the university. The week I finished, I got married and intended at that point to go on the stage but didn't because my husband was an actor and it just didn't work out somehow. I did do a year or two on the stage, but I also had a baby within the year. That rather cramped my style. So that was really how I began writing. I then wrote my first book during the year I was expecting my first baby. And now I have three.

Q. A significant characteristic of the young women in your novels is their inability to accept the values of their parents. Instead, they commit themselves to a search for "chosen" or "extended" families (friends, lovers, or perhaps children) with whom they work through their identities and beliefs. Clara Maugham of *Jerusalem the Golden* comes to mind. But there are other examples as well to be found in Jane Gray of *The Waterfall* and Rose Vassiliou of *The Needle's Eye.*

A. I've often wondered whether this is a problem that is particular to me in any way, or whether it's a problem that afflicts almost all girls, and men too—that one has to escape from one's own family and find substitute families or substitute patterns of living. I don't know whether this might well reveal my own feeling about my own family background. For many years my mother was very depressed. She's now not, thanks to, well quite frankly, thanks to drugs. So throughout my adolescence I was struggling with the fact that adult life seemed to be incredibly depressing.

Q. Perhaps this explains in part Clara Maugham's need for "a bright and peopled world, thick with starry inhabitants, where there was no ending, no parting, but an eternal vast incessant rearrangement" (*Jerusalem*, p. 224).

A. Yes. One had to find some image of liveliness or color or love that was different from what one had been brought up on. I don't know how I would have developed if I'd known my mother as she is now. She is so much more cheerful and active. I might have had a completely different view of needing to leave the family or having to find other mother figures. But I certainly do—did, I think—look for other mother figures. I think everybody does. What one is looking for is just patterns of living in other people. Clara Maugham is certainly looking for another pattern of life that she can go into, and in the book I have ambivalent feelings myself about whether she's found a good one. Clearly not. She's found something that suits her. She's going to turn into something fearsome, I think. I rather dread her future.

Q. Rose Vassiliou works through her values as opposed to those of her parents at considerable cost to herself. She says at one point: "But I'm determined not to make the mistake of most revolutions, I won't revert to what it was that I was fighting not to be" (*Needle's Eye*, p. 98).

A. Well, Rose finds a completely different image of domesticity—which is a nice little cozy working-class image of sitting in your own little house and minding your own business and being completely unaspiring. Her view is that wealth had destroyed her mother—a fairly reasonable thing to think. If her mother hadn't been so utterly idle, she might not have been so completely bored. So Rose psychologically sees her salvation in getting rid of the money and having something to do. She makes herself busy doing the ironing and so forth. What's more,

she says, "I do them all with love. Getting up, drawing the curtains, shopping, going to bed . . ." (*Needle's Eye*, p. 100). Interestingly enough, the person whom I partly modeled Rose on says she got it from her nanny in the true upper-class British way. She found heaven in a sort of big tatty old arm chair and a woman ironing and the little girl sitting watching this comfortable woman ironing, while, in her case, her brilliant mother chatted away upstairs to her friends, or so I imagine it. I left that link out in Rose's character. I wanted Rose to be a derelict child, not to be looking for a lost nanny.

Q. Would you say something about your views on the function of literature? Is literature for you a re-creation of values by which human beings can live?

A. I think I have a rather narrow, restricted, personal view of what I see and why I like and read books. I find out about living and about the values of living—and a lot of my beliefs in life and my feelings about people and what to do—from reading novels. Very often I meet a kind of person that I'm not familiar with, which a novelist has given me a guideline on. I think novelists do that. They give you guidelines on familiar, unfamiliar people. You can feel much more sympathy with them because you've met them in a book before or encountered their background in a book. I think this is important, to make sympathetic in a novel people who are perhaps not immediately sympathetic to everybody—to make their worries real to others. I do quite often make an effort to do justice to characters whom I don't possibly like or who in life annoy me.

Q. Yes. Whom are you thinking about in your novels?

A. I was thinking in *The Needle's Eye* of Simon Camish's mother. Simon was never able to give affection to her because she was an unpleasant woman. There is no doubt about it. She was unpleasant.

Q. How about Clara Maugham's mother in *Jerusalem the Golden*?

A. Clara Maugham's mother is exactly the same. They are unpleasant, hard, bitter, life-denying. Yet one knows exactly why they're like that. In a way they sacrifice themselves for their children. In both cases Clara and Simon have gone forward.

Q. You transform a variety of literary references into something very much your own. They become real within the context of the novel it-

self. For example, did you have Samuel Daniel's "The Complaint of Rosamond" in mind in *The Millstone*? Rosamund Stacey's tale seems a latter-day version of complaint literature. Also she is reading unspecified Samuel Daniel poems as she considers whether to get the abortion or not.

A. Presumably, I was reading Samuel Daniel while I was writing the novel. What I've found fascinating was that when I was teaching *Oedipus* recently, I was also looking back at *The Waterfall*. Now I think I must have just seen the Old Vic's version of Seneca's *Oedipus* because there's a whole passage in *The Waterfall* I could only have written just after I'd seen that. It's as though whenever I see anything or read anything, I take it as a directly personal comment. I can't read quietly or objectively. Well as I said earlier, I'm looking for meaning. I'm looking for guidance or help or illumination of some sort or another.

Q. I believe that you have stated in an introduction to a recent edition of *The Millstone* that the title refers in part to the verse in the Bible in which Christ says: "Whoso shall offend one of these little ones which believe in me, it were better that a millstone were hanged about his neck, and that he were drowned in the depth of the sea" (Matthew 18:6). Will you elaborate on your intention here?

A. I don't know what I intended actually, but I think it was a kind of double reference. The child was both a millstone and also a salvation because once it became obvious to Rosamund that she couldn't suffer any more harm from the child, the millstone was lifted from her. I don't know why nobody else liked that title, but it came to me just without thinking and it seemed to be appropriate. The more I questioned it, the less I knew why I had chosen it.

Q. I suppose you know that the American edition of *The Millstone* is entitled *Thank You All Very Much*. Is this your title as well?

A. No, it's not. It happened because a film was made which was shown under that title in the States and it's a line out of the film. There's a rather nice moment in the film when Rosamund is being examined by all the students in the antenatal clinic. There are about eight students standing around the bed and there is a shot of her sitting up very prettily and saying, "Thank you, thank you all very much," in a very British way. I liked the way she said it and so I didn't mind its being used.

Q. In *The Garrick Year*, Emma reads, among other things, Hume on morals. Has Hume influenced you particularly?

A. I don't know really. Hume says in his *Treatise of Human Nature* that "All human creatures, especially of the female sex, are apt to overlook remote motive in favour of any present temptation. . . ." For Emma, Hume sums it up by the word "all." In essence Hume said you've got to stay together because children need looking after—"that this union must be of considerable duration." Emma's trying very hard to be sensible. She is one of the women who suspects that her nature is really rather wild and dangerous. Emma says, yes, although I'm a mad modern woman, I will do this for a little bit. That's what she says in effect. I didn't know she was saying it. Looking at her now, that's what she would say. That's what she did. I'll bet she went off wildly as soon as those children were off at school.

Q. Doesn't Hume see mankind as acquiring knowledge by observation and experience. Certain contradictions of so-called "matters of fact" are allowed for in his philosophy. For example, Jane Gray says: "Logic might have indicated that this would be so, but I have little faith in logic. I await the impossible, the irrational, the grotesque, a Zoo without children, love from an empty heaven" (*Waterfall*, p. 172).

A. That's right. Yes, I was so deeply impressed by Hume that I still haven't quite got over him. There's another reference in *The Garrick Year* as I come to think about it—that if you drop an apple, why on earth should it fall to the floor. Indeed, it sometimes doesn't. Well, the apple drops but sometimes love descends from an empty heaven. There is a mixture of predictability and unpredictability in life which Hume was so interested in and which interests me. I'm very deeply affected by reading Hume because I remember struggling to get his philosophical concepts about matter and getting them. I've forgotten them now. Then the amazing, lovely way in which he said that having thought all that, "I'm nothing but a bit of a proper Scottish gentleman. I know that . . . I can't predict anything at all. Therefore, I might as well rely on the instincts of my heart." And that, I think, is splendid.

Q. Your characters are often confronted with the opposites of any given experience. It is as though they are both created and destroyed by diametrically opposed forces. Rosamund, for example, is a mixture of confidence and cowardice; Jane doesn't know whether her relationship with James is one of salvation or damnation; Emma and David watch their children with anxiety and delight; Rose presses flowers with anguish and delight, etc. Why do you stress these contradictions of fact?

A. The answer ought to be that I feel myself divided. One can see this in lots of people's writing, that there is a sort of divided self speaking. But I really can honestly say that, unless I am deceiving myself very profoundly, I don't feel that I am, and my characters seem to me not to be, schizoid. Even Jane, who says at one point that she's schizoid, isn't. Actually, I think that every person is full of such contradictory patterns, inevitably. But my characters seem to have got just enough force in them to stick together. There's a bit where Rosamund, when she's screaming about the baby in the hospital, says that she's almost, but not quite, breaking in part. Jane had exactly the same experience. She feels, referring to the sexual experience, that she must either break apart or die or be put together again now. She's put together again. Similarly Rose feels that her head's been split by a hatchet. But she's indivisible; that's her tragedy. Well, it's not her tragedy, but a character with possibly less natural integration would have split, would have gone mad or gone into a mental home or taken refuge elsewhere. I see my characters as glued together by personality. I feel myself to be and I often think that surely it would be more dignified to fly into a thousand pieces in this situation and give up. But in fact I'm incapable of it. I will go on relentlessly to the end, trying to make sense of it, trying to endure it or survive it or see something in it. I don't divide. I often wish I could.

Q. The will to endure is something that's really very pronounced in your characters.

A. It's something I admire very much in people. I admire endurance and I admire the courage to come back. I think that the kind of people I know tend to have this to a very marked degree. I'm sorry to go back to the children again, but I think that this is partly it—that you simply have got to be there in the morning. I know people who have gone through unbelievable torments and have still got up in the morning and got their children to school whereas unmarried women or men tend to have a lower breaking point. People often ask me why my characters don't just give up and plunge into the depths and be better for it. Yes, but they can't. I can see myself at the age of forty-five in a completely different domestic situation doing this, going through much more profound destructive mental processes, but I can't do it now.

Q. I find a great many references to predestined paths or to fated patterns in your novels. On the other hand, you often indicate that life is governed by accidents. For instance, Jane notes: "one is not released from the fated pattern, one must walk it till death and walk through those recurring darknesses: but sometimes, by accident or endeavor . . . one may find a way of walking that predestined path more willingly" (*Waterfall*, p. 172). Would you discuss these two concepts in relation to your novels? Aren't they basically contradictory?

A. The two concepts fit frightfully well together. The accidents are all planned, and one's fate is planned. It is going to contain certain accidents. There's nothing you can do about it. I was teaching *Oedipus* last week and, indeed, the idea that whatever you do is all written up for you and that the accidents are simply part of some bigger plan made at some other date by somebody else is fascinating.

Q. That reminds me of a couple of passages in which you mention Oedipus either indirectly or directly: "Often, in jumping to avoid our fate, we meet it: as Seneca said. It gets us in the end" (*Waterfall*, p. 103); "In seeking to avoid my fate, like Oedipus, I had met it . . ." (*Waterfall*, p. 243).

A. Yes. You're just completely at the mercy of fate. It's planned but accidental in some peculiar way. Jane tries to reason that she wouldn't have been so swept away by passion if she hadn't always thought that she would be. Whether that's true or not, I mean Jane talking of accidents or waiting for grace, Jane could have waited forever to meet a man like James who in fact not only seemed to answer her need, but did. It would have been far more logical for Jane to have had some successive, utterly unsatisfactory affairs. It should have been the pattern of Jane's life that she had an affair with somebody who turned out to be really not what she was looking for. Then she would have done it again and again and again until she would have given up. In fact by accident, she happened to meet the one man who really knew what she was up to and who truly loved her. Somebody told me yesterday I should never use a phrase like "true love." I have very naive conceptions of these things and I think that accidents do happen and that what has appalled me about the world is that some people have good luck. They meet the right person. Some people look forever and they try and they do their best to find God or a lover or a husband and never do. The lucky ones get it. Those that wait sometimes get it and sometimes don't.

I'm kind of Greek with a Greek view of the gods, I think. I mean, better keep on the right side of them because although they're not very nice, they're exceedingly powerful. One had better appreciate it.

Q. How do you use this concept of grace which you mentioned a few minutes ago? Jane would appear to receive grace; Rose Vassiliou to lose it.

A. Ah yes. I find this terribly difficult because I have a very strong conception of grace. Like Rose, I'm really not quite sure what my theological position is. On the other hand, I do have a sense of being in tune with the purpose of life. That sounds terribly vague, but being in harmony with some other purpose is a state of grace. When you're not fighting it, it might simply be being in tune with your fate, like Oedipus. It is then that you're in a state of grace. Once you set yourself up against it in the wrong way, you're out of grace. It is hard to explain how one recognizes a quality of grace or what it really is. But I feel it in a very strong way.

Q. Well, would you say that Jane receives something that is a state of grace?

A. She does, yes. She receives it through James. The thing about grace is that it does seem to come very arbitrarily. It descends from heaven like the muse, which is something that again worries me very much. It doesn't seem to be that you have to deserve it. It just seems to me that by accident you happen to fall into it, or stumble into it, or it happens to descend upon you like a kind of bird from the sky. I was talking about this to a Canadian writer, Hugh Hood, whom I found very interesting on the subject. He said that the seventeenth century had this concept of cooperative grace and operative grace; that you had to be prepared to receive grace, or you didn't get it—like the foolish and the wise virgins. If you were prepared to get it, then you did. If you weren't prepared, then you wouldn't notice when it came. So you can cooperate with grace. You can wait for it, but it need not necessarily come at all. I find it very worrying. You wait for the rest of your life and you might never get it.

Q. What about with Rose Vassiliou? Does she lose her sense of grace in the end when she chooses to stay with Christopher and the children?

A. I don't think she could lose it, really. She's choosing between two different kinds of grace. I think she's choosing the harder way. She loses her piece of mind. Perhaps she does lose her sense of grace just slightly. I think that probably she and Christopher would part again after another five years because she couldn't take it. That's why I wrote so as to make the position completely intolerable for her. Whatever she did, she was going to lose. She couldn't bear the torment of her conscience about what she had done to Christopher and she couldn't bear the torment of living with him either.

Q. It seems very painful for her to go through the process of denying that martyred aspect of herself. I'm thinking about the time she leaves Simon's office and is in the coffee shop struggling with this other part of herself. Does the martyr-self represent what a state of grace would really be for her?

A. I honestly don't know. I don't really answer this in the book at all because I don't know. I think Rose has several possibilities. She can stay with the children and continue to live as she does in a selfish state of grace that excludes the pains of the world. She can go off and become really martyred, an act which she is aware would produce a state of grace of another kind of selfishness, though one can be absolutely certain that if one does do something dramatic like go to help the starving, one will be redeemed in some way. A person like Rose might have found a deep spiritual experience in quitting and going off, but Rose has to reject that, too, and what she accepts finally is no less painful. Well, all the choices are painful for her except sitting at home and carrying on, which is what I tend to do. I wrote the book partly to explore which of these things was the right one to do. I think that I do see Rose in very simple religious terms. She's a girl who hungers and thirsts after righteousness and how difficult it is to be righteous, particularly when you've got small children. Duty can be terribly confusing once you've got children and husbands and you're personally involved with other people's sense of righteousness, especially when it conflicts with your own. There are simply no answers.

Q. Do you distinguish between grace and virtue? Is virtue synonymous with morality?

A. Virtue is a kind of morality that requires some effort from the person. Grace is stumbled into and is an accident. It is given. One must maintain virtue by one's acts while hoping for grace. Simon is virtuous, although he has never known grace. When Rose ceased to love her son, Constantine, it just happened. She virtuously maintained the relationship while waiting for grace. Love is meaningless without the sense of grace.

One of the things I was trying to say in *The Needle's Eye* is that you can't will to love. It's like Keats's statement about "the holiness of the heart's affections." When love ceases to mean anything, it becomes possessive or dull or ugly. There's a certain amount of ruthlessness in Rose. She has a surprising ability to forget and to carry on. One has absolutely no control over one's emotional response to somebody.

Q. What, exactly, do you mean by "spirit," a term you use rather often? Sometimes spirit seems to refer to the inner self, sometimes it seems to mean the Holy Spirit or God. For instance, you write: "but loss it was, and they could do nothing to revoke the death of the spirit. The spirit bloweth whither it listeth" (*Needle's Eye*, p. 112).

A. Sometimes I mean the spirit of the inward person and sometimes the Holy Spirit, the spirit descending. In that particular instance, I was referring to the arbitrary spirit of God. It's like saying some people are privileged from birth. And why? Just give me an answer, anybody, I'm waiting for it. It's a matter of faith, but there must be an answer to this problem because I can't really believe that my ideal of life is so superior to the creation of the world. Why should I be able to conceive of a life much more fair and just than God had? Even if you think of God as being a blind force, why should he not have been more intelligent or equitable? Why should man have such very fine perceptions of justice and equality and democracy and God in eternity, if they don't exist?

I suppose I was very much affected by the Quakers. One of the things that we were told constantly was that there is a light of God in every man. We used to discuss it. Was there a light of God in Hitler, Genghis Khan, and so on? There was, but it had been flooded out by ego. If it had been helped by forgiveness and love, then it would not have been so blotted out. God would forgive him in eternity. I was taught to believe that as a small child. It seemed to me to be true, that there must be a light of God in every man. God couldn't have created some people wicked and some people good. The other thing that runs through my books is the Calvinist idea that some are elected to grace and some aren't. But I can't really believe this. It's intolerable, especially if one is bound to believe that one is among the elect.

With Rose "the spirit bloweth where it listeth with vicious negligence and malice." That's when she and Christopher don't fancy each other anymore. Things have been piled up against them just once too often. The Holy Spirit has withdrawn itself from them. It was simply a description of what happens, but I think that I partly meant that it wasn't their fault. The spirit was negligent. They tried and missed. It was too much for them; the spirit shouldn't have left them. It should have stayed with them. Partly I was just trying to say quite simply that sexual love is completely unreliable. What seems to be a profound matter of the spirit is simply a passing matter of the body.

Q. You also seem to present the image of the spirit in a more personal manner as a feathered thing or as a bird: "He was caught. And his spirit would hunch its feathered bony shoulders, and grip its branch, and fold itself up and shrink within itself, until it could no longer brush against the net . . ." (*Needle's Eye,* p. 126); and "as myself stretched and put out damp, bony wings. . . . This was me, this was myself, this hungry bird who was ready from some unexplained famine to eat straw and twigs and paper" (*Garrick,* p. 118).

A. That's the spirit of the person. In fact, it's a dual image. The spirit of a person is like a bird trapped in his body. The cage is the body— definitely a Platonic notion.

Q. You also describe a desolate and forlorn spirit. Simon wonders how Rose turned out the way she is: "Perhaps it was the spirit of desolation that hovered with dark wings and a vacant spiritual gaze over the polished wooden dining table . . ." (*Needle's Eye,* p. 312).

A. Yes, that's Miltonic. There's a passage in *Paradise Lost* about the spirit brooding over the water during the creation of the world. I don't know what my images mean, but I know they mean something fairly involved to me and I use them because I don't know what I mean in words. But what I think I meant by that particular image is that Rose was made to be what she was; she has a special quality marked by the fact that it was a creative spirit of desolation hovering over her birth and childhood. This spirit was so oppressive that Rose had to rise up and become good because of it. It was as though she had to make herself out of this nothing world.

Q. Another thing that interests me is that you also have an occasional reference to Bunyan. The interior landscapes that you sometimes describe have a Bunyanesque quality to them. Has Bunyan been an important author to you?

A. I think I've read all of Bunyan. I read some of him when I was younger, and he really did knock me over, because he was a complete obsessive neurotic like me. When I was a child, I felt exactly that thing about wishing that one were nothing at all and wishing to undo oneself. I can't quite interpret it in terms of awakening sexual guilt. It was too big for that, but that certainly was part of it. Really, what could be more in one's bones than sex? A woman said to me in the middle of a frightful publisher's party that the trouble with her was that her mind was absolutely shattered at a very early age by masturbation and guilt. In a way that is what it's about. But in another way there's so much more pouring itself into this very simple Freudian explanation. Because why should one child take it so overwhelmingly and another not? And I felt that this woman had got a clue. I think she did mean that her mind had been wrecked. I think my mind was wrecked by something, but by what I don't know. It can't only have been that. What can it have been to make one feel so guilty as a small child? Was it that one was good at school? Was it that one was jealous of one's sister or that one's father was away during the war? I don't know what it could have been.

Q. Sarah points out that "what happens to one, and what one does, one becomes" (*Bird-Cage,* p. 143). This in turn reminds me of your reference to David Hartley's belief that "moral character is not born with us but develops . . . as a direct result of our physical experiences and the pleasure and pain they cause" (*Wordsworth,* p. 83). Would you say that Hartley has influenced your views of personality and character development?

A. Well, it's certainly something I worry about a great deal. I don't know whether I agree with him or not. We were doing *Mansfield Park* yesterday, which is so interesting about heredity and environment and inborn characteristics, but I don't know what I feel about that. My father produced this nonserious view that the reason the United States is in such chaos is that the land doesn't suit the people. The romantics were right. It's not a land you can live in and Americans are all being tormented by the fact that they're living in this hostile environment. But I wonder whether there's any truth in it or not. I've got this new theory which I'm going to put in my new book that there's something wrong with the people living in the North of England. They're all depressive. They're all sour and it's something either in the water or the chemicals or in the environment that is hostile to human happiness. I'm no scientist, but I do feel that there's something in these things that certain environments are more conducive to good qualities than other environments.

Q. Are you working on your new book now?

A. I haven't started it yet. I'm finishing up a biography of Arnold Bennett which I hope to complete by Christmas. I've been working on it for ages. Then I'm going to start this new book in which I think I'll try and tackle hereditary depressions that run through three generations of a family. It would fit in very nicely with my interest in pre-destination and fate and whether you can escape your destiny—whether it's right to escape it by taking drugs or just being happy in other ways; whether it will get you in the end anyway.

Q. Are you suggesting then that perhaps one doesn't have the right to try to escape depressive cycles? Doesn't that imply a fatalistic view that one is depressed because one is decreed or doomed to be depressed?

A. There's a very strong element of that in me because I really wish to believe that God has ordered the world correctly and that if he ordered you to be a depressive, then he meant something very significant by it and that if you be depressive, then God will illumine you in the end. Whereas if you try and cheat God by taking pills or doing this, that, or the other, then you won't get what God planned for you, which is something very special. I see no reason to suppose that God cares about individuals at all. To believe that one should have an individual destiny is really a form of hubris. Something that worries me tremendously is that fate has really given me a wonderful deal, a magnificent hand of cards. It is tremendously unfair and it's leading to disaster. Anyway it can't be fair because everyone else hasn't got it. I'm really egalitarian at heart. I think everyone should have the same hand of cards when they're born. I can't quite get over the fact that they haven't. These are the things that go through my mind constantly.

There is a passage in which Jane Gray says that she wouldn't have been able to lie around being so helpless and hopeless if she hadn't known that she would get James as a result of her depression, that somehow in her heart she knew that she was going to win out. In a sense she knew all the time that she would have James. "The Ace of Hearts," I believe she says.

I'm lucky too. I can't understand why other people don't have the same luck I do. I don't think it's fair and I don't think it right. I wish to handicap myself.

You know, I have a very involved correspondence with a man I never met. He told me about his inability to sleep and his asthma and various other deficiencies, and I wrote back that I used to have a terrible stammer, which I indeed still have at times. He replied that the reason I stammered is that I was guilty about doing well at school. That never occurred to me. It could well be true that I was afraid of voicing my views in class because I knew that they were good, that I would get approbation. I felt that wasn't fair.

Q. To change the subject, in at least two of your novels, *The Millstone* and *The Needle's Eye*, you handle in an almost documentary form descriptions of the workings of the National Health Services or African relief programs or Camden Town. Both Rosamund and Rose come to know from their own growing awareness of themselves and of others "the bond that links man to man" (*Millstone*, p. 79). Do you consider yourself to be a realist?

A. Yes. I think I probably do. It didn't occur to me even to question why I put them in. I included them because that's what life was like. It is such an odd mixture of emotional experiences and self-analysis and going to the post office. I suppose that mixture is something I wanted to indicate. I wanted to record what it was like.

Q. On the other hand, it also seems to me that part of the life experiences of such characters as Clara, Rosamund, Jane, and to a certain extent Rose are marked by extreme subjectivism and a sense of aloneness. There seems to be a feeling that only the self is important and that other human beings exist only insofar as they are perceived or imagined by the character. Perhaps some of your characters could be described as being imprisoned in their solipsist universe.

A. Very much so. I do see them like that, but I also see them as struggling to get out of it. That is one of the reasons I'm so keen on the episodes about the National Health and the post office. I mean in the National Health episodes you see Rosamund coming up against a world which she is aware goes on without her and that she has a peculiarly distorted view because of her own background. I wanted to make those documentary episodes real in their own right. Although they tell you something about the character, they also say, "and meantime life is going on in the post office." But Rosamund is certainly a solipsist, and so is Jane. In fact, Jane is the dottiest, the nearest to madness, of all the characters. And she, through James, learns to go out and down the street and that kind of thing. I mean she has got in such a narrow world that she is more or less unable to face the outside world. Rosamund, through the baby, is forced to encounter the outside world. The idea is that once you're forced to make contact through your lover or your child, then it's all right somehow. The other people are there. They're not just part of the images of your own imagination.

Q. Frequently you use water imagery (*Garrick Year, Waterfall, Needle's Eye*). Is there a symbolic intent?

A. Well, yes, I think water is symbolic. Beyond that, in *The Garrick Year*, they all go on about drowning themselves. Now I know exactly why; at the time I didn't know why. *The Garrick Year* was about a year we spent in Stratford-on-Avon with the Royal Shakespeare Company. The River Avon is very dangerous; while we were there at least two people were drowned. Adam was a baby and the best park to go for children was just by the water. Children used to crawl in all the time. I was in a perpetual state of nervous apprehension. And that's why that book is all about drowning. I wrote it in the dressing room when I was in the Company. I was understudying Imogen in *Cymbeline*, playing a fairy in *Midsummer Night's Dream*, walking on in *The Taming of the Shrew*. I think I must have been quite depressed because I was doing this really awful job in theater. It's very hard to remember precisely how one felt. I must have been feeling pretty gloomy there. It was a kind of defiance. I realized halfway through the book that drowning was what was going on and therefore at the end it would be most suitable if Julian drowned himself. But I hadn't realized how deeply oppressed I had been by the thought of children drowning themselves.

About the waterfall image, I'll tell you something that will amaze you. In *The Waterfall* I had no idea that I'd got a double image of the waterfall. I'd no idea that I'd pulled the card trick, the waterfall, and that they went off to the waterfall at the end. It occurred to me later when I was looking for a title and I thought "the waterfall," damn it, there's two of them, how suitable. I can seen it all looks incredibly deliberate, but it just isn't. I think Mary McCarthy said something very nice about imagery in novels. She said that naturally all the leaves on the same tree are the same kind. Well they would be. You start with the tree and the leaves grow from it.

Q. An organic whole whereby each part is necessary? Don't you have a passage that deals with just this topic: "perhaps people choose their own symbols naturally. . . . I should like to bear leaves and flowers and fruit, I should like the whole world . . ." (*Bird-Cage*, p. 73). Another point that interests me is Jane's comment when she and James visit the waterfall: "it is real, unlike James and me, it exists. It is an example of the sublime" (*Waterfall*, p. 251). Do you mean "sublime" in an eighteenth-century sense? The rest of the passage really puzzles me. It is almost as if Jane is looking at the two of them as characters in a passion tale.

A. Yes, I do very much have the eighteenth-century concept of the sublime in mind. In fact that particular waterfall was the real waterfall, Goredale Scar. Thomas Gray went to look at it and he said it was sublime. He said he stayed there about a quarter of an hour trembling. I thought it was very charming. And the scene was also painted by one of those early romantic painters. I'd longed to see it. In fact I went to see it; I'd nearly finished the novel when I went to see it. I went expressly in order to write the ending of the novel. I went with a friend of mine who in fact had got a bad leg, like James, so everything fit in very nicely.

As for "It is real, unlike James and me," I can give you an explanation of that though it's bound to be a rather personal one. Goredale Scar does exist and I went to it. It is an example of the sublime. The passions of Jane and James were meant to be an example of sublime, romantic passion. I'm aware that this is a novel and that many novels contain romantic passions which are not real and when Jane says that, what she is saying is a kind of double bluff. What she is saying is that Goredale Scar exists and is sublime. You may well think that James and I do not exist because we are characters in fiction and this kind of thing happens in fiction all the time and isn't true. But if you think a little more, you will realize that we exist. It exists and this could only be a record of a true experience. Otherwise why should anybody want to invent it. That's what I meant by it. But I put it in a kind of apologia.

You know I felt terribly guilty about writing that book—not only for the obvious reason that it was possibly upsetting other people—but for a more profound reason—that it was describing an experience that is not universal. Now *The Millstone* is an honorable book in that everybody knows what it's like to have a baby and to respond to this very basic situation. It seems to me that sublime, romantic passion is something very special and that perhaps everybody expects it, but very few people get it. The lucky ones get it. Those that wait sometimes get it and sometimes don't. At one point when they are discussing whether one knows about sex or has to learn about it, James says that you do it through knowledge, but God help you if you're that kind of person.

The Waterfall is a wicked book, you see. I've been attacked really very seriously and I can only respect the attack by people who say that you should not put into people's heads the idea that one can be saved from fairly pathological conditions by loving a man. People say that's not how I can approach my life. There's no guidance in that for me. And that's true. As Doris Lessing would say, there are not all that many men in the world these days who are worth looking for. She said in *The Golden Notebook* that the Englishman isn't worth tuppence and that no Englishman knows how to love. Well, that's very true. And if a woman happens to meet one of the few men available, good luck to her. But I mean it's luck.

Q. Each of your novels is distinctive in style. In *The Waterfall*, for example, the reader experiences the mind of Jane Gray from two points of view: Jane as objective narrator, describing her life to us, and Jane, as first-person narrator, participating in her life before our very eyes. Could you talk about the form of *The Waterfall* and why you develop the shifts in narrative style in that manner?

A. It really wasn't deliberate, you know. It just happened that way. I'd been wanting to write the first section of that book for a long time and I wrote it and I was intending to turn it into a novel. When I'd written it, I couldn't go on because it seemed to me that I'd set up this very forceful image of romantic, almost thirteenth-century love. Having had the experience or describing the experience, one had to say what is this about? I thought the only way to do it was to make Jane say it.

Q. What about the style in *The Needle's Eye*? Do the longer, more flowing sentences there perhaps reflect the quality of Rose's mind? Does the reader in a sense become a participant as Rose grows, changes, develops before his eyes?

A. No, it's never as simple as that. I do it because when I'm thinking about the book and Rose and my own feelings about life, at this stage in my life, it all sticks together. I wouldn't make a conscious decision to write long sentences about Rose. The whole thing comes from somewhere unknown. I think the very long sentences are just something I've learned to handle and couldn't handle earlier—partly daren't have handled earlier. I was possibly afraid of writing dully or alienating an audience. My first novels are much more ingratiating and made far more concessions to the reader. That was because I didn't know how to write a good long sentence and it seems to me if you're trying to express what seemed to me some very complicated concepts, you're bound to get involved in your prose while you're doing it. Following it through is going to be a fairly painful, complicated process in itself. So presumably the reader goes through what I went through when I was writing it. There's one sentence in *The Needle's Eye* that I've forgotten what it meant, but I do remember while writing it that I had some vague sense of having grasped very fleetingly some incredibly difficult and nebulous ideas about Simon's and Julie's marriage and the woman that he thought she was when he married her. I just don't know now what it means. But I know that it means something and I left it in. This is something I wouldn't have had the courage to do a few years ago. I left it in because someone, somewhere is going to know exactly what that means. I did for about five seconds and I let it stay there.

Q. Would you comment on your personal life view? It is difficult to know where you are in works which are so rich and varied.

A. Yes. It's very hard to say really. I mean obviously the books are expressions of different aspects of me. I think that probably from book to book I've tended to have the same kind of slightly manic-depressive reaction that I have in my own self against myself. I tend to write a comic book, then a rather sad book, then a strong book, then a weak book. I think that they've alternated between strong and weak characters fairly consistently. The *Summer Bird-Cage* girl is rather confused; the *Garrick Year* woman is strong; the *Millstone* girl is pretty defective; the *Jerusalem the Golden* girl is go-head, lively, a grabber; the *Waterfall* woman is feeble; the *Needle's Eye* woman strong. I think there's something in me that is going between these two poles all the time. In the novels I tend to be tossed to and fro between these two aspects of myself.

Some of the characters are better than me. I think Rose is a better woman than I am. But I'm not sure at all that's not simply because I desexed her slightly. And so I have Simon. Jane is over-sexed obviously and always behaves rather worse than I would. She's more irresponsible than I would ever be, I think. Rose is more responsible than I would ever be. I'm somewhere, striking an uneasy balance between the two all the time. And it's as though in the novels, I feel a compulsion to go to the end of each line, but alternately, which logically would mean in the next novel, I'm going to produce an extra-dependent and weak woman. I don't know whether I will because I think I might have grown out of having a single female protagonist. I think I might be far more kind to her in the next book. No, I can't deny that I've used an awful lot of incidents out of my own life. I think all novelists do. But I've also used again and again other people. Other people obviously see themselves as being specific and rigid or always being schizoid. I don't see myself as either. I see myself as being various.

An Interview with Kingsley Amis

Conducted by Dale Salwak

Since his first novel, *Lucky Jim* (1953), Kingsley Amis has become widely known as a novelist, poet, social and political commentator, and literary critic. Born an only child in suburban London on April 16, 1922, he was educated at the City of London School and St. John's College, Oxford, and served in the British Army (1942–45) as an officer in the Royal Signal Corps. He married Hilary Ann Bardwell in 1948, dissolved the marriage in 1965, and married the novelist Elizabeth Jane Howard in the same year. He has taught at various universities, including Swansea, Princeton, Cambridge, and Vanderbilt. Now a full-time writer and journalist, Amis lives in Barnet, Hertfordshire.

   Mr. Amis and I met on January 24 and 30, 1973, at the Travellers' Club in London. The sessions included two hours of taped interview each day. I must extend my deep appreciation to Dr. Gordon N. Ray, President of the John Simon Guggenheim Memorial Foundation, for arranging my interview with Kingley Amis; to Myrtle C. Bachelder at the University of Chicago, for financial aid in making my trip to London possible; and to Kingsley Amis, who treated me with the utmost generosity.

Q.   Considering your background and education, did you find it particularly difficult breaking into the establishment as a young writer?

A.   No. I want to record an emphatic no to that one. I started off with no social advantages at all. I acquired two very substantial ones. Having been to Oxford and having gotten a good degree at Oxford helped a great deal. And I'd heard there was a thing called the London literary racket which people used to talk about very much in the early

1950s, and that it was all an interlocking network in which Jones would review Smith's book favorably and vice versa, in which jobs were given to people you'd been to school with, and so on. That may have been going on but I never saw it, and it never did me any harm. I found my progress unimpeded by any external matters of that sort. Perhaps people have been stabbing me in the back all the time without my noticing it. But it showed me that what I had thought when I was younger (in my teens and twenties)—the view that Britain is a very rigid, structured, separated society, and that it is very difficult to break through from one class to another—was quite untrue. In my youth, England was not very stratified and it's less so now. It's always been alleged that the English, particularly the English as distinct from the other British, have an upper-class accent and various kinds of inferior accents, but even that is going now. It would be very difficult at any rate for a nonexpert to differentiate the way Princess Anne talks, for example, from somebody who is earning twenty pounds in a boutique.

Q. Looking back on your own career, can you reconstruct for me the way in which the "Angry Young Men" arose?

A. As always, I think it was all certainly not one or two things. Rather, it was a combination of accidents. One was that it so happened that three or four writers (myself included), none of whom were from upper-class backgrounds or had been to public schools in the British sense, emerged at about the same time. And they were all roughly of an age, and it so happened that there had been a kind of delayed action effect after the war. John Wain appeared, it so happened, in 1953. I think there was a feeling of exhaustion after the war. The older writers were still writing, but for some reason no new writer of any fame, any note, had appeared for seven or eight years. I think this was partly because people were busy putting their lives together again.

I was twenty-three when the war ended, and I spent the next few years trying very hard to get a good degree at Oxford, overwhelmed by getting married, finding almost simultaneously there were suddenly two babies in the house, and getting a job and working hard at it. There was this lag of eight or ten years after the war when nothing happened. Then by a series of coincidences, within three years, John Wain appeared, I appeared, John Braine, John Osborne, Iris Murdoch, and Colin Wilson all appeared. And others. Now that looks like a movement, and I can quite see, since there was this business of non-upper-classness (middle-class, middle upper-class perhaps, but certainly not upper-class) people could be forgiven for mistaking this for a sort of minor revolution or turning point in English writing. I don't think it really was that, but it had the look of being one.

Another reason why the thing was made to look like a movement is the fact that the novels and the plays were to a large extent about people at work. The hero of *Hurry on Down* wants to know where he fits in, where he's going to get a job, and changes his job a lot. The hero of *Lucky Jim* isn't sure what he wants to do, but we see him at work and a lot of his difficulties come directly from his job. Jimmy Porter in *Look Back in Anger* isn't employed very much but how he earns his living is important. *Room at the Top*, perhaps to a greater degree than any, is about a man getting on in the world. In other words, someone said that the weakness of the English novel of the twentieth century up to the time he was talking about (could be 1939) was that nothing happened until after 6:00 P.M. or on Saturday and Sunday. It wasn't that the people written about were of the leisure classes, it was just that we never saw them doing anything, apart from committing adultery and getting drunk. What they did at the office or at the factory, except for a very few self-consciously proletarian writers, we know nothing about.

Q.   What are your feelings about the political novel? Norman Mailer has made a way of life out of this for the past ten years. George Orwell occasionally used the convention of the novel for political statements. Do you see any similarities between yourself and Orwell?

A.   I'd be flattered to think there were any similarities between myself and Orwell. I think that with the exception of *Animal Farm*, which is an incredible freak of nature—unique—I don't regard Orwell as much of a novelist at all. A fine writer and a man with marvelous ideas, but look at his novels. *Coming Up for Air* is absurd as a novel. *1984* has got some marvelous ideas, but no narrative pressure. You get one situation and then another situation and another, and that's about it. It's repetitive. You get it also in his best novel, *Burmese Days*, which is nearest to being a novel. A man is in a hopeless situation, meets a girl who he thinks is going to pull him out of the hopeless situation, and she lets him down. Same thing as in *1984*.

As regards Mailer, I think that's a wonderful example of self-ruination by going in for politics. When I read *The Naked and the Dead* I thought wow, look out chaps, here's somebody on the scale of Dickens or Eliot, better watch him closely. But I needn't have worried, because he's systematically destroyed his talent by being rather silly. Very intelligent man, brilliant gifts. He was a novelist in the very sense that Orwell isn't—he could narrate and develop. All this semi-political rubbish has made Mailer just a hollow shell. I can't read him anymore. This is what often happens to American writers; they cease to become writers and become institutions. Too successful, too much money and something happens to them. There is so much temptation to become a national figure that you can become one, as has happened to Mailer and to James Baldwin (in a rather different way), although I don't think Baldwin had anything like Mailer's natural talent. Or you can disappear like Salinger, whose doom I lay squarely at the door of the *New Yorker* magazine for paying him the retainer. There are some people who flourish on being paid retainers because it stops them worrying about how they're going to pay for the groceries next week. Very few, however. I think most people need a little pressure like that.

Q.   What is there to write about in England today?

A.   Anything. That question brings up the whole question of what the novelist is up to. And this brings up another thing which I think is in favor of the British writer here—he is not distracted from his proper task, which is to write about human nature, the permanent things in human nature. I could reel you off a list as long as your arm, beginning with ambition, sexual desire, vainglory, foolishness—there's quite enough there to keep people writing. Of course the terms in which these qualities express themselves must be contemporary, unless one's writing a historical novel, and I see nothing against that. If you say, for instance, I'm so interested in the anatomy of ambition or jealousy that I'm deliberately going to take it outside the present context, so there'll be no distraction, and I'm going to go back to the eighteenth century—there, nobody's going to say what a true comment on the present scene, because I don't want them doing that, I want them to concentrate on my subject. The dress in which these abstractions are clothed must be contemporary, unless the writer is detaching them deliberately, and the contemporary details must be right.

But it's not the job of the novelist to represent the contemporary scene in any sense. He may turn out to be doing that, if he's any good he may turn out to be portraying the contemporary scene, and perhaps later be a source for social historians, but that's not a thing you can try to do. If you try to do that you become either propagandist or trivial. Dickens, for instance, had certain things which he wanted to say about his contemporary scene, although most of that, the sort of social reforming element in Dickens, was a little bit behind the social clock. He would not take up a cause unless it had been pretty heartily taken up by the people in advance. What primarily interested him, I'm sure, was how extraordinary people are. What extraordinary things they can do and say when they are very hypocritical, when they're very respectable, and when they're very mean. And, incidentally, of course he will show them being hypocritical and mean and so on in a contemporary fashion, wearing contemporary clothes in all possible senses of the term.

Q.   Turning specifically to your novels, are you consciously aware of using comedy as a critical device?

A.   In a sense, yes. It's essential from my point of view that the bad people should be ridiculous as well as bad. In my novels there are good people and bad people, which is very rare these days. There's often a lot wrong with the good people, and one must also lay off by making the bad people say good things or be right about things that the good people are wrong about. There are bad people, and it is essential to make them ridiculous. So that Professor Welch [*Lucky Jim*], who is a bad person because he treats Dixon very badly, is ridiculous because it is essential that he should be. Bertrand is rather a bad person—pretentious, rides all over people's feelings, women's feelings especially. But he's also a ridiculous person. The bad people have got to be funny, so that's critical if you like. But then of course when it comes to the good people the thing becomes a little more complicated, and also the question of whether the good people are really good becomes complicated, too.

To make a good character prominent is very difficult. This has been a perennial, incurable problem ever since literature existed. I think that one would find in my books that it's much more likely that an important good character would be a woman rather than a man. I think that Jenny Bunn is a good character, and Patrick Standish is a bad character [*Take a Girl Like You*]. He's in a way, I think, the most unpleasant person I've written about. I have sympathy for him, yes. He has his good points—when he pays for the other girl's abortion, for example. As a good character, Jenny is quite opposite to what Patrick could ever possibly be like, a good character who comes to grief and who has faults that one cannot get moral about. They are faults of foolishness, perhaps, indecision, but she is a person with wholly good instincts, generous, great humility, too much really. There's also Julian, who is all that Patrick ought to be and isn't, because although immoral sexually, let's say (many people would disapprove of the way he conducts his life), Julian actually knows what one should do and what one can do and what one should not do. And it's Julian who denounces Patrick for his behavior.

Those are in a sense my two favorite types. One is the person who is naive and shrewd (Jenny), in other words inexperienced, sees things for what they are, would never be wrong about a person even though she might be taken in by some things about them. The other admirable person is the person who is like Julian, entirely his own man, not preyed upon by anxieties, guilts, doubts, but nevertheless, in fact, is sufficiently so that he can afford to behave morally. I mean by that, he would never have treated Jenny as Patrick did because he'd just have decided he had to leave her. He too might have been confronted by Simon [*I Want It Now*], but would have said, "Sorry, this is too much; there'll be another one along in a minute."

Q.   In "A Memoir of My Father," you speak of the early training in morality you received. Could you elaborate?

A.   All the standard Protestant virtues (of course I know these overlap with Catholic virtues and Jewish virtues, and so on) were put forward and taken for granted—conscientiousness, thrift, hard work, patience particularly. That is to say, one mustn't expect to run before one walks nor to be a success at anything to start with. Everything worth doing is going to take time and trouble, unstinting and unceasing trouble. These were very good lessons. But God never came into the conversation. God was never actually referred to or appealed to, and there was no question of displeasing God by my actions or trying to please him. My parents would take me to church on Armistice Day, sometimes at Christmas, but these visits got less and less frequent as they grew older. In the last ten, perhaps twenty years of their lives, they never went into a church. They had suffered, they said, from forceful religious indoctrination, being forced to go to chapel when young, and I think my father regarded himself as a rebel in a mild way, mild certainly from today's standards. He had broken away from a very inflexible Christian kind of upbringing. When I saw my grandparents they too seemed to have come out on the other side. God didn't come into the conversation much.

Q.   Anthony Burgess, in his review of *I Want It Now*, comments that with the appearance of this novel a moral philosophy begins to emerge. How much stock do you put in a remark like that?

A.   Quite a lot. Again, I think it's improper perhaps to talk about one's self in such terms, but I've always been a moralist, which doesn't mean of course that I behave any better than anybody else. If I weren't a moralist I might behave even worse than I do in ordinary life. I

think—and this goes back to dad and mom and so on, if you like—
that because of my strong views that some kinds of behavior are admirable and others are despicable, hence I have this fairly rare phenomenon that there are good and bad characters. And very often they're
not at the center of the stage, but minor characters who are completely
good (Moti in *The Anti-Death League*, for instance) and completely
bad (Dr. Best).

I think that it's become more obvious, if you like, that there's a
moral concern at work. But I would have thought that it had been
there from the start. If Jim is such a slime, why doesn't he tell Margaret to leave, as he could do. Admittedly they work in the same
department and it would be awkward. Bertrand would have no trouble
at all getting rid of Margaret. Jim hates it and at the same time
laughs to himself about it, which is a thing some people miss; the only
way he can bear it is by joking to himself about it. There is a responsible concern, and if you like, at the end he says, well there are limits,
and as a Catholic would say, the individual's duty is to save his own
soul first.

Q. Do you see any time during your career when you have consciously modified the way you look at things?

A. Yes, I think so. At any rate that's what it looks like. There's been
an increase in the dim view which is taken of life, and the element of
horseplay and high spirits decreases. But I'd say that I've always been
a writer of serio-comedies, and I wouldn't be fair in ignoring the Margaret theme in *Lucky Jim*. I'm not claiming any merit for this, only
trying to describe what it is—an attempt at studying a neurotic person
who brings pressure to bear by being neurotic. It's true that Jim's
response to this can be taken by the reader as amusing, as comic, but
he doesn't think it's comic. He talks about it to himself, reflects about
it. What he is trying to do is cheer himself up, to make it more bearable
by trying to be funny about it. But that's quite a serious bit.

Even in *I Like It Here*, which has very little to say about anything, there are two fairly serious moral moments. One is when Bowen
goes over to Strether's side, having regarded him first with uneasy contempt, and becomes protective. The incident which is supposed to
show this is when he adjusts Strether's false teeth that had been half-knocked out of his mouth. The other thing is when he discovers something more about his wife than he thought, that she couldn't be a
blackmailer's girl, something he'd never put to himself before, and that
that was the most important thing about her.

Q. I notice that Jim Dixon makes a distinction between the "nice" and the "nasty" people, and that that distinction is referred to in your later novels. What does Jim mean by the "nice" life?

A. That is an attacking rather than a propounding remark, against *nostalgie de la boue*. It's a critical remark, saying don't let's pretend that it's a good thing to starve in a garret, that the painful experiences are good for you, the disagreeable experiences are good for you. Let's just face the obvious truth that you're probably a better person and nicer to your fellows if you are reasonably contented, reasonably well off, and have a reasonably comfortable time. It's not a materialistic remark, nor is it a spiritual uplift remark, but it's an attacking remark.

Jim and I have taken a lot of stick and a lot of bad mouthing for being Philistine, aggressively Philistine, and saying, "Well, as long as I've got me blonde and me pint of beer and me packet of fags and me seat at the cinema, I'm all right." I don't think either of us would say that. It's nice to have a pretty girl with large breasts rather than some fearful woman who's going to talk to you about Ezra Pound and hasn't got large breasts and probably doesn't wash much. And better to have a pint of beer than to have to talk to your host about the burgundy you're drinking. And better to go to the pictures than go to see nonsensical art exhibitions that nobody's really going to enjoy. So it's appealing to common sense if you like, and it's a way of trying to denounce affectation.

Q. Jim also manages to emphasize the division of classes and is constantly reminded of his lowly status. Is this an exaggeration?

A. He'd be the first to exaggerate it to himself, and I don't know how conscious I was of this at the time, but he's blaming his origins for things that his origins aren't to blame for. He's rather an uncouth person anyway; he could easily be more couth without his origins being changed. But I think that the proportion of that in *Lucky Jim*—the social climbing aspect—is not very important. For instance, Gore-Urquhart, who is Jim's eventual savior and benefactor, is certainly a man of the people who has made his way, but of heavy Scotch accent and therefore not one of the Scotch upper crust.

Q. In *That Uncertain Feeling*, an important question is raised when John Lewis turns down the promotion, presumably for reasons of integrity. However, Jean berates John for turning down the job and says economic security is more important. Is this ever resolved?

A. I think that Lewis' scruples about turning down the promotion because it has been rigged are only half-scruples. I'm pretty sure if we could run the thing through again up to the point at which the promotion is offered, and Lewis had had a sudden burst of self-confidence, he'd say, "I'll take the money." What is at work is partly scruples, but not enough alone to make him act in a scrupulous way.

What is also at work then is an attack of sexual panic. Despite his views of himself—which are partly ironical, as a striding, sneering Don Juan—when he finds himself behaving like that he realizes he hasn't got what it takes; he's afraid of getting really involved with Mrs. Gruffyd-Williams, and he's afraid of what this will do to his marriage. It's very largely a selfish fear which he then dresses up partly with scruples. But he uses them as a cover for his feelings of panic. He's in deep water, he's out of his depth, he's in a situation he can't handle. Then he strides in to Jean and says, "I'm a knight in shining armor, my integrity is at stake, I've turned down the promotion." He receives a well-earned kick in the stomach by Jean's obviously sensible retort, "What about the money? And what's so scrupulous about you in other fields?" That is a rebuke that Lewis has fully earned.

Some of Lewis' guilt feelings are sincere. He talks near the end about not giving up, not surrendering to one's desire for comfort, for sex, pleasing one's self all the time, and realizes that given his character, one can't hope to keep all those selfish desires in check all the time, but what he must not do is to stop trying to keep them in check, which means at least he won't be behaving badly all the time. This is, for him, a very realistic conclusion to come to.

Q.   Take a Girl Like You, on the other hand, seems a little more complex.

A.   Yes. I began that in 1955, and put it aside to write *I Like It Here* because it was obvious that *Take a Girl Like You* was going to take a long time to write. I was already behind in a sense. I was very nervous after it. I started making notes for it in Portugal in 1955, then put it aside in 1956, and wrote *I Like It Here*, then took up *Take a Girl Like You* again. I was very nervous because it was going to be a new departure for me; I even made about twelve drafts of the first chapter. I compared the first with the latest, and realized the only difference was that the later draft was ten percent longer. So I went on with it at an increased rate.

People say, "I laughed like hell at your book," and in a sense this is the nicest thing anyone could say. But when somebody said to me about *Lucky Jim*, "Thank you for your serious book," I thought, "Ah, you see what I intended." When *Take a Girl Like You* came along, it was saying, to put it very crudely, I hope they'll go on laughing, but this time they won't be able to escape the notion that I'm saying something serious. I don't mean profound or earnest, but something serious.

Q.   You speak of becoming grimmer in your view of life. Do you see any change in values, in Jenny's speech at the end of *Take a Girl Like You,* for instance?

A.   That's meant to be a very sad moment, because in fact, compared to Standish's behavior, she's a better person than he is, and the Bible-class ideas are better than his, even though they are quite inadequate. This is her trouble—she is presented with a great moral imperative or prohibition, without being able to understand the reason for it, without being able to work out the reason for it, and without wanting it, without being temperamentally on the side of it. Although Jenny is working-class, this would not be the right term for the earlier heroes. I think Dixon would say indignantly, "What, working-class? I'm middle-class." I imagine Dixon's father as being a small shopkeeper, or a man in some commercial firm, a lowly position but still white-collar person, obviously lower strata. Lewis' father—I doubt if he ever went down into the mine—is probably an office worker.

The same sort of thing applies to Bowen. Jenny, however, had to be working-class, not for any kind of political or social reason, but purely for strategic literary reasons, in that she had to feel on arrival, and the reader must feel this, too, that she is out of her element altogether, and she feels that her element is inferior to the one that she's in. In fact, it's not, but she feels it. This has got to be emphasized by first a geographical shift—she has come south (things have gotten more mobile since 1958 in England, however). In those days for a working-class girl to come south was something of a step to take. Therefore, she is socially isolated; there's no one to go to see, everybody's a stranger, has advanced ideas, more money than she was accustomed to, and they all seem more glamorous than people at home, certainly. So she'd have to be working-class.

Also, since the book is about the bit of morality—what happens when people can't give any emotional backing to their beliefs—this wouldn't be plausible except from a working-class milieu where people are more backward in that respect. I'm expressing neither approval nor disapproval when I say backward—backward in a chronological sense. You'd certainly find people with that sort of morality in Wales during that period. But I'd just done Wales, so she had to come from somewhere else. I could have made her Scotch, but that would have raised other problems I didn't want. I already had a Scotchman in the story, and so forth. Northern England is a very varied place, but it is believable that in the smaller towns, in Yorkshire for example, a girl could have been like that, born in 1938 or so.

Q. Beginning with *Take a Girl Like You*, I notice more of an emphasis upon sex. In light of your review of *Portnoy's Complaint*, in which you said the novel was "unfunny," how do you feel about sex in the novel?

A. Sex is a very important topic and most people are interested in it. I don't mean by that that it does no harm to one's sales; there is that, that is so. But it's also an immensely painful topic, and for that reason to laugh about it is important. This does not mean laughing *at* it, but its comic aspect is the only one one can hope to put into fiction. But to write about actual sex activity—what people do in bed, as opposed to people's sexual interests, schemes, seduction campaigns— except comically, I think, is impossible. I'd find it impossible. The moment I feel myself about to write a sentence which gives evidence of my sexual excitement, I stop. I don't much want to actually, but I would never do so because of how I feel when I feel that a writer is doing that to me. I become embarrassed. I've nothing against pornography provided it's well-presented as pornography, provided the writer says, "Look, you and I are going to have a jolly romp together, I'm going to tell you a story all about what people do in bed, and you're supposed to become sexually excited about it. Okay?" Fine. But if he says, "I'm telling you now a serious, also perhaps funny story, but anyway my aim is to entertain you and possibly to edify you," and if he starts trying to excite me sexually while he's doing that, it turns me off.

The other thing is if it's written about seriously, not pornographically but seriously—this is when I think the most embarrassment arrives. In some of the works of D. H. Lawrence, for example, there are serious attempts to portray a marvelous f—. I don't think it can be done. It's much funnier in its effect than anything I could possibly produce, but it also produces embarrassment. I don't mean sexual embarrassment, but the embarrassment one feels when one's heard something out of place, the wrong sort of thing is said.

Regarding the increase of sex, there is quite a lot in my latest novel, *The Riverside Villas Murder*, which is in part about an adolescent boy and the woman who lives next door. There's none at all in the novel I began recently, at least I can't see there being any. This is partly what a lot of writers do, their desire to elude categorization, to disappoint expectations. So I'm a funny writer, am I? This one, you'll have to admit, is quite serious. Oh, so I'm primarily a comic writer with some serious overtones and undertones? Try that with *The Anti-Death League* and see how that fits. So I'm a writer about society, twentieth-century man and our problems? Try that one on *The Green Man*. Except for one satirical portrait, that of the clergyman, it is about something quite different. So there is a lot of sex? Try that on the one I've just begun, in which sexual things will be referred to, but they've all taken place in the past because of the five central characters the youngest is seventy-one. So you dislike the youth of today, Mr. Amis, as in *Girl, 20*? Try that on the one I'm writing now where all the young people are sympathetic and all the old people are unsympathetic. This can be silly, but I think it helps to prevent one from repeating oneself, and Graves says the most dreadful thing in the world is that you're writing a book and you suddenly realize you're writing a book you've written before. Awful. I haven't quite done that yet, but it's certainly something to guard against.

Q.   Roger in *One Fat Englishman* is certainly shown to be a ridiculous character, largely because he is taken out of his social element. However, near the end it seems you express sympathy for Roger. Is this part of your concern with treating all characters fairly, even the bad ones?

A.   One can't write about anybody that one hasn't got some sympathy for. A reviewer remarked that "Roger behaves badly in more different ways than is usual, even for an unsympathetic character in a novel, but that I can't help feeling that the author likes the character, and so do I." Yes I do, I do feel a lot of sympathy for him because, I think, he's awful all right, and he knows it, and this is no excuse. But it does point to a perennial human problem, I think, that I tried to pin down in Roger's character and experiences—that if one behaves badly, it's no help to realize it.

Roger is a bastard to a very large extent, and he understands it, and yet he can't be different. One isn't asking for sympathy for him exactly, but we all have our crosses to bear, and being a bastard and realizing it is a kind of cross which he bears. Right at the end, the author steps forward, so to speak, to sympathize with Roger, and Roger weeps because although nobody says so, he was actually in love with Helene, or loved her as much as he is capable of loving anybody, and now he's lost her. So yes, I sympathize with him, I invite the reader to also, without condoning anything that he does.

Q. How did you feel about *The Egyptologists* after completing it?

A. I've always enjoyed it. To fill you in, Robert Conquest wrote the original draft which had the idea in it, and most of the characters in it, and a lot of the dialogue, and the science fiction dream, the Nefertiti statue, and so forth. I put in the plot, I introduced the women in fact, and the television debacle. But again, you see that horrible old morality keeps peeping up from time to time, when Schwartz falls in love with the treasurer, or starts to, and goes away. She sees that you can't run your life like that, it won't do for her, because it's a choice of what she is—she's either too starry-eyed about what life can be, or too decent and sensitive a person.

Q. Concerning Dixon's distinction between the "nice" and the "nasty," is Ronnie saying the same sort of thing in *I Want It Now* when he calls himself a "shit," or when Churchill in *The Anti-Death League* looks at the world and sees everyone as "nasty?"

A. I think they overlap a bit, but I think that Churchill is voicing what Moti would call selfish self-indulgent *contemptus mundi*—why is the world so bad—as a way of making his (Churchill's) sufferings seem more important. I think that covers that remark, because Moti is not the voice of the author exactly (how could he express the author's view totally, being an Indian with a totally different religious background). However, in that scene he is putting what the author would say when he says we must all try to become men.

As regards Ronnie, I think this is rather separate on the whole. He's making a remark purely about himself, and I think when he says he hasn't got the determination or the guts to be a full-time shit, to be a successful shit, I think this is perfectly true. It's like the man who doesn't sincerely want to be rich—he hasn't got the continuity of effort. In fact, Ronnie likes pleasure, and this is the thing about him from the start—at least I kept trying to introduce this notion. It's not a conscience at work. He has this habit of being efficient by saying what he thinks sometimes, a very bad practice if you want to be a success (never say what you think; rather, always think before you speak).

But Ronnie also likes pleasure, and he likes women, and this is emphasized several times, and power seekers, in my experience, don't like women. They may sleep with a lot of them, but that's a different matter altogether. And almost at once he starts liking Simon (much later he realizes he can't do without her). If he wasn't capable of liking her, none of it would have happened. He'd have said, "Oh the hell with this, this is too much trouble. I'll find someone else." Obviously there's something wrong with that book, because a lot of people said they find that Ronnie's sudden conversion is unconvincing and suddenly he starts behaving well. I thought that it was unconvincing because it was so obvious that that's what he'd do, because the early part of the novel is full of pointers in that direction.

Q.   How seriously, then, should we take Ronnie's conversion at the end?

A.   I don't think it's a conversion. Rather, it's the plot that comes into importance here. If things had been different (what we say about any drama or literature) none of this would have happened. As Milton says—to compare the great things to the small—if Othello had sacked Iago in Act I of *Othello*, Othello and Desdemona would have got on perfectly well for the rest of their lives. That's a grand example but I give it because it's such a well-known one. If Ronnie had been different, he wouldn't have bothered with Simon at all. Right from the start of their relationship he is concerned with her, before he knows that she is rich and this is very important.

The turning point in the novel comes far too early from my point of view. He sees her at the party, he likes her, tries to take her on, is separated, she reappears in the street without any shoes and such, he tells her to clear off, she says she has no money. He then says he has to do something about this girl, and after they've been to bed (unsuccessful as it is), before he finds out that she has money, he's very angry when she won't go but is also concerned, I think. It's not as if a last minute Dickensian change of heart occurred, where Scrooge suddenly says, "Come on, let's bring out the turkey and the plum pudding and let's all be generous to each other." I would like to think that it's there from the start.

Q.   I notice that your novels often conclude with the two central characters turning to each other for support: John Lewis and Jean, Ronnie and Simon, and Churchill and Catharine, for instance. Is this intentional, or did it just work out that way?

A.   I hadn't really considered the point before. Perhaps it happens to work out that way. Two going off together is a very common ending for all sorts of movies and books and so on, and perhaps that had its influence on it. But I suppose it's a rather sentimental feeling, if you like. Among all the disasters that have taken place and all the people that have been disappointed, these two have at any rate got each other, which is some sort of consolation. Also, if you like, the idea that one can't be happy on one's own, you can only be happy with another person, and so I suppose in a sense I am saying that by these endings.

Q. How earnestly should we take the supernatural in *The Green Man*?

A. As earnestly as possible, I would say. It all really happens; none of what is recounted happens only in the hero's mind. It's all literal in that sense. I think we can fit the supernatural part into the natural part by saying that the hero is made aware of his own deficiencies by finding out that the reason he's being picked on by the dead wizard to fulfill his designs is that the wizard feels Allington's character is essential for the wizard's purposes, Allington being a man who doesn't care for people and manipulates them for his pleasure. That's the link between them. I think it should be taken very seriously; I took it very seriously. And naturally I enjoyed doing it, and brought in some devices that had been in my head for years. I'd always been interested in the supernatural in fiction; here was a chance to do a ghost story.

As always, when you start to construct with plot it turns into something else, such that the ideas about the supernatural that you had in the past seemed to have somehow produced ideas in the natural world that fit in with them. I'm a very firm believer in the idea that the unconscious does two-thirds of the work. For example, the idea about opening the window and seeing it is light inside and yet dark outside, and the idea that everything stops outside, and that you can't move, can't leave the room because you can't get through the air molecules (it's like concrete). That too had been in my head somewhere. The idea that it is dark outside became an obvious link in the chain of supernatural circumstances. And the idea that everything stopped outside became attached to the idea of God or His emissary putting in an appearance. In what other way could God visit a mortal human being except by making everything stop outside? Otherwise, somebody might come in and we can't have that. It's God's security measure that makes everything stop, if you like.

Q. Is your portrayal of God in *The Anti-Death League* different from the being in *The Green Man*?

A. These are two very different incarnations. In *The Anti-Death League*, it isn't an incarnation at all in a sense. This is a view of the malignant God, who is very well described in Empson's *Milton's God* where he states practically, I think, that the orthodox God of Christianity is very wicked, and gives reasons for this. He sees God playing in *Paradise Lost* not altogether a dissimilar role from the role God plays in *The Anti-Death League* (although, of course, Empson's book was written before my novel ever appeared). I think if you were to look at that, this would throw some light on *The Anti-Death League*. In the novel, God is showing his malicious, malevolent side.

The Green Man takes a rather different view, and I'm not sure if they are really reconcilable. *The Green Man*'s God is slightly malignant, doesn't at all object to inflicting suffering, but that is not his main concern. He's running a game that's much more complex than that. He's admitting that he's not omnipotent, and that what may strike Allington as very arbitrary is in fact forced upon him because of the rules of the game. The chap in *The Green Man* does get tempted occasionally (let's throw down one dinosaur into Picadilly Circus and see what will happen), and that's the sort of thing with the being in *The Anti-Death League* (let's give her a cancer, smarten them up a bit; so that priest thinks he's in communication with me does he—all right, let's sort out his dog). Of course I incarnated God in *The Green Man* as a young man simply because he can't be an old man with an enormous white beard. The idea of a young, well-dressed, sort of aftershave lotion kind of man, I think, made him more sinister. That was the intention, anyway.

Q. Turning away from fiction for a moment, what do you find satisfying in the writing of poetry?

A. It's a higher art, and there's still even today a certain almost mystical status which attaches itself to a poet which the prose writer hasn't got. Many of us would be poets full time if we could, but we can't. Auden can do it, although he writes a lot of interesting prose as well. If one's mainly writing fiction, one would think that all one's creative energy goes into creating fiction. Some subjects, however, are not suitable for fiction. I'm delighted when I can write a poem.

There are several compensations for growing older as a writer, as you get to know yourself better, in your writing inclinations and so on. One gets more cunning, improves one's technique slightly as one gets older. You realize you get a little bit better at making transitions, such as realizing what a handy word "later" is (saying, for example, "What a marvelous old chap that fellow was," Roger said to Bill, later — thus eliminating the need for describing the end of the party, the departure of guests, and so on). You come to identify more precisely when to start a novel, and this is again not a conscious thing. It suddenly dawns on you that you know enough about your characters to start, and you understand your central situation to start. That means a certain amount of what you are going to say is already arranged in your mind. The same applies to political journalism, for example. Having written the first sentence, one ought to be able to take a rest, because one has done half the work. The great besetting fear is finding yourself with nothing left to say. I've tried to hedge by trying to write different sorts of books, partly because I like ghost stories, detective stories, spy stories. *The Riverside Villas Murder* is a detective story, set in 1936 in the middle of the great period of detective stories. My latest novel which I'm working on now is very orthodox.

Q.   I understand you also wrote a novel, still unpublished, during the early 1940s while attending Oxford. Can you tell me something about it?

A.   It's not really interesting. A novel that I'd admired enormously, and which is quite unknown (an English novel), called *The Senior Commoner*—about life at Eaton—made a tremendous impression on me. It's one of those curious novels in which absolutely nothing happens at all. Smith goes to see Jones and they talk, and then Jones goes away and runs into Brown and then Brown goes away and runs into Smith. It's about school life with no story to it.

I fell under the lure of this. There is a very crude and absurd story in my novel, called *The Legacy*, which again has a moral line in it in that it starts off with a young man who has inherited some money on conditions that he enters the family business (which is frightfully dull—accounting or something) and marries the girl his elder brother approves of by a certain time. He wants to be a poet and he has a nice girl, but by the end says to hell with poetry and marries the nasty girl and that's all that happens. I suppose there are some mildly amusing bits of observation, when he goes to live in a boarding house for a time and the people in the boarding house are studied. It's really no good and not funny.

Q.   John Gross wrote a fascinating book entitled *The Rise and Fall of the Man of Letters*. How do you feel about being classified as a man of letters?

A.   To him the man of letters is the man who gets most of his income from journalism and writing memoirs of people, collecting their letters, and all that type of stuff. I think that for me nothing really important had taken place since about 1880, in the sense that while lots of interesting books have been published, I think of myself like a sort of mid- or late-Victorian person, not in outlook but in the position of writing a bit of poetry (we forget that George Eliot also wrote verse), writing novels, being interested in questions of the day and occasionally writing about them, and being interested in the work of other writers and occasionally writing about that. I'm not exactly an entertainer pure and simple, not exactly an artist pure and simple, certainly not an incisive critic of society, and certainly not a political figure though I'm interested in politics. I think I'm just a combination of some of those things.

An Interview with Edward Dorn

*Conducted by Roy K. Okada**

Q. Could we begin by talking about your association with the Black Mountain College? Was this simply a community of artists or did you share aesthetic values?

A. When I went to Black Mountain I didn't have any aesthetic values. I was a work-scholarship student. I had learned how to print, working on the hometown newspaper, and so part of the possibility of my being there was that I could run the Black Mountain printing shop. It was a small shop and they did their own programs for dances and a little bit of poetry. It was all new to me—these people at Black Mountain. For one thing, I don't believe I'd ever met a person from the eastern part of the United States. A lot of people were from New York. The information they had all came into me as a flood.

Q. When did you go to Black Mountain?

A. It was in 1951, during the Korean War. A very important event in my life before Black Mountain was meeting the man who told me about Black Mountain—Ray Obermayr, who was from Milwaukee and had gone to graduate school in art in Madison. He was teaching at Eastern Illinois University and when I left the University of Illinois, I took some courses there. So I met him and he's the first person in my education who has remained important to me. He told me about things that were so exotic I couldn't believe it. One of them was Black Mountain.

---

* The interview was held on May 2, 1973, in Madison, Wisconsin.

Q. What about Charles Olson? What part did he play?

A. I didn't meet Charles until the second time I was at Black Mountain. I went there for a year the first time and then I left and wandered around the west—that was the first big odyssey I made. And I got to understand that there was more to the west than Route 66, which led to L.A. I spent some time in Wyoming and wandered up eventually to Washington and worked in the woods and met loggers who had been Wobblies or were old enough to have known people who were. And I met some people in the woods who had been trained by Marxist unions.

Then the second time that I went, I actually had met Charles because he came through the summer at the end of my term there and did a lecture. That thrilled me very much. His whole passion for a scope of knowledge that I hadn't dreamed of gave me a clue to what the extent of the mind might be. I'm speaking now more in the poetic sense, as enthusiast, really more than in the scholarly sense, because by the time I reached Black Mountain I knew that wasn't a real possibility for me. I also began to understand the distinctions between intellection and other ways of knowing things.

Q. What was the point of the bibliography that he compiled for you?

A. That came out of a tutorial arrangement. I told him that I wanted to read about the west, but I was very vague and wanted him to guide me. So one night he delivered this thing to my window. He worked at night and I already had a wife and children at the time and kept regular hours. So it came to me for breakfast. In fact, there were two versions. Donald Allen published the typed version, but the first one that Olson gave me was handwritten and I lost it in the shuffle when I gave that typescript to Allen.

Q. Did Olson and the Black Mountain School have a specific conception of geography? Were your ideas on the subject similar to theirs?

A. I don't know that I have any ideas as such about it at all, but my curiosity, the questing after what will identify the west in some big conceptual sense, certainly comes from there. I was ready for it anyway because, if you grow up on the plains, you're already on a geography—I mean it's such an overwhelming geographic term. The social basis of the central Illinois farmer is extremely thin and it's also characterized by a kind of skepticism—a social skepticism. You know farmers tend to be skeptical about both weather and people.

Q.   Williams once said "to what shall the mind turn for that with which to rehabilitate our thought and our lives? To the word, a meaning hardly distinguishable from that of place. . . ."[1] Would this more or less coincide with what you have been saying—that poetry results from the kind of geography that the writer grows up on?

A.   I have trouble with that one. I wouldn't argue with it in any basic sense but my own practice has shown me otherwise. I think there's a much more complicated terrain of the mind that is not necessarily a simple metaphor for the thing he's talking about. In a way, in the east, where he was, I think language has a different impact. On the prairie there's a certain evasion—a linguistic evasion—of the word as such. I suppose in New Jersey people might be more called on to pay attention to what the words are. One's social instincts become much more crucial where I come from, and they're not really linguistic.

Q.   In "Idaho Out," for instance, there's a section where you talk about the difference in response to young people, between the people of Idaho and those in Montana, and the fact that the Montana people seem to be much friendlier:

> My son rode with me
> and was delighted that a state
> so civilized as Montana
> could exist, where the people,
>
> .   .   .   .
>
> could be so welcoming to a lad,
> far from the prescribed ages
> of idaho where they chase that
> young population out, into
> the frosty air. There is
> an incredible but true fear
> of the trespassing there of such
> patently harmless people aged 13.[2]

A.   Well, I don't know whether it's contained in the poem or not, but what's back of that, as I now think of it, is that there's a kind of simplicity of human relationships in Montana that you wouldn't find in

[1] Quoted in Donald Davie, "The Black Mountain Poets: Charles Olson and Edward Dorn," *The Survival of Poetry*, ed. Martin Dodsworth (London: Faber and Faber, 1970), p. 221.

[2] Edward Dorn, *Geography* (London: Fulcrum Press, 1965), pp. 29–30.

a more complicated context like Idaho, the Snake River part of Idaho, which is immediately north of Utah. There's an entire population in Utah and Idaho that could qualify without any question to be Nixon advisors. On the other hand, for instance, Mansfield is an interesting man in that he's like a raw, leathery western kind of Montana pragmatist. His politics are—they're not liberal, they're not right-wing. What are they? He seems to have maintained a kind of sensibleness. It's difficult to find that kind of thing coming out of Idaho and Utah. So, I don't think the poem says that, but that's what the condition is that I'm speaking from.

Q. You use a statement from Sauer's *Morphology of Landscape* as an epigraph to "Idaho Out": "The thing to be known is the natural landscape. It becomes known through the totality of its form." Sauer also writes that "the natural landscape is of course of fundamental importance for it's applied to material out of which the cultural landscape is formed. The shaping for it lies in the culture itself."[3] *Geography* seems to agree that the culture does shape the natural landscape.

A. Well, by now we know that man has an effect. It's not just in Idaho and in fact my stepfather, the last time I was in Illinois, told me that—he's a farm machinery mechanic, he's really very in touch. He's watched what's happened to the soil, for instance, in central Illinois—he's watched that for forty years, and he says in effect that the soil is empty now. And that's speaking of some of the richest land known in the world.

Q. I think what I'm trying to get at is in the poem, "Inauguration Poem 2," where you talk about men being "spooks." Are you saying that there is something inherent in man himself which causes the soil to be "empty"?

A. Well, not necessarily, but in a programmed society it's true that we can want too much. This is not true only politically but in every sense possible.

Q. Could we talk about the form of your poetry?

A. I think, increasingly I find, that I have always been a narrative poet.

---

[3] Carl O. Sauer, *The Morphology of Landscape* (Berkeley: Univ. of California Press, 1929), p. 46.

Q. Many of the poems in *Geography* are songs.

A. Yes! But, in a way, they fit into . . . for instance, the songs in *Geography* were fed into a narrative of my life. Maybe that's stretching the term a bit. It doesn't become technically useful in that sense, but still it's part of those shorter love songs and lyrics. They form a disconnected narrative really because they're all about my own life and the life of my friends in Pocatello, in the case of *Geography*.

Q. They're either love poems or nature poems; you've said that you don't consider yourself to be a nature poet, as such, but the subject very often is nature.

A. Michael McClure's take on nature is more inside it because he's been interested in penetrating a certain biological awareness. Although, again, he's not a nature poet either because he can be social and cultural too. Nature's a magazine. I mean *Geography* isn't really geography, strictly speaking. I thought of the title not so much as the discipline as the word "geography," the writing of the earth or earth writing.

Q. In *The North Atlantic Turbine* on the dust jacket, you talk about "working out a location." Is the idea of a "location" more abstract than "geography"?

A. When I was in England the distance in perspective made me realize that I was a western poet. I mean a poet of the west—not by nativity but by orientation. It sounds pretentious to say that you can feel it, but I could feel that geography. I was impelled westward.

Q. Geography in a mystical sense.

A. It's kind of gold-rushing, except that there wasn't gold everywhere. The sun is the gold, in a way. The east—the eastern United States—was Europe as far as I was concerned. I mean Europe started in Indiana and New England was the heart of it. And so, in fact, I even felt like when I finally got to England that I wasn't in Europe.

Q. You were in the eastern United States. You were in some place out of Idaho.

A. It was England which was again still not the connection, although England doesn't feel that way about itself. If you follow the Common

Market business there've been obvious difficulties in the psychological differences.

Q. You wrote a review of Tom Raworth in which you say, "Manner is what the English have had and what they have largely become."[4] Is that part of your perception in *The North Atlantic Turbine*?

A. "Perception" might be a heavy word to use in that case. There are specific English people whom I feel so close to. I think foreigners are not really very trustworthy on the English.

Q. In "The first note (from London," for example, you describe a very delightful setting in which you and your wife are flirting and you write: "We considered of course making it then and there / while moving / but settled for a quiet kiss when halfway through it / abruptly and to our amazement / we found ourselves . . . smiling / into the equally smiling face / of a railway man idling / . . ., nonetheless we were sober and chaste / and slightly disappointed."[5] It's that "sober and chaste" which I think I find characteristic of the other incidents in "Oxford."

A. I suspect that an American can feel himself the most phoney person of all in England in a strange way because of the difference in national habits and there's a certain kind of directness about an American that you won't happily find in an Englishman. They do impose a kind of—well, I don't know what it is even—it's like deportment.

Q. "Sober and chaste" could not have appeared in *Geography*.

A. No! I don't think so because, you see, the terms are different. If you go into a bar in northern Idaho and you immediately try to find out what's happening, depending on the willingness of the proprietor or the bartender, you find out everything about the place— where they came from, where you can look for work, where you're going. It's all extremely superficial, but it's information that's vital in one sense; in another sense it covers up any real questions you might have between yourselves. That's the American thing. You just ask questions like a gatling gun.

---

[4] Edward Dorn, "On Tom Raworth," *Vort*, I (Fall 1972), 57.

[5] Edward Dorn, *The North Atlantic Turbine* (London: Fulcrum Press, 1967), p. 12. Parenthetical page references to this volume will be preceded by *N*.

Q. Part IV of "Oxford" begins with "An epistolary comment: knowing none of it accurately, the world can be surveyed." The poetry begins "I come to Oxford / not with the literacy with which / I could be / accused, but with eyes / closed most of all to the blandishment / I was most ready / at first / to assume more appropriate" (*N*, p. 31). Is that restating your point, that the assumptions are different?

A. Right! There's a certain kind of cultural substance in Cambridge or Oxford that I never wanted—that I was very intrigued by and captured by in a strange way, but I never wanted it to be easy in that sense. I didn't want it to be easy at all. That's an extremely difficult question. I think I was trying to discover . . . again, that poem sort of leads into *Gunslinger*, although it doesn't look to have any connection at all on the surface. I start using the poem as an instructive device for myself. For instance, with *Gunslinger* I'd been reading in the western material for a long time. It doesn't necessarily lead anywhere. I set the poem up in one sense, once I became conscious of it, as the instrumentality of my own instruction about it.

Q. One of the last poems in *The North Atlantic Turbine* is "An Idle Visitation" which does in turn become the beginning of *Gunslinger*. Is this all part of the dust jacket statement that you're moving from "worrying about working out a location to a spiritual address"? I think the word you use there is "intensity," which for me means the landscape of the imagination.

A. Exactly. My attempt there was to compel those materials. The thing happened late at night. It turned out to be a hundred or so lines and I dropped it.

Q. The "Idle Visitation"?

A. I published it in this book and then later I saw that it was the start. It was so open-ended that I recognized it later as being there for me if I wanted it. I mean I had left it there for myself which I didn't recognize right off. I didn't start out with the intention of writing a big poem. But I saw it later as a structure that was built in such a way that it could be extended.

Q. Was that the reason then that you moved from the natural landscape to intensity? That it seemed to be more open-ended?

A.   I don't feel that geography itself or a human preoccupation with the geography or a concern with the aesthetic properties of landscape and so forth necessarily leads anywhere at all and in fact most of that material is more or less interesting perhaps but inert. Until it's infused with the whole dynamism of human movement, I think its meaning is trivial. After all, the appreciation of landscape and geography is a human involvement.

Q.   The inscription to *Gunslinger III* talks about the "inside real" and the "outsidereal" (or "outside real"?).

A.   It's the outside real also.

Q.   The inside real becomes the focal point and the outside real, even linguistically, changes its form; it becomes outsiderial—in effect, a new word, which is, I think, characteristic of the shift from geography to intensity.

A.   I felt that. I later ran across a book that's become very important to me: *A Model of the Brain* by James Young, who takes as his main analogue the octopus brain. Apparently the octopus and ourselves had much in common way back. The octopods went one way and the anthropods went the other. But there's a lot in the nervous system that's still common and apparently the large part of the seat of memory in the octopus is in the eye. I believe that's a true motto for the poem—that it does represent that circuitry and that really outfront residence. He's not saying that the seat of memory is in our eye, but obviously the eye is a very complex thing and it has been thought of as the exposed part of the brain. When I look at you, in a sense, I'm looking at your brain so far as I can see your eye. So, I think that little formulation is my own sensual feeling for that mechanical truth:

The Octopus Thinks With Its Third Arm (after Young

Out of the total of some 500 Million nerve-cells
300 Million and more are in the arms

The script in the memory
Does not include the recognition of oblique Rectangles

In the optic Lobes of an octopus
We meet the first Great Section of the visual computing system
A Mass of 50 Million neurons behind each EYE
The optic Lobes themselves can be regarded as the classifying
And encoding system and as the Seat of the memory

The male Octopus Vulgaris fucks by putting the tip of the Third Arm
Inside the Mantle of the female
Who sits several feet away
Looking like nothing's happening
for about a half hour
The females are impregnated before they are mature
The Spermatophores survive until the Eggs are ripe
During the session
Both Animals are covered with Vertical stripes

And move not at all[6]

Q.   So reality is basically the thing that you perceive?

A.   Yes, it's difficult to put it. I have the sense that we know totality all the time through our senses and what part of that totality we can capture is the definition essentially of our sensate capabilities.

Q.   Well, Slinger, in Book I, asks very basic questions: "Are these men men?"; "Is my horse a horse?" He says, "bullets are not necessarily specific."[7] The fundamental questioning of reality is important in attempting to gauge the limits of this new world.

A.   That part does get very linguistic; I'm trying to grasp what the words can mean. I don't know whether this goes back to that idea about intensity or not. I threw that out as an obligation to myself to get out of that kind of soft dependency on the description and therefore, hopefully, the implication of myself and what was in front of me. I wanted language to do the same thing, in a way, except that the language then would make it real as the object was real. The subject would be as real as the object. This is necessary for me because I've always been confused by those attempts to make language the same thing as the thing. I don't want to say again what Williams said ["No ideas but in things"]—in fact I don't want to say that at all.

Q.   Getting back to *Gunslinger* and the question of the imagination. In Book II you have the "Literate Projector," which in effect reverses the film-making process as the image on the screen gets fed into the

---

[6] Used by permission of Edward Dorn.

[7] Edward Dorn, *Gunslinger Book I* (Los Angeles: Black Sparrow Press, 1968), pp. 20, 37; *Gunslinger Book II* (Los Angeles: Black Sparrow Press, 1969); *Gunslinger Book III* (West Newbury, Mass.: Frontier Press, 1972). Further references will be followed by volume and page number.

projector and comes out a film script. Is this reversal a characteristic of the *Gunslinger* world? Some of the names, for example, are reversed: instead of Houston, we have Notsuoh.

A. I know what you mean. It's the most arbitrary thing in Book II. In some ways it violates the forwardness of the book. I was interested in the idea, at the time, and while I was writing I got into it. But I think it mars the poem because it's only an occasional idea. In fact, when I republish the whole poem I think I might extract that.

Q. You mean the "Literate Projector"?

A. Maybe not entirely. I might find some way to leave . . . the idea is interesting to me but I don't plan to do anything with it. At one time I thought that I'd actually get into it and show it. In fact, I wrote a film script for Stan Brakhage. As it turned out we couldn't come up with the money and for one reason or another we decided not to do it. It's a western. He was interested, not from a director's standpoint, but to be the cameraman on such a project. We worked together on it and talked it over for about a month.

Q. Is it related to *Gunslinger*?

A. Well, the characters aren't the same, but the motif is similar. It's like a theological western. The characters are Dios I, Dios II, and Dios III—Father, Son, and Holy Ghost.

Q. Are they on a journey?

A. They're in Abilene, Texas. The first part takes place there. It's called "Abilene, Abilene" and the second half, after the intermission, is the cattle drive to Abilene, Kansas. That had a connection with the "Literate Projector" at one time, but then I lost it because I got more interested in a real film. This was 1968.

Q. Was this your first film script?

A. Yes, and it isn't actually finished. Maybe I'll finish it soon.

Q. *Gunslinger* could be a play: "The curtain might rise /any where on a single speaker" (I, 1).

A. Except that the characters are really a constellation of one body. They're not—I don't think they're discriminated enough to be a play in the theatrical sense. There's a guy in Seattle (Michael Wiater) who's turning it into a series of half-hour radio programs, like the Lone Ranger. Now, I'm interested in that because it probably has more relation to a radio serial than. . . .

Q. It's psychological drama.

A. It is!

Q. "I" dies and the "Biplane" enters, but I can't think of very many other scenes in which you could really film *Gunslinger*. It seems to me very internal. . . .

A. That's why I was interested in writing a film along those lines. But the "Literate Projector" really is a kind of intellectual trick, which I found interesting at the time. But it seems like a dead-end inside the poem. A lot of things are set up in a poem that could be major routes for it to take.

Q. For example, "I."

A. Yes! Although I think I can manage him okay—or her, I don't even know really.

Q. This is very basic, but why does "I" die? It's interesting to me that the first-person singular should be the one to die.

A. I wanted the narrative to operate by itself, if possible. "I" is dead actually. I think now the ego is pretty obviously dead. One of the most obvious facts of present life is people talking about themselves or referring to themselves or being preoccupied with themselves. That's about the most boring thing around. It's a habit that really has seen its day. It's not that it doesn't persist, but it turns out that everybody's everybody else. All our stories are so interchangeable. If they're significant they seem to be more interchangeable.

Q. But "I" returns in *Gunslinger III*. He doesn't actually return but we get a night letter or are the messenger and "I" the same person?

A. "I" is in communication.

Q. But he's a very fancy "I" on the printed page.

A. That's like a gothic "I," isn't it? That's a printing thing that I didn't have any control over and I don't object to it, but it puts an inference into the letter itself that's not. . . .

Q.   It changes the whole character. It's like the resurrection of an entirely different, very fanciful imagination.

A.   I can appreciate it from a certain Germanic standpoint. After all, I am interested in Heidegger and that whole basis of mentality that you can hardly avoid in the Western world. It's a mistake, but it wasn't my doing. It was given to me by the printer.

Q.   When you publish *Gunslinger* as a totality, will you change that "I" back to the original?

A.   I very well might. I won't change it back to anything. I might make it a different one. I think it could be gothic but not necessarily that one. It's kind of a crude . . . I think you could find one that might be absolutely right.

Q.   Why Heidegger and Parmenides and Lévi-Strauss as the names of characters? Partially because you are in the Western tradition, but what specifically about these writers or thinkers?

A.   None of this depends, in my mind, on how I feel about them.

Q.   Have you drawn on them as philosophers to be used in your poetry or is it as structured as that?

A.   No! My views of structuralism or Heidegger's phenomenology are not important to the poem at all. I want these characters to have the possibility of such names because they are widely understood and widely evokable intellectual signs. After all, this poem is addressed to the community in which I move, which is educated. My own audience might be small, but it's potentially comprehensive because the intellectual community is a mass community as much as the cotton picker's community, or the trucker's.

Q.   So then Heidegger and Lévi-Strauss become as important or as unimportant as Howard Hughes, or Hughes Howard?

A.   I'm more interested in activating those characters as believeably in possession of those names rather than demonstrating my take on their systems. In fact, I've been worried that some people have wondered if I've got the names right. That's not the point. I think that's self-evident. I feel very close to the mind of Lévi-Strauss—very respectful of it because I like the kind of mental nets that he sets up, but again that's irrelevant.

Q.   How about Howard Hughes?

A.   Howard Hughes is another category. He's more direct as a persona, although I'm increasingly not talking about him. I think he is a rather pure metaphor of a kind of primitive, entrepreneurial capitalist take of what America is, which is still embedded in the political and social instincts of a lot of American activity. He's a great singular—in a strange way like a dinosaur, but nevertheless his lineage in speculators goes back to the seventies and eighties of the last century and I do see him as an extension of the earlier, nonelectronic, financial geniuses like Fisk and Gould.

Q.   Is this the American dream gone bad?

A.   This is a danger—Hughes or Howard, whichever—I really don't mean the specific person, represents a very provocative sublimation. I suppose you could say dangerous. It's like the tip of the iceberg—what's back there is so hidden and so secret. The [Watergate] scandal is healthy and refreshing in American life—a cliché everyone can subscribe to.

Q.   Isn't one of your recent poems a comment on the subject?

A.   Of course this is more by way of notation than "poem":

> They won the election
> But lost the president
> Isn't it marvelous
> Corruption has saved us again—
> In America nothing goes to waste![8]

Q.   Could we, for a moment, go back to the third *Gunslinger*? Is the fourth coming along by the way?

A.   It's in notes. I keep a thing called the "iconic notebook." It's that sometimes short memory factor. I keep a mosaic of conversations—things I'd like to hear said. The books have been, to a certain extent,

---

[8] Used by permission of Edward Dorn.

assembled from that trash heap or whatever you want to call it. It's there—it's a kind of record.

Q.   The question I was going to ask about *Gunslinger III* was on a passage that I think is one of the most explicit that you've written about the poet. Slinger says, "To a poet all authority / except his own / is an expression of Evil / and it is all external authority / that he expiates / this is the culmination of his trait" (III, [16]).

A.   I believe that.

Q.   To follow what I was saying earlier about moving into your imagination then—is that, in a sense, defining the world of the poetic imagination as being "what is not evil"?

A.   I mean "evil" in the classical sense; everybody's got it, except that there is that kind of potential in the poet to not have it, and I think that's what he believes in. That's the connection with the whole burst of glow in the cosmos. And this gets back to what resides in things. This is another reason why I can't be satisfied with such a diminishing of potential. And I'm not misunderstanding what things are. It's just that the cosmos is not a thing.

Q.   So in the beginning of *Gunslinger III* when you talk about hitching onto the cosmos. . . .

A.   That means hitching onto the possibility of that occurrence.

Q.   In *Gunslinger*, you said that "I" could be "he or she." How do women fit into the *Gunslinger* world? There's Lil.

A.   I love Lil, but she gets to seem more like a resident woman. It's a true reflection of what's actual—the woman in a man's world, which is an occasion you don't have to walk far to find. I treat her with all the respect I have for her. That is a problem actually. I've been at pains for some time to see what she wants to do in her own life. I'm keeping a thing called "Lil's Book." It really hasn't come to much— I take it down as it comes and I'm anxious to pay attention to it, but I don't know whether it'll get done or not.

Q.   What place do women have in a poetic world?

A.   I don't have any special attitudes on the subject. I've always had a very good relationship with my mother, whom I respect very, very much. I've always lived a really very monogamous life. I haven't discovered in myself any impulses to do otherwise, although I certainly respect them when they occur in other people. I'm in total sympathy with anything a woman wants. I'm not very conscious of women as all that unique. When I meet a woman, I'm interested in her, but I can say the same thing for a child or a man. For some reason, the question doesn't turn me on that much. I feel extremely comfortable with the way I feel about women—I adore them.

Q.   Could we talk about *Bean News* for awhile? One critic has called it "transitional." I don't think it is. It seems to me that *Bean News* does a great deal to establish the intensity that you began with *Gunslinger*.

A.   I was anxious to have the form of the newspaper because it's an open form. Once the structure is set up—and I work very closely with one of the most excellent printers in the country now, Holbrook Teter, who was interested in doing a newspaper—and a lot of the work was getting the structure right, not that it was going to mimic another newspaper, but it was going to look super-newspaper, somehow. After that, anything can go into it. So I included a lot of things I didn't feel I could say in the poem because I held to a certain internal rhythmic relevance. I then used the newspaper as the vessel for that. I was also trying to work out for myself in editorials and some of the articles exactly what I meant by "Sllab." I was intrigued with Kubrick's use of the main deific principle in that film. In fact the most interesting thing in it for me was the stone with the music.

Q.   With magical writing on it.

A.   And then you can get elaborate in various ways. Like the rosetta stone is an extreme elaboration of what's basically the Sllab.

Q.   What was the format of *Bean News*? It seems to operate on the same principle as the "Literate Projector"—the lead stories, for example, are on the last page. There seems to be a great value on reversal.

A.   The thing that was exciting in doing *Bean News* for me was that it was kind of a community project. My wife Jenny, Michael Myers, and Holbrook Teter, the printer, had a lot of conferences about it in our apartment down on Pierce Street in San Francisco. In one of the sessions it came up—how different can you make a newspaper? What is there left that would be distinctive? Reverse the order. But to us, I must remember, nothing was reversed. Michael wanted to cut some cuneiform, and that's the way those numbers go. Michael Myers, the engraver and off-the-wall ideologist, and Holbrook and myself were all working on a product, a poem, which is a collaboration, a product of effort, and it's difficult to say where it comes from, ideally, whereas a poem by a one-and-one identity is a result. Everyone who was even in slight touch with *Bean News* became part of that belt of ideas so the list is a joke participated in by everyone on it. It's like any list of names; there's no reason for it to stop there.

Q. How much of it did you actually write?

A. I'd been in correspondence with Jeremy Prynne at Cambridge, when I was in Mexico, and he was interested in doing certain kinds of linguistic forgeries in biology. So, he provided all of that material, which is a certain fraction of it, and I did a lot. Then, to round it out, Tom Clark did the sports page. The people in the print shop themselves came up pretty much with the advertising page—that time thing—the slot machine or wheel of chance again ties back in with being, which is going to the shell game to me.

Q. There seem to be two different areas of concern. There is the world of the Bean News Service, for which Ed Dorn might or might not be the editor, the founder, the publisher; there are also poems which include a more direct social commentary. Are these two separate areas that you're developing or do the two worlds overlap?

A. I think if you're engaged in writing a long poem and it stretches over a period of time, the situation is peculiar. It does get to be two different things to a certain extent. I continue to write what might be called, in the simple sense, poems. They're not necessarily very connected at all with my big poem. Because in the long poem I've established a way of speaking that tends to rule what I say, because I'm anxious to keep a rhetorical tension there. So the poem doesn't break. It's really like building—it's a big structure. You don't have that problem with a short poem—diction fulfills another obligation to the ear. But with the long poem you've got to make it clear that this thing isn't falling apart or, if it is falling apart, that it's supposed to.

Q. Could we talk for a moment about your prose? You said that *The Rites of Passage* was reprinted with a new title. Could you relate the history of the novel?

A. It was first printed by Harvey Brown in Buffalo and didn't get around that much when it was published. I could feel that people might still be interested in reading it. So it was reprinted and I was happy to put another title on it. It wasn't meant to be deceptive or anything. It turns out that people are surprised when they discover they're the same thing, but in a way, it's not the same thing. People since have read it who don't actually know my work and certainly had never heard of it the first time around and so they read it in a different sense altogether. *By the Sound*, I think, is a good title and is equally true. In fact, it's more true to the ground of the novel than *Rites of Passage*, which is a kind of an intellectual pretension, which I was capable of at the time but have happily become increasingly incapable of.

Q.   I like *Rites of Passage* as a title because it suggests two levels. First of all, Carl Wyman and Billy are definitely going through initiatory experiences and become men. I also thought of the poet, Ed Dorn, being confronted by images, themes, ideas of his time. So he writes a novel which acknowledges Steinbeck, Faulkner, and the other masters; in a sense writing the novel becomes the novelist's own rite of passage. In another interview you called your prose "practice writing"; it seems to me that *Rites of Passage* wasn't "practice writing" in the very basic sense, but it was the poetic consciousness making its nod in the proper direction to acknowledge the masters of the field before striking out on its own.

A.   I like the way you feel about it. I don't mean to say that I repudiate that title for that edition. I don't mean that, but I was only really insisting that I also liked the new book and the new title. One of the difficulties, I suppose—what I'm really getting at is the fact that you know it's not a middle-class novel and I was not a middle-class person; however, it's a middle-class title.

Q.   You mean the middle class is concerned with such things as initiation and. . . .

A.   Well, I'm talking about the intellectual middle class. They're the only ones who would recognize it—the title, I mean—certainly not the characters in it. And I felt, actually, that the title was more—it finally allowed me to pay homage to the people that, in fact, I drew my story from and I was pleased to do that. That's really all I mean because it was *By the Sound*, and they were *By the Sound*, and it was their Sound. And the Sound actually is where it was at. That's almost the character, an implied character to that body of water. I mean it's a provocative body of water—Puget Sound.

Q. What about now at Kent State? What do you teach?

A. I teach a writing course and a literary history course of the American far west, which is mostly a reading course—you know, people use the library. I've encouraged them to go into figures that attract. It's a sort of a regular teaching job. Technically I'm "Poet-in-Residence," but I teach a load; it's been a nice experience being at Kent because it's like a national shrine and I was interested in that.

An Interview with Alain Robbe-Grillet

Conducted by David Hayman

The interview took place on June 13, 1973, in Alain Robbe-Grillet's Paris apartment in a good sized room, conservatively furnished, with Japanese prints on the walls, a number of well-stocked bookcases, and books piled randomly on the floor by the windows. Robbe-Grillet lounged in a corner of his couch behind a long coffee table containing an odd assortment of books, including one on repressed homosexuality. Though the original topic was to be the most recent novels (*Maison de rendez-vous* and *Project for a Revolution in New York*), we were soon on to other, less obvious topics.

The following translation tries to capture in English the conversational flavor of an intentionally informal encounter characterized by a maximum of free exchange. To this end I have even retained passages in which Robbe-Grillet rather obviously cannibalizes his own pronouncements. Certain gaps in the logic are due to telephone calls, but in general the conversation picked up smoothly after these interruptions. There are no long silences on the tape; there is no stuttering. Unfortunately, I cannot give the reader a sense of Robbe-Grillet's resonant voice constantly changing register, frequently breaking into guffaws or chuckles as he warms to a subject.

Q. Where would you locate your reader in terms of your fiction? Is he witness to or a participant in the action? Is it possible that he is aware of himself as a part of the creative process?

A. Perhaps that is the difference between the modern novel and the novel of the last century, and between modern art in general and the art of the last century. You know it was Marcel Duchamp who said that it is the viewers who make the painting. I think that is true of a painting by Marcel Duchamp or of later painting, American pop art, for example. The spectator before the canvas creates the painting. The canvas is nothing without that presence. On the other hand, it's easy to see the art of the last century as a closed universe which has no need for the spectator, or the reader in the case of the novel.

One could say that the reader of one of my novels or the spectator at one of my films is not really in front of but within. The work does not exist except through his presence. That is, unless there is someone within it who can reproduce the creative process. The relationship between author, work, and public is no longer the relationship between someone who creates a finished work and another who receives it. We now have a work which can exist only in a creative motion, which has its primary existence when the author writes or makes a film and exists a second time when the reader, the spectator, or in music the listener, is again within the work as if he were himself creating it. That is something we often have trouble getting the public to admit. The public is lazy and particularly the novel-reading public which likes to find itself before a work which does not imply its active presence and participation. But you can't enjoy a modern work if you don't enter into it.

Q.   You speak of a shift in aesthetic attitude and we all make a good deal of that change. Would you date the shift from Flaubert, from Mallarmé, from Lautréamont . . . ?

A.   Usually, when speaking of the novel we date it from Flaubert. That is, we have the impression that between Flaubert and Balzac something occurred, that Flaubert was the first novelist who asked himself the capital question, "Why and for what do I write? What is the power that I exploit? Who is speaking in my books?" etc. It is almost as though Flaubert was the first to realize that writing is not innocent, that it is an activity in which both writer and public are fully engaged, not only by virtue of the anecdotal content but also by virtue of the manner in which it is written.

Q.   Then it is a matter of verbal surface?

A.   Rather a matter of what [Roland] Barthes has called "*écriture.*" That is, we have the impression that for Balzac the problem of *écriture* did not exist. He used the third person past tense, writing a continuous and chronological causal narrative in a natural manner, or as if it were natural. He acted as though he believed it was natural. Flaubert, on the other hand, seems to have realized that nothing is natural, that there is nothing natural in the act of writing (*l'exercise de l'écriture*) just as there is nothing natural in the use of any power. And the sociologists immediately compared this with what was happening to, for example, political morality. The middle class incarnated by Balzac really felt that the bourgeois order was the natural one, therefore right and eternal. It appears that after, say, the revolution of '48, the idea was suddenly born even in the bourgeoisie itself that the use of power was not at all natural, that there was nothing natural about the workings of the established order. And, in fact, after 1850, there was a parallel degeneration of bourgeois political order and narrative order. It amounted to a declaration of liberty.

Q.   Would it be possible to push those limits back a bit? When I read, for example, your last two books (*Maison de rendez-vous* and *Project for a Revolution in New York*), I think even of seventeenth-century novels, novels by Furetière, Sorel, Scaron and the rather complicated games those authors play.

A.   Yes, you know one could say that modern art has appeared very revolutionary in relation to what we could call bourgeois art. I am not giving this term any precise political sense because these middle-class values and this sense of order are as current in Moscow as they are in New York and even in Havana. In fact, this middle-class order shaped itself slowly and had a century of predominance, the end of the eighteenth and the first half of the nineteenth . . . and also the end of the nineteenth, if we think of writers like Zola. But if we take the art which preceded that period, that is, even some authors you haven't mentioned, the great writers of the baroque period, for example, we do find a view of *écriture* and the nature of art which is much closer to the the one we hold today. Even though the bourgeois values finally triumphed, they were not really in effect during the earlier epoch.

Q.   I'd like to return to something you said before. You mentioned pop art. Is there any relationship between pop art and what you are doing?

A.   Yes, there probably are some connections, since on the one hand I personally feel their presence, and on the other hand the great American pop artists also feel it. You know, I had a very strange experience. Last year I spent six months in New York because I was teaching full-time at New York University. During that period, one thing struck me, that is, "*littérature*" paid much less attention to me than "*peinture*." Of course I was well-received in university circles, not only at my own university but also at Columbia and at the other universities in the area. But no important American writer sought me out. It was the painters who seemed positively drawn toward me. And for my part I had the same desire. I didn't want to meet writers like, I don't know, say Norman Mailer or the great lights of the literary world in New York.

Q.   They are doing something very different, aren't they?

A.   Completely different. But you know I really wanted to meet the pop art painters, and I did meet them thanks to art dealers, friends, art critics, etc. I met, and I saw a good deal of Roy Lichtenstein, Rauschenberg, Rosenquist, and I am even working on a book with Rauschenberg. That is, we're collaborating on a book which will consist partly of texts hand-written by me and reproduced photographically, and partly of lithographs by Rauschenberg which will respond to my texts. There will be a dialogue between pages of text and pages of lithography. I have some of the proofs here which I can show you. Now, what rapport? I don't know, but there is a common attitude toward realism, certainly. What's odd is that in literature I feel closer to the novelists of the last generation, to Faulkner, or even to Dos Passos, you know, *even* to Hemingway. There are two American writers who fascinate me because I find them close to what I'm doing: Burroughs and above all Nabokov.

Q.   Yes, but he isn't American.

A.   He writes in American! He is as American as Beckett is French! Look here, I'm rereading his *Despair*, which appeared in French in '33 but has just now been reprinted. A book like *Pale Fire* comes very close to expressing my feelings. And Nabokov himself feels very close to my books.

Q.   Is it a matter of style, of voice?

A.   Of *écriture*, a concept of literary creation completely different from the pseudo-realism of Saul Bellow and Mailer.

Q.   That reminds me of Roussel, who is after all very important at this moment.

A.   Ah, Raymond Roussel! I have one of his books here, the last one to come out, *Epaves*. I'm reading it right now. And you see, when a contemporary French writer like me spends time in New York, he feels very close to the painters and close also to what is happening in theater. The New York theater is very lively, more so than the French theater. The painting milieu also, even though there have been signs of life here lately, slight signs, and American inspired. French painting today is strongly influenced by American painting. So, when I am in New York, I see a lot of art shows, visit galleries and artists' studios. I see a great many plays, not Broadway, of course, not even off-Broadway, but off-off-off. But, as for literary circles, I find more life in Paris.

Q.   Which Parisian writers interest you now? After all, the *nouveau roman* is already twenty years old.

A.   Yes, the *nouveau roman* is twenty years old, but it can't date, since, for me, the *nouveau roman* is perpetually changing. If you read the latest book by Claude Simon, *Triptyque*, or *Le Corps conducteur* which preceded it, you'll find them extremely different from what appeared twenty years ago. In the same way, if you read *Project for a Revolution in New York*, you find it very different from *Jealousy*. I feel that all of the writers of the *nouveau roman* have evolved. And there are some to whom I still feel very close and whose evolution interests me very much, particularly Simon and Pinget.

Q.   But apart from that, there are certainly other movements. What about the *Tel Quel* group?

A.   The *Tel Quel* movement is very hard for me to discuss because, first of all, I was once very close to it. I was its father, if you wish. They say as much in the first collective volume they've published, *Théorie d'ensemble*. Of course, in the paternal role, my relationship with them has been "oedipal," especially with Sollers, who had trouble liquidating his. . . . But what they say about me I can't take very seriously. The *Tel Quel* movement is extremely hard to define because it has always been in flux. It hasn't shown the sort of revolutionary evolution we find in the work of Simon. It keeps shifting its ground and often for very personal reasons. The latest transformations of *Tel Quel vis à vis* the French Communist Party are completely mad. For three years Sollers swore only by the Communist Party and you couldn't say a word against the Party without having Sollers accuse you of the worst crimes. And then suddenly, in a fit of pique, he drags the Party in the mud. He says that it was never worth anything anyway. Oh well, there are far too many curious little events for us to be able to speak of a *Tel Quel* movement. Quite apart from all that, there are many members of the group besides Sollers himself who are writers.

Q.   There was Jean Pierre Faye, but he's with *Change* now.

A.   He *was* one of them, yes. There is Denis Roche, very much on the fringe of the movement.

Q.   Yes, and Maurice Roche.

A.   But Maurice Roche dates back to way before the *Tel Quel* movement.[1] He was writing much earlier. He was a friend of Henri Pichette and he was also a musician. He's not at all a creation of *Tel Quel*. I think there are no fundamental differences in our preoccupations and aims, and besides, I find Sollers grouped more and more with the *nouveau roman* by academic critics and even by Jean Ricardou.[2]

Q.   I think he wants to slip out of that category.

A.   Yes. He tried it once, but I can't see the point. Really, we have the same enemies. So what's accomplished by this sort of in-fighting? I don't find it very interesting. I just noticed a list of books on the *nouveau roman* in the *PMLA* bibliography. Sollers is always included in the *nouveau roman*. After all, where else would you put him? The *Tel Quel*ists don't exist as a category since they are always changing camp.

Q.   You know, I think, and Ricardou seems to agree, that there is another lineage. That is, they have other forebears. Perhaps we should group them in terms of their roots.

A.   Yes, if we ignore our little squabbles, all the *nouveau romanciers* show an abiding interest in the problems of fiction, in what we could call novelistic forms and their evolution. On the other hand, when Sollers places himself among the descendants of Antonin Artaud, we have a very different thing, and, in fact, an important difference.

---

[1] Actually, Roche began publishing fiction under the auspices of *Tel Quel* in 1966.

[2] See Ricardou, *Problèmes du noveau roman* and *Pour une théorie du noveau roman*.

Q.   In your latest novels, and also in the fragments you published in *Minuit I*, there is an interesting erotic aspect, an eroticism which is almost anti-erotic since it seems to deny eroticism. I wonder if that effect was intended and what you expect the erotic to accomplish in your work?

A.   I can't talk about the theory. It's the practice that interests me. By practice, I mean the literary practice, the textual practice. The other sort of practice (of the erotic) interests me too, but that's something else again. In my current films and novels the erotic is a privileged subject matter [*matériaux privilégés*]. As a matter of fact it has appeared more frequently and it has become increasingly distanced from what we've traditionally called erotic. That is, for all practical purposes amorous relationships, sexual relationships, are absent. What we find is not bodies but images of bodies. They are quite often not even images but images of images since the bodies. . . .

Q.   In "The Secret Room". . . .

A.   And also in *Project for a Revolution*, the images are mannequins, often. I'll show you some stills from my last film where I shot that sequence of the tortured mannequin [from *Project*].[3]

Q.   You seem to be turning a bit toward surrealism, don't you think?

A.   Perhaps. There are some resemblances with surrealism. What I'm doing is very sophisticated, very calculated, very staged, very much the spectacle, perhaps also, rather icy [*glacé*].

Q.   That's funny. Just recently, I read a review of an English history of the modern novel. The author of that book speaks of you as an "icy playboy."

A.   Icy! [Laughter] You know, people are often surprised to find me much less icy than my work. It's really hard for me to say anything abstract about my [erotic] images. It's true that I am interested in manipulating them, and it's true that one sees them appearing more and more frequently in my writing and in my films. The fragments you

---

[3] After the interview, Robbe-Grillet showed me the promised stills from his current film featuring a mannequin with bloody nipples like the manequin-girl in *Project*. The camera is used to create a similar ambiguity when it pans in on a live nude posed as though inanimate over whose *mons veneris* someone breaks eggs. Robbe-Grillet remarked to his wife that the actress managed to simulate waxy stillness during the pose.

read in *Minuit I* originally accompanied photos by David Hamilton. They belong to a much larger narrative which will come out next year. As pieces they belong for the moment to art dealers since they accompany either the lithographs of Rauschenberg or the engravings of Paul Delvaux. They are only fragments of a larger novel of which certain elements were written for Rauschenberg, certain for Delvaux, and others for the photographer Hamilton.

Q.   It seems to me that we have there the three thematic axes of your work. There is the element of pop art, the element. . . .

A.   Surrealistic, yes. . . .

Q.   And the erotic element. The erotic begins with *The Voyeur.*

A.   It's already there, yes. And it's the heroine of *The Voyeur* who appears, only with a much bigger role to play, in the *Project.* She's a little girl, still pre-adolescent. She belongs to a race we call Lolitas.

Q.   Yes, and she reminds me also of Zola's heroine Catherine in *Germinale.*

A.   Of course, but there are a number of literary heroines who resemble the little girl in my books. There is certainly the Lolita of Nabokov and also Lewis Caroll's Alice. There are, by the way, allusions to Alice in the text. Then we have Sade's Justine, a very strange little girl, and why not also Raymond Queneau's Zazie?

Q.   Perhaps we don't pay enough attention to that aspect of Queneau.

A.   I never forget to say when I make public pronouncements that the official list of *nouveaux romans* is fairly meaningless for me. Certainly, if I were to make up a list, I'd put Raymond Queneau on it, particularly books like *Le Chiendent,* which appeared in '33.

Q.   Yes, and Céline? He's something else.

A.   Céline too. It's strange how Céline's opening sentences resemble Beckett's. Have you noticed that? Listen, "Here we are again alone. . . ." Really, you'd think you were reading the first sentence of a Beckett novel.

Q.   Yes, and it's also the opening line of the traditional clown when he steps out on stage, "here we are again."

A.   Ah yes. Let's compare the first line of *Malone* to the end of Céline's paragraph,[4] "I shall soon be quite dead at last in spite of all." What's strange is that we have a first line which emphasizes the word "finished."[5]

Q.   I find the relationship even more remarkable in one of Céline's later books, *Féerie pour une autre fois*, three-fourths of which consists of an underground monologue that resembles nothing so much as Beckett's *Unnamable*. But I have another question. What is the rapport between the films you are making and have made for ten years and what you are doing now in the novel? I find that your novels are much more scene-oriented now.

A.   Because of the films?

Q.   I don't know, because of them or perhaps for other reasons.

A.   No, I don't think so. I think that there has been an evolution in the novel and that that evolution is quite naturally reflected in the cinema. For me these are two very different mediums [*matériaux*]. What is remarkable is that thematic aspect. You know I really enjoy not so much adapting my novels to the film as employing identical thematic materials in both, like, for example, the tortured mannequin we were speaking of earlier, or a broken glass, or blood. These are really. . . .

Q.   Motifs which are repeated. . . .

A.   Yes.

Q.   But there is another question. Your cinema is a sort of anti-cinema.

A.   Ah yes, there is an attempt to destructure [*déstructurer*], to subvert the narrative, an attempt at deconstructing as they say now.

Q.   The effect is almost literary at times.

A.   What do you call literary?

---

[4] "Soon I'll be old and it will finally be over." Céline, *Death on the Installment Plan.*

[5] The emphasis intended here is probably on the concept "end" rather than the word, the idea of beginning with death and completion.

Q. I'd say that the effects are effects of texture.

A. Yes, but I don't call that literary! Those are cinematic textures. You know they claim that our experimental cinema [*cinéma de recherche*] is a literary cinema. It's as though there were a norm, a naturalness about certain types of narrative, but I don't believe that is so. For me the most literary cinema is the cinema of Truffaut, Chabrol, the novelistic cinema which in fact reproduces literary forms of the last century. That, for me, is literary cinema. On the other hand, the cinema which manipulates the cinematic textual materials is really cinema.

Q. And in your novels, where the descriptive passages use effects of *tromp l'oeil*, there are visual qualities which suggest an attempt to undo the narrative.

A. Yes, in fact there is an effort to undo the code of the narrative, that is, the normal practice, the established order. There *is* an established order for the novel, which I feel must constantly be put in question, destroyed, subverted. At the same time we must subvert the illusion of realism.

Q. In *Project for a Revolution* I sense that you are toying with a particular novelistic convention, namely the convention of situating the action in an America of the mind (the dream). For example, the apartment you describe, far from being an American apartment, is completely Parisian. Even the door. . . .

A. A door with a key hole! There is no such door in New York . . . and a minute-miser in the hallway. There are no minute-misers in New York. And when you hear the firetrucks, you hear the noise made by Parisian firetrucks.

Q. And then I have a feeling that all the imagery of the novel is inspired by the paint patterns on the door, that ugly imitation-wood-textured paint one finds on all the doors of Paris.

A. Yes, of course, and that one finds in every one of my books. There is also one in *The Voyeur*. And the subway itself. In the New York subway the benches run parallel to the sides of the train, whereas here they are arranged in rows, like in the Paris Metro.

Q. That too makes me think of Céline and of Kafka.

A.   Of course, Kafka's *Amerika*.

Q.   But while Kafka never visited America, Céline and you have both spent time there.

A.   Yes, and it was all the more important that I knew things are not like that. You know, oddly enough, I've received letters from American readers, men, and particularly women, living in New York, who tell me, "Really, it's extraordinary how you manage to describe the anguish of this city. I live with that anguish and now each time I pass the window over the fire escape, I check to see if it's really fastened shut, etc." You see, they have lived the book totally in terms of the realist illusion without being disturbed by the accumulation of details that are completely, historically, false.

Q.   But you are, in fact, thinking of New York.

A.   Yes, I'm here, in Paris, thinking of New York.

Q.   And perhaps you are thinking of the tales.

A.   Of the mythology of the subway where people are raped, yes, of course. Yes, I think that my city is Paris, but all of the big occidental cities are moving in the intellectual direction of New York. It is a sort of supercity where all the qualities of our cities are exaggerated, pushed toward the limit. Richness is richer, but dirt is dirtier. New York is richer than any rich city in the world, but it's dirtier than any dirty city in the world. Poorer also; poverty is greater, richness is greater, splendor is greater, fear is greater, anguish is greater, freedom is greater too. It's one of the cities where freedom is really greater, don't you agree? It's a city which really excites me.

Q.   I think it is a city which fascinates.

A.   Yes, but why? Simply because it's the horrible projection of our city of the future.

Q.   In your latest books I notice an increasing tendency to include personages from the earlier books. The effect is rather Balzacian, but it is oblique Balzac.

A.   Oblique Balzac, yes.

Q.   Nevertheless, I find that these characters, who are about as unreal as they can be, become real. Perhaps the literary conventions are so strong that the reader permits himself to complete the vision.

A.   That's true enough to a degree. There is a more or less fraudulent reading which categorizes as credible characters who are not believable. But there is also the fact that my novels and my films are quite tricky [*retors*]. That is, my relations with "realism" are not simple. I think there is a constant tension in my books between a sort of ideal abstraction to which I give voice and, despite everything, the sort of empirical reality we find in novels of the last century. I feel that things are not as simple as Ricardou would have them when he speaks of a fiction which has become almost mathematical. I think rather that my books maintain subtle and more or less fraudulent relations with what one could call the "traditional novel," relations which at times appear like pieces in a collage more or less distorted, but only more or less, sometimes a bit less, sometimes a bit more.

Take *Project for a Revolution in New York*, which is as realistic a novel as is possible, given the fact that the book does not concern itself with New York, and that the action is incredible, etc. There are fragments which seem unexpectedly to belong to the still-possible literature of a still-possible novelistic mode. The character of the little girl has at times a presence similar to the one she might have in a traditional novel. And it is that which interests me. If you wish, it is these unresolved tensions between two poles, a tension between the subjective and the objective, the realistic illusion and total abstraction, and between the erotic which functions as such and another which would be impossible within the domain of the erotic. Such unresolved contradictions maintain in the book or in the film lines of force, and I think if there is a possible reading, it's thanks to this quality.

Q.   I find that this quality becomes very personal. Perhaps that's what is most important about your work. The whole apparatus of impersonality, while not completely false, is a façade.

A.   Yes, there is also a tension between the personal and the impersonal, because, in the last analysis, my books, which appear to be so impersonal are also very personal.

Q.   That's clear enough today, but in the beginning it wasn't at all clear.

A. There are plenty of things which were not evident in the beginning. For example, they have finally realized that there is a good deal of humor in my books. But in the beginning nobody noticed it, with the possible exception of Beckett. One sees more humor now, but it was there from the start. There were things in *Jealousy* which made me laugh heartily but which amused no one else.

Q. What sort of things were they?

A. Ah, that's very difficult since it concerns the text itself. At times, for example, textual impossibilities which can go almost unnoticed but which are for me particularly funny.

Q. I find quite a few instances in *Project*. That book seems funnier than the others and so do the fragments you did for David Hamilton. As I read the passages I kept the photos in mind. They are pastoral in mood, pictures of soft young girls in misty settings. But the texts poke perverse fun at all that. They are jokes.

A. Yes, and Hamilton, who has a sense of humor too, liked that.

An Interview with Abé Kobo

Conducted by Nancy S. Hardin

A scientific education and a keen and lively imagination underlie the creativity of Abé Kobo. As a writer of novels, essays, plays, as a director of films and theater, and as a photographer, he seems to have an uncanny ability "to contemplate the unimaginable" (*I*, p. 100).[1] By examining the nightmarish atmosphere of modern life, Abé alters attitudes toward reality much as Lewis Carroll dealt with complicated nonsense in order to make sense. Whereas the dreaming Alice's confrontations with "a land/Of wonders wild and new" shifted her perspective of reality, so too can one veer out of the endless flow of people on a Tokyo sidewalk and drop down, down a steep underground parking ramp—down into another reality of the Abé Kobo Studio. If one arrives during the rehearsal of a play such as *The Fake*

---

[1] Abé Kobo's novels have been translated by E. Dale Saunders and published in hardback editions in this country by Alfred A. Knopf, Inc. At this time only one of his plays, *Friends*, trans. Donald Keene (New York: Grove Press, 1967), has been published in this country. *Four Stories* (n.p., 1973), a bilingual edition translated by Andrew Horvat, includes "The Deaf Girl," "The Dog," "The Dream Soldier," and "The Cliff of Time." *New Writing in Japan*, ed. Yukio Mishima and trans. Geoffrey Bownas (Baltimore: Penguin Books, 1972), contains "Stick" and "Red Cocoon."

Page references throughout the introduction and the interview refer to the following paperback editions: *W—The Woman in the Dunes* (New York: Vintage, 1972); *F—The Face of Another* (Rutland, Vt.: Charles Tuttle Co., 1967); *R—The Ruined Map* (Rutland, Vt.: Charles Tuttle Co., 1970); *I—Inter Ice Age 4* (New York: Berkley Medallion, 1972). Page references to *B—The Box Man* are from the Knopf manuscript, which was translated by E. Dale Saunders and will soon appear in a hardback edition. Quotations from *C—The Crime of S. Karma* are from the manuscript translated by E. Dale Saunders.

Fish or *The Briefcase*, one feels as did Alice that the world has become curious. Indeed, one's observation of the world can never again be limited to the simplicity of the purely rational, but must hereafter incorporate a more complicated vision, much as that reflected by the compound eyes of insects.

In his plays Abé relies not only on words, but also on a physiological mode of communication that draws from the temporality of dance and movement itself. It is through drama, a combination of words and dance, that Abé is able to bridge the more conventional time/space art forms. For example, one of Abé's techniques of acting which aids in this endeavor is found in what he calls "neutral position."

To achieve "neutral position" an actor is encouraged to choose a place and pose that is comfortable. He then listens to the sounds around him, erasing one after the other until finally he is concentrating on only one sound. When he concentrates on this single sound, other parts of his body are released from tension. In this state the actor is then open to all forms of expression. He may imagine himself, for example, being watched by someone who is holding a gun while standing behind him. His concentration on the original sound is then modified as his attention alerts to the danger behind him. He thus moves from the "neutral position" to a position of tension—reaction to an enemy. That tension is suddenly broken and he must return to an awareness of the original sound. Through the sense of repetition evoked in his mind as he moves back and forth between the extremes of tension and neutrality, the actor is able to experience the depths of a given time/space situation.

Abé uses this technique in his own plays which are frequently characterized by the theme of man's tragicomic situation and his inability to transcend it. At times the humor of Abé is that of psychological manipulation and the dramas become games people play with one another. But Abé also uses a sometimes surreal humor to counterbalance the irrational fear that is so much a part of his world. This humor includes metamorphoses in which people are changed into insects, briefcases, and fish. Closely aligned with the humor associated with change is a sense of terror: "The most fearful of monsters is the well-known friend slightly altered" (*I*, p. 167). On this score Abé has been compared to Kafka, for both writers deal with a changed reality; Abé's protagonists, however, do not experience horror to the same extent as Kafka's characters. Moreover, the Abé adversary is known, whereas the Kafka adversary is not.

In both his drama and his novels Abé's characters know no specific nationality. They are contemporary men in contemporary times, confronting problems that have yet to be afforded solutions. Abé crosses cultural boundaries to deal with universal themes; his mind is not limited by the rigidities of a given cultural framework. One looks in vain for the influences of the more traditional Japanese literary forms such as the *Noh*. When asked about this, Abé responded: "You know I have an education in the scientific fields, so I haven't had much education in literature. I think, of course, I have an unconscious influence from traditional works." Neither does he seem to be influenced by Zen Buddhism: "The Japanese rediscovery of Zen was introduced by Americans."

Abé's novels draw much of their imagery from detailed descriptions of the properties of sand, of the varying characteristics and adaptations of insects, of the workings of computers, of the precise measurements of a potassium alginate mold to make a skin-like mask, of the mazes and labyrinths of the city, and of exact instructions for making and existing in a box. All of these images, selected out of a realistic as well as a psychological scrutiny of life, are interrelated with themes that pertain to those moments of crisis when the loneliness and terror which erode the lives of contemporary man, particularly urban contemporary man, become the total reality. In "a world where people were convinced that man could be erased like chalk marks from a blackboard" (*W*, p. 67), Abé's characters accept this loneliness and fear as essential realities in their lives and then move on to questions of mystery and ambiguity beyond the facts themselves.

For human relations in the Abé novel are, if not bankrupt, frequently suspended "like some algebraic equation that does not include such diverse items as name, occupation, and address" (*F*, p. 190). His characters for the most part find themselves "periodically overwhelmed . . . by an unspeakable sense of loneliness" (*B*, p. 190). Abé charges modern man with such crimes as that

of having lost one's face, the crime of shutting off the roadway to others, the crime of having lost understanding of other's agonies and joys, the crime of having lost the fear and joy of discovering unknown things in others, the crime of having forgotten one's duty to create for others, the crime of having lost a music heard together—these are crimes which express contemporary human relations, and thus the whole world assumes the form of a single penal colony. (*F*, p. 149)

Because of these losses and the emptiness that accompanies them, the fate of the Abé character is frequently as bizarre as the situation that leads to it. For example, in *The Crime of S. Karma*, the protagonist's emptiness is of such magnitude that when feeling a sense of affinity with a picture of a desert plain, he sucks it into his body simply by looking at it. Later he is arrested when a camel at the zoo, smelling the desert within him, wants to come into his eyes and into that arid landscape he senses there. Undergoing an irrational trial which is as distorted as that of Carroll's King and Queen of Hearts, and having lost all his badges of identity, as well as his name, an exhausted hero is no longer a human shape but something changed into a wall: "The plain extended as far as eye could see. On it I am a wall growing endlessly and serenely" (*C*, p. 126). In *The Woman in the Dunes*, Niki Jumpei, while defined by society as a missing person, by enforced confinement in a sand hole redefines his life and becomes a more authentic individual: "The change in the sand corresponded to a change in himself. Perhaps, along with the water in the sand, he had found a new self" (*W*. p. 236).

Meaning in the protagonist's existence can be found only in moments of creativity; his loneliness is otherwise unrelieved. Love in this world is either nonexistent, not to be trusted, or of slight duration. For Abé's study of human relations reveals a world wherein individuals cannot truly believe in one another, so that if an emotion resembling love exists, it is perverted by either rage or fear. The protagonist of *The Face of Another* finds his isolation compounded by a facial disfigurement that encourages his ambivalence toward his wife: "Thus both the desire to restore the roadway between us and vengeful craving to destroy you fiercely contended within me. At length I could not distinguish between them, and drawing the bow on you became a common, everyday thing; then suddenly in my heart was graven the face of a hunter" (*F*, p. 93). In *The Ruined Map* the hunter becomes the hunted and the quest for a meaningful relationship ends in a denial—a surreal dissolution of self into an unknown and impersonal world: "Nothing would be served by being found. What I needed now was a world I myself had chosen. . . . She searched; I hid. . . . I began walking in the opposite direction from her . . . perhaps in order to reach her. I would forget looking for a way to the past" (*R*, pp. 298–99). *Inter Ice Age 4* focuses on the constancy and impersonality of change. Dr. Katsumi, the principal character, must acquiesce in the success of a computerized society over the older human values, of the future over the present: "The most frightening thing in the world is discovering the abnormal in that which is closest to us" (*I*, p. 221). The packaged protagonist's alienation of *The Box Man* is almost total, yet he manages to survive by his own form of creativity, the notes that he scribbles inside his box. Of love he comments:

I think we had simply abandoned hope from the beginning. Passion is the urge to burn oneself out. . . . We were afraid of stopping loving before burning out, but we were not sure we wanted to go on the way people usually do. We could not imagine things so far as a half year in the future, as when the room would be full of garbage. . . . Words themselves had already begun to lose their meaning. Time had stopped. Three days, three weeks were all the same. No matter how long our love goes on burning, when it is burnt out it is over in an instant. (*B*, p. 184)

Questions put to Abé about his past are not always answered. He grew up in Mukden, Manchuria which he describes as "a frightening place in many ways. There was no law in the streets, where sometimes children were sold as slaves. It was nonetheless a fascinating city, a maze, a labyrinth with very dirty buildings made of black bricks. Outside the city, if one took the train which was very slow, the scenery was endlessly empty and monotonous. There were only a few trees scattered here and there." Abé now lives in the suburbs of Tokyo, commuting to his studio in the center of the city. It is not surprising to find the theme of labyrinthine mazes so prevalent in his works. Nor is it unusual to find him describing and writing of the city so vividly: "The first beat of the city's heart is a signal; within a five-minute period hundreds of filing cabinets are unlocked at one click and swarms of different but indistinguishable workers, like a wall of water released from the floodgates of a dam, suddenly throng the streets . . ." (*R*, p. 20). Abé is an M.D., as was his father, although he has never practiced. His wife, Machi, is a talented artist who has illustrated several of Abé's novels. She is also a successful stage designer who is very much in demand in Tokyo theatre. She does the stage settings for all the Abé plays.

The following interview took place at different intervals in November and December 1973 in Tokyo. Serving as interpreters were Hagihara Nobutoshi, a historian, and Hamada Tomoko, a graduate student in sociology. Abé himself is a warm and gentle person who laughs often. Our conversation ranged over topics including his reading interests, which are international. Of American writers he is particularly interested in Bernard Malamud (*Pictures of Fidelman*) and Susan Sontag (*Death Kit*). But our literary discussions varied from Mayakovsky (*Bed Bug*), Chekhov (*The Cherry Orchard*), Beckett (*Happy Days*), Vian (*L'Automn à Pékin*), and Henry Miller (*Dark*

Spring) to mention but a few. Talking with Abé is full of surprises, for his mind is constantly making imaginative associations. His creative virtuosity only begins with writing, for he has as well that rare ability to stimulate and provoke creative growth and excellence in the people around him.

There is one description from out of his past that captures the love of movement that one sees so much in his theater:

The Japanese, you know, learned how to ride horses from the Mongolians and it was also the Mongolians who expanded the local culture to a world wide one. Have you ever seen real Mongolians? They are very tall, stout, physically strong men. Once I saw some Mongolian soldiers on horseback. It was at the end of the war in 1945 when I was in Manchuria that I have that memory. It was in winter and the road was frozen so that one could ice skate on it. But the Mongolians on horseback opened their legs and dashed. It was spectacular and very frightening. With one hand, they handled the horse; with the other, they carried a rifle. Some crows were flying in the sky and the Mongolians started shooting. With legs wide apart, the soldiers balanced. When their horses suddenly stopped, the men stopped with them. The horses and the men rode as one. It was unbelievable.

Abé Kobo's agility as a creative artist is equally as spectacular.

Q.   Before I came to Japan, I had thought of you primarily as a novelist. One of the most delightful surprises has been watching you direct the actors in the Abé Kobo Studio. How did you become interested in drama?

A.   To direct human beings is a kind of pleasure. It is fun to handle various personalities. It is something like the sense of driving a powerful sports car. As a director one has the same feeling that a professional racer has when he controls a fantastic machine perfectly. Because, you see, all actors are mad.

Q.   The striking thing to me is that your theatrical world relies not only on words, but also on a physiological mode of communication— on dance and movement itself. How exactly does this work?

A.   Simply speaking, there are two types of art: one is spatial and the other one is of time. For example, in order to make time objective, we use a watch. That is to say, we make time into something spatial. The act of making time a spatial entity and the act of verbalizing are very similar. For example, people read a novel and after they finish they can repeat that experience again in themselves.

There are, however, other types of art where people recognize time itself directly. While listening to music, they are experiencing that art. It is a form of "-ing" being. When the music ends, for instance, they cannot reenact that experience.

There is a tremendous gap between spatial art and time art. Drama is the bridge that crosses between them. On the one hand, when one concentrates on the dialogue, he is doing something akin to reading a novel. Yet really to experience drama, it is necessary for the audience to watch the stage where the movements of the actors are ephemeral. There are two ways that drama can affect the reader or the audience. One involves the actor's words and the other his body to express some meaning as an "-ing" form. In this sense drama is dance as well as music, for dance can also be music using the human body. I am very much interested in drama and as a result I ask physiological things from the actors.

Q. This certainly would appear to be true from three of your most recent plays: *The Eyeglass of Love Is Colored Glass, The Briefcase,* and *The Fake Fish.* In *The Eyeglass of Love,* for example, it seems that you are rejecting any kind of interpretation or even any pretense of knowing what makes the characters act or feel in a certain way. One of the main points would seem to be that there are no clear distinctions between what is real and what is not. One is left wondering who is sane—the actors or the audience? Or even perhaps what sanity is?

A. When we practiced the play I gave different situations to each actor. In one sense it is like a technique of montage so it has a kind of double effect. The audience somehow gets some kind of story or plot, but nothing exact. It is a rather whimsical way of treating the audience. As for an answer, it does not come until the very end of the play. I don't know either who is sane or insane. [Laughter]

Q. Could you tell me something about how you conceived *The Eyeglass of Love Is Colored Glass?*

A. The title is sheer nonsense. It might lead one to expect a romantic love play. A person with such expectations will get a headache; I am amused by his getting sick and going home in confusion. This is what I really want. It is just like Boris Vian's *L'Automn à Pékin,* a book in which he writes all about Africa and nothing about Peking.

Q. I know that in the Abé Kobo Studio you produce only your plays and those of Harold Pinter. Why Pinter?

A. Because first of all Pinter's plays require the most effort from the actors. They are all demanding.

Q. Would you mind elaborating? Does it, for example, have something to do with Pinter's use of nonverbal levels of communication? His use of silences?

A. Partly this is true, yes. However, according to my interpretation of Pinter's plays, it is difficult to separate silence and nonsilence. Both are treated as equal. What interests me is that the world created by Pinter is very different from the world of traditional acting. Pinter's world is impossible to express by conventional means. The actors are quite at a loss about how to perform Pinter's plays.

For instance the relationship between being watched and watching something is changed. In a traditional play the actor is a man to be watched. But now in Pinter's play, the actors cannot perform in the same conventional manner—just to be watched. So I, as director, cannot produce Pinter's plays just to be watched either.

Q. I'm not sure I follow you.

A. Perhaps I could begin by saying that one characteristic of Pinter is that in his dialogue time does not flow. Rather time is a spiral. The relationship between time and space is changed. From that concept of time as a spiral, and how it affects the actors, arises the problem. For the conventional actor who plays the conventional way, this aspect of time is not a problem.

Take music for instance. The basic element for music is rhythm because this indicates time in the "-ing" energy form. When one adds to that sense of time spatial elements, then one has created a melody. Melody was very much required in a conventional dramatic technique. But when one wants to perform Pinter's plays or those of Beckett, actors are required to express themselves as more than just a melody.

As for the relationship between seeing and being seen, strictly speaking "to be seen" is an abstract concept. We imagine the situation that we are seen. The consciousness of being seen is very human. If there are two dogs and one dog watches the other being operated on, unless there is a rapid movement, the watching dog never shows any response to the operation. That implies very important things between the relationship to see and to be seen. The dog never recognizes itself as the other. In that operating room the dog to be seen should be the dog on the operating table. People, however, can never separate to be seen and to see. Only one combined entity exists. There is always to see *and* to be seen together. That is the principle.

But we often tend to regard "to be seen" as a kind of concept or idea. On TV or in a movie, there is an actor who is seen. But those of us watching him recognize that concept "to be seen." Therefore we understand to be seen as a kind of stereotype. And as such we don't allow ourselves to be seen literally. We wear armor. Conversely, abandoning that stereotype, we are able to be seen literally. It is necessary to give up this pretense only once, in order to gain the true position of being seen. All this is closely related to the idea of space and spiral time.

Q.   Watching and being watched, seeing and being seen, peeking and being peeked at seem to be important motifs in several of your works. In particular I am thinking of *The Woman in the Dunes, The Ruined Map*, and *The Box Man*.

A.   Yes, there are passages in *Woman* and *Map*. It is true that in *Box Man* peeking is a very important subject. A man is in a box and has no personality. He just peeks at the world from inside, and the people outside consider him to be just a box and not a human being. So the relationship between to be seen and to see is a very important motif here.

Q.   Critics say that in this work you have murdered the novel form— perhaps even that the end of the book signifies the death of literature.

A.   I do admit *The Box Man* is an unconventional novel. The structure is quite unique. There are many tricks, but I don't think they can be understood, even by the careful reader.

Q.   What do you mean?

A.   Loosely speaking, *The Box Man* has the structure of a suspense drama or a detective story.

Q.   In the same sense as *The Ruined Map* or *The Face of Another*?

A.   Yes, but this time it is an extreme case. I think I committed a crime to write that novel because the man who writes that novel is the man who committed the crime. But people never know who that man is. I tried in *The Box Man* to give people an idea of what it is like to live in a box. I even gave directions on how the box is made in case people wanted to build one for themselves.

Q.   Aren't you afraid people will write to you with all their problems about making and living in boxes?

A.   Well that actually happened. I got a letter from a man from one of the poorer sections of Tokyo. He said a friend of his has been wanting to live inside a box and he was quite at a loss what to do with him. What this man wanted to know was how I had heard about his friend and how I could have written about him. [Laughter]

Q.   Did you reply?

A.   I didn't. What if the man inside the box actually came to see me.

Q.   While we are talking about *The Box Man*, perhaps you would say something about the eight photographs that accompany the book.

A.   The photographs are a kind of montage. They are rather difficult to explain.

Q.   I like their ambiguous and hazy quality. They are moments captured in time and they offer, as well, a sense of "found art." You seem particularly attracted to impersonal places, to objects discarded by society, and to people regarded as outsiders. It seems to me that the music of such photographs is sad and lonely. I am reminded of a passage in *The Face of Another*:

True, I must make special mention of this music. Ornamental neon lights, blanched night skies, girls' legs that expanded and contracted with their stockings, forgotten alleys, corpses of dead cats in trash cans, tobacco ashes, and then . . . and then—I cannot name them all—every one of these scenes made its own particular music, its own particular noise. And for the sake of this music alone, I wanted to believe in the reality of the time I was anticipating. . . . (F, p. 154)

A.   Praise of my photographs makes me happier than praise of my novels.

Q.   Certainly they are intriguing and unexpected photographs. Each in its own way is a lonely scene, indicating a melancholy reality of a particular time.

A.   I took them at lonely times, and yes, of lonely people. The photograph of the family with the child in the wheelchair was taken in front of the Russian pavilion at Expo in Osaka. I took the family taking photos of a memorable family gathering.

One is of a man looking at a lottery poster for a lottery that has already been drawn. He is an honorable, respectable gangster. It was taken at about six o'clock in the morning. A very lonely time of the day.

One is of a man pushing a bicycle. He is a beggar and he carries all of his property with him.

Q.   That photograph is particularly blurred and ambiguous. Its caption says: "Here is a town for box men. Anonymity is the obligation of the inhabitants, and the right to live there is accorded only to those persons who are no one. All those who are registered are sentenced by the very fact of being registered" (*B*, p. 151). How do the poetic captions relate to the accompanying photographs?

A.   The captions are not really relevant. These poems only emphasize that I think the photograph as a whole should be a poem.

Q.   Is there then any particular reason for the order of the photographs or that the one of the discarded trucks comes last?

A.   Whether there is meaning or not I have forgotten. Each photograph resembles a poem. As for the gangster, he is just a typical gangster. The mirror at the street corner shows a clubhouse of the navy officers in the fashionable style of the 1930s. The freight train is just a freight train. The room is a special one for critical TB patients to be examined and to have emergency oxygen. In that ward on the walls there is a sign: "No Smoking." The photograph of the public urinal with the men urinating was taken at Ueno Station, one of the largest and bleakest stations in Tokyo. I have not talked about these photographs to anyone. The only one I have told before is the editor of Knopf, Harold Strauss, who is a semiprofessional with a camera. But he didn't like them. Maybe you could explain them to him. [Laughter]

Q.   Certainly there is a poetic quality in your novels as well as the photographs. Have you written poems as such?

A.   I think there is a tendency toward poetry in my works, but I am hesitant to say that I am a poet. There is a kind of contradictory element in the novel as compared with poetry. It is the function of the eye of the novel to observe the area between those things which are poetic and nonpoetic.

Q.   Do you mean realistic?

A.   No, I don't mean that nor do I mean objective. On the one hand, the object passes easily through the mind and, on the other hand, it is often hindered from doing so. There comes a time when one can see it as a kind of identifying object of one's own. At other times, one sees the object as an obstacle against one's mind. It is the function of the novel to see between these two extremes.

Q.   I've wondered if Rilke has been a poet that you've been interested in?

A.   When I was young I read Rilke. During the war I was very much interested in him—his poems of course, and *The Notebooks of Malte Laurids Brigge*, as well. I liked the *Notebooks*, but found his philosophy too egotistic. I do think that Rilke has a genius for seeing the object between things poetic and things antipoetic.

Q.   I have also been fascinated by your use of images, such as mazes, labyrinths, cages, boxes. Certainly a sense of poetry emerges from these objectified images that happen before our eyes on the stage and in the novels.

A.   Compared with the feudalistic society of the middle ages, we now have an open society. But in another sense we have made for ourselves a cage, or a kind of prison. As a writer one of my efforts is how to deal with an object as object itself. If I try to use these objects as means to express a philosophy, then the story becomes extremely dull. The important thing is *to think into the object*, to allow the object to be an obstacle to the mind and not, as most people do, allow it to pass easily through the mind. Once one thinks into the object, he gets a kind of surprise. Let me say again that Rilke has a true genius for doing this kind of thing. I don't like his philosophy, but I feel his power, his ability as an artist.

Q.   Sometimes I think of Lewis Carroll's *Alice in Wonderland* when I read your novels or see your plays. Not that the content is the same, but there is something about the approach that gives me the sense of a world turned upside down.

A.   I like Lewis Carroll very much, perhaps next to Edgar Allan Poe.

Q.   Perhaps one thing that reminds me of Carroll is the fact that you use so many mathematical references throughout your novels. You do seem to have an intriguing knowledge of pure mathematics which one finds in your poetic usage of mathematical concepts. I choose at random: "Where in God's name should he start on this equation filled with unknowns?" (*W*, p. 125), and "In mathematics there are 'imaginary numbers,' strange numbers which, when squared, become minus. They have points of similarity with masks, for putting one mask over another would be the same as not putting on any at all" (*F*, p. 94).

A.   Your point is a pleasant surprise. Although I went to medical school, I might have gone into pure mathematics. *The Crime of S. Karma* was written under the influence of Lewis Carroll—not under the influence of Kafka as so many thought. Although Carroll was a mathematician, *Alice in Wonderland* was written in a nonmathematical way, just as my books may use mathematical terminology in a poetic sense.

Q.   I am curious to know how you go about writing. What are your sources of energy? At one point in *The Face of Another* you say, "For the act of writing is not simply replacing facts with arrangements of letters; it is a kind of venturesome trip. I am not like a postman on a preordained route. There is danger, and discovery, and satisfaction" (*F*, p. 150). Isn't writing, or for that matter anything creative, a matter of energy? How do you create your energy? What are its sources? You are a man of so many talents: novelist, playwright, director, photographer, mathematician. . . .

A.   Always I think I have a sense of amazement about myself. Afterwards, I wonder how I was able to create what I did. I judge other novelists by only one standard: the author's control over his material and his ability to give it a life beyond himself. In other words if a certain work surpassed its author, I regard it as very good.

I can say the same thing about my own work. During the time I am writing a novel I remember everything that I write. I remember even on what part of the paper I wrote that paragraph or phrase. But at the moment I finish writing, I forget everything and then I get depressed. On the other hand, if I then read that work again five years later, I am often happily surprised by what I've written. That doesn't mean all my works are superior. Let's put it this way, in case my work is good, just in case, I don't think the author is that good. What I mean to say is that a work should be at least better than himself.

Q.   But how do you create the energy for so many things . . . photography, directing, writing?

A. I really don't know. I don't think in actuality I have that much energy. It may be wrong, but the creativity seems to come out of a sense of scarcity—something like the sense of a "shortage of oil." It is a negative pressure, a sort of emptiness. To make it perhaps more concrete for you I can name two authors, Edgar Allan Poe and Franz Kafka, who seem to me to have the same negative feeling. It is not, you see, entirely a matter of myself, but it is more a matter of what others want. I feel that everyone has a hole, a kind of emptiness. And if I can, I want to fill up the hole.

Q. Will you elaborate on Poe and Kafka as meaningful writers for you?

A. Poe was really the first person to inspire me to write. I was about fifteen years old at the time. This is a story I don't usually tell. I was born in Manchuria where the winters were very cold. When I was a mere school boy it was so cold that I was unable to go out during recess and I had to stay in the classroom. I read Poe's stories and I told them to my classmates. I had to read one story a day in order to maintain my standing, and there was still a demand even after I had finished all the translations. I then found myself having to invent stories during the whole cold winter. That was the first time I began to write the kind of story that could entertain other people.

I read Kafka after I had become a writer. I was really shocked when I read him for the first time. I felt a sense of relatedness, of someone very close to me. Kafka's way is different from the ordinary way of approaching ideas. Both he and Poe disclosed to me how to share something with other beings, outside the conventional pattern. It seems to me that Kafka's search has to do with how two absolutely lonely, solitary beings can make conversation with each other. In that sense Poe and Kafka create a sense of being in accord, each sounding the same note. It is a question that I concern myself with—this theme of loneliness.

Q. Yes, it is true that in each of your works your protagonists seem lonely, isolated, alienated personalities. . . .

A. I think first of all that loneliness is universal. Rilke's basic theme is loneliness. And it is one of my central concerns. But you know, as a matter of fact, it is a new theme for the Japanese. The reason is that the concept of loneliness appeared in the urban mode of life. The oldest examples in literature must come from England where urbanization began the earliest. Also in China. Unless the cities were established, the theme would never have emerged. I have discussed this in *Itan no Passporto* (*Pagan Passport*).

Q.   Do you consider yourself an existentialist?

A.   Perhaps so. I remember that when I was in high school during the war, I was a pacifist. At that time I read such people as Jaspers, Heidegger, Husserl, all of whom undoubtedly influenced me to some extent. I was spiritually and intellectually supported by Dostoevsky.

Q.   Have you also read Sartre and Camus?

A.   I did not like Camus at first. Only now do I understand what he is suffering from. I do wish, however, that he had more of a sense of humor. I don't like Sartre at all. He doesn't have any sense of humor. Without humor we cannot bear reality.

The reason that I was so attracted by existentialism initially was quite simply that I was persuaded that "existence precedes essence." In the case of militarism, essence precedes existence. Perhaps the idea of fatherland or motherland really belongs to the category of essence. So from the existentialist's point of view such an idea is really a sort of subordinate one.

Q.   Could you apply this to any of your novels in particular?

A.   I am not Sartre. When I write I can't be so analytical. When I am preparing to write I can be analytical and detached. But once I start writing I am not. It is strange but I become subordinate to what I am writing, and I can no longer dominate the work I am writing. After a certain stage I lose a certain control.

A good example of the nonphilosophical workings of my mind has to do with *The Ruined Map*. To tell the truth the opening scene appeared in my dreams and I continued to write. Just before ending I was unable to finish. I struggled for a few months and finally the ending scene appeared in my dreams, and I transcribed it. After all a novel is not so logical a thing.

Q.   Could you comment on the fact that, in the end of *Fake Fish*, the man isn't able to come from out of his dream. He dies within the dream.

A.   He died in his dream, that is to say before he got out of it. He cannot get out of the dream because he is still in the dream, forever as it were.

Q.   Is this like Sartre's "bad faith"? That is to say, are you dealing with a person who does not live his life in an authentic way?

A.   *Fake Fish* is a kind of black comedy, British style. One man dreams of being a fish, simply speaking, and dreaming of being a fish he dreams too deeply. He makes every effort to get out of that dream, but as I've said during those efforts he dies, and therefore he dreams forever. On a beach after a storm there are many dead fish. Maybe among these dead fish some of them are dreaming men who couldn't get out of their dream. All this, I suppose, is total nonsense.

Q.   Then what will you do next?

A.   I always ask myself. What next? I am scared just to think of it.

Q.   Do you get frightened before you begin to write?

A.   The most enjoyable time is when I suddenly get the idea for my work. But when I start writing it is very, very painful.

Q.   I can believe it.

A.   To write or to commit suicide. Which one will it be? [Laughter]

Q.   Better to write.

A.   Many people ask why a writer commits suicide. But I think the people who ask don't know the vanity and the nothingness of writing. I think it is very usual and natural for a writer to commit suicide, because in order to keep on writing he must be a very strong person.

Q.   I have noticed that in your work the individual is frequently sacrificed for the good of the group.

A.   You are right. I don't want to lecture, so I will keep this to the point. Writing a novel is very different from thinking something through logically. Whereas now we operate under new social relationships, our inner selves still cling to the older values. Thus there is a conflict between the self who seeks a new social relationship and the self who tries to maintain the older form. Regardless of what one wants, one still must face the new relationship, although the older self rejects it. I suppose that this has been a common literary theme forever. Whether man will survive or not is also an eternal subject, though more pronounced in our time. I think that a characteristic of modern literature is this uneasiness regarding human existence which has been superimposed on a desire for new human relationships. That is to say, there is an uneasiness as to whether the quest for new relationships is meaningful or whether human relationships are worth seeking at all. They might simply disappear altogether. That is what I am facing now. Say, for example, in Beckett's play, *Happy Days*, all human relationships are stagnated. But Beckett put that theme in a play and a play in itself is a means of communication.

Q. Although your own plays may deal with some levels of non-communication, they do communicate.

A. Yes, I think that is a characteristic modern theme. Pinter also pursues it. Thus we communicate the theme that we are unable to communicate with each other. We terminate our communication. And that's self-contradictory.

Q. One novel we haven't mentioned at all is *Inter Ice Age 4*. You say at the end that one of your purposes is "to make the reader confront the cruelty of the future, produce within him anguish and strain and bring about a dialogue with himself" (*I*, p. 221).

A. One word for explaining it. I am not against revolution, but would emphasize that revolution frequently takes a form that kills or hurts the people who want it. As long as a revolutionary recognizes that he will suffer for the sake of the revolution rather than for his own happiness, I agree with the revolutionary in his wish for revolution. Unless one has the confidence to take his life at risk, to be killed in revolution, he cannot make revolution. On the other hand, if one has that strong belief, one should do it. That is the theme of *Inter Ice Age 4*.

Q. Earlier, I was extremely interested in what you were saying about space and time. You spoke mostly of time, however. Could you comment on your use of space in novels such as *The Woman in the Dunes*? It seems to me that you use space differently in your plays from in your novels.

A. We feel time only when we see the changes of space. Unless we can catch that change of space, we cannot feel time. For example, the animal without language seems to live very much in time but in fact is controlled by time and can never control time. But human beings, because we have words, can see time as a kind of wrinkle or some shade of space. The human being has the power to imagine. By using imagination as a function of change, the human being goes beyond time. If we have only music, we wouldn't have much civilization or culture. Music is always in the form of "-ing" time. Music is to live in time but never to be able to look at time. Novels and drama, on the other hand, are forms of creativity that allow man to look at time.

Q.   Does imagination then rely much on memory?

A.   What I have said is a form of reading space. Memory as a form of imagination is to be found in old folk stories, old folk songs. These older tales give us various kinds of time. For the past, that was fine. But the relationship we have now between time and space is much more demanding. For example, there is the law of cause and effect, the idea that the present moment is the result of the past and the future will be the result of the present. Now because the relationship between time and space has become much more complicated, it is impossible to apply the law of cause and effect to everything. The collapse of the simple belief in the law of cause and effect let modern literature suffer in the twentieth century.

I became interested in the *nouveau roman* and Robbe-Grillet precisely because such writing destroys the law of cause and effect. Robbe-Grillet used the conflict of time and space as a theme, but I think it is rather a method.

Q.   Whereas Robbe-Grillet's novels indicate this collapse of time and space as a theme, you attempt to demonstrate this collapse in the structure of your novels?

A.   In Robbe-Grillet's static space, there are wrinkles and shades in which we can see the technique of conceiving time. I try not to overlook time. Gazing at static space very carefully, so that it seems as if no time is going on, is a process that deeply concerns me. For example, take this white wall. I must be able to gaze steadily at this white wall— that is, look at it with a special eye—if I want to make a single book about it. That is what I mean when I say the novel is a struggle against time.

An Interview with Stanley Elkin

Conducted by Scott Sanders*

Q. In *Boswell*, your protagonist says, "There had been a time when I had responded to the bizarre without understanding it, feeling only the need to be curious, to remember, as though anything truly outlandish were a kind of signpost, an indication of a sort of clumsy, cloudy truth." As a novelist, you are evidently interested in "outlandish and bizarre characters." Are you interested for Boswell's reasons?

A. I think the passage you just quoted is probably an example of the writer trying to fastgun, outdraw his reader and potential critic. A writer always knows more about what the hell he's up to, more about what is going on in his work, than any reader or critic; consequently he becomes suspicious, self-conscious. Because *he's* suspicious, he develops a kind of paranoia about the suspicions of others, so he'll sometimes do a sort of on-going critical bowdlerizing in the book itself, in order to preclude the criticism he has coming to him. This is always a bad idea.

Q. A bad idea to try to preclude criticism?

A. A bad idea to write yourself into corners you then have to write yourself out of.

Q. What of the outlandish and bizarre characters?

A. I'm attracted to the extreme. The air-conditioner on super-cool and the steak bloody. I'm attracted to extremes of personality, too. When I was a graduate student, I was a reader and admirer of William

---

* The interview was conducted on December 11–12, 1973, at Bloomington, Indiana. Mr. Elkin kindly consented to edit the interview.

Faulkner. Ultimately I wrote my thesis on him. It wasn't a good thesis and it had to do with religious symbolism in Faulkner's work. What I then took for religious symbolism, I now see as a kind of religious *awe*. I'm not comparing my talent to Faulkner's of course, but it seems to me that as human beings, we may both be hyper-impressionable. I stand in awe of the *outré*. Those characters who are exaggerated seem, to me at least, more vital than the ordinary character, certainly more energetic. It's this energy which engines my work.

Q.   It seems to me this awe that you're describing, this fascination with extreme figures, although present in all of your works, is most evident in *The Dick Gibson Show*, the latter part of which presents a collection of exaggerated figures. The book becomes a record of extreme voices, of eccentrics who call into Gibson's talkshow from all over America.

A.   Yes, but those are figures who are out of control. They're amok men. Gibson himself, like myself and Faulkner, is interested in the outrageous. But when the outrageous becomes the *italicized* outrageous, it becomes dangerous. When Gibson makes a speech to his callers and says, "What's the matter with everybody? I'm sick of obsession. I've eaten my ton and can't swallow another bite. Where are the ones who used to call with their good news and their recipes for Brunswick stew and their tips about speed traps between here and Chicago? What is with the crabgrass? What'll it be this summer, the sea or the mountains?" he's getting scared, denying the very types to whom he'd originally been attracted.

Q.   Your fiction is full of hustlers, con men, and salesmen. Feldman's father, for example, in *A Bad Man* or Lome in *Boswell* sell their wares by overwhelming their listeners with language. Is your prose also in places a kind of pitchman's rhetoric, a way of persuading an audience of the outlandish or the unlikely? I'm thinking, for example, of the wrestling scene with The Grim Reaper in *Boswell*, or the kangaroo court in *A Bad Man*, or the bear rape scene in *The Making of Ashenden*.

A.   It's not so much a question of persuading an audience of the outlandish or unlikely, as of persuading them of the possibilities inherent in rhetoric. Rhetoric doesn't occur in life. It occurs in fiction. Fiction gives an opportunity for rhetoric to happen. It provides a stage where language can stand. It's what I admire in the fiction of other people and what I aspire to in my own fiction. I'd rather have a metaphor than a good cigar. Certainly there's a pitchman aspect to my prose, but *I'm* not trying to sell anybody anything. I *am* trying to upset the applecarts of expectation and ordinary grammar, and you can only do that with fierce language. You can only do that with aggression: the aggression of syntax and metaphor, the aggression, really, of actual, by God metered prose, which I try for from time to time in my novels. But there's an element, too, of the other thing—persuading people of the unlikely. To take what today everybody is so fond of calling the conventional wisdom and to show that there is no conventional wisdom. That truth comes in fifty-seven day-glo flavors.

Q.   You described Lome, for example, persuading people on the sidewalk to buy clay from him because he "breathed meaning into it." In the spell of his words the clay becomes real estate. Is that phrase a key to your own notion of the function of rhetoric?

A.   That's precisely my notion of its function. Rhetoric is there, not only to perform for us, to show its triples and barrel rolls, but to introduce significance into what otherwise may be untouched by significance.

Q.   You've said elsewhere that shoptalk and specialized jargon fascinate you. Why is this?

A.   Let me answer your question by not answering your question. In a writing class I'm teaching now, there's a young man named McGuire who picked up on my notion that, when you don't really have a situation, you try to get somebody with a somewhat out-of-the-way occupation. And he wrote a story for me called "The Cutter." The cutter is a man who edits movies. Now what the cutter is doing— the premise of the story—is that he can't abide the notion of discarding these swatches of film-clips of great movie stars, so he salvages these out-takes from different films and puts them all together in a self-contained crazy quilt of film. Mr. McGuire evidently did a tremendous amount of research because he's got the vocabulary of film-editing down pat. In this way he establishes a powerful authority and authenticity. In a kind of way, the authority is more interesting to me than the authenticity, and in another kind of way, the authority is more interesting to me than the story itself. The secret of a bestseller, I suppose— though I've never written one, alas—is that it takes you backstage. It shows you a closed world. I'm not talking about "gossip," I'm talking about mystery. And what I mean by "shoptalk" is the language that is spoken in that closed world, the funny foreign accents there. It's like hearing people speak a different language. Even if we don't understand what they're saying, the sounds themselves are so strange as to make them valuable.

Q. Earlier you used the phrase "aggressive metaphor." I wondered whether you meant by that your ability to draw together areas of experience which are ordinarily so far apart that their conjunction shocks us: for example, the phrase "skate on his eyes" from *The Bailbondsman.*

A. Yes. In *The Bailbondsman*, which I happen to have in my hands, when Alexander Main, the bondsman, witnesses the ravaging of the Phoenician's tomb, he perceives the opening of an amphora in these terms: "He makes one deft, powerful stroke. The thick shaft goes in neat as a needle, but he was wrong to have worried about the flow. The amber liquid, whatever it is, is viscous, slow and thick as glue. It comes in measured plops, filling the chamber with a sweet sick smell, the odor of vital essence, of human butter." It's the "human butter" that is particularly attractive to me.

Q. That phrase also pushes the language beyond the point at which most writers leave their metaphor.

A. Sue me. No—let me give you another example. Here's a passage from *The Bailbondsman*, where I'm describing the sarcophagus and the mummy of the king: "their eyes travel up the long horizontal shell of the dead king—this priceless golden Easter egg of a Pharaoh which seems to float in its sarcophagus as in a bathtub—taking in each detail, its crossed arms and big golden gloves that grasp the shepherd's crook and flail, Pharaoh's and Osiris' carrot and stick, its great head in three dimensions like some coin of ultimate denomination. . . . The first tomb robber gazes at the long blue faïence beard that looks like a plaited hockey stick." It's not just the yoking of disparate objects, it's the *rightness* of the yoking. The Pharaoh's beard—I was looking at a photograph of Tutankhamen's death mask when I wrote that—is *exactly* like a "plaited hockey stick."

Q. So far you've talked about the role of personality and language in your fiction, but you haven't mentioned the abstractions that other writers commonly mention—social issues, politics, ideology. What is your feeling regarding those other concerns of fiction?

A.   That they're off-limits, out of bounds. The writer doesn't have the moral authority to prescribe for others. A novel's function is not sociological. A book doesn't have to sell people anything but language. Style, yes; lifestyle, no. As for ideas, it seems to me that no writer I can think of—there are exceptions—*thinks*. He comes to ideas late. The writer uses the techniques of other arts. For example, "Nude Descending a Staircase" precedes Joyce's stream-of-consciousness technique in *Ulysses*. Freud precedes Joyce. Writers pick up on ideas, perhaps, and use them in their work, but they do not invent them. Writers come to the idea of community only after the notion has occured to some social scientist.

Q.   Is this tardiness, do you feel, due to the fact that the writer's medium puts up a greater resistance than, say, the musician's or painter's?

A.   No, it's because, if the writer is doing his job, he is thinking only in terms of sentences and metaphor and syntax. These are the only things that are really real to him. That's all I care to be admired for.

Q.   What writers, living or otherwise, offer you models for this passionate interest in language?

A.   Well, I've mentioned Faulkner, who is "otherwise." Living writers? Certainly William Gass—above all others, probably. Then John Barth—though when I say John Barth I mean early Barth, the Barth of *The Sotweed Factor*. Gass has said that his art is the sentence, that he knows more about the sentence than any other living being. It's not a boast; it's simply a statement of fact. When I was a graduate student, and working on *Accent* magazine, I shared an office with Bill Gass at the University of Illinois, and I used to watch him scribble scribble scribble, and what he was doing was practicing his sentences, doing these endless, silent scales. He had a kaleidoscope on his desk, and he would turn it to the window to catch the light, and then try to write down what the kaleidoscope saw. You know, taking from the one medium and translating into the other. That's a marvellous thing. It's much more important than the writer doing the social scientist's job.

Q.   This focus upon syntax, this close craft of the sentence, seems uncharacteristic of American fiction.

A.   Certainly. As a matter of fact, when a popular critic becomes aware that a writer *is* handling language, he tends to write off that novelist. For example, John Updike for years has been criticized as a man of no substance, as a man who *"writes well."* The criticism of Updike's novels is that they are *written* well. That's absurd.

Q.   Because language is the one domain that no one else but the writer masters? Other people tell stories—film-makers, for example— but no one else performs in the realm of language except the writer?

A.   Right. I've yet to read a review of my own work—maybe it's not *true* of my own work, but I hope it is; it's certainly the thing I most strive for—where the reviewer simply says, "This man writes well."

Q.   Is "writing well" in part a question of accuracy, fidelity to your impressions of the world?

A.   When I was writing *Searches and Seizures*, I was living in London, and I needed to describe a hotel room. I've been in lots of hotel rooms, of course, but I didn't want to depend upon my memory. And so I went to the Royal Garden Hotel in Kensington and rented a room, simply to study the furniture there, to feel the glossy top of the wood that is almost not wood, to get the smell of the shower, the textures in the bath, to look at the rhetoric on the cards on top of the television set. This is stuff that I could not invent, and it was important to me to have it down very, very accurately. So I took notes. Somebody watching me would have thought I was a madman, a madman or an appraiser, going around jotting down notes about the upholstery. I looked like somebody casing the joint. But it was very important to me, and very exciting too, to look at things closely, so that I could get those things down in my writing and have them absolutely right. Now unfortunately there's a law of diminishing returns. Probably when one is doing one's best work, one is turning the reader off.

Q.   Because one's own interest in a subject exceeds the reader's?

A.   Yes, it's a kind of absorption which almost excludes him.

Q.   Was the hotel room, for example, your kaleidoscope? That is, was it an example of a place or an object which you tried to translate into prose?

A.   That's very good, I hadn't thought of that. I was doing with the hotel room what Gass was doing with the kaleidoscope.

Q. Your fiction is full of things observed—like that hotel room—with a specificity which suggests that you had to be there, you had to be the precise observer. For example, the teeth in *The Bailbondsman.*

A. Yes, there I had gone to the Natural History Museum in London, across from the Victoria and Albert. I hadn't gone there for that purpose though. I was with my kids. And finally I found myself in a room with cases filled with teeth, and because I was very taken with these teeth, I knew that I would have to come back, and somehow get their precise look. So I did. I returned the next day with a notebook. I came back with a clipboard and a bluebook and a bunch of pencils, and just went from case to case, writing down in notes to myself what it was I was actually looking at, and then in other notes what these teeth *looked like to me*—making up my metaphors on the spot, to work with and refine later. But making up the broad metaphors and similes right there in the museum. Then I went home and carefully constructed these similes and turned them into English. Elkin, the tooth-sayer.

Q. Is this a habit of yours, translating your impressions of people and things into metaphor on the spot?

A. It's the only kind of research I do.

Q. You seem to have a fascination for the *stuff* of modern America, of consumer America—the ticky-tacky highway culture, merchandise . . .

A. That's only because I *live* in modern America. If I had lived in seventeenth-century Germany, I would be fascinated with stuff in palaces, the swords and steins and dueling scars.

Q. The reason I ask is because many contemporary American writers feel hostile toward precisely those features of our society which fascinate you and fill your fiction.

A. Not only fascinate me. I *approve* of plenty. I dig cornucopia. I eat excess up. In the same way that I'm attracted to the bizarre personality, I'm attracted to overstatement of all kinds—whether it's material overstatement, the overstatement of the neon signs on our Broadways, or spiritual overstatements, which others see as spiritual understatement. It seems to me that all these *things*, all this *crap*, is the true American graffiti, the perfect queer calligraphy of the American signature—what gives us meaning and makes us fun.

Q. Roth and Bellow, among others, have complained that contemporary American reality beggars the writer's imagination, because the reality itself is more fabulous than any fictions they can generate. You as a writer seem to thrive on the fabulous, on the extreme, in American culture.

A. I hope so.

Q. Whom do you think of as your audience, as your readers?

A. Primarily I try to please myself. Next, Bill Gass. After that, no one.

Q. Do you mean that when you're writing, you're not conscious of, you're not trying to affect, some larger audience?

A. That may sound arrogant, as if I'm not concerned with my audience. But if I were to tell you about my concern for my audience, it would sound even more arrogant. Obviously I want people to like what I do, but primarily I would like them to understand that what I'm doing is *writing*, and to appreciate the work for the quality of the writing. Now most readers are not accustomed to reading that way, they really aren't. I teach literature in a university. And obviously, because it's the easiest thing to do, because it provides a kind of handle to the book, one talks about themes, one talks about symbols, one talks about ideas, one talks—in a vague way—about characterization and personality. But that isn't really what we ought to be talking about. What we really ought to be talking about is the individual sentence. I teach creative writing, and for a long time I taught it by trying to get the student to recognize a viable situation. Recently, I've learned that I can teach a kid how to write far more efficiently if the student comes to my office where I can take a page of what he's written, put it down on my desk and rewrite it for him. Then I hand him the page and get him to admit that what I've done is better than what he's done. Then I give him another page and have him do to that page what I've just done to the other. Then I get him to do it again. This takes about an hour and a half, and he learns more in that hour and a half than I could otherwise have taught him in an entire semester.

Q. Although the language is dense throughout your fiction—and by dense I mean it offers resistance to the eye and the mind—it seems to have become even more intricate recently, more dense, especially in the three novellas which you've just finished. Do you feel this is true?

A.   I hope it's true. And I hope it gets truer. My next novel—if I live and nothing happens—is going to be a book which I'm tentatively calling *The Franchiser* (though I think that this title is a particularly ugly one), about a man who goes out and buys franchises across the country. He's the man who's responsible for making America look like America, and to the degree that that's so, according to my lights, that makes him a hero. Because he makes plenty look like plenty. Or because he makes plenty look like plentiest. And this will give me an opportunity to check into a Ramada Inn, which is a franchise organization, and make my notes, as I did in the Natural History Museum, and do for the Ramada Inn what I hope I did for teeth. It will give me a splendid opportunity to discuss thirty-two of Mr. Howard Johnson's flavors, and to try to get the colors of his ice creams down. It will give me an opportunity to get down the late forties quality of the Fred Astaire Dance Studios, which still exist as franchises. So, hopefully, I have a form which will serve intentions I've had all my life. Not just a form—a concept particularly serviceable to me, the beauty that sleeps in the vulgar.

Q.   Do you anticipate that *things* will displace personality in your fiction?

A.   No. I'm no admirer of the French *nouveau roman*. No people live there. Things are a necessary backdrop to personalities and character, but personality must be the organizing principle of the novel. You can't have a novel about a television set. You can't have a novel about the texture of towels. It would be unbearable. So you've got to invent people to use those towels, you've got to invent a guy to watch that television set. You see, to the extent that there is a persistent theme in my work it's the theme of the human being as consumed consumer.

Q.   Would your franchiser be in some sense a transmutation of Feldman, who at his trial in *A Bad Man* talked about those aspects of America—highway strip America and mass culture America—which "moved him"? In a way which I find it difficult to account for, his catalogue *is* very moving.

A.   And so it should be. Because after all, once we have done our work, our function is to be comfortable. And Feldman's catalogue—

or much of Feldman's catalogue—is a listing of those things which make us comfortable.

Q. Do you feel that critics have contributed at all to your work?

A. No. I don't. They've simply made me defensive. They invariably call me a satirist. Clancy Sigal, the man who wrote *Weekend in Dinlock* and *Going Away*, a writer whom I respect, recently reviewed *Searches and Seizures*. And one of the things he said is that he finds that America *uses* satire—the Establishment uses satire—as a kind of release valve, so that the Establishment can continue to get away with being the Establishment. The burden of what he was saying is that we have free speech in order not to have freedom. Well, that presupposes that I am trying to change the status quo. As a matter of fact, he criticized me precisely for not going far enough in changing the status quo. Well, I wasn't satirizing a god damned thing in that book. He says that the guy in *The Condominium* who jumps off the building jumps because he is driven to it by the mundaneness of those people whom he's forced to live with. That's not why he jumps off the building. He accuses me of things which I haven't tried to do. I'm not a satirist. I don't enjoy satire myself and certainly do not aspire to it.

Q. When you read your own work aloud, you do it with an obvious pleasure, not simply because you've written it, but because the language itself has an excitement and an energy to it. In your actual composition, is listening to speech, or reading aloud, an important part?

A. Not listening to speech. But I do have a tendency to read my stuff aloud as I'm writing it. As a matter of fact, I read other people's books out loud if I'm enjoying them.

Q. You've mentioned some of the other writers you enjoy, because of the density or energy of their language. Are there writers who interest you for other reasons, as storytellers or simply as human beings?

A. Saul Bellow. Saul Bellow is clearly a good guy, a nice man. I don't mean that to sound patronizing—well, how could it sound patronizing to call someone a nice man? (And anyhow who the hell am I to patronize Bellow?) He's a great writer, probably the writer who has influenced me most deeply. While I admire Gass tremendously, I don't think I imitate him. And while I admire Barth, I don't think I imitate him either. To the extent that I imitate anyone, I think I may—in dialogue—imitate Saul Bellow. That rich kind of Constance Garnett mix of the formal and the vernacular: that's what Bellow does better than anyone else in the world, in dialogue. And that's something I try to do.

Q. This mix of what linguists call register, added to the aggressive metaphor we've already talked about—the yoking of incongruous images—gives your prose a free-for-all quality. Any kind of language seems to be available to every character. Any given sentence might combine language drawn from radically separated realms of experience.

A. Yes. And I suppose what you're also saying is that there are people in my work who may suddenly speak like Ph.D.'s or Ph.D.'s like slumlords, but this is simply a convention of fiction and drama. Did the people in Elizabeth's court speak blank verse? Did the children in the nineteenth century speak the way that children in Henry James speak? I allow every character my diction. And may it serve him better than it serves me.

Q. That diction includes a variety which would not be available to anyone but the writer?

A. Probably, though writers do not own the language. We may copyright only what we use.

Q. Morty Perlmutter, who appears in a couple of your works, an anthropologist and Nobel Laureate, defines morality as "the awareness of others." Is Stanley Elkin, like Perlmutter, a kind of fictional anthropologist, a man who takes all humanity for his subject, and on equal terms?

A. Well, it's a question which is self-serving in the answer. The answer being yes. On the other hand, maybe it's not so self-serving if stated in another way: which is, human beings amuse me. But they *do* amuse me, and I do *like* them. One of the things that gets my back up—I'm still thinking about your question concerning critics—is that when critics aren't calling me a satirist, and when they aren't calling me a black humorist—a term I reject—they're saying that my characters are losers. I don't regard them as losers. The fact that they may be unhappy doesn't mean that they're losers. The fact that they may be outrageous or immoral doesn't mean that they're losers. The fact that they're obsessed, that they have obsessions which would get real people arrested, doesn't mean that they're losers. It means that they are simply demonstrating the kind of extravagance—the kind of *heroic* extravagance, if you will—that makes them, in my view, winners—winners, inasmuch as they *impress* me. Alas, they put others off.

Q. By saying you're not a black humorist, I take it you mean that you do not set out deliberately to ward off tragedy through humor. Yet your works are very funny in places, all of them. Is that humor a by-product of your amusement—to use your word—over your extravagant types?

A. I never deliberately set out to be funny. As a matter of fact, I didn't even *know* I was funny until a friend of mine told me that I wrote funny stuff. This was years ago, before I wrote my first novel, and before I had very much published, and I became very self-conscious about being "funny," and began, I think, to cultivate those aspects of my work which were amenable to humor. But I don't distinguish between race, creed, and color regarding comedy. I mean I do not know what the hell "black humor" even *means.* That's why I resent the title. Humor is humor. A joke is a joke, whether it's performed on a vaudeville stage, or in church, or on a gallows. As a comic writer I think I'm something of an opportunist. That is, I write X, then discover two or three pages later that X is susceptible of being turned into a joke. Even if it is destructive of structure, even if it is distracting, I make the joke. I take the money and run, as it were. I make the joke because it amuses me to make the joke.

Q. You mentioned that even at the expense of structure you would make the joke. One criticism that might be raised against your novels is that they tend to be episodic; you seem to be less interested in structure, in the sense of plot or sequence of events, than you are in personality, or in rhetoric. Do you think this is true?

A. I think it is true. But I see nothing *necessarily* negative in that. I'm incapable of writing a detective story, which requires, it would seem to me, a knowledge of the end before one begins the first sentence. I'm incapable of long-distance plotting. I plot as I go along. This is true of my novels, not of my short stories. Something happens when I write a short story. That is, I have the entire story in view before I begin to write it. But it is not true when I am writing a novel. When I'm writing a novel I begin with a character, and with a character who has a particular occupation, an unusual occupation, and then I find out about the character, through the disparate episodes in which the character is involved. One discovers what one wants to say by saying it, as other people have pointed out.

Q. Is this another way of saying what you have said before, namely, that, because your prime interest is in the energy and impulse of the language, you have to follow the momentum of the language wherever it leads, regardless of structure?

A. Yes. The language blinds me to goals. It blinds me to ends, and that may very well be a flaw in my work. Certainly I admire what I cannot do. I also admire, as I've indicated before, what I *can* do. But I admire, let's say, a writer like Iris Murdoch, whose novels are superbly plotted. I admire a writer like William Trevor, whose novels are masterpieces of plot. An attention to writing ought not to exclude an attention to plot. In my case it does. Here's an example. In *The Condominium*, Marshall Preminger is sitting in his father's apartment and the doorbell rings. A woman comes in. I have it here: "Closing the door behind her, she stepped into the apartment and looked around. 'I'm sorry about your father,' she said nervously. Preminger nodded solemnly. Though he'd never seen her before her brief errand, there was something familiar about her." Now, only *after* I wrote that did it occur to me what was familiar about her, and I let myself go. This is what was familiar about her:

A large woman in perhaps her early forties, she wore her hair in a weighty golden beehive and seemed as imposing as the hostess in a restaurant, a woman men kidded warily. He could see her with big menus in her hand and wondered if she was a widow. She was the age of the men and women who'd been his parents' friends when he was in high school, in that long-gone postwar prime time when his father earned more than he ever had before or since, when his parents had begun to take vacations in the winter—Miami, cruises to the Caribbean, others that grazed South America's long coast, nibbling Caracas, Tobago, Cayenne. Seeing this woman, he recalled those trips, how proud he'd been of his parents, how proud of the Philco console television and Webcor wire recorder and furniture and fur and stock brochures that had poured into their home in those days, a high tide of goods and services, a full-time maid and a second car, his father's custom suits, his mother's diamonds lifted from their settings and turned into elaborate cocktail rings like the tropical headgear of chorus girls in reviews. It was at this time that there had begun to appear new friends, this woman's age, people met on cruises, in Florida, at "affairs" to which his parents had eagerly gone, bar mitzvahs and weddings—he'd seen the checks, for fifty or a hundred dollars, made out to the sons and daughters of their new friends, children they'd never met—and dinner dances where his father pledged two or three hundred whatever the cause. Proud of *all* the checks his father wrote, of all the charities to which they subscribed—to fight rare diseases, to support interfaith schools, the Haganah, the Red Cross, Schweitzer, Boys Town, the Fund for the Rosenbergs, the Olympic Games Committee, the Democratic Party and Community Chest—proud of his parents' whimsical generosity that bespoke no philosophy save the satisfaction of any need, the payment of any demand.

Well, that passage hasn't got a damn thing to do with the flow of the story. Indeed, it interrupts it. Here's a woman, standing in a guy's doorway, to whom he's sexually attracted. And suddenly he just waffles on about women that he has seen before in his parents' house. This leads to memories he's had of his father's first making it, and then to a description of the organizations to which his parents had belonged, the checks his father had written, *ad infinitim, ad hoc, ad cetera, ad astra.* Clearly it interrupts the dynamics of the plot. Yet it seemed to me at the time, and seems to me now on rereading it, to be more important than anything that happens in that scene.

Q.   There's another form of momentum in your language, where one metaphor seems to generate a whole series of metaphors.

A.   Yes. Well, this is the old business of cataloguing. I'm fascinated by catalogues. I love making them up. What Gass is to the sentence, I would like to be to the catalogue.

Q.   You've mentioned some of your experiences and practices as a teacher. I wonder if you feel your experiences in the university have affected—or enabled—your work in any way?

A.   Well, it has permitted my work in one way by cutting the work off at the pass. What I mean is, I am not one of those people with unlimited sources of energy. I cannot conceive of having to write all the time. I hold to the Hemingway notion of recharging the batteries. The ideal life, it seems to me, would be to write for nine or ten months, then teach for even more than that. Then write for another nine or ten months, teach for another year. I couldn't teach all the time. So the one thing reinforces the other.

Q.   While you are in the process of writing a work, you've mentioned elsewhere, serendipity plays an important role in providing you with new materials. Could you talk about that?

A. Why, yes. Certainly. Absolutely. Sure thing. Try and stop me. Catch me before I kill more clock. Anyway, after I finished *The Dick Gibson Show,* I began to write a short story. I was on the English Department softball team, and I thought that I'd write this story about how a man not only is what he eats, but what he hits. And I sort of nattered away at this story for about three months, putting in a lot of time, and building up a huge backlog of pages. But not getting anywhere. I mentioned before that a story has to come to me all at once or not at all—unlike a novel, where it comes piecemeal. I has having lunch with my editor in New York. He told me an anecdote about a friend of his who owns a gambling casino in London, and who had been mauled by a bear. (The friend has an estate where he maintains a private zoo.) He had gone out to inspect the animals one evening, and put one of the animals, a bear, in a cage because she was in oestrus and dangerous. The bear was due to be let out the following day. Well, he miscalculated, and got into the cage with the bear. The bear was still in oestrus, and even though he had raised her since cubhood, the bear was about to kill him. It was only with the help of his wife and other people on the estate, who managed to distract the bear by poking poles at it, that he was able to escape with his life. It occurred to me as I was listening to this story, "My God, what I'm being told is not in itself a story, but *if* the man had to fuck the bear in order to save his life, *that* would be a story!" Now it would never have occurred to me to write *The Making of Ashenden* had I not been told that anecdote.

The idea for *Boswell* came to me while I was talking with a friend of mine named Phil London, who was regaling me with stories of how Boswell got to meet Voltaire, and I got the idea for *A Bad Man* talking with my friend Al Lebowitz who was telling me a sad story about a lawyer pal of his who was about to be put away for a year, thrown into jail for malpractice or something. And I thought, gee, what would it be like for a middle-class man to spend a year in a penitentiary? So I guess I would never have written *A Bad Man* had I not been told this story. That's an accident. They've all been accidents. You can tell my critics—"Leave him alone, he didn't mean it, it was an accident." Anyway, yes. I believe in the muse. And Her name is Serendipity.

An Interview with Charles Tomlinson

*Conducted by Jed Rasula and Mike Erwin**

*Q.** In *The Poem as Initiation* you write, "there is no occasion too small for the poet's celebration—Williams' red wheelbarrow, or Wordsworth's 'naked table'—all ask, through the insistence of the poem's ritual celebration, to be recorded by us in their deeper significances." Is this an archetypal reality, something touching on the primary basis of existence (whatever your sense of that is); or in other words, does the particular contain the general or does the particular exist primarily in its own "isolate intensity"?

A. In *The Poem as Initiation*, with twenty minutes or so in which to say my piece at the Phi Beta Kappa ceremony, I didn't really have time to differentiate the kinds of celebration that are possible for the poet. Rather than call the celebration that of an archetypal reality *tout court*, I should want to come down to the individual poet, the individual poem. For Williams, "so much depends" on the red wheelbarrow— but already I'm deforming by paraphrasing what he wrote:

> so much depends
> upon
> a red wheel
> barrow. . . .

Cut out the doubled preposition of "upon" and substitute "on" and you cut back the verbal force in the doubling, ignore the split between

* This interview was conducted through correspondence during January 1974 and was edited for concision. Questions asked by Jed Rasula will be indicated as *Q.* and those by Mike Erwin as *Q.**

"wheel" and "barrow" straddling the line end and you are ignoring the fact that the dependence he's talking about is involved in slowing down the appearance of the separate words of the poem, letting them come into view only bit by bit. It's the form of language—the speed of meditation through written language *depends* on the wheel/barrow. The celebration here is not only a celebration of objects but of the forms of language we choose to articulate the sense of objects bodied over against us.

Now, Wordsworth's "naked table"—"snow-white deal,/Cherry or maple" as he goes on—is one of the domestic objects in Book One of *The Prelude* and it has its part in a life rich in essential things and unmindful of luxuries—"plain" and "seemly" are two other adjectives Wordsworth uses in this context. They play cards round this table in a cottage while winter is raging outside—rain and frost and splitting ice. So Wordsworth's contact with primal things and (I suppose) archetypal things. I suppose the very different sorts of celebration in Williams and Wordsworth do touch on "the primary basis of existence" as you call it; for both, the particular radiates outwards (and inwards), for both there is an ethical awareness approved and enacted by their verse, and the particular ballasts the ethics in common daily existence.

In my own case, I should add that the particular, rather than existing in its own isolate intensity, means first of all the demands of a relationship—you are forced to look, feel, find words for something not yourself—and it means, like all relationships, a certain forgetfulness of self, so that in contemplating something, you are drawn out of yourself towards that and towards other people—other people, because, though the words you use are *your* words, they are also *their* words: you are learning about the world by using the common inheritance of language. And once you are moving on into your poem, rather than "isolate intensity," you are aware of belonging among objects and among human beings and it is a great stay for the mind, this awareness. And a great chastener in that you realize that you in your *own* isolate intensity would be an egotist and a bore.

Q. *   There seems to be a noticeable lack of myth in your poetry. Why? What are your feelings about the use of myth in poetry in general, and in your own work (i.e., what can it convey, or does it tend instead to obstruct)?

A.   I think there's a lack of myth in my poetry because it usually arises directly from something seen. I want to register *that* in all its clarity or in all its implications. The nearest I come to myth is that word "Eden," which I can't seem to get rid of and that fits what I'm doing with its implication of primal things, fresh sensations, direct perceptions unmuddied. In a recent poem, "The Way In" (in the first number of *Poetry Nation*), I describe the demolition of parts of Bristol —humble and rather fine streets in their unpretentious way, neighborhoods never to be restored. I catch sight of an oldish couple dragging away scrap iron, old magazines, odds and ends in a battered perambulator and this I suppose is a use of myth, though I dislike the word "use." It's a use of myth in so far as I see them as Adam and Eve long-banished from Eden, but I wouldn't want to expand the thing to Wagnerian proportions.

Over twenty years ago I wrote in *The Necklace:*

> A dryad is a sort of chintz curtain
> Between myself and a tree.
> The tree stands: or doesn't stand:
> As I draw or remove the curtain.

This tends to be very much the case now—it is temperament, I imagine, plus the fact of also being a painter. In getting rid of the dryad I'm trying to realize something that has been left out of consciousness—we are great fixers of the contents of our consciousness and hence great fixers of our egos: we'll have it all on our own terms. . . . So I get rid of the dryad to see what is there. And this, I say, is in part temperamental; I could imagine a different sort of artist keeping *in* the dryad to realize something that has been left out of consciousness—which, I suppose, is why dryads first arose.

That dryad passage was a reference to the marvelous section in Buber's *I and Thou*, "I consider a tree," where he talks about various attitudes to trees seen as objects, then the moment when one becomes bound up in relation with the tree. I have that battered copy of *I and Thou* still on my shelves. Here's the passage:

Everything belonging to the tree is in this: its form and structure, its colors and chemical composition, its intercourse with the elements and with the stars, are all present in a single whole.

And he goes on: "The tree is no impression, no play of my imagination, no value depending on my mood." That's what got me: "no value depending on my mood"; if you've ever tried to draw anything accurately, respecting its structure, you suddenly see how much mere mood would have left out. So, yes, I first worked out of a suspicion with myth, trusting sensation; and sensation, as people have been telling us for a long time, isn't just the naked impact of objects but already a grasping for significance.

In a recent article Donald Wesling isolates that astonishing passage from Coleridge's *Biographia Literaria*, where Coleridge seems to be agreeing with Hobbes and Hartley "that all real knowledge supposes a prior sensation" and suddenly moves out of associationism into phenomenology with "sensation itself is but vision nascent, not the cause of intelligence, but intelligence itself revealed as an earlier power in the process of self-construction." So in our trusting in the language of the senses we are constructing our selves. So much, once more, for "isolate intensity"—how could it ever exist? How much we bring to our moments of perception—how much our moments of perception bring to us—awarenesses already extensible, always offering new facets. Perhaps myth would have been mere superfluity for me, beginning where I did, and moving from the moment of perception into a world that was visual, geographical, historical.

Q.   In "Swimming Chenango Lake" there is much attention paid to the sense of flux and permutation of form, usually thought of in terms of the passing of time. In two other poems in *The Way of a World* there are references to an arc; in "Tout Entouré de Mon Regard" the lines: "To see, is to feel at your back this domain of a circle whose power consists in evading and refusing to be completed by you." And in the poem "In the Fullness of Time" you speak of

> . . . That hesitant arc
> We must complete by our consent to time—
> Segment to circle, chance into event:
> And how should we not consent? . . .

Is there an increased concern for this problem of permutation of form through time (with increased attention to water, also) in *The Way of a World* and *Written on Water*? In other words, has the arc that resists completion become a central image in your work?

A.   I think there are two arcs in question here: first, the fact that, as I said, things are not given *absolutely*, so that there is much (necessarily) that escapes us, escapes the forms of language. And in this I rejoice. If you could close *that* circle, if language or consciousness could completely possess their objects, there would be no more room for literary endeavor and there would be no surprises, no discoveries. The second arc I speak of in that "Fullness of Time" poem is one we can convert into a circle by accepting things as given—in this poem by not attempting to escape from time or transcend it or search for the moment of intersection of the timeless with time, as Eliot does. The poem celebrates my friendship with Octavio Paz. Many chances led to our meeting; we had corresponded before but finally met *by chance* at Rome airport, then travelled together to Spoletto. Our friendship ripened through chance and time but we chose it also—and the arc became a circle and chance became "event," which in the poem rhymes with "consent." So my poetry is aware of time as a necessary medium for such things, and it's also aware of the flux of time though it pleads that there *are* human fidelities that survive mere flux and that they *need* the passage of time to become what they are.

The other arc that *resists* completion has been there implicitly since the early Stevens poems based on "Thirteen Ways of Looking at a Blackbird"—thirteen, the odd number, the series that could go on forever. My second arc—the conversion of chance into event also links up with the fact of my painting—oddly enough the first booklength publication of some of my pictures in '75 will be introduced by Octavio Paz. Since 1968 I've done a lot of pictures, many of them based on chance beginnings—using decalcomania, the surrealist technique— then building out of that, choosing, either by use of brush and extension of the given idea or by use of scissors and extension via collage. I've also used photo-collage—destroying or transforming images and dis- covering other images among them quite different from what the original photograph was supposed to be. . . .

I do quite agree, though, that the question of time is very much there in *The Way of a World* and *Written on Water*, but it was there in early perceptive poems like "Sea Change" in *The Necklace* and it was there in the poems about ruined buildings in *Seeing is Believing* in a more specifically historic way. And history is certainly an arc that resists completion, though men are always trying to fix it through revo- lution or mystical transcendence. I see the assassination of Trotsky in *The Way of a World* ["Assassin"] as an attempt to transcend time, almost as a caricature of mysticism, an attempt to have the future *now* on one's own terms and the result of trying to complete *that* circle is inhumanity—as when Che Guevara for whatever "good" reasons decided "We must transform ourselves into cold and efficient killing machines."

Q.*   Are you much moved by world events? What responsibility do you feel the poet has for writing a political or publicly minded kind of poetry? Do you feel the private and the public impulse can be reconciled in poetry?

A.   I am much moved by the event of revolution. And I am anti-revolutionary. In *The Way of a World* there is a poem called "Prometheus" about the Russian revolution and the shadow it has cast over our history. I was much moved by the recent events in Chile, and now that Allende put back the cause of reform there by God knows how many years by pressing on dogmatically in the face of realities, I imagined people might see there are certain pragmatisms that ought not to be ignored. However, Allende has now become a martyr.

People tried political poetry in the '30s, didn't they? The only poem that comes anywhere near bringing it off to my mind is Hugh MacDiarmid's second of his three hymns to Lenin, but even MacDiarmid ends up in this poem by saying that poetry includes politics and should be "the greatest power among men." He thinks what Lenin is up to is pretty fine but concludes in praise of poetry: "Ah, Lenin, politics is bairns' play./To what this maun be." I wouldn't exactly put it that way myself. I prefer Marvell's "Horatian Ode on Cromwell's Return from Ireland,"² which tries to sum up a whole phase of politics very close to the events. Then there's Dryden's *Absalom and Achitophel* written much more decidedly than Marvell's poem, from a given political point of view. I think these are indisputably fine poems but neither of them settles for easy partisanship.

What political poetry tends to more now is urging liberal sentiments (on Vietnam, for example, not so long ago) that everyone already agrees with anyway and, of course, as in Bly's political poems, heaping on top of that very ugly and inflated rhetoric that mistakes itself for poetry when all it is doing is enjoying a bath in its own righteous indignation. I see no reason why you shouldn't write a political kind of poetry but I don't see it in terms of merely urging opinions, or merely supporting the New Left, or trying with horrible self-conscious enthusiasm to ride along with youth as in that disastrous volume of Denise Levertov's *To Stay Alive*. Initially a lot of Vallejo's poetry is political, but it gets far beyond merely urging solutions—you have only to compare it with the naive point of view in his prose reportage of Russia in the 1930s where he seems to have swallowed every cliché.

I very much understand the feelings of my friend George Oppen, who did live through the 1930s, was very much of the left, but reticent to write "political poetry." He saw that men needed feeding and as there was no easy way of doing that for them by writing poems he worked in poor relief. If that is the way one sees the priorities, that is what one does. Alternately, I am maybe the writer for whom it would be possible to see men were being fed *and* to go on writing poems. Ultimately, I think the private and the public impulse are reconciled in one's care for language—one's duty towards that is a duty to a thing at once public and private; one will so deal with language that insofar as it is in one's power, one will not issue a debased currency.

Q.*   In "Comedy" in *Written on Water* you write:

> . . . If you sat still
> The horizontals plainly said
> You ought to be walking, and when you did
> All you were leaving behind you proved
> That you were missing the point. And the innumerable views
> Kept troubling him, until
> He granted them. Amen.

Are you implying that you believe in the overwhelming complexity and relativity of things (which the complexity of your own poetry would seem to belie) and that a unilateral political position is inadequate?

A.   What I was saying in that poem in *Written on Water* was chiefly a philosophic comedy, not a question of politics. If expressing a unilateral political position means expressing a view on a given issue, I imagine a pamphlet, not a poem, would be the most effective weapon. After all, "expressing a position" means you more or less know in advance what you're going to say, whereas writing poetry is a less predictable undertaking. The views in that poem are views of landscape, not political views.

Q.   In an interview with Peter Orr in 1961 you spoke of Ruskin, Wallace Stevens, and Marianne Moore as being of use in giving you an "openness to the creative universe in looking at the surfaces that it offers one." How exhaustively do you think the surfaces can be pursued? For instance, in one poem from *The Necklace* you write "Six points of vantage provide us with six sunsets," and in another poem: "To define the sea—/We change our opinions/With the changing light." In *The Poem as Initiation* you have said "There is no occasion too small for the poet's celebration," and in "A Process" in *The Way of a World* you mention

that speech of islanders, in which, we are told, the sentence is never certainly brought to an end, its aim less to record with completeness the impression an event makes, than to mark its successive aspects as they catch the eye, the ear of the speaker.

Is your own work an attempt at such a language? How much can a certain area of material be covered before a change of consciousness is necessary, or a different sensibility in ways of perceiving?

Also, you seem to have been aware, perhaps, of the complications of these beliefs behind your poetry in the lines: ". . . And the innumerable views/Kept troubling him, until/He granted them" ("Comedy" in *Written on Water*). Has this been in fact a problem for you?

A.   We seem destined to keep returning to this little poem "Comedy." It merely expresses in comic vein what I said perhaps more urgently in "Antecedents" in *Seeing is Believing*: "Let be its being"—an attempt to calm the desire to be always anxiously seeking. After all, one doesn't always want to be wondering how many ways there are of looking at a blackbird. There ought to be times when one way is enough or the existence of *that* blackbird is enough. Consciousness that becomes merely a disease of prying, a bullying assertion of its own dear self, can be not merely obtrusive but comic—I think of some of Proust's more excessive moments.

That "speech of islanders" in "A Process" refers, I think, to the characteristics of the language of (I may be misremembering this) the Trobriand Islanders. I had been thinking of the way the structures of Hopi and Navajo speech give one a so very different sense of space and time than our own language. Then a friend came up with this example from these islanders. The sentence "never certainly brought to an end" does remind one of the open-ended structure of much modern poetry which, in its turn, is very much aware of the way language stylizes our perception.

Q.*   How much does poetry, because of medium or practice or historical role, tend to shelter rather than stimulate? Or is the balance tending toward stimulation? Are these functions incompatible?

A.   When I look at all the pain that poetry has been able to admit and cope with in its long history, I don't see it as sheltering in any sense. Of course, some poems are more comfortable than others, as some moments are more comfortable than others. In painting there is Goya. But there is also Matisse. I think Matisse is stimulating as well as full of "luxe, calme et volupté" because his formal means are never just indulgent. You see something new in these oases of luxurious possibility he creates. Some poems of Eluard have a similar effect. There's room for patience and accepting the good that is given and art should not slight these.

*Q.** You suggest that aggressiveness or defensiveness toward the world is up to the reader in "Poem" from *Seeing is Believing* in the line "I leave you /To your own meaning, yourself alone." How does this relate to the problem of presentation/stimulation?

A. "Poem" is about a fallen tree striking an impossibly romantic pose. I'm talking to the tree and the people who also fall into attitudes. The last line you quote has a misprint in the first edition and should read not "I leave you/To your own meaning, yourself alone," but "I leave you to your *one* meaning. . . ." It is a reflection on the way posturing means bad faith, means loss of integrity in relationship and *that* applies to daily life or to writing a poem. For me, what you call the problem of presentation/stimulation can only be solved in poetry by the chastity of the formal means.

*Q.** In the poem "Beauty and the Beast" you write "Beauty is neither/Truth nor truth's reflection." Do you think art is more concerned with truth or with beauty?

A. You may not have noticed, but I removed "Beauty and the Beast" from the second (British) edition of *Seeing is Believing* because I had come to feel that there was a lingering Nietzscheanism in that formulation, "Beauty is neither/Truth nor truth's reflection." I find it hard, also, to go on using that word "beauty" because it always seems to be heading you towards a stereotype—*Vogue*, the ghastly child on the back of the Pears Soup package, "preparing to be a *beautiful* lady": you know if she keeps that up she'll be finished by eighteen or whenever. I think art is concerned with truth and that truth begets beauties ("a terrible beauty," if you like, to use Yeats's formula) which were unforeseen. The very wrenched, compact poems of Ungaretti have a beauty that no one would have thought beautiful in, say, 1890. But we have killed that word: how can it adequately define the satisfaction one gets in Ungaretti's war poems from the exact fit of language and the event?

Q.* How much inspiration do you draw from your painting when you write poetry?

A. Poetry and painting are interdependent for me because I am the same person conducting both. They are different because painting is a silent world whereas poetry only uses silence to measure sound. At times—perhaps the teacher's occupational disease—the sheer vanity of so much talk, talk, talk, discussion, verbal evaluation, weighs one down. Take up a brush and then you are almost sure to do a good picture. But certainly my poems and pictures do come back to the same area of imagery: water, stones, light, space.

Q.* Many of your poems seem to be in the form of an address. Do you have a reader in mind?

A. To quote George Oppen once more. Some years ago he wrote me a letter on this topic of one's imaginary reader. I suggested that he could break up the prose into a verse lineation and this was the result:

> One imagines himself
> addressing his peers
> I suppose. Surely
> that might be the definition
> of "seriousness"? I would like,
> as you see,
> to convince
> myself
> that my pleasure in your response
> is not
> plain vanity
> but the pleasure of being heard,
> the pleasure
> of companionship, which seems
> more honorable.

Yes, I do always feel I'm speaking to someone. Though it may, of course, take some time to reach him. There is quite a lot of humor in my poems, though the reviewers never seem to notice it, but I go on hoping it will be heard.

Q.* How much does *what* you choose to write about determine length, form, and manner of poem—i.e., what limitations does the material itself pose? Do you think there is material that is definitely limited or limitless?

A. As to length, I can rarely predict it. As to form, I often use a four stress line—basically four stress but capable of variants up to six and down to three—because it gives me something of the breadth of the iambic pentameter line, yet leaves me free to use as many unstressed syllables as I want. I like this medium. It has roominess and can carry a lot of internal rhymes. I never really know what limitations the material itself imposes until I'm a good way on with it. As to manner—"a man speaking to men," starting as foursquare as possible, no special pleading, a clarity of utterance and sometimes an urgency, no bludgeon, a respect for the adulthood of the reader, no "howling," no theatricality, but these aren't determined by what I *choose* to write as you put it. These are the ethical base. I choose surprisingly little. It usually hits me. Or you see something and decide to explore the situation—hawks mating, a madwoman dancing on a London underground platform—but is that in any exact sense a "choice"? There's an early poem, "Chateau de Muzot" [*Seeing is Believing*] which goes:

> Than a choice of subject
> Rather to be chosen by what has to be said
> And to say it . . . .

Yet I always want to unfold the subject, lift it up into consciousness as far as I can, see its facets, set it into a perspective of place and time.

Q. In the poem "Reflections" in *Seeing is Believing* you say that nature and habit are blind and that they lie—that we can get close to the truth of things because what we reflect we *choose*. Do you think, then, that the best and truest representation of experience in poetry is achieved by an arrangement of perception, a control exercised by the poet in trying to strike a balance between the surfaces of what his eye sees and the depths that the whole man perceives?

A. Your quoting from "Reflections" seems to half refute what is said in "Chateau de Muzot." Actually, "Reflections" was an early poem and I kept feeling the need to argue with its rather brusque formalism. We can, of course, choose one point of vantage, choose to write or not to write, but whether choice versus habit is the best way of putting the matter I had come to doubt by the time I wrote "Chateau de Muzot." Some balance, as you say, has to be struck and an achieved poem in which the stresses, say, have been counted and the rhymes rhymed is scarcely just a direct slice of description. And yet many of my poems have arisen by writing done very swiftly, before the object, before the actual scene, what was perceived, just as a painter might do a preliminary sketch from nature.

Often the thing seen embeds itself more and more in an historical context or a context of thinking about what we see or a context of memory. The thing seen (or heard) has to beget its song, but that act of seeing and the act of getting it over into words in the preliminary sketch are also acts of thought—already in taking purchase on nature, on attending to what Wordsworth and Coleridge call the language of sense, the whole man is involved.

So I don't see it as a question of striking a balance between the surfaces the eye sees and the depths that the whole man perceives. Surfaces are already leading one into depths: surfaces already are involved in space, light, texture, color, resistance. The surface, say, of an Edward Weston photograph are *all* he has to say—and they are deep enough for his purposes—evaluative purposes, purposes of thought and feeling. I dislike making a dualism of that pair. "Sensation is but vision nascent," to get back to that Coleridge already instanced. And, for me, the moment of sensation, the taking hold on the physical moment, the melting of person and presence, are what comes first in my poetry.

I'd always wanted to find some way of explaining how we build our structures on the sensed and the given. Then one day, in a friend's flat in New York, I turned up Merleau-Ponty's *The Primacy of Perception* and the little essay in that seemed to say all I'd wanted to say. It says it for poetry and much more, and it makes one see how poetry is of a piece with other human activities. I return, time and again, to the central point of that essay where Merleau-Ponty says,

By these words, the "primacy of perception," we mean that the experience of perception is our presence at the moment when things, truths, values are constituted for us; that perception is a nascent logos; that it teaches us, outside all dogmatism, the true condition of objectivity itself; that it summons us to the tasks of knowledge and action. It is not a question of reducing human knowledge [and here I put in "poetry"] to sensation, but of assisting at the birth of this knowledge, to make it as sensible as the sensible, to recover the consciousness of rationality.

That, for me, with the whole essay behind it, is one of our great defenses of poetry.

An Interview with Michel Butor

Conducted and translated by Marianne Hirsch

"For me writing is a spinal column,"[1] said Michel Butor in 1959 at the height of his success as a new novelist. (*L'Emploi du temps* was published in 1956, *La Modification* in 1957, and *Degrés* in 1960.) This statement still applies today after Butor has abandoned the novel to write essays, *études*, dialogues, illustrations, a capriccio, a radio play, a stereophonic study, an anecdote for the cinema, and an opera. Throughout these various formal metamorphoses, however, his writings remain personal quests for knowledge and discovery, literally guidebooks for survival in a multifarious and fragmented modern reality.

Unlike the writers of *Minuit* and *Tel Quel* who continue to classify their texts as "novels," adding "new," "new new," or even "new new new" in order to call attention to the contradiction between their deconstructive activity and the traditional novel, Butor uses generic classifications that are as descriptive as they are accurate. Seeking structures which correspond to current geographic, social, and political phenomena, he is convinced that new forms will enable us to see, perhaps to create, new worlds.

Butor's formal experiments with open and mobile forms of narrative, mixed media, alphabetical order, discontinuous layout, and multiple typography resemble those of his contemporaries. For example, a recent Butor text looks much like a Roche and even demands similar kinds of reader participation. Yet while the writers of the new and the new new novel are generally known for their creation of hermetic and self-reflexive verbal worlds which explore, through formal play, the possibilities of literary discourse, Butor's work distinguishes itself by its representational impulse, by the im-

---

[1] "Intervention à Royaumont," *Répertoire* (Paris: Minuit, 1960), p. 272 (my translation).

portance of the referent, and by the consciousness of speaking to and about an extratextual reality. In Butor's view of literature as an instrument of knowledge about the world, formal (re)search and innovation are necessarily motivated by the needs of representation.

The impulse toward representation and inclusiveness has led to continual expansion in the work of Butor and accounts for the encyclopedic techniques he has developed, as well as for his interest in multiple authorship and in the interrelation of places discovered through travel. Well known as a critic and teacher of literature, Butor reads and uses the work of other writers as a ground on which to continue building. It is the conjunction of text and world that interests him, the manner in which others have chosen to represent reality, and the possibility of adding to or of correcting their vision. From more common forms of intertextuality such as allusion, quotation, and the description of art works, Butor has moved to actual collaboration, thus profiting from the expanded and perhaps more accurate vision of several individuals.

In his effort to include in each text as full and varied a vision as he can, Butor makes of his texts worlds to be explored like cities and cathedrals.[2] Each text exists in space as well as in time; the book is an object, the page a tableau. Strict rules ranging from the realms of biology to those of mathematics govern the organization of each text. As if eager to free the work from the control of its creator, Butor experiments with effects of chance. Each text is a place to discover, a labyrinth in which to find one's way, a storehouse of information. The act of reading thus duplicates the act of discovery, the quest that each work enacts. Butor's realism is based on analogy: to learn to read his books, that is, to participate in their creation, is to succeed in orienting oneself in a complex and heterogeneous environment not unlike the world in which we live. Butor's texts thus become true guidebooks.

Butor's fascination with places is due to his sense that they need to be discovered and written about. "The world, both in its totality and in its details, is a cipher,"[3] he once said, and for him literary creation is an act of deciphering and illumination. To discover the world in its totality is to trace relationships between individual units,

---

[2]See "Recherches sur la technique du roman," *Répertoire II* (Paris: Minuit, 1964), p. 98.

[3]"Le point suprême et l'âge d'or à travers quelques oeuvres de Jules Verne," *Répertoire*, p. 134 (my translation).

an essentially structuralist project. Throughout his works, Butor experiments with relationships between individuals, between individuals and groups, among groups, as well as with relationships between texts and between texts and worlds. Hence his continued and special interest in America, the seat of cultural multiplicity.

Butor's work is now in what might be identified as a third stage. His early works, the novels *Passage de Milan* (1954), *L'Emploi du temps, La Modification*, and *Degrés*, are centered on individuals and their defeat by an overwhelming environment. Then, with *Mobile* (1962), *Réseau aérien* (1962), *Description de San Marco* (1963), and *6 810 000 litres d'eau par seconde* (1965), the focus shifts to the interaction of groups made up of nameless, repetitious, stereotyped individuals who, together, are better able to master the environment. A celebration of the multiplicity that equates humans, artifacts, natural objects, and places has replaced the anthropocentric values so desperately upheld by the characters encountered in the novels. In the most recent works of Butor's third stage, *Où* (1971), *Illustrations IV* (1976), *Matière de rêves* (1975), *Second sous-sol* (1976), and *Troisième dessous* (1977), the individual has mysteriously returned, but not until after the firmness of selfhood has been shattered, dispersed, and absorbed by the setting. There is in Butor's work an expansive movement out to the world. His settings range from Paris to the Mediterranean, from America to the entire Northern Hemisphere. Although the individual self is no more than a crossroads where various geographic, political, and social forces meet, the depths of the self continue to be explored through dream, fantasy, and imagination.

Butor's texts themselves follow the movement from individual to group in their format. The individual novels and "spatial poems" have increasingly given way to serial works, such as *Répertoire* I-IV, Butor's series of essays, and *Illustrations* I-IV, which are collections of short texts originally published as verbal illustrations of visual art works. In addition, the early *Le Génie du lieu* has been transformed into a series by the publication of *Où, Le Génie du lieu II*, to be followed by a third volume. Most recently, *Matière de rêves* has initiated a new series which will be composed of five volumes.

As some of Butor's shorter texts are republished or anthologized in different collections, they are renewed by their interaction with other texts. Similarly, the works of other authors are metamorphosed when they appear in Butor's texts. As his ordering of the issue of *L'Arc* devoted to his work demonstrates,[4] he is particularly fasci-

---

[4] *L'Arc*, No. 39 (1969).

nated by the organization of each of his books. To place Butor in this collection of essays devoted to the new new novel should create a renewal full of just such surprises and insights.

The following interview was conducted in French in May 1976 at Butor's villa, "Aux Antipodes," in Nice. Michel Butor speaks slowly and deliberately. His comments, interspersed with "eh bien," "alors," "si vous voulez," are often punctuated by a final "voilà." Butor has a loud and contagious laugh. Friendly, helpful, and relaxed, he visibly enjoys talking about himself and his work.

Q. Your work is thought of as unusually innovative and you once said that formal research and invention are the *sine qua non* of a greater realism.[5] Do you feel that your continued interest in innovation constitutes a criticism of traditional forms?

A. Yes, in the sense that such innovation shows that it is possible to do something other than what was done before. At a given moment there are forms which are imperialistic, which pretend to be the only ones possible; novels are written like this, say, or drama like that. There is no use looking for anything else because we have found it. When we do something different, it shows that something different is possible and, consequently, these forms which presented themselves as the only ones are no longer the only possible ones. This difference allows us to see why, at a particular moment, these forms were chosen instead of those. If there is only one way of writing, there is no problem. We often have the idea (it was the idea of our ancestors) that, of course, there are many ways of writing but there is only one that is right, that formerly there were nothing but primitives, savages. And then, little by little, the true way of painting, the real manner of writing were found and that was it—except, of course, that there was always the possibility of falling back into barbarism. Thus, from the moment one shows that there are other possibilities, one forces questions to be asked. One begins to ask oneself why the people of the seventeenth and eighteenth centuries, for example, were obliged to write their tragedies in alexandrines. They didn't ask this question. For them it was obvious: this was what they had to do. For us today it is an oddity; it seems a bit crazy.

Q. Is it your goal to find forms to correspond to our world today?

---

[5]See "Le roman comme recherche," *Répertoire I,* p. 9.

A.   Of course, among other things, that's it, because the old forms force us to see things a certain way and prevent us from understanding a very great number of things. So, it is not a matter of substituting a new classicism for a preceding one. No, it is a matter of arriving at a much more mobile and open conception of literature.

Q.   And yet, in your work you utilize many other authors; your work is truly intertextual. Would you stress the continuity between your work and what comes before it, or is there a break here? How does innovation fit in this context?

A.   I am, above all, sensitive to the continuity, but it is a continuity in which certain adventures take place. I see literature as a fabric, but it is a fabric that twists and turns and makes knots. I may be at the place of a knot.

Q.   If we speak of what has come to be called intertextuality, it seems that you are trying to arrive at a new conception of authorship, one that involves a composite of several authors. Are you trying to eliminate the single author?

A.   I cannot totally eliminate the notion of authorship; that is impossible, that is a wrong way of expressing oneself, to speak of eliminating the author. But the notion of author changes considerably from the moment ones becomes conscious of the fact that a text is never the result of a single author, that there is always a collective author. This collective author is, first, language—society and language—and all a writer can do is to work within a language even if he transforms it considerably. This is absolutely basic. Thus, a writer expresses not only personal thoughts or feelings, but also what is in the language; he shows the possibilities of the language and makes it evolve. And then, let us say that there is an individual who writes, who prepares a manuscript for a publisher: that is the author. But he always works on a collective ground which is the ground of language. Between that ground and this last manipulator who prepares the manuscript for a publisher, there can be all sorts of intermediaries. There can be collaborations, naturally, where other writers or other artists intervene; and then this relation of the language and the author can focus itself through the intermediary of a certain number of authors who are individualized. This is what happens when there are quotations in all the different shapes they can take—either the literal quotation, or, of course, parody, transformation, allusion.

Q.   And yet it seems to me that this notion of the collectivity of authorship fascinates and preoccupies you even more than other contemporary writers and I would like to know why.

A.   I am particularly conscious of this phenomenon because I am myself a teacher of literature.

Q.   And what about the notion of literary genre? On the one hand, you clearly go beyond all the genres we still consider canonical, and on the other hand, you consistently define your works in generic terms. Do you see some of the generic notions you use, the "illustration" for instance, as a new genre or as a personal form, unique to you?

A.   There are two levels here. I believe very strongly in the notion of genre because, at a given moment, literature particularizes itself into a certain number of functions; each genre corresponds to such a function, to a social ceremony. That is the reason for rules in the first place. But the genres generally taught in literary studies correspond, on the whole, to the literature of the mid-nineteenth century. They embody a conception of genre that was based mostly on French literature of the mid-nineteenth century and that is adapted, as well as possible, to the literature of other countries and of other periods. So, this classification is well suited only to a certain period. It has immense shortcomings as far as our period is concerned, because it actually prevents us from seeing a great many aspects of contemporary literature.

The genres that are used today are not those taught at the university. The radiophonic text,[6] for example, is something entirely new which is linked to a new technology that gave rise to an extremely important social ceremony—listening to the radio. I will not even mention television. From the point of view of general ethnography, Westerners are people who, every day, at given periods of time, are seated in front of it, and nothing, or almost nothing, will disturb this kind of prayer. So, the texts that are made for these technologies are of a very different nature than those made for the theater, for example, and yet they are still defined and studied according to an old generic classification. Thus, it is extremely important today to delineate the genres that are currently active and to abstract their rules. We must study the genres used today in opposition to the older

---

[6]See Butor's radio play *Réseau aérien* (Paris: Gallimard, 1962).

classification to see the weight of ancient structures and the blinding they can cause.

And then there is something else as well, a second level. It is not enough to determine which genres function today. It becomes a matter of seeing if it would not be possible to invent something else— that is, invent forms which would end up generating social ceremonies other than those which function today. These would lead, eventually, to a much more profound social transformation than, say, elections within a given political system. The "illustrations" are things I propose; others can adopt them or transform them.

Q.   What interests me very much in your work is the abandonment of narrative. . .

A.   The abandonment of narrative, what do you mean by that?

Q.   You wrote novels, but since *Degrés* you have not written anything that might be called a novel.

A.   Yes, but that does not prevent me from writing narrative—a kind of narrative that is, however, organized differently.

Q.   Is your departure from the novel form an implied criticism, a break?

A.   Oh no, the great novelists of the eighteenth, nineteenth, and twentieth centuries fascinate me. I read them, study them, and teach courses about them. They brought about considerable transformations in their time. We must continue in the same vein, transforming that which precedes us. I don't believe in innovation for its own sake. I don't just try to do something because it looks new. It is by doing things other than my predecessors did that I do the same thing they did. It is precisely by trying to do what they were doing that I am forced to do otherwise, because of the difficulties I encounter, you see.

For example, I plan to spend two months in Australia this summer. I have already gone to Australia twice, and it is a country that fascinates me. I can explain why, a little, but not well. In talking about Australia, I must succeed in showing why this country fascinates me, but for the moment I still don't know how. When I first went to the United States, I did not at all think that I would write a book like *Mobile*. I thought that I would speak of America as I had spoken of the Mediterranean cities in *Le Génie du lieu*. In fact, when

I was first in the United States at Bryn Mawr College, they asked me to write a piece for the Bryn Mawr *Alumnae Bulletin*. I wrote something I have never anthologized since. It is called "Première vue de Philadelphie,"[7] and is very much in the style of the first *Génie du lieu*. The longer I stayed, the more I realized that it just did not hold, that I had to find something different. This realization produced *Mobile* and subsequent books. Well, for Australia I still have to find the means of saying what I have not been able to say, because the literature about Australia is quite limited. There is one interesting Australian writer, Patrick White, who writes very beautiful Australian books; and then there is D. H. Lawrence's *Kangaroo* and a very nice travelogue by Mark Twain, but that's all, and these works don't express anything; they repeat.

Q.   And yet in your book about Niagara you don't attempt any new description of the falls; you simply use that of Chateaubriand.

A.   Yes, I use Chateaubriand's description precisely because it is something very, very classical, but the transformations that I impose on this text result in a description that is totally new. That description is what I want because, in my text, the water flows; in Chateaubriand's it doesn't.

Q.   You make it flow *in* Chateaubriand's text. That is the remarkable thing about *6 810 000 litres d'eau par seconde*.

A.   Yes, and in the existing descriptions of Australia the desert is not red. . . . So I want to write a third *Génie du lieu*. I have been thinking about it for years; it is vital to me that there be texts about the Southern Hemisphere. There will be a text about Australia and one about Brazil.

Q.   And Africa?

A.   I have never been in black Africa, although I know Northern Africa quite well. And yet I would like to include in this volume a text that will not be a travel text, and which will be called "Jungle." It will be a kind of forest with descriptions of animals moving around in it. And that will replace Africa.

Q.   Will it be like Conrad's jungles?

---

[7]Reprinted in *Les Lettres Nouvelles* (Dec. 1960), pp. 153–55.

A.   No, it will be rather like the jungles of the painters, like le Douanier Rousseau's jungles.

Q.   An imaginary jungle then?

A.   Yes.

Q.   You write about places. Have you ever written about places you have not visited or about imaginary places?

A.   No—they are in the dreams, of course, but otherwise, no. I have always written about the places I have visited.

Q.   The United States seems to be a special place for you. Why?

A.   For two reasons. First, because it is the most powerful country in the world by far and for many years to come. It is a country that has today an incredible power of cultural diffusion. It is a country which is in a privileged position; that is a fact, but Europe has had difficulty accepting it. In France, the picture of the French street has been completely transformed by an imitation of America, completely. Secondly, it is the country where I have lived longest outside of France. If I add up all my visits, I have lived there nearly four years. There is no other country through which I have traveled as extensively.

Q.   I think America is a country that is difficult to know for a European. Has your vision of America changed very much since you wrote *Mobile?*

A.   Not very much. What has changed is America itself. It has developed in the photographic sense, like a negative that develops. There are many things that were not very apparent fifteen years ago, and which have become more and more visible. *Mobile* surprised many people when it was published; now it no longer does. There are many things in the book that Americans have become aware of in these last few years, which means that the evolution of the United States has actually confirmed the book. Nevertheless, there would be many new things to say, of course.

Q.   The value you place on knowledge in your works has always intrigued me. In *Mobile* and the other books written in the early 1960s (*Réseau aérien, Description de San Marco, 6 810 000 litres d'eau par seconde*), the knowledge of our surroundings becomes the basis for a collective vision, and what you just said about *Mobile* demonstrates the important role that literature plays in this communal awareness. And yet recently you speak more about the writer's solitude. In *Illustrations IV*, you use the expression "more solitary than a writer."

A.   The two are not mutually exclusive. We said before that the writer is not the only author of his work. He is a kind of point of coagulation, a knot in the social and linguistic fabric. But it is the fact that he is a single point, as they say in mathematics, that makes a difference, and that difference is painful. Even while writing for others, the writer feels isolated. He speaks for others; not only does he address himself to others, but he also succeeds in saying what others would like to say. But this function makes him solitary. It is because one suffers more than others that one begins to write, in order to find a means of expressing that suffering. It is because one is at the center that one is alone. And it is because one is at the center that one is marginal. You see, there are many metaphors one can reverse, but it is this very solitude that allows society to change through the writer.

Q.   In your novels you repeatedly dramatize the sacrifice of the individual seeker. In the books after *Mobile*, however, that sacrifice is avoided as knowledge becomes collective and more open.

A.   Yes, yes. One of the purposes of these forms is to make things less tragic, to find happiness in all this; and thus, let us say, the writer is no longer the only victim.

Q.   Knowledge for you is always knowledge of the outside world, and it is always knowledge that serves others. Never does it become exclusively self-knowledge; never is the outside world absorbed to enrich the self. Is that what distinguishes you from other international writers like Henry James, for example?

A.   Yes, these are two sides of the same coin. If you imagine the self as a sort of container, then it is obvious that you cannot put everything in it. That would be gluttony.

Q.   Do you see the notion of the self changing as a result of the kind of knowledge gained in your books?

A.   It is not only the self that changes, but it is also the conception we have of the self, the conception of what it means to say "I," that is changing. Perhaps psychoanalytic notions could help us here, if we use them with caution.

A new conception of the self is not separate from a new conception of society. There is a point which is very important to me—the decentralization of today's world. Formerly, the Western civilizations imagined that the world was organized around a center, and since Rome, that center has always been a city. In France this idea is particularly strong; we cannot get rid of the opposition between Paris and the provinces. The French just cannot understand that Paris is no longer the center of the world. Paris has, of course, been the center of France for a very long time, since the seventeenth century, and it has been maintained so with a violence that has never existed anywhere else. And this Paris, center of France, dreamt itself center of the world; and it almost came to be that, first with Napoleon, then in the first half of the twentieth century with Paris, center of the arts, Paris, capital of painting, etc. Well, that is finished. It does not work any longer. One of the things that interests me so much about the United States is its nomadic side. People move much more easily. Not only are communications easier, but there is a kind of life in the car; people bring their houses with them. That fascinates me. There are dreams of imperial cities in the United States as well. New York, the Empire City, and then Washington, the dream of a Roman city. How prodigious! They even needed a Frenchman for that. In addition to a capitol, they needed an obelisk which was the most Egyptian of obelisks since ancient Egypt. It is not only the obelisk of the city Washington, but also of the man Washington, of a deified man. It is extraordinary, fascinating. There are fascinating phenomena of centralization to study in the United States, but there is also all the rest, all this great movement, this great nomadic life—very instructive for the French to study.

Q.   And you yourself have chosen not to live in the center.

A.   I live in Nice because I want to be at the periphery. I need it. I need to be at the frontier, to be perpetually elsewhere. Centralization in France is just terrible.

Q.   There has been a lot of criticism of American mobility in recent years. People have no roots.

A.   Well, people have roots, but with a difference. There is a system of roots which is much more supple. We can imagine an outline for a spatial organization that is much more interesting than the radiating organization I have just described, and it is the only one which allows us to imagine peace on earth. As long as there are centers to attack, there can be no peace. And that is where we still are: we say Washington and Moscow, for example, and yet we can well conceive that in the United States, in Russia, and in China new organizations will be developed wherein there would be a balance of points in a much more supple network. Communications would be much facilitated by the fact that one wouldn't always have to go through a central point.

Q.   You spoke of this in connection with the self, and that is very important, isn't it?

A.   Yes, it is all related, of course; it is our relation with the other. We still have an imperialist conception of the self, whereas we could well see ourselves as elements in a pattern in which others are just as important as we are.

Q.   Don't we lose something in doing that? Isn't it painful to give up that individuality, that interior depth?

A.   We lose only illusions. There are still things we don't say to others, that we don't tell ourselves, and that creates depth. But depth is not only interior, it is exterior as well. The others also have depth.

Q.   I would like to come back to the importance of formal research in relation to that of representation in your work. Jean Roudaut, for instance, has said that your books must be read as a series of transformations imposed on an initial formal plan.[8] Many other critics as well emphasize the formal plan in your work (e.g., André Helbo's recent book *Michel Butor: Vers une littérature du signe*).[9] I feel, on the contrary, that unlike many other new or new new novelists, you are very much concerned with representation, and that formal research works in the service of representing reality.

A.   The two are inseparable. You can emphasize one or the other, but you fail to understand anything if you forget one or the

---

[8]Jean Roudaut, "Parenthèse sur la place occupée par l'étude intitulée *6 810 000 litres d'eau par seconde* parmi les autres ouvrages de Michel Butor," *Nouvelle Revue Française,* 28, No. 165 (Dec. 1966), 500.
[9]Brussels: Editions Complexe, 1975.

other. Formal research for its own sake is no longer interesting. If you emphasize the formal side of the new novel exclusively, you get things that are interesting and absurd at the same time, like those of Ricardou, for instance. The way in which he speaks of things is at once very ingenious and entirely wrong.

Q.   There is an emptiness there . . .

A.   It is not entirely empty because even though it is superficial, the surface itself is rich—it is deep, one could say. One can go on finding things at the surface indefinitely, only touching a small part of the subject. And, similarly, if you wanted to study only the content without paying attention to the manner in which it is presented, you would find only platitudes.

Q.   Would you agree that the difference between you and the other new and new new novelists is precisely this impulse to represent an external reality?

A.   Of course, I am very different from the others. There are points of coincidence, of convergence, but it seems to me that I am very much alone, to come back to something we spoke about a little while ago.

Q.   In a recent interview you said: "My entire work is representation, even if the density of transformations, the generalization of processes prevents us in certain cases from seeing what could thus be represented."[10] What are these transformations?

A.   You can cut something into many small pieces, paste them together differently, put on another coat of paint, and the result is very different from the original. That is immaterial, since, as I have said in several other places, it is representation not only of that which exists, but also of that which does not exist. And the two are equally important. Dreams, desires, etc., are part of reality because reality is a trap door: it is not full, it does not even exist in the usual sense of the word. It is something which exists and does not exist at the same time, and the holes are as important as the solid parts. I look for the holes, for that which hides and that which we desire without knowing it. Thus all my books are dreams, but they are not dreams of me, they

[10]Helbo, p. 11 (my translation).

are dreams of reality. Others dream my dreams. I am only their scribe, their typewriter.

Q.   Would you say that your works are very personal?

A.   They are personal in the sense that they are different from those that were written previously, but that is not an individual quality that ends with me. I am not interested in myself. I am interested in myself only as an instrument, just as to do certain things I have to know how to use my typewriter. In the same way I have to know how to use myself, my family, my four daughters—none of this is unimportant. So I write with my daughters. I write with my head, with my hands, with my typewriter, but also with my daughters. I write with this dog.[11] All this is related. This means that there can be more and more autobiographical notions when I write, because that locates me as a writer. Not everyone has four daughters. For readers it can be interesting to see that the person who produces the book has four daughters. When you have four daughters there are certain things you see that you do not see when you have three daughters, and vice versa.

Q.   You say that water flows in your book and indeed it does; the wind blows, and so on. Would it be possible to use the notion of imitation instead of, or in addition to, representation to describe this phenomenon?

A.   Oh, yes. There is imitation of reality, imitation of other writers. I would like to compete with certain things—with other authors, for example. Often, when I read something, I would like to write as well as that. And then, I want to compete with painting, music, also with the sea, with clouds, with locomotives.

Q.   I would like to come back to the development of your work. The novels (the works called "Romanesque I")[12] are structured in a rather traditional manner, with a single point of view: a subject who is revealed as insufficient and who is sacrificed so as to be integrated into a larger, collective vision. That sacrifice is painful for the subject, who gives up his central place to become no more than a medium. In the books associated with *Mobile*, which have been

---

[11] Jonas, Butor's dog, was present and barking throughout our conversation.
[12] *Passage de Milan, L'Emploi du temps, La Modification, Degrés.*

grouped under the category of "Romanesque II,"[13] something new is announced, a celebration of a new existence within a collective— collective dreams, a collective identity. A new epistemology and a new writing are part of this, and the self as we know it is surpassed. In more recent books, in contrast, the self returns, narrative returns, and the deciphering of space becomes more and more frustrating and difficult. How do you account for this return to the self?

A.   In these recent books there is, in fact, a return to the self, but with a great novelty. That self has a name; it is called Michel Butor. This is really different, because when you write a novel, you write so as not to say your name. You say, "I am giving you this but I am not the one who is saying it. You cannot challenge me on this because it is Ivan Karamazov, it is Louis Lambert who says this, not I." In my last books there is a situation in which an individual, Michel Butor, says "I am the one who is saying this." Amid all of the collective givens (phonebooks, dictionaries), the manipulator of these elements can be identified because of such and such a particular sign; just as inside a painting, the painter puts his portrait in a given place. You can sign with your own portrait. That is at a great distance from the first novel, where the transposed autobiographical character was very obvious, I think. Today I can say, pronounce, write the name Michel Butor as I could not at that time.

Q.   And why?

A.   I don't know why. I was full of complexes and taboos and I still am, but my books have worked out some of them. So, there are things I can say today that I could not say ten or twenty years ago. And I can speak about myself differently. Here there is certainly an important evolution.

As for the place and the deciphering of the place—places are difficult to decipher at any rate, aren't they? There are places which have, one might say, a clear historicity. They are historical places— there are documents, the work of other writers. That does not prevent them from being very complex. Let us take Delphi, for instance. We have Greek literature. But there are other places which tell you something, remind you of something, Mount Sandia, for example.

---

13 *Mobile, Réseau aérien, Description de San Marco, 6 810 000 litres d'eau par seconde, Où, Intervalle* (1973), as well as the first three *Illustrations* (1964, 1969, 1973).

Here there is no literature, or rather very little, because Sandia does figure in Indian legends and in guidebooks. That becomes much more difficult. The choice is not the same. In the first *Génie du lieu* we go around the Mediterranean. That is as cultural as you can get. In the second *Génie du lieu (Où)* we leave Europe. We still refer to Paris and all things in France, but we leave Europe. That poses very different problems, and with Australia it is even worse.

Q.   Then you attribute the difference between the two *Génies* to the difference between the places you chose to visit in each?

A.   Yes, and it would be tremendous if I could make the third book as different from the second as the second is from the first, but that would surprise me. That is what I would like, you see.

Q.   Is there a great difference between "Romanesque II" and "Romanesque III"?

A.   What do you mean by "Romanesque III"?

Q.   Your most recent books certainly seem to announce a new stage: the self returns, narrative returns. The previous works seemed to have superseded all that. Is this a break, or do you see it as a logical development: the self returns, but it is situated within the collectivity announced in the sixties?

A.   Yes, certainly it is totally logical. The second stage goes from *Mobile* to *Où*, and now with the latest *Illustrations*[14] and with *Matière de rêves* there is possibly a third stage, one which I see as more obscure. There is a great deal of obscurity in most of my books, but I strive to present myself with as clear a conscience as possible. It is obviously impossible to have a clear conscience in the case of obscurity, but I used to display clarity anyway, even if it was really, really difficult. Whereas with *Matière de rêves* I say that I no longer know what I am doing. I am still in control, but I take different risks.

Q.   Here you speak of imaginary places, don't you? There is no longer an attempt to understand that which exists but, as you said, to penetrate that which does not.

A.   Yes, of course, and it is all announced. There are many dreams in the novels, and *Mobile, 6 810 000 litres d'eau par seconde,*

---

[14] *Illustrations IV* (1976).

and other works of "Romanesque II" are full of dreams as well.

Q.   But are not these collective, less individualized dreams clearer?

A.   Yes, yes, but I don't think that my recent books are difficult books, *Illustrations IV, Matière de rêves*. I have already finished the proofs of the second *Matière de rêves* called *Second sous-sol* and I have completed the manuscript for the third *Matière de rêves*, called *Troisième dessous*.[15] These books are more obscure, but I hope that they will be less difficult to read. I have never believed that my books are difficult to read.

Q.   People find them quite difficult, you know.

A.   Yes, yes, well I admit that, but I don't believe that they are difficult. It's not true.

Q.   They are difficult, I think, because we are unwilling to abandon the central self, the individual, the particular. Isn't there a risk in emphasizing, as you do, all that is general, collective? In *Mobile* you speak of what Americans have in common, not of what might distinguish an individual American. Isn't there a risk, particularly in view of the book's formal games, that your book will become a kind of Freedomland, a kind of Clifton's Cafeteria, that it will imitate what is reprehensible about America? How do you avoid this risk?

A.   I would say that these structures do produce the particular; that is how the particular comes to be. The particular American lives in Hanover, Indiana, buys his curtains at Sears, and dreams at night after turning off his television set. Besides this crowd there are small individualities that appear and this individualization is reinforced by the historical individuals (certain Indians, Jefferson, Carnegie, etc.). But, for instance, the way in which Jefferson appears destroys him as an individual. We see very well that, in fact, it is not he who speaks, but it is the rest of America which speaks through him. But he could not avoid saying certain things which appear monstrous to us today. Jefferson's individuality, his talent, Monticello, are reversed in some way. The same thing happens to him as to all the others.

Q.   What choice does your reader have? Does not this book, as

---

15Both volumes have since appeared, *Second sous-sol* in 1976 and *Troisième dessous* in 1977.

well as all the others, demand of the reader a very personal kind of response, an individual self-definition in relation to the book?

A.   Yes, sometimes there are things that needle, things that are deliberately provocative and that cause the reader who circulates within the book as he would in Freedomland to become aware of what Freedomland is. That is the reason why this book leaves no one indifferent: the reactions to it are very violent.

Q.   Could you tell me about your recent *Bicentennaire-Kit?*[16]

A.   I will show it to you. I think it will amuse you. It is written for French readers who can afford such an object (F. 8800), for rich Frenchmen, therefore, who are fascinated by the United States and who play at being Americans. So the book sets itself up against this imitation of America, and it strives to make certain things scream. It must be read as a French book to get at its full irony. It is an irony whose object is the French imitators and, by way of them, America itself.

---

[16]Michel Butor and Jacques Monory, *USA76* (Paris: Ed. Philippe Lebaud, Club du livre, 1975). This "livre-objet" appeared in a limited edition of 300 copies. The blue plexiglass box contains a collection of objects, twenty serigraphs by Monory, and Butor's commentary. The text itself will be reprinted in the third *Génie du lieu: Boomerang.*

An Interview with Robert Duncan

*Conducted by John R. Cohn and Thomas J. O'Donnell**

Robert Duncan is conventionally associated with the Black Mountain Movement and the experimentalism of postwar American poetry, and is specifically linked with Charles Olson. In this interview Duncan recalls that at the end of his life Olson saw that "we'd been on a great twenty-five-year adventure, and he also saw that I was excused and was at the end of that adventure." Despite his sense that the "Movement is no longer current," Duncan holds that its "spiritual imperative is one that even today will be felt." The following pages suggest the poet's own literary program, his place in his poetic generation, and make clear the romantic and spontaneous character of Duncan's temperament. He analyzes the relationship between his homosexuality and his choice of poetry as a career, emphasizes that he "read Freud straight across," offers his unique view of Olson and the Black Mountain Movement as well as his general conception of the development of American poetry in the last fifty years, and explains his theory of the collage (and conglomerate).

As revealing as the substance of Duncan's responses was his entire manner of participating in the interview. It was begun at the University of Kansas, where Duncan was serving as poet-in-residence for a week. Wearing a black cape against the early spring air, he looked the part of the poet and seemed to enjoy his various activities immensely: meeting with classes, lecturing on Yeats and Whitman, reading from his own work, and conferring with students. His extraordinary energy was apparent during the interview; in answering a question he would speak until interrupted or redirected. The range

---

* The interview was conducted in February and July, 1976.

of his conversation and the intensity of his expression were often exhausting to the interviewers, if not to Duncan himself. In a single response he might mention—and interrelate—Dante, Milton, Pound, Olson, Williams, Eliot, Pindar, and Krazy Cat. Duncan's talk was equally compelling and intense when he completed the interview in San Francisco a few months later. He shares an impressive four-story nineteenth-century house in the Mission District with the painter Jess Collins. Duncan met us at the locked, ornate iron grille before the door of the house and led us immediately into a library just beyond the entryway. Here his most valuable books are stored, and he stopped to show us rare editions of William Morris. The interior decoration of the house Duncan aptly characterized as a collage and said the house was "always making presentations, like a lyrebird." During the actual interview sessions Duncan seemed completely unaware of being recorded; whether the machine was on or not, he spoke with the same intensity and rapidity. He would circle around a subject, start a sentence, break it off, backtrack, begin another sentence, then digress suddenly to an arcane subject—which he would again begin to circle. No topic was taboo, including the death of his mother in childbirth, his adoption by an architect's family, and his homosexuality. Duncan seemed to respond to the questions spontaneously, as if he were considering them for the first time, or genuinely reconsidering all these matters. Not only was he generous with his time during the sessions, but the house as well seemed to open easily to his friends and to people making pilgrimages.

Toward the end of the interview Robert Duncan declares that "there'd be a hole if I disappeared, a small one." Most readers of postwar American poetry would find that hole much more significant than Duncan acknowledges. Although the difficulty of his poetry and the learning it displays evoke the image of the genius, the exceptional man, Duncan himself argues that he does not give feeling and meaning to the object of his poetry. Rather, "*it* gives me passion, *it* gives me the identity of my passion." In the best of Duncan's work the reader experiences this passion and renews his own faith in poetry as a way of knowing and being.

Q.   What do you see as the relationship between an individual poet and poetic movements or groups?

A.   Well, I think there are some things I'd like to use an interview to clear up a bit. One of the larger ones is, What was the Black Mountain Movement that I've been identified with? What do groups mean to me, and what do movements mean? Particularly since the death of Charles Olson I feel I'm not a part of "current literature"— and don't have to be. I feel that somebody concerned about the "current," in exactly that historical sense, doesn't have to bother about my work at all, because I don't write as if there are any more movements, and that's a decision that I know many poets of the past would have recognized. In my case it's made deliberately—not with an antagonism to history, but with a much more deliberate sense of what's really going on. I'm a little puzzled by the fact that we have such rapid changes and such rapid dialectic going on in poetry, but I know that while I may use it or not, I am very happy to have the sense of timing back in my hands and not have to be out there. And so I feel my readers are off the beat when they land on me and ask, Where is the H. D. book, or where is this or that? That book's going to come in its own time. I'm not writing a *Finnegans Wake* in the H. D. book, but I am writing something; and it does have a plan, and I'll know when it's finished. Why are they breathing down my neck? History's not breathing down my neck; if history were breathing down my neck, the book would be there.

Q.   When Olson was alive did you feel that you were a part of "current literature"?

A.   Oh, yes, yes, absolutely in the current. Olson called us to order. Previous to that I felt I had full permission not to be. I could do anything; I could ransack it; I could play in my little kindergarten all I wanted. But Charles called everything to order with "Projective Verse" in 1950. I had met him before, in 1947–48, but I didn't even know he was a poet. We talked about history and the clear emergence of what Charles would have called the sciences of man, and that is the coordination from which you approach history as a question about how you live. You're not paying attention to national history any longer. It's a history of cities and countrysides. Well, our first conversation was about them, because I was wound up in my thought at that time about how in every pattern, of either the Russian Revolution or that of the United States, the cities are ripping off the countryside because they have to have the food; but the countryside doesn't have anything, so you civilize them so they need the refrigerator that

you're making. You make a lot of junk to sell to them, but the junk
has to be ingenious, because it has to be something that makes them
dependent. Well, that was what we talked about the first day, although
he had looked me up because Muriel Rukeyser told him about a poet
who had done something with medieval scenes—that meant history
in it—and so he was already thinking of me as a poet, and I didn't
return that interest. Consequently, when he sent me *y&x* in his first
correspondence (and now you know you'd have a fortune if you had
it) I was outraged. I mean, here's this guy in history, and why does he
load his poetry off on me? I threw it into the wastepaper basket.

Q.   But from 1950 to 1970 were you influenced greatly by Olson?

A.   I'm wondering if we would even call it influence. Well, no; I
played heretic often to Olson's position, and he had a position in
which heresy would sharpen my own sense of things. This is a familiar
role; I've never been able to have a single figure, and Jack Spicer also
was, for some time, an entertaining, an instructive person to play
heretic to. I might have been more confused in the area of
Manicheanism—about the glamour of Manicheanism and Calvinism
—if I hadn't had somebody who was really very solidly *that* to disagree
with. What I needed very much was someone who was serious about
what the thing meant, and whom you wanted to be able to reach the
final line of difference with. In Charles's case, the aftermath of my
study in the Renaissance and Medieval periods was an enormous
sense of the intellectual excitement and power of Roman Catholic
thought; and Charles really behaves in poetry as the Pope. I don't
mean that his thought is all orthodox, but it is charged through and
through with analyzable Catholic origins, transvaluation of Catholic
content. This vivified my own activity, which is always to transvalue
the things in my parents' religion that I wanted to take with me
because they made life vivid. And they can only be transvalued by
being questioned and kept, arriving at a place not where they're
acceptable, but where they're actually alive and not deadened by the
terms and governance they are given when they're in the religion;
and Charles was in the same process in relation to his Catholic
content. He found a synthesis because Jungianism—he and Denise
Levertov were both Jungian—allowed him to preserve his Catholic
content and be at the same time current.

Q.   But you're Freudian?

A.   Yes, I'm a Freudian, and Jungianism drove me up the wall with a good deal of fury; but it would have been an abstract fury had I not met a mind that I was always going to contend with as really being there and, moreover, a mind that would have to contend with me. And so when Olson wrote "Against Wisdom as Such," some people thought this was an attack and we must not be speaking to each other; but everything is absolutely accurate to me. We had been in conversation for some time; as a matter of fact, in the original that's a letter to me, he doesn't *not* know how I'm going to read every line, and then I can return and stretch my imagination and imagine how he's writing every line. I think you see part of what this is.

Eventually Spicer's Calvinism and Manicheanism became a drunken obsession. (I sometimes wonder if alcohol causes such breakdown and damage in the brain circuits that they become locked in a kind of stupor in which our activity that keeps ideas vivid and moving fails.) Eventually Spicer's propositions that had been *méchant* originally of demons of outer space became no longer propositional; they became necessary to believe, so that he couldn't move the idea around. (And, by the way, there were possibilities *I* entertained; I keep alive the notion that angels and demons might possibly exist.) It's no fun to play heretic to a fanatic. I play heretic so that ideas are moving, and I'm entertaining their ideas, and I know they're entertaining mine. My correspondence with Spicer dropped off when I realized that he wasn't entertaining my ideas; and while I could picture his, they no longer would move around. There was no play left.

Q.   You have spoken of a sense of freedom now that Olson's dead and a sense of freedom before you met him.

A.   I said freedom from history. Toward the end Charles saw where it was, but initially he wanted to be like Ezra Pound, a mover; and he was a mover, of course. He came charging in; and also he saw his man Melville as a mover of his mind and was really sort of shaking his poor old head as to how come Melville didn't move anything else. I mean how come Melville didn't move his own time? Well, maybe one of the explanations would be that Melville didn't get out there and do it. Charles was going to get out there and do it, no matter what, but he had a lot of reasons to do it. He did do it; projective verse really called us. We might have had a hazy memory about a lot of what Köhler was saying about composition by field and vector and so forth. But projective verse landed in our world and made a proposition that you have to start doing something. And, of course, it didn't come in nakedly: it came as a second proposition. Pound had not made a proposition that came into our world since the somewhat scattered proposition of the ideogram, at the stage of culture in 1936, and the real propositions were back in 1910. All this intrigued me as far as history is concerned; I knew I came out of the Pound propositions of 1910, and I knew that I was waiting at the bookstore door when that book *Kulchur* was going to appear. And the way that it was put together was through the ideogram, and the ideogram was the last stage that I had to think about and maybe incorporate. But incorporating something that's a proposition is not the same as what happened in projective verse. It was supposed to be a change.

Q.   Did you discuss these views with Olson?

A.   When I had one of the very last sessions with Charles at the hospital, one of the first things that I said to him was, "Well, Charles, we felt like we were moving the world, but maybe only you and I ever were interested in composition by field, although *Pieces* was written. And Dorn's doing something different." Well, that really hurt Charles. By the time he got to Buffalo and was thinking of dying, his graduate students there were very different from those at Black Mountain. At Black Mountain he had genius as a teacher, but that isn't going to be carrying Olson's program. When he got to Buffalo, he wanted young men who would do his work. Well, they are now lost young men, because there doesn't exist any "his work"—except what Olson did. And his first remark was that we'd been on a great twenty-five-year adventure, and he also saw that I was excused and was at the end of that adventure. It was a quest.

Q.   Do you conceive of poetic movements as a series of quests?

A.   For a very good reason poetry has had the matter of King Arthur as very central to it, because it's *quests*. Britain may try it on and think it's calling for a new Britain; but one thing we know it calls for is something about the way a poem goes. You go on a quest, and when you complete the quest—and it can be a failure—you bring back the bloody head, or you follow the maiden with the bloody head, and you don't have a good time. But when you come back, you come back to that round table of poets sitting, and from no other round table do any of the Arthurian things start. Poetry wasn't written by kings or actual knights; even when people were playing their actual little jousts, poets weren't there. You come back, but you can still be writing poetry. You've done your quest, and that's what I mean.

Q.   But it was a great quest?

A.   Yes, I think that was a tremendous experience, and so I have an Age of Charles Olson. The ones who were in the Age of Auden (and for much of the time that I was in the Age of Olson, the Age of Auden was still going on) did not read that as a quest; that was something else. I don't know what it was, but it makes for such a division of poets that they glare at each other as if one came from cannibal Africa and the other one from the Victorian parlor; and only two gentlemen went down to discover the source of the Nile. You can look through projective verse and look all the way through Charles; he always wanted to unlock a code. I don't go along with those projects; that was his quest; I don't think it was put on us. He did put it on the students. Charles Doria, for instance, who had just gotten out, finding his assignment, had gone on to a thing called *Origin,* where we've got very active translations of the key creation texts— not the myths, but the texts themselves, trying to get the direct feel of what it's like to be right in the Hittite. Well, what Charles wanted at Buffalo was for his young men to get the Hittite or to get the Mycenaean Greek and then get all the Lattimore stuff thrown out so that you're actually looking at the way it feels when you read it.

Q.   Did your homosexuality affect your work? Were there aesthetic effects?

A.   Aesthetic effects? No, well, originally when you take *Medieval Scenes,* Spicer was very concerned about building up and reproducing something like a George Circle [from Stefan George (1868–1933)], which he knew about when I first met him. It was probably 1946, so I was about 27, and I guess Spicer would have been about 21. He could also have been in his teens; he had come to Cal from one of those Quaker colleges. I'm not sure what college he came from, but he was a strange-looking kid. And he would want to sit during the entire day and learn everything I knew, so I know what it was he wanted to know right away—had I ever heard of the

Maximin cult of George? And I had indeed. I had a very strange lead
to that because just in 1945 I had had an affair with a German poet
who was about ten years older than I was, and who felt he should
initiate me into the inner ideas of what the George cult was.
His mother had been in the George group; as a very young boy he
had, then, been quite familiar with the George Circle. He had just
gotten his degree in Mallarmé, and he eventually became the official
German translator and editor of Yeats. I had a very personal, and
actually still to me strange, initiation into the cult and was then very
much in correspondence with it. Well, Spicer had a good deal of
feeling about me all the way through this. And you find that even at
the end, when I had not seen Spicer for two years or so (and in
Vancouver he was trying to propose that his serial poem would
supplant my work), I was occupying the position of a master to him,
though I was only six years older. But I had been writing, of course,
and I was the first poet he ever met that was an actual poet. More
than that, I was certainly an odd animal because I wasn't teaching
and I was entirely a poet, only a poet. I'd wash dishes or do anything.

Q.   Did your homosexuality determine your being "only a
poet"?

A.   As a matter of fact, the reason I really was only a poet (it was
clear even in high school that I wouldn't have a second profession,
and that I would be just a poet, which was very distressing to my
family) was that I was incapable, absolutely incapable, of living in
the double standard. I would just blabber too much; I'm not talking
about some great moral courage or something. I was literally
incapable, and I didn't read myself wrong. So, without thinking
about it, I understood that no one cares who or what is washing
dishes—but by the time you're a busboy they care, and they're
patting your bottom or whatever—and nobody cares who's typing
his manuscript, and that's where I was and never asking myself. But
if you would try to get an office job! I would take a Civil Service
examination and would be A-1 or whatever is the top bracket; but
when you'd go to get the job that's at the other end of that, they
simply read you out, in no time at all. You never got the job and,
more than that, they'd ask you to tell them why. And you'd meet a
hostility that couldn't be described; so no wonder I didn't, luckily,
remotely believe that I might grow up and be a teacher, maybe, as
well as a poet. Well, I could already see when I was a freshman in

college, no, you don't grow up and be a teacher. I was living with a French professor who lived in absolute terror. Three years later he was a French professor at the Naval Academy in Annapolis, and I could go out, providing it was after ten, and walk the dog. I got a lot of reading done; I read all the way through Proust and Trollope, but I couldn't go out of doors. And I had to exist as if I didn't exist. And then the hysterical other side of this is—because that's the backswing of absolutely abnormal double lives—people were just losing their minds at parties. Again they had to be very wealthy, where you had eight walls and whatever. Smoking pot was nothing compared with the simple sex lives in those days.

Q.   Yet despite this legal and social pressure your poems are at times openly homosexual.

A.   The fact that I didn't have inbuilt any religious or negative formulation about homosexuality meant that my poetry didn't have to be covert. It's perfectly apparent from the start and, more than that, I had some models; I loved Marlowe and very soon found *Edward II,* but could also read what was going on in *Tamburlaine* and several other places. In the late 1930s there were key texts like that. Long before an English course would bring it up, I'd be starting out reading my Melville that way. *Moby-Dick* was always a little key text given to kiddies, because if you could read straight at the beginning of *Moby-Dick,* you could learn quite a lot—I mean the little bedroom scene. There were such key scenes in literature that gave you something straight on mores and human responses, something not distorted by your having to read faggots. If you read the scene with Queequeg and Ishmael in their first night in that hotel as written, it tells you as much as *Edward II,* because it's decent and straightforward and presents certain areas of feeling that you can inherit without being an ugly, distorted human being. Whereas, if you read novels of the 1920s for your information, you'd think you'd come on like a freak in a parking lot.

Q.   How do you think this enforced separation from the conventional affected your poetry or your ideas?

A.   Only in the fact that my education then was very much my own and that my formulations in poetry, of course, were completely free from the formulations I would have had if I had been teaching

English, although later, if I thought of teaching, it would have been history. Ernst Kantorowicz at Cal had very much wanted me to go on; at the point that I met Jess, as a matter of fact, I had got my mother to back my going to Germany, and Kantorowicz had it charted out. So it was by a very slim margin of a month or two that I met Jess; otherwise I would have been off to Germany, where I would have chugged through to be an historian in medieval history. I was not unconvinced that I couldn't have been both an historian and a poet. I mean, I was a poet, but I had done papers and certain work in seminars. Things got straightened out; I am an artist. But it was so entrancing a prospect; this is again the George tradition: one of the closest ones to George was the great historian Friedrich Gundolf, who was Kantorowicz's immediate mentor. And that whole transformation of German history was a transformation that could have taken place in American history. When I met Charles Olson, by the way, what I didn't know about him was that he also was on the verge of a similar development; he had been in American studies that, under F. O. Matthiessen, were increasingly history and "science of man" centered. And Charles, reading Melville, began to realize, "Melville has all of this and is transforming the novel; I can transform the poem, and I get to be a poet; I am a poet, and my long training and history-centered mind do not disqualify me." I think you realize that the entire tenor of having an English department was that history was an extraneous concern of the poem, as, for instance, God was extraneous.

Q.   How did this attitude toward God affect you?

A.   I remember, when I was a freshman at Cal, that they didn't have classes in poetry, but poets, the ones who felt they were poets, met and talked about poems in an evening session. And Jo Miles came to a session and rebuked me for having stars in a poem because they were too big, for having the universe in it. She's a funny kind of objectivist; she relates to Williams' poetry in the early stage. And everybody objected to the fact that I was God-headed; I had gotten it off Marlowe. I hadn't really stumbled on Shelley; that would have been even worse. Shelley was a really bad name there.

Q.   To return to homosexuality, when did you first publicly declare it?

A.   There was a battle sense at Cal; and partly out of that I wrote, in 1942, the first article on homosexuality in which it isn't just apparent; I state that I'm a homosexual. I was twenty-three and it was published in Dwight MacDonald's *Politics*; it's called "The Homosexual in Society." James Agee had just written an article on blacks and the fact that their form of comedy, and their only area of social acceptance, was one in which they made it amusing to whites that they, the blacks, were hostile, and that their blues were, as a matter of fact, amusing to the whites—that they were blue and were sold as such. And Agee rightly found this a very dangerous social symbol. One of my contemporaries that I've known the longest, Pauline Kael, was very interested in political writing; one of the reasons I came to know her so well is that arguing back and forth with Pauline, who was very sharp on Marxism and who strongly questioned the anarchism that I was proposing as a political position, gave me a challenge to build ideas around. That article was very much written with a sense that I had people who would judge what I was saying there. Agee was recognizing a symptom, and it struck me that I could talk about another symptom of another hostility that is perfectly acceptable and absolutely amusing to everybody, providing it presents itself in the way that it does, and everybody in the whole society likes it. One thing I knew about our friendly University—of course, I mean the set of people that I've seen crippled by it, such people as I was in love with in the early period—when that was their environment, I saw them absolutely done in by it. It was always known that the whole department would love its pet queer; what they didn't like was the challenge that demanded intellectual respect and not on the grounds of *this*. If it was always on the grounds of *this,* that was fine; but it would really alarm them if it was pointed out in ways that didn't ask for some special social position, or didn't say I'm hurt over here, or didn't excite a sympathy.

Q.   What did you achieve with this article?

A.   One of the immediate results was that I also escaped from being acclaimed at that point. John Crowe Ransom accepted effusively a poem of mine called "An African Elegy" and then wrote that because a major poem by Stevens was coming out in the fall issue, he's transferring me to the spring; he wanted this poem by a poet who had not appeared before to be a lead poem and it would not otherwise be a lead poem. The article on "The Homosexual in Society" came out and I got a letter from Ransom, saying that he had not realized that this was a covert advertisement for homosexuality; *Kenyon Review* was not a journal accepting this sort of thing. And then I wrote back, "Would you prefer an *overt* one?" And then I got a letter, and he said he did not know what the law provided, but he believed that homosexuals should be castrated so that they wouldn't breed more homosexuals. Among our many odd versions of what is likely to happen, I think the castration document is strange indeed. So scratch a Southern gentleman and you'll find something awfully interesting. So I was *out,* just read out, out, out, at a point when I would have been *in* at the wrong place. When the issue came out, I would have been *in*: Auden, Paul Goodman, Parker Tyler; I mean the place looked like it was a coffee klatsch. I'm glad I wasn't in there; I would have been read not as an advertisement but a conformist of the first water.

Q.   You said that you "escaped from being acclaimed."

A.   Well, let's call it "claimed" because I very much wanted to be in the current when I was young. I did understand that there was an immense impetus that would be important to me in the sense of having contemporaries—I wouldn't have to cover everything in my own writing. I could be increasingly on my own, providing there was a Creeley also writing and people would be reading us together. Let me give an example, a concrete one, of the opposite of this. I began to run across a few poems of Bill Merwin's that looked something like *Structures of Rime,* but they seemed awfully fake to me, and I couldn't find any verifications when I was reading them that the poet had actually had visitations. I think you can begin to see what a difference it must make. Does the poet dispose of these visitations as poetic fancies and as an ambience in which something poetic happens? Or is he having (and I think he was, but not ready to put his mind there) something like a master of rime appearing and talking directly, and certain figures as would be in a dream, but others as persons of poetry? We would have no questions with Stevens, would we? We don't have to run around and ask him; the poem makes it very clear. But something was unclear with Merwin. While I actually find some of them pleasurable to listen to, they also make me angry because it will be possible for someone who is reading in the Merwin sense to turn to *Structures of Rime* and get them wrong. Mostly I make it impossible for somebody to get it wrong. If you don't pick it up right, you can't go anywhere. This is the way I read lots of things that happen in the *Cantos*; as a matter of fact, scholars were beginning to observe that the modern poem is making it impossible for somebody to read it wrong. And so my first question was that in Merwin nothing was forcing me to read it in some particular way; it was beautifully available, and I began to wonder, "Can this possibly be?" And he can still produce poems; they simply remain back there where the English gradually taught themselves a poem should be: it's a form that a gentleman writes. Disastrously it happened to Wilbur; Wilbur's first book comes with an amazing force. And my first book —not only was Ezra Pound embarrassed when he had to read it, but he said, "Why are you doing this?" when he knew from correspondence. But Wilbur's first book is truly a first book, and from there on he erases it, and he's writing those poems as you're told to write; maybe only a war gave him the context of the straight stuff. So this was one of the meanings of the Black Mountain Movement: you don't get mixed up. Think how important it was to Coleridge and Wordsworth that they weed out and that they not get mixed up with Southey.

Q.   What you've said, then, suggests that the Black Mountain Movement is over for you personally.

A.   That's not quite what I said. I think that the Black Mountain Movement is no longer current; consequently, I'm not current because it's very much what I do. But I think the Movement took place; its beginnings are 1947–1949, and clearly by 1960, when Don Allen's anthology appears, it's there. What my life work will be is entirely there at the point when I begin *The Opening of the Field*. You find its content and its propositions are in the preceding period, from 1952 to 1956, and it takes place in the book *Letters*; and from there on I have a work assigned, and it's, as Charles would say, a vector. When I say I'm not current, I don't mean my work might not be of influence, but the influence will not be the vital one going on in *Letters*. However, our spiritual imperative is one that even today will be felt as the continuing spiritual imperative of the 1950s.

Q.   You've spoken about visitations and your interest in occultism. Have you ever participated in a séance?

A.   Oh, I did very early; in the period when I left college—that would have been 1937–38 or so—and was living in Woodstock, we had séances during the winter. We had no mediums; I think I have references in poems to a "fireman" I saw at that time. After we had been meeting for about three months, and only at the beginning of any kind of manifestation, I felt the muscles in my lower leg going in a whole series of pulsations, rising clear up, and I got quite alarmed. As it was happening, I saw sitting by the fireplace a man entirely of fire, and I reasoned it and reassured myself, well, that's Sanders Russell, and I'm seeing him in the glow of the firelight. Then I began to realize that I was talking and the talking was getting remote, and I didn't want to lose consciousness, so I lurched up (like lurching up from sleep) and put on the light. And there was no Sanders there at all, so that would be an example of seeing. Another example of seeing; Michael McClure was taking drugs, and wanted me to take LSD, because he was very excited about what had happened. I was sitting in their dining room, and they have a big plane tree in the back. And I said it was not a plane tree. And Mike said, you'll see this great flowing something or other. And I was going to say, Mike, you don't realize that it's too easy for me to let go, and every leaf on that tree was a crawling, faintly hostile animal kind of thing, as I looked right past him at the tree. And I said, in reference to LSD, Mike, if I'm going to go to hell on a visit, I want to be sure I'm on a visit and not on a trip. None of those drugs; it's only too easy for my chemistry to shift.

Q.   How does your poetry relate to such states?

A.   Actually, I think poetry may also have been, very clearly, a protective way for me. Why is the poem surrounded and why does the intellect happen to be so much present in my poetry? This may be an enormous protection against the seizure of the poem itself. My sense of my poetry is that it's extremely anxious. Large portions of it will be in a rhythm that's built up of almost machine-gun-like stutters, all of them keyed as highly intellectual propositions, before it starts to flow. The flow would be very dangerous for me. I don't have any psychotic periods, and I have very few hallucinatory periods that I can remember, and yet in *Passages* there were disturbing dreams. The one in the Victor Hugo poem is a reference to pillars of light (moonlight) that came in the night; Jess woke up and I was whimpering, and he realized that this was not just a dream to be wakened from, because I might have been frightened, and that he had to sit through it and I had to go through it. And it was experienced as a visitation of angels, mothering angels, and one was actually my adopted mother, and one was H. D., who was adoptive, because I had come to know H. D. in correspondence. But it was an experience I didn't doubt. Everybody thought when I wrote "The Carpenter" it was perfectly apparent that I say, you came in a dream and I knew I was to write to you, not pose like I'd made you up. And actually that was another dream visitation. I was never sure who the Carpenter was; in the dream, or in the visitation, I raise the question myself, "Is it Christ?" But it could also have been Christopher because it was huge and I was little. I clearly was running from God, as in "The Hound of Heaven," which would be exactly where I would be today. So the intellectuality we're talking about is also the form of running from God.

Q.   Do these poems seem to come from inside or outside?

A.   When lines come to me, frequently it's not clear that they aren't outside my head. Now that would be a psychotic symptom, but I never experience it as such, nor do I quarrel. I don't set up something about this is "inside my head"; I will work with it as if it did come from "outside." I'd work with things that come from somebody talking, reading. Learning that Joyce had gone to bars and used conversations was one of the encouraging things that we knew. As a matter of fact James is getting whole novels out of a little sentence or two in a newspaper and calling them a "germ." We read that when we were little and understood what it was; I mean James's germinal theory of the novel is one of the origins, lo and behold, of how Duncan proceeds in poetry. And while Pound doesn't reflect on it in his essay on the poem, probably it's prevalent. Lawrence proceeds as if people who belong to the novel came to him, and then he says, once he started them, he can barely write it down as fast as *they* do it. So all of that would be in the territory you're talking about; and, consequently, when I read testimony of saints, I take that as testimony, and certainly it's a little more dependable than Nixon.

Q.   You say you write only when you have to?

A.   Well, as a matter of fact, yeah; actually, it's quite compelling.

Q.   You mean an internal compulsion.

A.   Well, no, it's almost always an external one. Many of my leads toward writing come from applied Freudianism out of *The Psychopathology of Everyday Life.* I go by a series of omens, these leading to the point where you have to deal with them in the poem.

Q.   A series of what?

A.   Omens—of compelling directions that certain things are no longer. Things that you would ordinarily take, in a Freudian context, to be parts of your psyche I take to be parts of my poetic projection. For instance, I am not in my derivation from Freud; I have not been psychoanalyzed; I am not remotely interested in my psyche. It's not an interest in psyche when I speculate upon the primal scene. The primal scene bare is exactly like the primal scene if you're dealing with the Fall; and the way I read my *Paradise Lost,* Milton's angels instructing his Adam and Eve on the nature of the Fall are way over there where my Freud is. If you were in the course of a psychoanalysis instead of in the course of a poetics, then if something happened you would recognize the dream was telling you to do certain things, and you had, for instance, a thing called the dreamwork. In the first Freud I ever read, *The Interpretation of Dreams,* he's already talking about a thing called dreamwork. That is, he sees his patients as if they're in the course of an analysis; immediately I took that over. That poetry-work was like dreamwork was premise number one when I was seventeen and started reading my Freud. And it went along to things that had been in my family's occultist tradition, because if they talked about their alchemy, they had work to do. They taught me that dreams told you things you had to do. Freud produced in his psychology analogous structures to the ones that had been present in the whole Jewish mystical tradition. But it was a tradition of things you had to do, of ways you read things of being significant of more than they said. And I grew up in an atmosphere where anything written always meant more than it said. And the dream is certainly polysemous. I'm not building a psyche; I'm building a poetry. I find myself in profound aversion when faced with close friends who were in Jungian or Freudian analysis and doing things with their psyche. I feel as Joyce does: they're playing with their icky, or something. Little games, psychodramas—and yet what is a poem?

Q.   But how does the process of writing compel you?

A.   You don't initiate themes; the themes are there all the time, but you recognize that they're leading and drawing. One thing is certain, that my internal chemistry changes, because I feel a body change. Well, I would not need a poem at all in order to be involved with mythology, in order to be involved with most of what you take to be the content of a poem, but a poem has an entirely different thing going on in it that is proper to it, and so that it is poetry. The fact that you're working with language and making something with it is far different from the pursuit of ideas or the study, and yet all my poetry incorporates, tries to incorporate, the ranges of my personality in its work. That is, it's study—study is *au naturel* for me—so my poetry also will show it. At the point when I take up a work I find frequently I'm in study, within the poem. But they're conceived of now as building; I think we talked about this one thing from my father.

Q.   Your adoptive father was an architect?

A.   Certainly it's my judgement, then, that he was not a true architect. Then I had to ask, okay, am I a true poet? No, I wouldn't want to have to be, so I decided I was going to make up poetry the same way I would make up love. If I'm incapable of loving, as my mother told me once, then I'll make it up; I would prefer to make it up than be real me. No wonder I don't want to go into psychology. I read Freud straight across. I also discovered in Jakob Böhme, a philosopher, the idea that the whole universe is grounded in wrath, and love has only one root, which is wrath (it's a transformation of wrath and not the other way around). Or now I'm attracted to Heidegger, because he says *Dasein* is rooted not in its possibility but in its impossibility, so all of life is rooted in death. Isn't this for our whole period our apprehension of what's involved in the third thermodynamic law? Our entire energy world is rooted in zero energy and ordered by it throughout, and coming to it, *not yet,* so we live in what Heidegger called the *not yet.* These are not things that influenced my poetry, but recognitions so like what I felt was the nature of the poem, rooted in its not being true. So the poetry seems true to me, whereas I would be as abashed to say I was a true poet, and abashed if somebody made that announcement, as I would to say, "I love you," which is also an announcement I can't make. And essential. So there are essential points when the dread of language leaves you in such an abyss as what the Lie is. Much of my poetry's gone into all those areas in which we learn that the word "poem" means "to make it up, make up what is not true." And fiction, then, means to me something more severe than Wallace Stevens proposes to us, although I think, since he has roots in Hawthorne, he's not so jolly as Whitman, from whom he also stems. Wallace Stevens doesn't have the confidence in language he sometimes proposes. Whitman has a confidence in language which I'm certain I don't have. It's the one place I am not like Whitman.

Q.   You take the idea of *making* quite seriously, then?

A.   I'm making buildings and architectures frequently. So I go back to build something, and my intuition of when it's time for me to work is when the whole language proposition appears to me as intuitions of building a building. A poem to me is a building of this kind: it's got very specific properties and it can be intricate; but it always has a suite or a number of rooms; it always has current that goes through. As a child I was making floor plans with choreographies. And I had very elaborate floor plans and choreographies that move from my head as well as ideas; and they can never come into activity, except when I'm making poems. Now all the rest of the so-called verbal area, the so-called content, constantly comes into conversation, but the floor-plan aspect of it comes in only in the art, so again it's the architectonics of the poem that seems to me one of the crucial things. The minute that comes forward, then I'm writing, feel a call to it (doesn't mean I can do it). I'm as often stranded in impossible architectures as anybody else, I would presume.

Q.   Would you discuss a specific poem? Perhaps "Often I Am Permitted to Return to a Meadow." How did you write that?

A.   I had for some years told the story that "Often I Am Permitted to Return to a Meadow" was a poem in which I recognized the beginning of the book it belongs to, *The Opening of the Field*. And so *The Opening of the Field*'s got a plan. It is continuously illustrating itself throughout, and, more than that, it has thematic propositions moving out of the idea of "field," which is constantly found and re-found, and has a drama that moves through it. But initially I didn't have any such proposition of what was going to be—just a determination that the initial poem would be nuclear to be a book, and it would contain themes and I would be called to them. Well, I had two poems, and what I remembered in the legend, then, was that my first two poems that came were poems in which angels were present, and I wanted to be sure that I didn't have any involvement with angels.

Q.   Why the prohibition against angels?

A.   Rilke's *Duino Elegies* had been an overwhelming conversion for me, and I dreaded, and still dread, any angelic invasion—I'm not talking about angels as they invade religion, but angels as Rilke found them invading poetry. And I would say the same thing: my difficulty with the proposition of angels is that they are so much a proposition of poetry; they must be the same danger there that they would be anywhere else. They're not a proposition about Do I or do I not believe in them, and would it be disturbing if one walked into the room? All those doctrines of angels, about how they move our lives, are beside the question I'm entertaining here. I did know that if they come into a realm of poetry we're in very heavy trouble, analogous to what happens in the *Duino Elegies*. I actually did pray that I'd be excused, in other words, be permitted to. And so, when I wrote the opening line, "Often I am permitted to return to a meadow," I recognized that this was my permission, and that this meadow, which I had not yet identified, would be the thematic center of the book. In other words, what's back of that opening proposition I understood immediately: twice *you* wanted to compel me to have a book that would have angels at the center, but *now* I am permitted, often you have permitted me, to return to a mere meadow. But I was also flooded with meadows from childhood, and I also knew immediately that I was permitted to return to a dream, a dream which appears in this poem and also appears in the Pindar poem. Typically, the dream is an absolute experience for me—that is, it is not illustrative of something—so when Rosenthal, who wants to make a confessional poem out of it and to find a personal psychological extension of that dream, comes to it, it's merely those children dancing in the circle on the hill. But to me it is a generative symbol, and revelatory in the sense it throws me forward to a question, not to an answer, and it is not relevent to a psyche.

Q.   The opening sentence contains meanings, then, that are far from apparent.

A.   And if we take just that opening sentence, "Often I am permitted to return to a meadow," at the same time that I recognized it meant you have permitted me now to return to this meadow (I will be safe from angels) that is not what happened by the time I'd done an "eternal pasture folded in all thought." I knew the idea of a "folded pasture" or a "folded field" as a proposition given in the Zohar for the Cave of Machpelah, so my field was identified initially in this poem, in its very first version, with the cave that Abraham sees, and he recognizes before he buys it that it is the center of the universe, and also that the forefathers are gathered there, are buried there, of whom he is going to be the fourth. You find in the same period, in my writing to Olson, I was building a picture of the quartet; I had kept trying to picture what was happening in the generation of Pound and Williams and Lawrence. The quartet, as I finally designed it, was Williams and Lawrence and Pound, and then Olson became both an ancestral figure and a fellow figure, and I got to be the son. In other words, I am recreating a father and fathering myself. In the H. D. book I talk about poets mothering themselves in the language, in the loss of their mother, and frequently I have father constructs, just as I construct an architect almost immediately.

Q.   The "first version" you mention is a manuscript version of "Often I Am Permitted to Return to a Meadow"?

A.   The manuscript version and the press publication are only a couple of weeks apart, so you can read the first version. What I did that made for a second version is that when I began to see the theme of the woman appearing (which may have been as late as "The Maiden"), I redid the first poem so that it included "Queen Under The Hill." I'd also begun to see that the theme in the matter was going to make a union of the Judaic, the Classical, and the Celto-Germanic. In medieval studies I'd had a seminar in Celto-Germanic art, and I'd had—back of the medieval studies—quite a lot of delving into a picture of what parts of European consciousness were really Celto-Germanic. I put the two together; there's a negative feeling about the Germanic I want in there. And so this book develops—by the time it comes to the end—the idea that there's a kind of rope in which these are thoroughly entwined, and consequently it is the growth of a single vine. In time it comes to be the whole Semitic, because I make a union between the Moslem and the Judaic and then the Semitic back of that; and if that's broken at all, you have catastrophe, which is how I read what happened in Nazi

Germany.

Q.   What specifically is added?

A.   It is the "She it is Queen Under The Hill / whose hosts are a disturbance of words within words / that is a field folded," and it makes most intolerable to both parties a union in which the Celtic and the Judaic are combined. And the queen then becomes a Shekinah. But I already knew, of course, from the Zohar that there was such a queen folded in the fold of God and that while we pose this father—right into the center of this poem which has its hidden reference to that Cave at Machpelah, which is fathering yourself again —you pose inside the queen who becomes the queen of the whole hive. Well, that's all I had to do to have enough. Once that was there I saw I had everything that I was going to unwind/wind in the book. The field very rapidly is identified with another source of the field I knew, and that is in Fustel de Coulanges' *Ancient City* (his description of Rome and the Roman field), so that in the midst of the Beat Movement, by lovely synchronicity, while they're talking about squares, I am dealing with a *square*: my field is square. It gave me great elation to be building a fourfold square field, but the thing that haunts the book is that at the center, I knew, of that where the hearth is built, something has to be lost. What it was is the cat and the death of the cat. As I came toward the end of the book I became more and more apprehensive about the death of someone, and at one point I asked what had happened to my closest friend in the Second World War. I was told he had died, and you have a poem which really addresses his death; and when it was printed in a magazine in Chicago, it turns up he wasn't dead, so I came to know him again. But "A Storm of White," the death of that cat (of the cat Pumpkin, who was very close to us indeed), produced a paroxysm of grief because it was a necessary sacrifice to this field.

Q.   There's another connection with the idea of the field a bit later, isn't there?

A.   Oh, you mean where the title of the book comes in. Well, that's actually in "The Structure of Rime II." That's where I recognized the title of the book: "He brings his young / to the opening of the field. Does he so fear beautiful compulsion?" My poetry is a process of opening. Of opening meanings out of meanings out of meanings, with a confidence that there's closure. In the question of closure—you know at the present time physics has still not decided whether we are an endlessly opening universe with no possible proposition of closure at all—I'm sure about life that death can't be experienced as closure. There are no terminal experiences. So I think of it as altering; that's all I can think of it as. I don't mean the eternal: it does not interest me in the least. I was raised in reincarnation, and I tend in crisis situations to behave as if that's where it was. But when I'm talking about death's being an opening, I mean it can't possibly be a closure. It is not a terminus, because experience itself has closure, whereas a coma is not experience.

Q.   In "The Structure of Rime II" you attribute observations to a lion who appears in several guises. What does the lion symbolize?

A.   Well, "lion" and "line" are always analogous to me; my puns are not puns because they're entirely in the world of language. And it is presumed within the world of language that language is always specific. A difficulty I notice is that if we talk about speech, then we don't have to talk about English or French or any other kind of speech. And under speech we've got many kinds of languages. Speaking is a very great activity and, in the English speech, that is a real limitation on my poetry: that it inhabits the English language as if it were speech. Translators have to give up on a word like "sentence," because it is crucial in the whole structure of my world that a "sentence" in a law court and a "sentence" in grammar are identical. That's not true in German; it's not true in French. God gives his sentence upon the earth but not in any other language but ours, I think. So here "line" and "lion" are at every point. Sometimes I wonder, "That again?" But my artistic feeling about it—I'm not sure at all where my aesthetic's going to be—is that if I am continuously intrigued with "line" and "lion" I can do it as often as Mondrian's intrigued with his propositions of light and dark, and so forth. I don't save myself with "line" and "lion," but I'm surprised how often new terms enter in the pattern. And we don't have to talk about hierarchies because often my own perception of the poem, when I'm working on it, is very close to putting together a patchwork quilt. And I refer to myself as a jackdaw in some—and frequently ask, "How do we lyrebirds build nests continually on top of themselves?" My house, for instance, is frustrating because you fill it and you get into certain sets and you keep wanting to add house on top of house because you're always making presentations, like a lyrebird. So a poem to me is a lyrebird's presentation to an imaginary reader. A "lyre" is one I run all the time. I never write "lyre" without the other "liar" around.

Q.   I understand your approach to writing "Often I Am Permitted to Return to a Meadow," but I'm interested as well in your general practice. When you're working on a poem, do you do several manuscript versions?

A.   No. Manuscript versions are in notebooks, and by the time I'm working on passages I have a method of composition so that when I'm typing them I make new developments; but I don't write them twice in order to arrive at these. At the present time, in working on a complex recital from a translation from Pindar, I am actually having to work the recital. Now the recital is written in one notebook, and then in preparing it to be typed for publication, for being part of a composition, I have to use the material of the recital. The recital is a series of mistakes, and I did not want to worry at all about whether this is unwieldy. So the first writing is a sketch. In the middle of the poem it's lyrical; it's a long essay recital of the translation of the Pindar passage, making all the possible mistakes that can be along the line of "line" and "lion" in order to find extensions. Okay. Now, that becomes material which I now have to work, also still in the notebook, in order to shape it in relation to the suite it belongs to. And then, once that's there at the typing point, I call that almost like orchestration—more and more, as I listen to music and learn how composers and music proceed, I'm to a good degree composing. It's themes that enter that poem to change it, not improvements, and I understand what I'm doing with those themes, because they make possible the large structure of the book. The recital has long held up this particular poem from being finished, because the last two lyrics can't possibly come into existence until I have got the complex web of this recital to where I've got the gist of what it is that's in that poem. I mean the lyrical passages would certainly not be the maze that the essays are.

Q.   We've tried to relate you to the Romantic notion of the artist, the artist drenching what he sees with feeling and meaning. In "Dejection: An Ode" Coleridge looks out and sees nature, sees the green light and the storm, and says, "I may not hope from outward forms to win / The passion and the life, whose fountains are within."

A.   I see it the other way around: *it* gives me passion, *it* gives me the identity of my passion. I used to feel, "Am I not maybe empty or have no identity at all because I'm all out there?" I was mentally excited when I started Whitehead, which is the same time as *The Opening of the Field* begins. Olson came in the spring of 1957, and he was just reading Whitehead, so I began not so long after him reading *Process and Reality.* And I had that feeling that the world illustrates *us,* that we were the *tabula rasa.* I had always been baffled by the Berkeley proposition. Are we going to worry about, "Is it there when we're not looking?" My question is, "Am I there when I'm not looking?" And I vote for Aristotle's view that a soul is simply the life experience of a lifetime. It is the shape of the lifetime. Now that means, "Am I there when it isn't there?" No. The "I" can be the universe, because there it is out there. And then we get, "What about this world?" Every imagination of the universe extends this universe for me, so none of that is unreal. I make no choices among it, so science forms a more generative idea; a perfect one, where I really do know my center, is strict, straight-line Darwinism—which is *no purpose.* And there damn well better not be a purpose, because you're lost if there is. You find Darwin entering early in *The Opening of the Field* and in *Letters,* where I'm trying to propose, "Okay, if the biggest generative process is *no purpose,* how do I remove purpose from a poem when I'm working at it? How do I actually evolve as I begin to understand life does?" Because my model of how a body is most viable—how its life is most going to survive—no longer resembles the one you have if you are a paradigm that might be extinguished. When the DNA appeared you'd have thought you'd written it yourself!

Q.   Could you explain the symbolic significance of that discovery for you?

A.   DNA is a biological analogy derived from the very linguists we were reading. Cybernetics is the birth ground of the DNA—of seeing biology as if it could be a code which they then assumed language was. And it's my generation who got it for the very first time—could even imagine language as a code. The watershed by which I am not at all the same species of poet as Robert Lowell is that Lowell knoweth nothing of cybernetics—knoweth nothing of a language which is a code. Language doesn't behave that way; that's not the world of language that his mind addresses or from which he comes. Pound himself couldn't address it. He also knew nothing of a cybernetics, so he feels that the *Cantos* have a logic, but his mind isn't going to go to their logic; his mind rushes to fascism in order to boss that big form. So he feel it's formless at the last, at the very time when it's actually significant. For how do we think language behaves? He thinks it's falling apart and he can't use it; but actually being entirely contemporaneous with Norbert Wiener and the people who are all in the language field (but not reading them), he has no idea. He could have gone to Schoenberg to find out what was happening in music, but he couldn't because of his anti-Semitism; he could have gone to Freud to find out what was happening in a new psychology, but he couldn't; so he behaves as if he were a wandering Voltaire writing the wrong thing and inherits all the anti-Semitism of the eighteenth-century mind trying to get itself clean.

Q.   Where would the world that's mediated by your poetry be if your poetry didn't exist to represent it?

A.   I'm *a* locality of what's happening in poetry, as I am personally a locality in the universe. Well, if I weren't here, we wouldn't worry about that locality's being missing. I do understand there'd be a hole if I disappeared, a small one. No, I'm a development in a language, but I certainly didn't develop the language, so I refer to myself as derivative entirely. And at the same time I am the only place where that derivation can happen, so I don't resemble what I derive from, couldn't possibly because there's only one locality for something going on. Where would the language be? The language is the source of all the possible poetries. It's like asking where the DNA would be if your own local sperm hadn't connected with this local egg. Well, there's millions of sperms that don't connect, and there are lots of eggs that don't connect, and we could build whole imaginary worlds about the missing bodies. No, I don't think it's a jigsaw puzzle like that. I'm sure that the field of language is as destructive of its individual occasions as literature clearly is of its. But I do build myself large enough that I might leave a fossil, if only a bone somewhere in the debris.

Q.   In "A Letter," addressed to a carpenter, you speak of working with wood, planing it down. In your poetry are you trying to expose the grain of that wood, the grain that is in the external world, the pattern or form that's out there?

A.   Yes, I bring out a content as you would bring out a grain, that's true. Frequently you'll find me taking a quotation because there's a promising grain in it. Marquetry is referred to often in my work; it also bears a relation to carpentry, and you're not just bringing out the grain but relating it to contradictory grains. The place where I've seen it as being impressive is in the marquetry of the eighteenth century, or the seventeenth century, where it's really elaborate. And the elaboration fascinates me; but again, though it's fitting and contrasting, you bring out what's there in the text. And I'm always bringing out possibilities of language, even in that initial poem in *The Opening of the Field,* and eliminating other things, in order to bring out a promise toward things that will happen later. But you're bringing out the qualities that are there: I don't think of myself as giving the quality to the language.

Q.   To take it one step further back, you're not, as a Romantic would be, imposing that order?

A.   Oh, no. The order is there and I bring it out. I have an aesthetic about the composition of the poem; this would not describe what I think a poem arrives at, but what governs its coming into shape. Specifically, it was a decision made—I don't know why I made it, because I'm not sure I had a talent for what I thought I was rejecting— against the kind of artful, orchestral coloring that goes on in Hart Crane's use of the language. It sounds poetic because it's not located. And then there were things described in the 1930s and talked about as being ambiguities, where they really meant not double locations or triple or polysemous, but simply that it was so vague that we could do almost anything with it. Certainly by the time I came to *Letters,* I began to articulate the line into even, short phrases; I determined that every part of the poem would be active at the conscious, meaningful, directed level, and that my business would be to recognize how many meanings were present, like "line" and "lion" and so forth. And so I became a recognizer. This is the grain of the language: you *recognized* all the activities that you'd ever known that would tell you. And, of course, the phrases became much smaller. Why the articulation of a line into a series of smaller elements? So the caesuras widen, and there's no longer a punctuation within a syntax. It calls attention to the fact that the mind is in full attention on the minutiae of the poem. In the formula of the poem it meant that the poem was finished when every part of the poem was significantly related to every other part. And in "The Dance," for instance, where I explore these propositions, inner lines, like dance that the "movement makes . . . co-/ordinate" and even the division of "co-" from "ordinate," are meaningful, so I insist that there are not terms of the poem that are not meaningful. Now I don't *put* the meaning in. There was a rumor at one time that Spicer, because he was trained in linguistics, had poems in which there would be whole areas that were front vowels and whole areas that would be rear vowels and so forth. Well, actually, every time I've tried to teach the feel of where the vowels are in the mouth, I've got very strong prohibition, and yet I feel it's essential that they be felt. But I could not *put* a vowel somewhere in a poem, because I'm bringing out a grain; I'm not *putting* a grain into the wood.

Q.   Could you illustrate how you bring out this grain in a particular instance or word?

A.   In "The Dance" I get a line right away: "The Dance / from its dancers circulates among the other / dancers." I'm not putting anything in there, but I've got, as fast as I write it, to recognize everything that's potentially in that. I'm not going to be able to recognize more that's in "circulates" than I have. So what do I do when I'm not writing a poem? I am constantly in study and recognition, not only of what's going on in other poems, but I know that *circ* means "circle" and a million such things about the word "circulates." I acquire language lore. What I am supplying is something like grammar of ornament, I mean grammar of design, or of the possibilities of design. I'm not going to produce everything that circulates, but I'm not going to be caught out of court with some activity of that word "circulates" that I don't want to recognize. We're talking about the negative possibility—if you're unhanded because you refuse to recognize how words work. But my ideal of the poem is that every word be viewed as polysemous, and it can only be governed then by its rhymes and the structure in which it happens; and if you don't recognize all of its polysemous activity it's going to break down the structure. So one of my ideas, then, of the structure of the poem is that it's a constant closing down of an absolutely protean situation until finally you have only one identity. If I'm strictly there, absolutely, not directing but bringing every attention upon every happening within the poem, then I know that everything will bear (what we otherwise would assume) a signature. The reader is also going to be attending to all these phrases; he's forced to attend to the phrases more and more in my poetry because he can't even hit the rhythm unless he is. And it moves faster. It's amazing when Charles talked about "instanter" as he did, because he had some of the same drive toward this insistence. I think all finely articulated poems have this insistence.

Q.   Is this insistence always an advantage to you?

A.   The language is not vague in its activities. This becomes a very severe limitation in my poetry; it doesn't produce certain atmospheric possibilities. I can get carried away on certain sensualities—color and several others; you get *lotophagoi* passages, fairly identifiable as coming from Pound, or ideas of enchantment. But I really picture an enchantment which, if you examined it as a Freudian does when he looks at the dream that he thought was an enchantment, you would find, when it's analyzed to its particulars, isn't an enchantment at all.

Q.   Do you feel that because the words are charged with multiple meanings you're coming closer to some original language lying behind English?

A.   No, no, not at all. Actually the charge is inherited from Pound's language charged to its utmost degree. The thing was laid down in Imagism in the very first rounds; poetry was language charged. And I read that "charged" as relating to every word, and you'd put the full charge of language as far as you knew. I "O.E.D." a lot. If I weren't fascinated with the language, none of this would be here. It's not *au naturel* that poets do it this way. Quite a few poets pick up "O.E.D."ing and I read it as just "O.E.D."ing. Particularly, of course, I'm quite divorced in feeling from poets that are inheriting some things from me: Robert Kelly and Eshleman and so forth, because they're projecting a personal psyche. I'm character-structured, not psyche-structured, so I find it quite abhorrent; I can't read them with any pleasure.

Q.   What do you mean in "The Dance" when you write, "Lovely our circulations sweeten the meadow"?

A.   I've got very much in mind there the whole tradition of the Morris dance and its sweetening the spring. I also view poetry as participating in certain energies that are present in the language and "sweetening." In my Dante essay I address myself to the sweetness and greatness of Dante. One of my contrasting points with Spicer was that he stood for bitterness as being a reality, and I stood for sweetening. Sweet and bitter, like chiaroscuro, the mixing of dark and light, is an insistence throughout my poetry. So sweetening the meadow is one of the beginning propositions. At the point where I write "sweeten the meadow" I don't have any memories that immediately flashed on the sweetening style of Dante. And the *dolce stil nuovo* is part of my idea of what my tradition in poetry was—clear from Pound's spirit of romance through to the courses in Kantorowicz to the whole idea of what sweetness meant to the Renaissance. So "sweetening the meadow" is loaded, although that's a very innocent poem; today if I wrote that line it would get heavy. It's not heavy in that poem.

Q.   When you "sweeten" language in the Renaissance sense, aren't you bringing something to it that wasn't there before?

A.   Yeah, you bring your dance to the grass. By the way, of course, you're sweetening the idea of the meadow; I would say if I were thinking analytically of it, all dance conceives of itself as sweetening the meadow. The meadow is a field of thought, isn't it, and it's a field of poetry, so you sweeten the poetry in dancing it. Spicer so much opposes it that you find in his poetry an elimination of almost all of the sweetening activities, melody and dance, and a hostility to it, so that in his final lectures he's saying that if a line seems beautiful, cut it out. Not stop it, just cut it out, take the whole line out. Take any area of the poem that seems beautiful out, and this is the contrary to sweetening the meadow.

Q.   Do you have strong views on the relation between poetry and performance? For instance, when you do poetry readings is the poetry you're writing ever affected? When you became prominent as a poet, readings were beginning to come back into force again, weren't they?

A.   By 1946 I started reading, and that's part of the reason why in the West we didn't publish. Printing was not the mode of the writing, but writing was still the mode. The performance of the poem was like the performance of a piece of music, and from the beginning I understood it that way. Beethoven exists in his notation, and he's subject to endless interpretation. But since I conceive of the poetry as notation for a performance, but not for a specific performance, certainly not for my voice, when I give a poetry reading I am not giving a poem that preexists; I am giving that particular reading of that text and it will change all the time. Sometimes, of course, I'm reading the poem and taking it for granted, but in anything as involved as *Passages* I'm always suddenly seeing more possibilities of what it means. I'm readjusting and the notation is fairly exacting; it already contains the whole pattern. One thing I don't dream I do when I read it is give it expression or more emotion than's there. I think the emotion's in the writing, so I object to the Dylan Thomas kind of rhetoric. I am very keen on rhetoric, and consequently object to the Dylan Thomas bathetic reading of a rhetoric, which destroys the structure by putting it across. I really object to expressionism, to *putting into* it something and or *putting in* more depth.

Q.   If your text instructs and directs your performance of that poem, and yet performances can vary, does that mean that the sense gets changed?

A.   No, I'm always returning to the text and the text is the one I'm performing, not some new possibility in that sense. And I haven't listened to enough tapes to know to what degree there is a shift. I know that my way of performing is characteristic enough that somebody else can perform it *au juste*. When I finished "The Soldiers" I sent it off to Creeley. Now I had not myself read it aloud; all of *Passages* grew up around the fact that you have an audience, so they're auditorium pieces. So I hadn't really read it aloud at home— sitting at the table is awkward; it just would be the wrong dimension. I sent it immediately to Creeley when it was finished, and he was teaching a course at Boulder or Aspen. And so within a week of its being finished he read it aloud and they sent me a tape back—and *au juste* a Duncan reading. Creeley, however, has a greater mobility in reading—and appropriately—other people's work than almost any poet I know.

Q.   What happens to some of the words that are polysemous, or ambiguous, when you render them in speech and so choose one pronunciation?

A.   My sense when I'm rendering them is that they go toward a neutral position, so they leave open their operation in other parts of the poem. And also I have certain places where the particular lines— and this is more interesting than the polysemous possibilities that are present—establish a kind of irony. And in Dante's case, since the actual world illustrates the spiritual world and also the intellectual world, these three are conceived of as being a harmonious set. In my case they may belong to different systems and one system may be in a kind of joking relation to the other. So a tone may change, and often when I read a passage, I wonder if in any way the peculiar pitch of it is conveyed. But then I hear this is a changing problem in music, as early as the shift between Brahms and Richard Strauss. Brahms's humor is notoriously rollicking—I mean if he's in a humor, he's in a humor; you can't miss it. Meanwhile, in Richard Strauss there are jokes that run through actually excruciatingly passionate passages, and they *are* jokes. There wouldn't have been a joke in Wagner at all. We do have a pitch and it's the pitch of what we're involved in. The thing that Pound so admired in Eliot was that he could contain certain jokes, which Pound really never could. In this Pound is not modern in temperament. If he could have seen a few jokes he would hardly have been enthusiastic about Mussolini; you have to take a second look at your hero to see the joke. Now, it's only if you *have* your hero; if it's not your hero, then there's no joke.

Q.   Some critics have suggested that the reader can skip the difficult parts of your poems.

A.   I've asked people writing essays on my poetry to approach the question of the several natures of the reading difficulty. They should ask two questions: "What do you imagine were your reading difficulties?" and "What do you imagine would be a reader's reading difficulties?" In general, a reader's reading difficulties will exceed your own. Well, let's just take the difficulty of reference. Why does Dante come into it? Why in my conversation do I presume that we know something about *Paradise Lost*? I come in heavy over and over again on Milton because Milton was disallowed by Ezra Pound from the main track of poetry, so in general I'm making it impossible for us to read Duncan without both Ezra Pound and Milton. Now, that forces Ezra Pound into a different court and it forces Milton into a different court, but it also forces a whole track of poetry into a different one. It was one Charles Olson would not accept; and Williams attacked Eliot for coming back to Milton, but Eliot came back to Milton to put a memorial on top of him. That's not the way I think of my Milton: my Milton is news, not memorial. Not commemorated anywhere. I do not commemorate with my texts, although I revere, I adore, I do a series of things. But I want the reader to be involved with my primary experience. And my primary experience has been not only in Milton or Dante, but also out in the novels of Charles Williams and in Pindar, a bit of a novel, of a thriller, I think it's still read as a thriller. I'm not talking about big stuff. And in Jess's mystery canvases we find Crazy Cat, which most people read as a cartoon, but that's not the way it's being seen. So it is a conglomerate.

Q.   Could you explain your use of that term?

A.   Dodds, in *The Greeks and the Irrational,* speaks of our crisis as being whether we carry a conglomerate. He sees the whole Greek civilization as having collapsed because it could not carry its conglomerate. And he says there's no guarantee that a civilization can necessarily carry its conglomerate; if it fails to, then it collapses. It knows the conglomerate is there, and it is no longer carrying it. And you get really serious rifts. The thing that bolsters all of the Baroque, the decision that Milton made, for instance, is contained in the *Areopagitica* in its insistence that truth is there throughout, and in everything it needs all occasions. That he keeps firm—that its occasion will be found even in things you would want to censor. So you need pornography, you need every part of the range, and Milton doesn't imagine that he's encompassing the range. He's supplying something that's needed, not at the center; it needs Milton, but he is not the artist encompassing the range. Shakespeare is building a world; Milton does not. He builds a stage set like Jonson, and the line from Ben Jonson to Milton is a much more sensible line and an actual one. And Blake is not building a world; he's in the same line as Ben Jonson and Milton.

Q.   It's interesting that you used the word "rifts," the same word that Denise Levertov used to describe the jumps one must make in poetry.

A.   Oh, yes; and rifts enter my poems. "The Continent," for instance, with its idea of the movement of masses going back to form a single continent.

Q.   And since we're trying to avoid the rifts that you suggest ruin any society not coping with the conglomerate, are the rifts in your poems micro-earthquakes to avoid the actual earthquake?

A.   No, they incorporate rifts as information of the conglomerate, as a way of containing the conglomerate. The *Cantos* had for me the promise of a way the conglomerate would be carried. And I see myself, by the way, as still carrying that conglomerate, so that when an actual poetic genius arrives at the place, it will be there. In other words, so far there is no synthesis of this conglomerate; that's one thing we don't have at all. So the collage actually carries it more adequately; its aesthetics reveal that it can be quite vivid for us. Cubism showed us that we can carry what we thought were contradictory elements in a large composition; but a composition means it's in your mind.

Q.   In developing your technique of the collage, were you influenced by what Jess Collins was doing?

A.   Well, his technique of collage has grown, along with my concepts of collage in poetry, since 1950, and in the big leap forward in his collaging period he incorporates many kinds of sources and materials and all of them have content reference, which many collages don't have in a polysemous sense. That's the same period as *Letters* and *Caesar's Gate,* when we were in Mallorca. And *Caesar's Gate* begins to be complex collaging, and during the build-up years of *The Opening of the Field* and especially *Passages* we talked about what was going on in assemblage and collage. And our general life style is collage. We don't have a decor in our house; we have an assemblage of objects which have one core of sentiment. A perfect example of the conglomerate—one of the efforts of modernism, which emerged as a style—was that it thought if it disposed of nineteenth-century sentiment, sentimentality as it began to appear, if it could just rip the nineteenth century away from itself, it could then form a conglomerate of *pure* elements, functional elements. And actually critics very soon found that *A Portrait of the Artist* is a nineteenth-century work, filled with aesthetic sentiments, so it wasn't modernist in this sense, and they began to observe that about *Ulysses*.

Q.   Is this true of Pound also?

A.   Pound never accepted that he wasn't a modernist, but his critics could see he wasn't. He was sentimental, a troubadour; he was a pure product of having read William Morris and so forth. Well, our conglomerate is not just a contemporary conglomerate. Our conglomerate is our feeling of continuity through time. And it is that which makes our predicament: a point of collapse can be shown to happen after Dante, because Dante doesn't start a Christian culture; he contains the conglomerate at a point when you couldn't believe it could be contained. After him it can't be contained again ever. He contains the conglomerate at a point when the evidence of the Albigensian Crusade was so bloody that you couldn't contain what was called Christendom. But what he did was not a typical medieval poem at all, and it's hard to place it in either the Middle Ages or the Renaissance. But in his imagination it occupied an entire time: it admitted all he knew of the pagan or pre-Christian world. And spacewise it admitted the Moslem world into its theological level; it wasn't *theologically* significant, although it may have been heretically. It was *compositionally* significant, because he made a collage (or assemblage of elements) in the Moslem world of the identity of God that was intolerable unless it was a collage to be in or to enter into the Christian theology. And yet, of course, this is a rather closed picture; the real assemblages of our time would be like *Howl,* where we've got Buddhism going along with Judaism. I find this phenomenon in many directions. Where I would differ from Ginsberg is that I see it not as that kind of amalgam, but for me in the poem it's experienced entirely as a compositional amalgam. I'm not that concerned about my spirit or soul, that's quite true.

Q.   I want to take you back to something you've said about language. In *The Truth & Life of Myth* you write: "In the world of saying and telling . . . , there is a primary trouble, a panic that can still come upon me where the word no longer protects, transforming the threat of an overwhelming knowledge into the power of an imagined reality . . . , but exposes me more." Does this mean that it's good that the language no longer protects and that it lets in more experience?

A.   No; it's just the very nature of it. You proceed along the line
of excitement, certainly drawn into the art initially by a series of
lures. Among them is one quite analogous with one's entrance into
falling in love and sexuality, in which an energy appears and then an
excitement which exceeds the one which you encompass in your
personality, so you are transcendent—transcendent in its whole
context. In general, in falling in love you feel identical with the
universe, so the entire scene changes all the way to the horizon. It's
the same thing being in love in the language, but all of those states
are perilous. Always the quarrel with being in love is your domesticated imagined reality, which is within the bounds of the actual. Our
word "suffer" struck me first in John Dewey; as a pragmatist, when
he's talking about experience, he talks about "suffering" something,
"suffering" joy, "suffering" grief. We suffer, so we're in John
Dewey-land; and you'd think a pragmatist was far removed from this
scene. Every bit of what we call experience is the Cross. Every bit of
actual experiencing is passional, and Dewey is not a Neo-Platonist,
who disapproved of passions. Kathleen Raine wants to make Blake
vote for the Neo-Platonists; it won't work, because Blake is entirely a
passional artist. And yet passional is not a pure position at all. It
threatens every level of your imagined reality, and the imagination is
not passional in its nature.

Q.   But you're attracted by that threat?

A.   Plotinus' is a sublime imagination, as if the imagination could
occupy all of creation, and I find it abhorrent and attractive. So the
lure is mixed. You go into a poem, and it promises more of you than
you know of, and a you more true to yourself, but it must promise
that to the reader as well. There's an opening in language in which
I'm going to be able to exist. But that opening is also an opening into
perilous difficulties which you don't quite feel at first. My poems are
all hopelessly inadequate. My early poems, of course, are in every
occasion hopelessly inadequate. In the beginning you think that they
ought to become adequate. Finally, in my case that's not what's at
issue; it's knowing what's happening, not its adequacy to a situation.
And to know what's happening in a poem is not to drive or control it,
but to know where it is, and the *where it is* is the condition of it.
And you almost sense it by the dread in every situation. My concept
of the minimum of the poem is a place where the complete poem is
happening, and in that place it apprehends and contributes to every

other minimum in the poem. So the total poem remembers all its parts and doesn't have the factor of going from one place to another. As you move from line 1 to line 2, line 2 begins not to have every opportunity in the world, because everything in line 1 is there. It's a decreasing series of opportunities, so it's coming into our imagined domesticity. It's increasingly domesticated. But it's also, because it's going along the line of risk, increasingly endangered. I do not picture any domestic situation—unless it was sound asleep—as not being more and more at the pitch of this dread. Why does it increase? Otherwise after twenty-five or twenty-six years we would not be more filled with protections against that dread, but we would have to let them go and be living rather habitually. Maybe we are.

Q.   You're saying that your poems need to go into a place where the word no longer protects?

A.   As the poem really gets there, the word doesn't protect at all. In the original lure you thought there might be something—the word promises. I think the poem is entirely a protective form. The realization of form that's in the poem is analogous to the use of a pentagram in magic, where you're going to call up demonic powers. You measure accurately and you close all the things and you have more and more complicated features of the poem to cover its situation. But I'm talking here, of course, about proposing a poetry that's going to be more open. If you open rifts and you still conceive that you're in this territory of suffering the situation of the poem, you are opening up rifts that you *have* to suffer for. They must be part of the lure of the poem. Of course, it is for me. The rifts are not merely open because I'm bored by going, or I *see,* but because I'm tremendously aware that what I see is not the only thing that's there. There's a reply from a Hasidic master; students ask, "Why don't you write, master?" And he says, "Because whenever I open my mouth to say anything, the world floods in and drowns me." And I say, "Yes, brother." Now that's the rift part of it—the world. You've got to be flooded by the world, and yet, more and more, *how* to be flooded by the world becomes the question of the artist.

An Interview with Jerzy Kosinski On *Blind Date*

*Conducted by Daniel J. Cahill**

Jerzy Kosinski's most recent novel, *Blind Date*, (1977) is a chilling examination of the adventures of George Levanter, a free spirit who recognizes that destiny is written concurrent with event, not prior to it. In this interview Kosinski expands upon the idea of what it means to become a personal "event" in a modern society that insists upon a predestined future.

Q.   In various places, you have stated that your previous five novels constitute a cycle—a special exploration of society and the individual's capacity or incapacity to survive in modern civilization. Do you still view your previous fiction as a cycle and is that cycle completed with *Cockpit*? Is the reader to interpret your most recent novel, *Blind Date*, as a continuation or a redirection of the cycle?

A.   Although each novel of this cycle reflects and comments upon the motifs of the others, only *The Painted Bird* and *Cockpit* concern themselves with its full archetypal spectrum. In *The Painted Bird* society refuses the individual (the Boy) a place within itself by waging a war against him; in *Cockpit*, it is the individual (Tarden) who, refusing the place society insists he occupy, wages a war against the institutions of society.

Blind Date is a redirection of these previous concerns; here the modern character George Levanter is engaged in the Socratic quest— one's obligation to examine and assume responsibility for *one's own*

---
* The interview took place on September 22, 1977, in New York City.

actions regardless of the societal framework in which they occur. Whereas in *Cockpit* Tarden is preoccupied with the impact of his own camouflage on others who either accept or reject his altered truth (and so does *Cockpit* as a novel), in *Blind Date* George Levanter reveals his unfulfilled longing to be able to examine one single human being, one single truth at a time. *Blind Date* examines the concerns of George Levanter. The question posed by Socrates, about righteousness and sacrilege "with respect to murder and to everything else," is at the core of *Blind Date*.

Q.   Do you view *Blind Date* as a radically different novel—in intent, structure, philosophical impact—from *Cockpit?*

A.   Yes, I can repeat after Browning that "my stress lay in the incidents in the development of a soul: little else is worth study." The development of the soul of George Levanter in *Blind Date* is of a different sort than that of Tarden in *Cockpit* or, let's say, the hero of *Steps*. Tarden perceives and lives his life as if it were a cumulative process. In *Cockpit's* opening sentence he sets up his predicament: "Although we have known each other for a long time . . . ," and the novel continues as a confessional *summa* of Tarden. To Levanter, life is composed of moments, each one commencing with one's awareness of its beginning. *Blind Date* opens with "When he was a schoolboy, George Levanter had learned a convenient routine," but for the rest of his life Levanter will rebel against routine. In *Cockpit*, it is Tarden's language, his narration that is the sole dramatic agent that recasts what the protagonist claims had been his life's experiences. In *Blind Date*, objectively narrated events of Levanter's life provide the novel's outward expression.

Q.   You have used two mottoes—one from Jonathan Swift and one from Jacques Monod. First, can you comment on the Swift quotation: "Remove me from this land of slaves. . . ." Who are the slaves and fools in *Blind Date?*

A.   To Swift, the land of slaves and fools meant Ireland. To George Levanter, it is Eastern Europe, the land of totalitarian oppression that he had left behind. Swift, by the way, has always been among my favorite writers, a master role creator with a universal imagination, able to comprehend and to portray the totality of societal forces that condition men's daily lives and thoughts. The author "reports" to the reader what George Levanter, like Captain Lemuel Gulliver, has

seen and done—in "the land of pygmies and in the land of giants"—
and he does it as a storyteller who claims to have had no share in what
he tells. His stress is on the characters and on the incidents, his
language simple and evocative enough for the average reader, and
his vision "the art of seeing things invisible" (Swift).

Q.   With respect to the Jacques Monod quotation, I know (as you
make clear in the novel) that he was a warm and affectionate friend, a
man whose mind and ideas you valued greatly. What special force or
shadow does he cast over *Blind Date?*

A.   Like Jonathan Swift, Jacques Monod is a historical figure and
his philosophical work *Chance and Necessity* (1970) is, like Swift's, a
historical document written by one of the greatest scientists of this
century. [Jacques Monod received the 1965 Nobel Prize in physiolo-
gy and medicine for demonstrating how the living cell manufactures
the substance of life.] The scientific discoveries of Monod and of
other biologists led him to postulate a fundamental theory that there
is no plan in nature, that destiny is written concurrently with each
event in life, not prior to it, and that to guard against this powerful
feeling of destiny should be the source of our new morality. George
Levanter, the hero of *Blind Date*, is dissatisfied with Marxism because he feels betrayed by the Soviet society that preaches "objective
destiny," proclaiming, in a travesty of scientific discourse, that Marxism offers access to the "scientifically" established "objective" laws
of history which man has no choice but to obey, and that the State
and the Communist Party have a moral duty to enforce at any cost to
the population. Thus, Levanter embraces Monod's scientific postulate that forces man to acknowledge his isolation, to utilize each
moment of his life as it passes rather than to dismiss it as a minor
incident in a larger passage or zone of time. This philosophy, derived
from and based on modern science, presupposes an ethic which bases
moral responsibility upon that very freedom of choice an individual
exercises in each instance of his life, an instance being dictated
entirely by chance, and not by necessity.

Levanter's friendship with Monod is merely a consequence of
Levanter's profession: he is a successful small investor whose activities are not limited to one country or any particular field or endeavor.
In the course of his life he has met and been befriended by many men
of accomplishment—Jacques Monod among them.

Q.   While all of your fictional work has contained intermittent autobiographical elements, these were always submerged or welded to the dramatic episodes of the novel. *Blind Date* strikes me as more frankly autobiographical. Is this a fair representation of the novel?

A.   *Blind Date* is neither less nor more autobiographical than my other novels. The inclusion of "real life" characters—Lindbergh, Jacques Monod, Stalin's daughter, the U. S. Secretary of State, the Soviet poet, the victims of the Manson murders—makes the novel in my eyes more, not less imaginative and perhaps less "subjective." In any case, these "real life" heroes are no more or less real than the novel's other "real life" characters: President Samael of Lotan, the Arab diplomat, Impton's Chief of Police, Mme Ramoz, the beautiful wife of the President of the Republic of Deltazur, J. P., the tragically punished greatest saber-fencer of all time, the corrupt court officials from Indostran, the Foxy Lady, the henchmen from PERSAUD, Weston of Pacific and Central. They all inhabit together the imaginative space of the novel that, by its nature, abolishes the ranking of "real-unreal."

The so-called "historical figures"—Lindbergh, Monod, the Manson killers—influence the way we perceive ourselves in a society, our moral and ethical values, our concept of justice, our fear of evil. And don't they influence us pretty much the same way fictional characters do—Hamlet, Robinson Crusoe, the Brothers Karamazov, Julien Sorel? Like World War II in *The Painted Bird*, television in *Being There*, or the financial trust in *The Devil Tree*, the "real life" personages of *Blind Date* only reinforce for the reader the novel's "objective referrals," providing the general climate for the personal story of George Levanter, the American small investor.

Q.   As a novelist, are you concerned that your reader will or should recognize these passages as actual elements in the life of Jerzy Kosinski?

A.   Whatever the reader "recognizes" in the act of reading the novel belongs, by virtue of his imagination, to *him*, not to the author. By its very nature language fictionalizes our "real" experience. To me, "recognition" by the reader—the semiconscious power of projection into another time, place, and identity—is fiction's foremost principle.

The stress on "what's autobiographical" in fiction (as opposed to what's imaginative) so dear to our popular culture has, in my view, its source in the Hollywood-made preoccupation with the life of the actor (as opposed to his ability to portray various roles). The popular culture shifts the source of celebrity from talent to that of simple visibility. Such attitudes applied to imaginative fiction simply mean its death.

Aiming for the greatest involvement on the part of their audience, Shakespeare, Swift, Milton, and Browning already realized the importance of the literary manipulation of masks, identities, inherited historical scenarios, dramatization—and the protective characterization of the authorial persona.

Q.   Few readers will know of your fateful escape in the Sharon Tate murders. Your account of that murder scene in *Blind Date* is both real and personal drama. Can you say how your dramatization of this tragedy served your novelistic intentions?

A.   Popular culture "immortalized," of course, the murderers—they are the best-selling heroes—not so their victims. My preoccupation has been with the victims. In *Steps*, published shortly before the Tate tragedy, I wrote: "many of us could easily visualize ourselves in the act of killing but few could project ourselves in the act of being killed in any manner. We did our best to understand the murder: the murderer was a part of our lives; not so the victim."

The victims of Manson typify, to me, the terrifying randomness of our modern existence. By including the fateful encounter of the victims with their killers, I wish the reader to be able to visualize, to recreate an atmosphere of serenity, peace, and prosperity brutally invaded by a gang of murderers who come to the house by chance to kill everyone in it.

Q.   There are certain sexual scenes in *Blind Date*—the rape of Nameless, the highly graphic and violent sexual episodes with Jolene, the bizarre encounter with Foxy Lady—these are all graphically intense scenes in which Levanter imposes his will on another person. Is he a dramatization of Monod's criminal without a definable crime?

A.   The only instances in which Levanter imposes on another person took place when he was a boy (the rape of Nameless) and a student (the kidnapping of Robot, the girl from China). He was willing to suffer the legal consequences for the first act, but the authorities refused to believe he was the rapist. Robot, of course, never felt abused by the two men: she had long before lost her capacity to acknowledge her self.

As a mature man, Levanter is increasingly given to acts on behalf of others—Weston, the shareholders, PERSAUD, the tortured intellectuals, Mme Ramoz, the imprisoned journalists, and many others. Even killing the hotel clerk is not only an act of revenge for what was done to J. P. the fencer and to countless other unsuspecting visitors from behind the Iron Curtain, but a way of breaking the chain of further denunciations and misery for them (as it was with getting rid of Barbatov, Levanter's Commander in the Army).

Even when Levanter is blackmailed and used—by Jolene, his out-of-town blind date, by Impton's Chief of Police, by Serena—he does not respond with malice. He makes no attempt at revenge—as soon as he is free, he merely steps away.

Q.   In an echo of *Being There*, George Levanter frequently acts as an invisible assailant in an atmosphere of nameless, faceless violence. Is *Blind Date* a warning against this future of violence?

A.   If *Blind Date* contains such a warning, it is not against our future but our present. It is a warning that, given the staggering proportions of violence in our society, life is, at best, uncertain—we might not live through the very next moment, our next blind date, so to speak.

Q.   One function of your fiction is to prompt "awareness" of self and the world. Today we see the fantastic popularity of "guides" for living, such as *Your Erroneous Zones,* and "religious literature": they are outstripping the usual top-ten best sellers. All of these books seek a continuity of human experience and they all represent a tremendous "search" for "totality of experience."

A.   In the parlance of popular culture, "totality of experience" is simply another label for a sort of popular religion, which is to people who feel lost in the midst of the so-called free economy what a Soviet version of Marxism is to the masses hopelessly locked behind the Iron Curtain. The popular religion's elements are all there: one's destiny is somehow "predictable"; just as one's life can be psychologically computerized, one's destiny can also be predicted, or, at least, "not escaped." For me, this trend represents a further repression of the development of an awareness of life as it happens in each of its moments, and that man must treat each of those moments as unique.

But, I guess, the society of parrot-like trained "consumerists" demands an easy assertion of the continuity of its psychological "spending" habits, emotional "investment" routines, sexual "wheeling-dealings"—briefly, a Master Charge attitude to life.

Q.   One of your critics has commented that the figures in your fiction have "a great capacity for barbarism" such as Levanter seems to possess. Yet he is also guided by contrary impulses—friendship, concern, affection.

A.   This is the kind of frivolous judgment that spokesmen for our Pollyannaized popular culture easily dispense against literature that portrays our everyday physical and moral reality, thus threatening their propagation of happy-go-lucky, life-banalizing philosophy, without which our rampant consumerism could not flourish. What consumerism needs more than anything else is the idea of the predetermined, predictable life that obviously invites predetermined investing and buying. Thus, popularization of the notion of a central plot to one's life does, to a degree, encourage the philosophy of the installment plan, long-term credit-based investing. . . .

A serious novelist's effort to confront a reality that is anything but rosy is quickly labeled "morbidity," "pornographic imagination," "lonely rituals." My novels and I get our share of such labeling. In most cases, though, such reviewers are not really critics; they are, rather, "cultural Kapos." They don't bother to examine the novel's (and the author's) point-of-view, they simply reprimand; they denounce, and all they seem to miss is an opportunity to kill his vision and put the writer in jail. Their counterparts in Eastern Europe do just that. . . .

To me, a serious novelist's task has always been to take society to task: he is no more answerable to his critics than to his publishers, family, lovers, or neighbors—he is answerable to the plausibility of his vision, to his construction of dramatic imaginative reality that intensifies readers' awareness and confronts the very areas steadily deadened by the popular culture, which, in its essence, is fundamentally hostile to man's real aspirations, fears, and joys. Thus, imaginative literature not only dramatizes life; above all, it enhances man's ability to perceive his own condition for what it is: a drama of which he is the protagonist, but a drama of particular, clearly delineated moments. Each moment is his blind date.

Q.   In the parlance of American dating patterns, a blind date is generally an innocent and harmless affair—two people brought together by well-meaning friends. Perhaps you will elaborate on your title and its implications in the novel?

A.   In Aristotle's terms, the most moving elements in human tragedy are *peripeteia* and *anagnorisis:* the first can be freely interpreted as working in blindness to one's own defeat; the second, the opening of the eyes. The American "blind date" is, philosophically, a complex invitation to both. It presupposes an invitation relying on chance; it postulates a willingness to go through an encounter arranged by a "third party" (who is, even if for a short moment, placed in charge of the destiny of the two other people who are about to meet); it reveals optimism—a belief that "the unknown" other might, in fact, become our "partner"—and also the fact of our isolation—a human need for an encounter, even with a stranger. . . .

Jacques Monod once told me that *Blind Date* would have been a perfect title for his philosophical book, with "An Essay on Chance and Necessity" as its subtitle. But the French don't go on blind dates; they don't have a corresponding phrase for it either. For that matter, only Americans seem to have the blind date custom—and because nobody else does, I have to come up now with another title for my novel in foreign languages. So far, the Dutch, French, and Germans will call it *The Unknown Partner.*

Q.   How is the reader to respond to the central character, George Levanter? Is he a creator of values or is he a clever opportunist who preys upon, and is preyed upon in return by, others?

A.   A reader must "decode" George Levanter on his own terms. After all, Levanter's acts are open to the reader's scrutiny and they invite moral judgment, which is implicit in any encounter—whether with a fictional protagonist or with a neighbor next door. The novel is written in the third person, past tense—the "tragic tense." If Levanter was happy, he is no more; if he was unfulfilled, he can't relive his life better. This stance places the reader in a relatively superior position: unlike Levanter, he can still attempt to be master of his character, of his "moment," and thus, to a degree, of his fate. In terms of my own reading of *Blind Date*, I can't see anything in the novel that would suggest George Levanter is "a clever opportunist." Rather, many incidents suggest that he is a true, self-appointed protestant.

If in life we're finally betrayed by what is false within, then I perceive George Levanter as free from such falsehoods—a man who, having learned some harsh lessons in his boyhood during World War II and as an adolescent in Stalinist Russia, has emerged greatly concerned with moral issues. As a small investor active in America, George Levanter is a classic "permanent reformer," preoccupied with counteracting social injustice. That's why he executes the hotel clerk and blows up the henchmen of PERSAUD, and why he exposes abuses of political power. He is aware and critical of the fraud and sterility implicit in the concept of morality perpetrated by the popular culture.

Q.   I have tested the ending of your novel on several readers— some were merely puzzled, some felt Levanter drifted in his mind and died on the cold ledge—a final blind date. Does Levanter "sell himself for naught"? Does his death become useless because he has exceeded the limits?

A.   Levanter dies with an image of a boy who wanted to hear the end of the story that Levanter had started to tell him. But the boy's American divorcée mother and her British suitor disapproved of the stories Levanter was telling the child, "an old experienced sinner instructing a young beginner. . . ." That's from Swift. Thus, perhaps Levanter feels his life—if its lesson cannot or will not be conveyed— has been wasted: "And since thy essence on thy breath depends / Thus with a puff the whole delusion ends." Swift again!

Q.   The reader of your novel is directed by the general flow and sequence, yet the novel dislocates time: for example, on page 92 we read, "It was Levanter's fifteenth Christmas in his new country." In a different episode in the same chapter, we read, "A few years after Levanter's arrival in America." What artistic purpose or authorial intent is served by keeping two or more time-frames operating?

A.   The novel has the order of a painting or a work of music. Its order is both circular and spiral, corresponding to the different parts of Levanter's memory. Its philosophical basis is the chance selectivity and randomness of our memory and our inability to say why we remember certain events and not others; and our reluctance to look for the principle of such ranking. The randomness of one's memory is an indication that unless each moment of life can be assisted by an emotional awareness of it, the moment simply flows in the stream of lost time. Perhaps one's personal history is indeed mainly the creation of others; perhaps we have been trained to see ourselves as we have been—not as we are. Unless one is consciously armed with a philosophy to undo this, a philosophy which refuses the notion of natural preordaining, one becomes entrapped in the best-selling notions of one's own predictability. The current fad of popular culture is selling the alleged predictability of life's patterns as opposed to the proven unpredictability of life's moments. This leaves man at odds with himself: he remains maladjusted and he waits hopelessly for the newest "maladjustment correction course." With a true sense of the randomness of life's moments, man is at peace with himself— and that peace is happiness.

An Interview with Angus Wilson

Conducted by Betsy Draine*

Angus Wilson is one of the great men of letters of our time. A distinguished critic, literary biographer, and playwright, he is now firmly recognized as one of the major novelists to emerge in England since World War II. In November 1979, when this interview took place, Wilson was on lecture tour in the Midwest, teaching at the University of Minnesota, enjoying unrestrained critical acclaim in the U. S. press for his third critical biography of a novelist, and working on his eighth novel. At 65, he seemed to be at an intensely creative moment in his career.

A chaotic childhood with a histrionic but lovable family instilled in Wilson a lifelong delight in passion, commotion, and verbal fireworks—a predilection that is directly reflected in the worlds of his novels. After irregular early schooling, due to his family's many wanderings, Wilson successfully studied medieval history at Merton College, Oxford. Upon graduation, however, he found himself restless in a series of jobs as a tutor, secretary, social organizer, caterer, and restauranteur. In 1936 he settled at last as a staff member at the British Museum, where he rose to become the Deputy Superintendant of the Reading Room, without ever quite finding fulfillment in the work. It was not until 1955 that he resigned to become a full-time writer.

Since in his early stories he dealt directly and often satirically with social themes, Wilson was early labeled a neo-realist. Although he at first accepted the label, he later stated—and he reiterates here—

---

* The interview took place on November 3, 1979, when Angus Wilson lectured at the University of Wisconsin, Madison.

270

that his realism is always leavened by an extravagant invention characteristic of his nineteenth-century mentors Zola, Dickens, and Kipling. (He has written biographies of all three novelists: *Emile Zola* [1952], *The World of Charles Dickens* [1970], and *The Strange Ride of Rudyard Kipling* [1977].) The fantastical element in his work has steadily grown over the years. His second and third novels, the widely acclaimed *Anglo-Saxon Attitudes* (1956) and *The Middle Age of Mrs. Eliot* (1958), do rely somewhat on the play of unlikely coincidence and exaggerated caricature, but the action focuses mainly on central characters who are given psychological depth and significant connection to a specific social milieu which Wilson is at pains to endow with the authority of history. The next novel, *The Old Men at the Zoo* (1961), took him into less safe but more exciting territory; there Wilson authenticates a material and social world through the devices of the realist while at the same time allowing the irrational forces of emotion and imagination to seize power over the text at the apocalyptic crisis of the plot. His brilliant execution of this technical feat was a crucial turning point in his career. Since then he has steadily pushed the limits of his basically realist narrative form in ways that are often as exciting for their subtlety and finesse as the radical violations of more experimental novelists.

During the interview, especially when speaking of his new novel, Wilson was fired with the energy of a man twenty years his junior. He is in person as vibrant, as startlingly dramatic, and as responsive to the moment as his own best work.

Q.   Your publication of *The World of Charles Dickens* in 1970 was a broad hint to critics that Dickens has been very important to you as a novelist. What makes him such a touchstone for you?

A.   I think he uses all the things that we have, you see. Joyce says what a debt he owes to Dickens. Proust says he owes to Dickens—and especially to the beginning of *David Copperfield*—his whole treatment of memory. And I think he was the father of the nontraditional novel—not of the Jamesian novel, but of the expressionist, theatrical novel. The first thing I did when I became a writer, when I did a radio talk, was an attack on Virginia Woolf, and that was in part because I felt that those Bloomsbury people had simply failed to see that there was this other whole strand in the Victorian novel. Dickens, Dostoevsky, Zola, this whole thing is something quite other than what Bloomsbury admired. I'm not now *against* the

Jamesian novel—I admire it very greatly—but this theatrical, Dickensian novel is something totally different, which I believe much more leads into Joyce and to contemporary possibilities for the novel.

Q.   And to your own work? The phrase "this theatrical, Dickensian novel" seems to fit your novels. I think of *As If By Magic, No Laughing Matter,* and *The Old Men at the Zoo.* Do you feel your work to have that Dickensian quality?

A.   What I want to have is the theatrical flair—an opera going on upstage with ballets behind—and the capacity to endow the stage with scenery, to give movement across both the main opera and the little ballets also. For example, for me the wonderful thing about *Bleak House* is that you have this vertical line right through society from Sir Leicester Dedlock right down to the little boy who "don't know nothink," which is Jo. And that's the practical thing. Then there's the story which goes across this vertical, social line—Lady Dedlock's story, ending in Tom-All-Alone's. This is the long, the horizontal narrative. And then, behind, as I say, are all these ballet people—Mr. Turveydrop and Mrs. Jellyby and Mr. Skimpole. Even when the book is ended, one knows that Mr. Turveydrop is still doing his dance, still walking along Regent Street and saying, "Of course, that's where the good Prince Regent spoke to me, you know." And Mrs. Jellyby is still writing letters to the Borrioboola-Gha mission, and Mr. Skimpole is still saying, "Money? Why I have no idea of money." This is to me the way in which the world is constituted. Another marvelous thing in that book is the use of the inner voice, Esther, and Dickens' own narrative omniscient voice. He doesn't finally succeed with this mixture, but of course it is very early on in such things. But when one thinks of the experiment of that! And the way the camera comes in and down on the city at the beginning. . . .

Q.   That wonderful theatricality is a quality I admire in your fiction. Have you always had a flair for the dramatic, or did you work consciously to achieve it?

A.   This is a quality that I have from my family. Daydreaming, stories, mockery, build-up, theatricalities, scenes—all this I live over a very great deal from my family time. Let me give you an example: My father used to run through his own money very quickly. He didn't ever do anything in the way of work, but he had a small income. My mother had more, and he used to run through her income as well. He would forge her name on a check or he would run up bills, and then there would be a terrible row. He was a very keen games-player and had a tennis bag. He would put a pair of socks into a tennis bag and he would shut the tennis bag and he would say, "I'm never coming back to this bloody house again. I don't intend to be talked to in this kind of way. Christ almighty, if my mother were still alive." And off he would go. My mother would turn to the cook and she'd say (we always seemed to manage to maintain a cook, God knows how, but we did, and we had a cook): "He's never going to come back. I'm sure he won't come back again. He'll never come back." And the cook would always say, "Oh, Madam, I think he will. You go and have a rest. That's what you should do." And then she would quickly make some bovril, and my father would slip into the house as if no one saw him, like a naughty boy, and she'd say, "Oh, Mr. Johnstone, nice you are back. Mistress will be pleased. There's some bovril there that I've made for you." Well, now, my brothers used to mock this. They were then fourteen, sixteen, seventeen, eighteen. They used to act this out. One day I, aged about six or seven, with the cook there, I said, "Oh, Cook, he's never coming back. I know he won't come back." And she said to me, "You, don't you talk like that. You'll be lucky if you ever have anyone as fond of you as they are of each other." But that didn't stop me from acting the scene out again. This is very important, indeed, to my writing, because this kind of thing, this kind of habitual play, is that thing that I call "the ballet," which is what makes me love Dickens so much. The narrative runs along in front, like a grand opera, and behind are the minor but wonderful characters doing perpetual little ballet dances. In my own writing, my characters do their little "bits" all the time, behind the narrative. This comes out of that part of my life in which there were little habitual scenes, the same habitual scenes acted again and again.

These were real scenes of suffering and shame that my parents went through, and the cumulative effect on them was terrible, but you certainly could say that they were play-acting as they went on. There's one great family riot scene I always have in my mind—all the family rowing. I must have been about six. My oldest sister-in-law was there and my youngest brother, then about nineteen. He was a very hysterical person, and I remember he took the planter pot and shook it over my sister-in-law's head and said, I thought, "You trumpet, you trumpet!" For years and years I wondered when she was going to actually play this trumpet. She never seemed to do so.

But I remember that as this was going on, my brother kicking his legs up in the air in a sort of hysteric state, my mother came in. She hadn't been in on the act, so to speak. She came right up to where he was and naturally got kicked in the shin. She then turned to my father and said, "You can sit there and see your own son kick his mother?" Now she had a role.

Q.   These family scenes and the dramatic energy in them are, then, a source of your own peculiar genius as a novelist. You have many characters who seem to have an analogous fund of creative energy from their childhoods but who become thwarted in some way and who fall into a terrible apathy. Why is this pattern so prevalent in your novels?

A.   In my life I have seen people whose creative powers were thwarted. They either become apathetic or they become marionettish-mimetic, with a kind of jiggling, continuous liveliness that really doesn't create anything. That's perhaps the kind of feeling I wanted to give in *No Laughing Matter* with all six of the children. One asks oneself about those children, What are they doing there even after the parents are dead? They're still playing the childhood game when they're re-ordering the house in London. The whole point of it is that they were people who really had never lived down properly their childhood. Margaret's career as a novelist was very serious to her, and Marcus certainly wanted to be a benevolent industrialist in Morocco, and Quentin intended to be a serious journalist, and so on, but somewhere or other—and here we come back again to this old thing—they're doing their little "dances" all the time, and when they come together they do the same dance that they did as children. They long to recreate that happiness which had been there, but which was never expressed, because although the characters of Billy Pop and the Countess in their own way attracted people, they them-selves were totally childish and thus prevented any of the real happiness that could have been made for the children. So the children are forever trying to reenact that past. Even right through to the end there they are, not totally fulfilled, not totally taken up into their own careers, because their creative energies have all been withered away in this continual reenactment of the past. So they are like "Here we go round the mulberry bush."

Q.   I see that pattern also in Inge of *Anglo-Saxon Attitudes* and in David Parker of *The Middle Age of Mrs. Eliot.*

A.   This is quite true. David is a very good example of the fixation on childhood. I love puns. All the early stories are named for ironic puns, and I'm still doing this with the new work, *Setting the World on Fire.* And with David, it's not for nothing that he runs a nursery and that he wants his sister Meg to come back and live there with him forever, "back to the nursery." It hasn't really worked with his friend Gordon. It's gone wrong. He thinks Meg's marriage has gone wrong. and in a sense it has. But her failure she takes to be a challenge to move on. I hope it's one of the better moments in my novels when he takes it for granted that she thinks the same and he simply puts his hand back to sort of take her hand and say goodnight, and she isn't there. All these people are playing children, and it's the child in people which I'm terribly concerned with and interested in.

Q.   When you do show people being thwarted, their life energy not being fulfilled, do you tend to see that thwarting happening for consistent reasons?

A.   You mean the same predominating weakness is there. Yes, but I don't like to think that that's too much so, because that would suggest that my characters are all "moralities" and not many-sided human beings. I'm not the one to judge that. It could be that if an adverse judgment were to be made on the psychology of my characters, it would be that there's not enough of the mixture of contradictions that makes up large numbers of people. But I'm not really very sure. Some characters in some modern novels—for example, some of Iris Murdoch's characters (and I admire her work greatly)—seem to be quixotic. She seems almost to have been anxious to make them seem like harlequins. And I don't consciously do that. She may feel, as many other writers have, that she must give to any character a myriad different guises before the character becomes a fully human being. That isn't my experience of people. People certainly are not all of one simple shape. But they do have predominating shapes all the same.

Q.   With your penchant for humor and with your desire to make that playful structure of the novel which you represent in the opera-ballet image, it must be helpful for you to have characters with clearly recognizable identities—in fact, almost the solidity and vibrancy of characters in an opera.

A.   Indeed. Well, this is probably why in *The Old Men at the Zoo* the actual directors of the zoo recognizably stand for one particular standpoint. And I suppose that one could say that the six children in *No Laughing Matter* have a rather concrete character.

Q.   And in this way your work has parallels with the stories of Kipling whose biography you have just published. I've wondered whether your writing *The Strange Ride of Rudyard Kipling* indicates an artistic affinity with him as strong as your affinity with Dickens.

A.   What really excited me about Kipling as I began to read him was that I found somebody who walks on thin ice. I suppose all the writers I really admire see the world in terms of thin ice, and so do I. And his way of dealing with this ever-present danger of life was unexpected to me when I came to look at it, and especially when I came to read *Kim*.

Kipling had an enormous passion for the variety of life, and he saw India as a rich, medieval, Canterbury-pilgrim world. And the reason why he was a star to the New Congress Movement and the liberal approach to India was that he thought that to impose western ideas there was to impose a kind of deadening puritanism upon a country that was rich and alive in itself. Now I think I share something of this. I found extraordinarily fascinating his struggle to express in his works at one and the same time first the excitement and love of life which he undoubtedly felt (and which he evokes partly through his prose style and partly through his use of animals and children) and then the sense of life's continuous and enduring danger. He felt, as I do (and I've talked about this in *The Wild Garden*), the lure of the wild and at the same time the desire to make some point of contact between the wild and the civilized. This concept that he had of a whole group of people, you might call them the professional men of the world (engineers, doctors, soldiers, sailors, district commissioners), being a kind of guardian of this law and order which has to be kept so that the rich and fertile world can continue to work—this is not my view of life, but I've found it a fascinating solution of a problem that presses upon me, as it has done on most English writers: the problem of nature versus civilization, the country versus the city.

Q.   You certainly address this theme in *The Old Men at the Zoo,* and in fact much of what seems to have been an issue for Kipling is also an issue for Simon Carter, the hero of that novel: When does the imposition of a human order on nonhuman life pervert nature?

When does the *failure* to impose a human order open the way to disaster?

A.   Well, there's this terrible fight, you see, between the love of the wild and the free and the natural life and the desire to protect ourselves, which is after all the impetus of civilization. Simon certainly is a man almost destroyed by his need to be a neat administrator—a civilized and civilizing man—and yet he has this passionate feeling for wildlife. And I purposely arranged it so that he goes again and again to observe the badgers in their natural state but he is never able to do so—until he has to kill them for food, and that's when he vomits it all up. And so that book ends on a question mark, as most of my books do. At the end Simon doesn't know whether he is going to survive or not. He's got these two talents—for nature and for civilization—and he has somehow wasted both of them because he couldn't give enough to either of them. Beyond the end of the book, will he choose to be the secretary of the zoo? Will he be able to do what he likes as a naturalist? Will his marriage last? I don't think he knows.

Q.   Was it partly to emphasize the uncertainty of such knowledge that you chose to use the first-person point of view in this novel?

A.   It's the only time I've used the first person, except maybe in the odd short story, and then I think I do use it in one called "More Friend than Lodger," and that's really in order that the woman should give herself away. But in this case it was not so. Yes, my aim here was to suggest the limitedness of human understanding. At the end of the book, when the little boy says, "Do giraffes kill?" Simon says, "I don't know." And he doesn't.

Q.   The handling of the first-person point of view can be a difficult thing in terms of placement of the characters. For example, your critics have differed quite markedly in their interpretations of Simon Carter's final statements. When you are using the first person, are there other technical devices that you attempt to use to make up for the kind of "placement" that authorial comment can provide in a third-person novel?

A.   I think I do purposely leave the moral judgment open. Clearly there is some judgment made, and that is that Simon is a man who is weak and indecisive—one can't say otherwise. But whether that weakness and indecision make him in some ways a better man than the old men at the zoo I don't know. They all too easily thought they knew exactly what was right and they usually were quite wrong in one way or another.

You know, of all my novels *The Old Men at the Zoo* has been the least talked of in England. It is so different from the other work. And then people got the idea—which had a certain truth—that some of the old boys were drawn from the keepers of the library of the British Museum when I'd been there, and so they would say things to me like, "Why, I didn't really like the novel awfully, but you've got the Museum out of your system now, haven't you?"

Q.   Perhaps one of the things people may be more interested in now than when the novel first appeared is the Armageddon image in the book and your wonderful handling of the quasi-fantastic material associated with it. You've said elsewhere that you admire Samuel Richardson because he builds up the details of experience, starting with the mundane but moving slowly toward the bizarre, until all of a sudden you're in a fantastic world and you never know how you got there. You do seem to be following Richardson's model in your building up to the Armageddon scenes.

A.   I feel very strongly about that. However, V.S. Pritchett, whom I greatly respect, reviewed *The Old Men at the Zoo* for *The New Statesman*. There or in an interview later, he said something like: "This is a fascinating book in the old manner, and the directors of the zoo are wonderfully odd characters, but Mr. Wilson fundamentally mistakes the English character if he can suppose that we can ever have—*would* ever have—gladiatorial games of the kind depicted in this novel." But, I'm sorry, Pritchett mistakes the English character—*every* character. Any country could have them.

Q.   I found myself comparing your treatment of the breakdown of British civilization there with the apocalyptic images in Lessing's *The Memoirs of a Survivor* and her *The Four-Gated City*. In her writing I sometimes sense a need for Armageddon to wash away a very painful consciousness which she, the writer, can no longer support and which the characters can no longer support—so that the final scene of destruction provides an image for the obliteration of consciousness, which is as much desired as feared. Your Bobby Falcon says in *The Old Men at the Zoo* that he was rather looking forward to Götterdämmerung. Were you using Bobby Falcon to embody a longing for annihilation that you find to be a common feeling among people today?

A.   I find *myself* divided about the matter. I walk on thin ice, and I pray that the ice will stick, and I think three things: I think how marvelous ordered life is. It allows me to do the things I want to do. Then I think, Oh, if I could only get away from this ordered life to the wild. And then I think, Oh, God help us—the best thing is if we'd all blow up. "A good old, rare old Armageddon!" So, I'm dealing with the appeal of the apocalypse very much in my present novel. It's called *Setting the World on Fire,* and the title does have a reference to Armageddon. The book is about a young man who lives in a house built by Pratt, who was a very good 17th-century architect, and finished off by Vanbrugh with a vast painted ceiling to the great hall, which is the fall of Phaethon. And this little boy from his earliest times made a hero of Phaethon. And it doesn't matter how much people tell him that Jove threw the thunderbolt, and so on. He says, Phaethon had the courage to ride the chariot and that's the thing. He then becomes a theatrical producer and puts on *Richard II:* "And down, down I come like Phaethon." And this is the moment of tragedy but it's noble, it's the great Richard. And then he comes into a world where "setting the world on fire" means something quite different, with terrorists and so on. But there are three sides to me: I'm very much one who could get on quite well having a cup of tea with Mr. Wodehouse. Then there's another side of me which would very much like to be Mowgli with the puma, and there's a third side which could say, "Oh, thank God, at last it's arrived—and out we go!"

Q.   Since you're speaking about your work in progess, *Setting the World on Fire,* I'd like to ask you about the state of contemporary fiction as you see it. What is your attitude toward the experimentalism of many authors writing at present?

A.   The whole obsession with narration and voice and point of view has really gone too far, especially in the university. I do a workshop for writers at the University of Minnesota. The students write stories and we discuss them. Again and again we have a story and they say, "But I don't think I too much see where that voice comes from." And I say, "Well, did you find it effective?" And they say, "Yes, I thought it was marvelous. It came just at the right moment." I say, "Well, so what if it was an armadillo screaming?

What does it matter whose voice it is? It's part of the poetry of the shape of the whole thing." And they go on voice-finding so much and being in such a state about it that it's quite out of proportion. I try to tell the students that television alone has trained people not to look for voices like that. The television uses all sorts of camera angles, voices, mixtures of music and images. The mixture of fantasy and realism is something that the television audience accepts far more easily than many of these students in workshops who feel that in their stories they must know exactly who and where the narrator is at every moment.

Q.   You seem to be saying that excessive ordering can be counterproductive in art. That reminds me of a speech in which you said that it is a mistake to ask art to provide order, especially order for one's own life.

A.   That's what I feel about it, very much so. I do not want to make myself out to be a pure aesthete. That would be quite wrong, as you can see that I'm an old moralist. But the fact remains that I don't believe that you could write novels if all you were was a moralist. Some part of you delights in art for itself—must do, otherwise you would have chosen another means, such as becoming a Sunday school teacher. Equally, on the other hand, if you are part of the community, as I feel myself to be, and a person very much concerned with other people, then I can't imagine that you could leave moral things out of writing altogether. In fact, if you did leave the moral dimension of life untouched, your audience would be most uncomfortable, as they were with Virginia Woolf. I don't believe that the American or English Puritan conscience can ever quite accept her work, because she's one of the only novelists I know of who is not concerned with the moral will. She's concerned with life itself, the enjoyment of life itself, sometimes the agony of it. All that makes for George Eliot's kind of greatness is just not there. People commit suicide, they go through agonies, but it isn't because they are deciding how they should use their will. Nearly always the will is dissolved into the general framework of the people and the relationships between them. And this I find very, very impressive. It couldn't happen with me because I'm too deeply embedded in some kind of will, but there is a side of me which is in sympathy with Woolf. And I do get turned off a certain amount, much though I admire them both, by both George Eliot and Lawrence, in different ways, because of the enormous degree to which they insist on imposing their will on us, especially Lawrence.

Q.   If you feel little sympathy for the novel with a moral purpose, how do you feel about the philosophical novel? If someone were to say of you that you write the novel of ideas, would that upset you?

A.   I'd be very surprised at it. Because for me the novel of ideas means a novel like those of Thomas Mann—a novel in which the ideas or philosophies are overlayed on the top of life, as is commonly the case with Sartre. And I wouldn't want to do that; nor do I think that I actually do do it. If there are ideas in my novels, they are subsumed into the life, I think. But I should say very firmly that I think I'm rather short on—I mean I'm very very poor when it comes to—analytical or philosophical discussion. Abstract thought is very alien to me and anyone who starts asking me what my philosophy is will get me into very deep water and I won't know how to get out of it again. Life in the particular is how I see it very much. It's true that my novels have been concerned with particular themes, and increasingly so, as I take a lot of trouble now about the shaping of them. But I would like to think that the working out, the relating of those themes and of the particular individuals in the situations in the books to any general proposition would be hard to trace, and I wouldn't be able to do it. I have, funnily enough, a lot of friends who are philosophers. I happen to have known Stuart Hampshire and Freddy Ayer and Richard Wollheim very well, but I'm constantly aware that my own thinking is ludicrously pragmatic beside theirs, and I'm constantly aware of it when I'm with intellectuals from Germany or France, because their thinking is so often so very much more abstract.

Q.   If you don't think of yourself as a philosophical novelist, do you see yourself as a social realist?

A.   No, I have never been wholly the realist writer that the public has seen me to be. I have a very good ear, though I say it myself, for dialogue. And dialogue in my short stories and later, but particularly in the short stories, is very exact. People felt this was a sign of neorealism, and also I have a strong sense of the social structure in England, so that was all there. But if you take a story like "Raspberry Jam," which is the very first thing I ever wrote, this couldn't really be called a realist story at all. And the same is true of a great number of my short stories. They are very far from realistic. But the ones that were *liked* seem to be much more realistic. Some of the early stories are very macabre. There's one, I think, called "Mummy to the Rescue" about a very enormous girl, a woman of twenty-five who's underdeveloped like a child. Yes, that faintly fantastical side is there from the start.

So, I don't think I am a social realist. This is why, for example, I infinitely prefer *Kim* to *A Passage to India*. I'm pleased to see the Indians are now doing so. I used to admire Forster's work much more than I do now. Forster has receded from me as a figure. I find *Howard's End* intolerable now. And the terrible patronage in his work so offends me. Forster says that Leonard Bast, the bank clerk, had one happy moment in his life. It was when a Cambridge undergraduate spoke to him in the train. It's so terrible to think that Forster could have supposed that any human being could exist on that basis. And he says about the daughter-in-law, "Dolly was a rubbishy little thing and she knew it." Now no person goes through life knowing they're a rubbishy little thing. What I dislike most is anything which is callous about people. I can be very fierce, but I hope I don't treat people as negligible. If I ever have done that, I'm ashamed of it, because to me that's the most awful thing you can do. You have every right to mock a character and you have every right to abuse him, but you have no right to treat him as though he were not worth putting in the book.

Q.   If that's what you would be most ashamed to have done as a writer, what would you be most proud to have done? What is your most conscious aim as a novelist?

A.   I would like to have produced a novel, more than one, which related individuals to society, but which also related individuals to the poetry of their lives and which intermixed laughter and tears. (This is the Dickensian thing in me.) I also want to find some solution to the connection between what might be called my humanism and my increasing concern for the nonhuman—for artifacts and for animal life, and so on. As I grow older, I'm more turned off from people than I used to be. I like people, but I get very quickly bored with groups of people, whereas I am passionately drawn towards watching bird life and going to look at buildings and so on. Now what is the meaning of this? When I was young, I never looked at buildings or birds or painting or anything like that. There were some parts of my life which had not been fulfilled, and that has come later, and I'm very much interested now. I would like people to feel in my novels they would find the world of people but also the world of things. And I would also like to make scenes live without introducing description in a very Scottian sense. What I want is for people to say, "Your novel seems to be very *total*."

An Interview with A. R. Ammons

Conducted by Cynthia Haythe

In "Grace Abounding," A. R. Ammons remarks, "Ah, what an abundance is in the universe." His work suggests that abundance both in its multiplicity—he has already published fourteen books of poetry and won the National Book Award for the *Collected Poems 1951–1971*—and in its inclusiveness. Refusing to limit himself to any single, static viewpoint, he prefers diversity and motion, seeking to "lean in or with or against the / ongoing so as not to be drowned but to be swept effortlessly / up upon the universal possibilities." In his attempt to explore "everything," Ammons not only experiments with a variety of forms that range from the tiny, circular "Small Poem" to the book-length, linear *Sphere,* but also willingly surrenders perfection to a wholeness that accommodates garbage, weeds, and rust:

> How does the pot pray:
> wash me so I gleam?
>
> prays, crack my enamel:
> let the rust in.
> ("Utensil")

At the same time, Ammons is unmistakably a Southerner—one of the South's finest poets. While his work transcends regionalism and speaks to everyone, it also reflects the stratified and neoclassical outlook of the traditional South. His vision is essentially moral in its advocacy of the classical ideal of moderation and in its recognition of the need for wisdom as well as for knowledge. Exhibiting a sense of degree reminiscent of Alexander Pope, Ammons cautions against excess in *Tape for the Turn of the Year:*

> rely on feeling—
> till it goes too far:
> then
> on sweet reason which
> recalls, restores, and
> levels off. . . .

He welcomes new scientific discoveries, but simultaneously sees the importance of reconciling them with timeless ethical and spiritual values. In "Discoverer," he juxtaposes "Kepler's equal areas in / equal times" with "the words of / the golden rule," and he warns all of us not to forget the past as we move toward the future: "feed the / night of your seeking with clusters / of ancient light."

In particular, Ammons remembers his own past. He misses the North Carolina farm which was his home before he married and moved to New Jersey and then to Ithaca, New York, where he has lived and taught at Cornell University since 1964. Ammons, like many Southerners, feels caught between tradition and change. Trying to balance them, he writes poetry "about" the modern South and about the way it might define its future: "too traditional is loss of / change: too changing is / loss of meaning & memory." Most criticism has emphasized his affinity with the romantics, often linking him to Emerson and Whitman, but the following excerpt about North Carolina reveals an awareness of his own limits:

> I stand on the stump
> of a child, whether myself
> or my little brother who died, and
> yell as far as I can, I cannot leave this place, for
> for me it is the dearest and the worst,
> it is life nearest to life which is
> life lost: it is my place where
> I must stand and fail,
> calling attention with tears
> to the branches not lofting
> boughs into space, to the barren
> air that holds the world that was my world. . . .
>
> ("Easter Morning")

My interview with Ammons took place in December 1978 in Ithaca.

Q.   I want to ask you a few questions about your connections to the South because so many reviewers have spoken about you as an Emersonian poet. In your *Diacritics* interview with David Grossvogel you spoke about discrediting the South religiously and intellectually, though you could not emotionally. I wonder if you could say a little more about that: religiously and intellectually you had to break away, but emotionally you feel bound?

A.   My father was a Baptist and belonged to the New Hope Baptist Church, which was about two miles from our house. And my mother was a Methodist since—well, I won't say since—her name was McKee. But there was no Methodist church near us in the country: the nearest church was a fire-baptized Pentecostal Holiness about a mile away. So I was located in at least a Trinitarian disposition with three churches. On Sunday, when no important sermons were to be expected, we would just go to the nearest church. I would always bring a penny, I remember. I never brought—that I can think of—more than a penny to Sunday School. Isn't that amazing? And we were lucky if we had a penny to bring. But anyhow, that religious saturation was very intense for me.

Q.   How long would a service last?

A.   Well, often we would only go to the Sunday School session, which would last, say, half an hour to forty-five minutes. And then if any of the adults in the family had come, we might stay for the sermon, and that could take anywhere from half an hour to two-and-a-half hours because they often did achieve high physiological levels of involvement and so sometimes would take a long time.

I was sitting on the bow of a destroyer escort in the South Pacific when I was nineteen, and we had anchored near one of the islands. For some reason the level at which the ocean was striking the island —which was a very sharp bank—made me begin to think of that early experience and to think of the details. I could hear roosters crowing ashore and could see little shacks made of fiber—bamboo or whatever. I had an intuition of what life must be like there without the war going on. And then there was the level of the ocean separating the top—the farm and roosters and hens and houses—

from the nature of the reality right under the level of the water. I guess that language would be submarine: shells and fish and all that. And it seemed to me that a personal god had not decided exactly what should be above and what below that water line, and that it had fallen out that way as a result of the way the world and the universe were made, and that whatever the nature of God, I would associate him with that, not with the incarnate shell, chicken, hut, coop, or whatever. The experience lasted for a split second but had an intensity that you never would forget it you lived to be a thousand.

Q.   It was like Proust eating the madeleine.

A.   Yes. You know just like that that something's different. But, you see, then I didn't know it intellectually, how it was to be different. When I went to Wake Forest, I began to read the histories of the individual books of the Bible to get some idea of where that came from—where that word came from—and I began to learn that there were three Isaiahs perhaps, that the style of this was different from that. I learned that Genesis was mainly traceable to Sumerian origins, to the mythologies of another culture and civilization, and that. . .

Q.   And the two stories of the Creation.

A.   Right. I began to work my way intellectually out of the framework that I had been raised in.

Q.   But emotionally?

A.   Emotionally, I was still there—and still am. I think there's no getting over the early hell-fire sermons. And terrorizing visions of the consequences of doing this, that, and the other are very deep in me and I'll never be able to get rid of them, unfortunately.

Q.   A sense of sin?

A.   Punishment. Sin and punishment, yes. It leads me to congratulate most of mankind, who must be very thick-skinned if sermons have to be that intense to reach them, because they could have been twenty-five times milder and gotten the message across to me. So I'm only too glad to get out of that particular aspect of the South. I don't live there. I'm not interested in it. And I wish I were freer of it than I am.

Q.   You also said that you come from a rural and defeated South. This sense of a defeated South . . . do you feel it has come into your poetry or into your sense of things?

A.   Oh, yes. It's the Civil War I'm speaking of. I knew that my great-grandfather on my father's side—a man named Joshua Ammons—was killed in the Civil War.

Q.   Do you know which battle?

A.   No, I don't. But I knew that he was educated in Ireland, and consequently was educated, whereas my grandfather, I think, was not, nor did my father go beyond the fourth grade. But there was an educated Ammons somewhere way back there, and he was the one killed in the Civil War. And he wrote home letters that were lost. They were in the bottom of my aunt's trunk, and a young child got in and destroyed them just before I heard of their existence. One never gets over the loss of a great-grandparent like that because he was from Ireland and had no involvement or investment in the things that caused the Civil War one way or the other. But he lost his life. So we were defeated. And I identify very deeply with that defeat, and it seems to me that the South did not become the thing it wished to be.

Q.   Which was?

A.   Which was whatever it wished to be. It wished not to be a part of the rest of the country, and it was not allowed to become what it wished to be. And I think that translates very quickly from national to personal feelings and reverberations. Then later, I discovered that a great-grandfather on my mother's side of the family also was killed, and that merely traumatized me further. So, yes, I identify very deeply with the South emotionally and historically, in some ways. How could I not? I was born in a house on a fifty-acre piece of ground—twenty-five acres of that woods, and twenty-five acres cleared—and lived the first seventeen years of my life there, and didn't leave the county even, except to go on a picnic when I was twelve years old. That was the first time I had ever been out of the county. So, no, I will never be other than that, such as it was.

Q.   How do you feel about living in the North? Do you have a sense of yourself as an exile?

A.   Yes.

Q.   Almost in the sense of a Joycean exile surviving by cunning?

A.   Yes. I was born in 1926, fifty years after the end of that war, but I still feel that the politics of the South went underground with its defeat and that the politics of the rest of the country is another matter. So here I sit in the North, not very much involved with the politics going on around me because it doesn't seem to me to be my country.

Q.   Why do you stay in the North?

A.   Except for some fairly early acceptances of poems for *The Southern Review* by Guy Owen, the South has never welcomed my poetry particularly, or encouraged it at all. But the North has. And the North has given me a job, has read my poetry, has been very friendly to me—in comparative terms, very friendly. And I live here rather happily, I think, but isolated.

Q.   Would you now be just as isolated in the South?

A.   I discovered that I was when I went back, after twenty-five years, for a year. It has to do with a twenty-five-year transformation of the self in another location such as the North. And then when you go back, you really can't go home again because *you've* changed, not because the home changed, although it did. I found myself as much a stranger there as here. So I'm now literally homeless.

Q.   What enables you to survive in that state?

A.   I survive by a kind of ambivalence of hiding and by such an extrusion of creativity.

Q.   If you see everything, you see nothing?

A.   That's right—everything having been so intricately presented that the revelation blinds out all penetration of sight.

Q.   You also spoke in that previous interview of a solitary individual who has a fury in him to go back to his own order and possess it somehow. One might even think of Allen Tate's notion of the Southerner taking hold of his tradition by violence. Don't you suppose that in the future when people teach courses in Southern American literature, you certainly will be on the curriculum?

A.   I already am.

Q.   You are a Southern writer.

A.   Yes, I am.

Q.   Do you want to be more recognized as such?

A.   When was that interview? That was 1973, wasn't it? Well, I went back and spent the year 1974-75 there.

Q.   At Wake Forest. Did you feel you possessed it?

A.   I did.

Q.   Tell me more about that.

A.   They told me that . . . I can't really say this. I possessed it enough and was glad to be re-dispossessed.

Q.   You were re-dispossessed?

A.   I re-dispossessed myself.

Q.   What did you do down there?

A.   I came the hell back to Ithaca. I think if I had remained in the South, I never would have written my poems about the South.

Q.   Do you feel affinities with any of the Southern writers?

A.   Not really. When you speak to me of literature, all regionalism vanishes from my mind . . . I don't associate regionalism or anything Southern with anything literary. I think they could be associated, but my concerns with literature are almost exclusively literary.

Q.   The sense of looking for a home, for instance, that figures so largely in your work: do you feel affinities with Thomas Wolfe's *Look Homeward, Angel*? I associated the skipper in your poem "Raft" with Huck Finn and his raft. But perhaps those are things you're not aware of, not conscious of when you're writing?

A.   I'm not conscious of them, certainly. But, number two, I'm not doing it because I'm Southern.

Q.   Do you think it could be almost innate?

A.   Oh, yes. I believe in that.

Q.   It seems to me that one could find all sorts of connections in your work with the Fugitive poets. And, looking at some of your very early poems, one might think of Edgar Allan Poe and Gothic affinities.

A.   I think so. And I'm going to show you some of the very early ones that confirm it even more clearly.

Q.   I want to ask you some questions about your readers: do they write you a lot of letters and ask for help and criticism?

A.   Yes, they do. I don't know how many a lot is because I haven't spoken with other poets. But I would say I get an average of three or four letters a week of that kind, which seems to me a lot. I can't answer it all. But the thing I get the most of are booklets and pamphlets of poems that are just sent to me, and I simply have become unable to respond. You know what that would involve: to sit down and actually read a pamphlet of poetry would take hours, and to think about it and try to respond in any way that would actually be useful to the person. . . . It's just out of the question.

Q.   In *Sphere,* you say that you don't understand your readers, that they complain about your abstractions and want you to be more political. Are you referring to some of the letters you receive?

A.   No, to reviewers. Reviewers nearly always say my language is conceptualizing rather than being experiential, and so on. And then I felt all during the sixties, as a Southerner, emotionally unable to make any commitment to what was going on around me. I felt very defensive about my lack of political involvement. When I was a kid, I thought the greatest thing in the world would be to grow up to be rich enough to buy a nice mule. Now I have money to buy a great mule. . .

Q.   Like Silver?

A.   Silver was an old, boney, worn-out mule and could just barely get along. And so I used to *dream* of having this frisky, wonderful mule. And it seemed to me the greatest thing in the world would be to be able to own one. Now that I could own several, the value is totally irrelevant. So there I was, standing in the middle of the sixties, unable to make any connection between my own past and the events that were going on around me. I felt very defensive and lost. That's what I was complaining about. They want me to be political, but what I do instead of individuating in that direction is to go just the other way toward the deeper layers that we all share, Northerner or Southerner or Easterner or Westerner—what it would take to discover a more generalizable human value rather than a surface, defined, political, issuistic, Movement value.

Q.   Actually, your poems are very political.

A.   That's what I say: All I mean to do is to overturn the Western mind! For that, you don't need a political movement: you need something more radical. That's where I would head—toward the deepest roots of the frameworks by which we dispose ourselves in social and political ways.

Q.   The dedication to *The Snow Poems* reads "for my country." And you showed me an article about you that was published in *People* magazine in 1975. Do you have a sense of wanting to reach everyone in the country? Do you want to be a popular poet?

A.   I do. In the deepest possible way. I would like for the people who are like the people I was raised with, many of whom could barely read or could not read at all, and who were not very well educated . . . those are people I would like to speak to.

Q.   Yet your poems are quite difficult.

A.   Are they really difficult? The corpus, yes. But individual poems can be very accessible, don't you think? I dedicated that book "for my country," which someone has pointed out is a gesture of such size that it's quite ridiculous. But that's not what I meant. Again, it was sub-political. I meant this land—the land I worked as a boy—as being land like other people work everywhere in this country. And I do feel a very deep connection to that soil. And I will say it's for "my country," meaning the United States of America. But if that's taken from me, then "my country" the South. And if that's reduced for me, then "my country" the farm I was raised on. But the nature of the connection is not one to be diminished regardless of the size. So it's for my country. I meant it absolutely. And I still do. My whole theory of poetics has been, as you know, to work out some centralizing means that will not lose contact with the *least* particular, democratically speaking—the coincidental, the single person in the farthest reach. And I have distrusted any centralizing means that is willing to give up whole regions and areas of experience. Yes, I would like to speak to the common man.

Q.   Does this wish to be a democratic or popular poet influence your level of language at all?

A.   I think the way it influences me is that when I have a choice, I choose the word most highly polished in use—that is, the central vocabulary, the monosyllabic often, though I throw in a lot of polysyllabic words. I don't throw them in because they're polysyllabic, but because they happen to be words that point to very particular things. But the main body of my poetry aims toward the use of the central vocabulary, I think. Daily usage. That's what I mean to do, anyhow.

Q.   How do you reconcile this wish to be a democratic poet with a wish to climb to the "top" or to go to a specialized and rarefied landscape?

A.   I experience a double sense about that. Number one, yes, I want to speak to the common man. Number two, however, is how do you do this? And it seems to me that it works the same way in personal terms as it does in poetic terms. The poem is at once a single poem and representative or symbolic or other poems or experiences. There's no doubt that the ambition in my poetry is unlimited. It's terrifying, in fact. But it seems to me that the way one represents the common man most broadly is to achieve the highest position from which to represent him: that is to say, if you speak to the common man as a common man, nobody's going to listen, right? Which doesn't mean that you aren't still speaking as a common man. You must simply write the best poetry you can so that what you think about the common man will be heard, rather than not. That's the way I feel right now: I would like to speak to the common man, but I would also like to represent him.

Q.   A lot of your poems are about mountains. How do you feel now that, in a way, you're a mountain?

A.   Astonished!

Q.   Do you feel any anxiety about reaching a height and then never again being able to achieve the same height?

A.   I think one suffers from that more earlier in one's development when the whole enterprise of your writing seems somewhat fragile. And then you do a really good poem and begin to fear that that was your height and that you'll never revisit that height. That's a terrible self-intimidation and anxiety of the early years. But I think now that I feel myself almost delivered forth, if I may use such language, and that what I do now, positive or negative, pro or con, will only slightly influence all the writing I've done.

Q.   Could you say something about the poem that recently appeared in *Epoch,* the one about society liking your unconventional verses best?

A.   This brings up a very complex area. First of all, let me speak about the readers again. I mentioned getting pamphlets and booklets from people, but I did not mention the personal letters I get from readers, and I get a good many of them. They are at a very intense level of participation with me and, as I identify them, they are from lonely people—people as lonely as I am in that essential sense in which one knows that one is one person and in one body. I get letters from people that are very deeply moving to me. So I have a very strong attachment to readers.

Now, on the other hand, if you live in a university community, you constantly hear things being explained. It gets to the point where it looks as if the explanation is going to replace the reality. You get articles about the role of the artist in society, and you hear that from so many directions that one day the opposite occurs to you, about the role of society in the artist. That was the title of the poem you speak of. That sets off, though, a prepared chain of reactions, I guess, in that it seemed to me that our society does push us away or keep us away or throw us away from its more rigid structures, wishing not to have them changed in any way, at first. So you feel really intensely alone as a young artist.

Then, however, you start to be accepted and known a little bit here and there, and you find the other side of society showing up. Though it has protected its rigid structure, it is also aware that it is trapped and wants to be changed to some extent. And then it begins to give you honors. This very person, formerly rejected, is now almost humiliated with honors from the society, to the point that he becomes disgusted with the very people whose praise he sought. This infuriates him even more, and he goes off and writes even more unconventional verse, which the society finds that it likes *even* better than it liked the original ones. And, at that point, the nausea is at such a level—and the fire and fury at such a level—that instead of having the society say, "To hell with you (the artist)," the artist says to society, "To hell with you." And that's a scary poem. But it plays through a system of feeling from beginning to end. It certainly doesn't represent all that I feel about society, one way or the other— it's that poem playing its possibility.

Q.   So, in a way, that poem is about success.

A.   Yes.

Q.   Society is almost something that devours you. In a sense, it won't let you fail anymore. Anything you do is all right.

A.   Using no more judgment now in accepting you than it used in rejecting you. That's the unpardonable thing, that society doesn't really expend any time on perceptual accuracy or judgment or exposure to the material either way.

Q.   In *Sphere,* you speak about "this sow century."

A.   Actually, I love sows! But let's face it, they can slouch around sometimes pretty much. It does seem to me that with World War II, the Korean War, the Vietnam War and so on, it's been a very troubled and horrifying century, especially in the middle, which is the middle of my own maturity. In *Sphere* I identified that with the long slouch of a sow belly.

Q.   If you had to pick a time in history in which to live, which time would you pick?

A.   I have no such choice, but I really think maybe it wouldn't be now. It would be about the early nineteenth century in America, or the seventeenth century.

Q.   Why?

A.   I think of America when it was rural . . . the village rural community without cars or that kind of transportation . . . with horses and streams and a nearly pure environment of streams and sky. It must have been very beautiful. Spiritually, I don't know. I think I would suddenly fly way back to something Sumerian or pre-Socratic. I would like to live in a pagan, pre-Christian society.

Q. Looking back now, how do you feel about your poems in *Ommateum?*

A. I like them because they seem to me very highly assimilated. That is, without my being very conscious of it at the time, they tell a little story. Each one tells a little story which is like a small myth or a small ritual. And it seems to me that the level of compression and emotional intensity that I was able to achieve by those stories was pretty strong. I certainly think I've written many looser poems since some of those early Ezra poems. I still like some of them very much, to tell you the truth.

Q. Do you feel any affinity with eighteenth-century England?

A. I do. I think that century plays out so beautifully some of the formal possibilities, from the high Augustan to the deliberately made ruin. I like that wide range, and I use it myself. I say in one of my poems, "We should all be a shambles." There are times in the world when it wouldn't be appropriate to be in any condition except a shambles. And I like the eighteenth century because it seems to me to support both poles of that extremity of formal value.

Q. Are there any writers in the eighteenth century that you particularly admire, novelists as well as poets?

A. I love all the novelists. I know them because I once had a course. The earlier part of the century troubles me more because it carries over from Dryden a little bit in a heavy way for me, although I just read Pope's "The Rape of the Lock" again the other night and enjoyed it a great deal.

Q. I find that sense of "mock" in your poems a lot. Do you have any notion, like the eighteenth-century writers, of wanting to write epic and of writing mock epic instead, simply because of the times we live in?

A.   Yes, I do. David Ray called *Tape for the Turn of the Year* a mock epic. I think I hadn't been very much aware of that when I wrote it, but then could see the justification for it.

I mentioned that I had this course in the eighteenth century with Bronson at the University of California. He was a very good teacher, and he brought into the classroom a good deal of material not in the text. Street cries of the sellers. And he brought in information about the jails, about the condition of the jails. The eighteenth century had that polarity—real elegance, but just the most incredible lower strata of society.

Q.   I think of Gay's *The Beggar's Opera.*

A.   Right. And you know Johnson's London poem, which shows a pretty rough style of life.

Q.   That discrepancy between high and low certainly does run through your poems. Do you think reviewers have made too much of you as an Emersonian?

A.   I don't think so. I really didn't read Emerson that much or that well before Harold Bloom started speaking of him. When Harold began to speak of my connection to Emerson, I went back myself to try and confirm or renounce this thing, and I found, in nearly every paragraph, a man speaking my central concerns more beautifully than I could say them myself. There's just no doubt about it. I would *love* to renounce it because no one wishes to be that much like or influenced by anyone. But Emerson says the very thoughts that I think I've come up with on my own. I certainly haven't paid much attention to him, but I can open his work at almost any place and see a better thinker and a better writer saying my material for me, for the most part. Thank God he didn't do water colors, as far as I know!

Q.   Well, your poems are better than his poems!

A.   (laughing) I think my poems may be better than his poems. But I admire them, nevertheless.

Q.   How would you reply to those reviewers who accuse you of being a cold poet?

A.   I would say they're right. There is an aspect of my work that's defensive. I should appear cold to almost anyone on first contact with my work. But it seems to me that the more of the work they know, the more it returns to them, the more another nature—welcoming and generous, I think—would begin to emerge. Because I don't offer myself quickly or easily to anyone. I'm very defensive and withdrawn.

Q.   What were some of the thoughts you had in mind when you dismantled the unity of *Expressions of Sea Level* for the *Collected Poems? Expressions of Sea Level* has its own order, it seems to me, so that the last poem, "Nucleus," looks back at "Raft" and the first poem, "Raft," predicts "Nucleus." One sees "Raft" differently after reaching "Nucleus" and one sees "Nucleus" differently when one remembers "Raft." Why did you dismantle that order when you put those poems in *Collected Poems?*

A.   Oh, my. It hurt me to have to do that. I think that *Expressions of Sea Level* is one of my best books. And they produced it beautifully. But I was controlled by that statement of Emerson's—or rather, I was controlled by a sentiment in myself, expressed by Emerson when he said, "In this life that God allows me, let me record from day to day my honest thought without prospect or retrospect." I've forgotten how the rest goes, but it's something like "I have no doubt that my days will appear to have been symmetrical," that some underlying unity will emerge if you remain loyal to the chronology and truthfulness of each day. So when it came time to do the *Collected Poems,* I went for chronology, thinking that I might misjudge the symmetries in making an individual book. I had to decide whether I would be loyal to the symmetry of the book or loyal to some symmetry in myself that I might not even be able to apprehend. I chose the latter because I thought it truer . . . deeper . . . truer to experience than the fabricated book.

Q.   Do you think of yourself as a major poet?

A.   It depends on the poets you name in that category. I would not put myself among the greatest poets. But if you mean by major poet "one who has found a sufficient means to deal with what he knows," then I think I have found that. Perhaps some great poets have written only short poems, but I think it is still true that our greatest poets have also written long works. Chaucer. Milton. Spenser. Shakespeare. You name them. They're big poets in terms of size and the dimension of the enterprise. In a lyric, you must aim at something essential because you only have time to capture a single thing in its essentiality. You're not multiplying your responses. You're finding the one central response that will find its pure tincture in that single poem. In a philosophical poem, or the larger poem, you're looking for something very different, it seems to me. You're looking for a structure that will satisfy *all* the responses that the human mind and feelings are capable of. You will want vivid images. You will want deep, controlling symbols. You will want a sense of a compressed, mythical narrative at the center. You will want to respond to ideas and statements about the world. You're looking for a controlling system that answers the human spirit in whatever way it shows up. But the lyric doesn't intend to do that. It intends to do something else, just as beautiful but, it seems to me, numerically slighter . . . smaller and purer.

Q.   I think of "great" poets as having written large poems that take in a cosmos.

A.   Which can have its own structure, hierarchy of value. And that's when tradition begins to be meaningful . . . how that hierarchy finds itself, which value outflanks another.

Q.   Could you say a little more about hierarchy?

A.   Well, for example, I know of a splendid poet who can write poems of such sensuous intensity that the theme or the object, usually in nature, that he's writing about seems to appear before the mind's eye. It's a beautiful talent and something Keats was so great at, remember? That's a single thing that we need, and he does it beautifully. But we need other things. We need for that sensuous vividness to be placed in another framework until we have a sense of an adequate system that will answer us spiritually and physically in a real way. That's all I mean about hierarchy. The human mind cannot get away from that, as far as I'm concerned . . . the idea that we do stack our values one way or another. And even more fundamental, we cannot handle all the million bits of information that we receive every day except by subgrouping them under controlling suborders and symbols. Otherwise, I think, we would be inundated by the capacity of our body to pick up so much information during the day.

Q.   Are the levels rigid or are they moving and changing?

A.   Changing. Changing all the time. I see it more clearly when I drop back to something like Sumerian civilization and see the priest there, occupied with—among other things—structuring the pantheon. Who's the top god? That is, what force is primary in their life? What's second? It was sky, air, earth—those very large, general entities. And then there would be more local gods. And finally the household gods, which have a very particular interest for one particular person. And he would have his little god on the shelf, right? I'll never forget that letter of Stevens when he's writing to somebody overseas and says "and get me one of those little wooden Buddhas about six inches high. And every morning when I wake up, it will do me good!"

I don't see how we can get away from amassings of that kind, and valuations. And I say that as a person who would run to the defense of the particular practically as fast as my legs would go. But I'll also begin to group them and say, "Now why don't you go off and do that" and "You go over here and do this."

Q.   We could talk about this in relation to your water colors. I had the sense that you're exploring there a landscape that you haven't really explored in your poems; a level you've chosen not to deal with as much as the sky or the air or the earth. You tend to avoid going below the earth or below the ocean. And yet, in the paintings, you seem to be exploring that landscape. Is it a landscape that's too dangerous to explore in the poems, but that somehow can be dealt with in your paintings?

A.   I think, at that time, I would not have been able to do it in words. And I can't do it now in words. But I can to it in colors and designs. For example, you know Ashbery's work. John Ashbery is able to write poems in which he has tonalities, surfaces, incoherences, things that I can do in paintings, but I cannot do in words—or I will not. There's something about sense that's communicated with something like the Bible—I think this is where the religion comes back in. I associate word and religion so closely that, to me, you do not have the right . . . I can't take upon myself the right to disturb the coherence of language. I just can't do it. But I can sit there and start a painting and almost deliberately and willfully do the perverse, the discontinuous, the nonorganic juxtaposition.

Q.   It is an unconscious kind of landscape.

A.   Yes. They are primordial forms, mainly chucked up: phallic and vaginal, and other deep forms of the energies.

Q.   Sometimes, you seem to see that landscape as a fearful place. Other times, however, you see there the very source of the imagination and creativity. You speak both of "subterranean fires" and "refreshing energies of the deeper self." You have to go there to receive energy and force. At the same time, it's a force that could completely overpower you . . . the conscious mind. Do you feel it's a region you have to go to? Do you feel that any poet needs to go periodically to that source?

A.   I think I feel just about what you've said. It seems to me if anything is *too* outlined and surface, then it may be drained of any intensity or forming energy. That's bad. The other side of that . . . if you should hit so deep a level of the mind that you have mere energy without structure or any kind of self-declaring means, that would be bad. And so there's some intermediate level that is mixed delight and fright where various levels of formal means announce fresh energies, summon those energies up truly, as much as possible.

I've always been impressed by Ashbery. When he was here, he said that he began his poems often in the most deliberate way. He would just sit down and jostle words around on the side of the page until something would begin to emerge. That doesn't sound like a very deep level of participation. But, on the other hand, it is a kind of conjuration of parts that could get up into a very complicated frame of mind. And it does. And very beautifully. I can't do that in poetry. I never come to a poem a little at a time. I wait until it possesses me. But, with paintings, I'm just like Ashbery. I can sit down and pour a little paint out on the paper, wiggle it around some, push it here, and after a while I begin to see emerge a possibility. And I'm not all that deeply engaged in it—at first, at least—as I think perhaps he may not be at first in his poems. And this may be something I've invented on my own.

But it seems to me incredible that I write poems in such a different manner from my paintings, and that I can't write poems the way I paint, even though I think they speak to the same energies. I just can't do it the same way. I don't want to worry this point to death, but it interests me because I can't understand it. I think I'm onto a little bit of descriptive truth about those two ways of doing things. . . .

An Interview with Richard Hugo

Conducted by Thomas Gardner

In "Stray Thoughts on Roethke and Teaching," as much a meditation on his own work as an account of his studies with Roethke in
the late forties, Richard Hugo writes, "Real experimentation is involved in every good poem because the poet searches for ways to
unlock his imagination through trial and error. Quest for a self is
fundamental to poetry. What passes for experimentation is often an
elaborate method of avoiding one's feelings at all costs. The process
prohibits any chance the poet has to create surrogate feelings, a secondary kind of creativity but in most poems all the poet can settle
for. The good poems say: 'This is how I feel.' With luck that's true,
but usually it's not. More often the poem is the way the poet says he
feels when he can't find out what his real feelings are." This is an
accurate overview; the "quest for a self" is Hugo's single theme,
and his books, read in sequence, are an elaborate account of one
poet's various attempts to unlock the imagination and find out
exactly "how I feel."

The technique Hugo uses most consistently in this quest has to
do with landscape and place. The "Contents" of his *Selected Poems*
reads like a litany of place names: "Near Kalalock," "Duwamish
Head," "Fort Casey, Without Guns," "Docking at Palermo,"
"Indian Graves at Jocko," "Letter to Levertov from Butte." Landscape in a Hugo poem is used as a version of a possible self; by recreating a town or a river, the poet is able to stumble upon "surrogate feelings." In his best poems, the result is not description but a
startlingly precise struggle to define an emotion: "my view . . . /
not the world photoed and analyzed, only one felt" ("Letter to
Goldbarth from Big Fork"). In Hugo's first books, the landscapes

302

often present versions of, and dreamed escapes from, the speaker's stalled inner life. The first and last stanzas of "At the Stilli's Mouth" are typical:

> This river ground to quiet in Sylvana.
> Here, the quick birds limp and age
> or in flight run out of breath and quit.
> Poplars start and then repeat the wind
> and wind repeats the dust that cakes the girl
> who plays a game of wedding in the road
> where cars have never been. The first car
> will be red and loaded with wild grooms. . . .
>
> Now the blackmouth run. The Stilli quivers
> where it never moved before. Willows
> change to windmills in the spiteless eye.
> Listen. Fins are cracking like the wings
> of quick birds trailing rivers through the sky.

"Degrees of Gray in Philipsburg," a poem from Hugo's fourth book, demonstrates a more complex use of the same device. Following a brilliant, bitter description of the town where "The principal supporting business now / is rage," the poet turns on himself, questioning this version of himself and the easy use of the technique. The last two stanzas read:

> Isn't this your life? That ancient kiss
> still burning out your eyes? Isn't this defeat
> so accurate, the church bell simply seems
> a pure announcement: ring and no one comes?
> Don't empty houses ring? Are magnesium
> and scorn sufficient to support a town,
> not just Philipsburg, but towns
> of towering blondes, good jazz and booze
> the world will never let you have
> until the town you came from dies inside?
>
> Say no to yourself. The old man, twenty
> when the jail was built, still laughs
> although his lips collapse. Someday soon,
> he says, I'll go to sleep and not wake up.
> You tell him no. You're talking to yourself.
> The car that brought you here still runs.
> The money you buy lunch with,

> no matter where it's mined, is silver
> and the girl who serves your food
> is slender and her red hair lights the wall.

The conversation which follows begins with Hugo's recent *31 Letters and 13 Dreams*. The letter poems are addressed to other poets and develop Hugo's concerns with landscape, memory, and imagination; in a sense, the poems are the working out of an aesthetic. Here, for example, is the poet on the imagination:

> . . . Hell, Bill,
> I don't know. You know the mind, how it comes on the scene again
> and makes tiny histories of things. And the imagination
> how it wants everything back one more time, how it detests
> all progress but its own, all war but the one it fights over
> and over, the one no one dares win.
>
> ("Letter to Matthews from Barton Street Flats")

here is the poet on grace:

> . . . But you know, Bob, how
> in the smoky recess of bars all over the world, a man
> will suddenly dance because music, a juke box, a Greek
> taverna band, moves him and how when he dances we
> applaud and cry go.
>
> ("Letter to Peterson from the Pike Place Market")

and here is the poet on taking up a stance:

> . . . I think some days I should be like you
> and embrace a religion, and hope to create for myself
> a definite stance that keeps people away while I keep looking
> for my real disposition, and not go to bed starving like I do,
> bitter and plotting revenge.
>
> ("Letter to Sister Madeline from Iowa City")

The dream poems, though following the same associational patterns as the earlier landscape poems, chart the poet's inner life in a purely fanciful world. In addition, the sequence of the dreams, moving from "In Your Fugitive Dream," "In Your War Dream," "In Your Bad Dream" to "In Your Wild Dream," "In Your Dream on the Eve of Success," "In Your Dream After Falling in Love," seems to suggest that a positive conclusion to the quest may have been reached. The imagination, of course, is never so easily satisfied; as

Hugo says in this interview: "There's some kind of need involved in the impulse to write, and it apparently never stops. It seems to be dependent on self-rejection when you're young. Yet the impulse is so strong that finally, when it's all over and you've transcended that feeling, you find you're still writing."

The result of that impulse can be found in Hugo's eight books: *A Run of Jacks* (1961), *Death of the Kapowsin Tavern* (1965), *Good Luck in Cracked Italian* (1969), *The Lady in Kicking Horse Reservoir* (1973), *What Thou Lovest Well Remains American* (1975), *31 Letters and 13 Dreams* (1977), *White Center* (1980), and *The Right Madness on Skye* (1980). Though several of the earlier books are now out of print, Norton has issued a *Selected Poems* (1979) which contains selections from the first six volumes. Also available from Norton is a recent collection of essays, *The Triggering Town: Lectures and Essays on Poetry and Writing*. Richard Hugo is currently editor of the Yale Series of Younger Poets and director of the creative writing program at the University of Montana.

The following interview took place on 19 April, 1979 in Madison, Wisconsin. Mr. Hugo has consented to read and revise our conversation.

Q.   I'd like to begin with *31 Letters and 13 Dreams*. I was struck by how often the letter poems become meditations on writing. For example, in "Letter to Birch," the state prison in Deer Lodge suggests what it means to be a writer:

> Some poets equate themselves with criminals. That may be
> because we share the same desolate loves, the same railroad
> spur along the swamp ignites some old feeling of self
> inside and when the sky comes gray late afternoon across
> the world on sunday, we know we're friendless and hounds bay
> in the distance sniffing for our trail.

And at the end of the poem:

> We find secret ways to play. No one
> except poets knows what gains we make in isolation.
> We create our prison and we earn parole each poem.
> Michele, our cell door's open like the dawn. Let's run and run.
> The day is windy and alive with fields.

Self, play, prison, parole—would you talk about the importance of those words for you?

A.   I think play must go back to a course I took in aesthetics. There were a couple of German aestheticians, Schiller and Lange, who had a theory of art as play. It's something that's always intrigued me, and as you know from *The Triggering Town,* I try to teach people to play with words, to almost treat words like toys at times, hoping that some wonderful accident will happen if they keep playing around. I live a lot of my life in fantasy. Outside of fishing and a few other things, I don't care much for reality. It bores me. I've always had a kind of vivid inner life that's going on all the time, converting things I see. I'll change an old town, for example, into a town the poem can use, then appropriate it. I don't choose to do this. It's just something I do and have always done.

Q.   "We create our prison"?

A.   I have a bad habit of mind, a rather neurotic habit, that I think a lot of writers have. It used to be called psychasthenia, which means, literally, "weak-mindedness," but that term isn't used any more in psychiatry. It's the habit of dwelling over and over on the same thing, at its worst moments, replaying incidents in one's life that are very painful. The hope is that one time I'll play it out and the pain will be gone, I'll have won over the situation. But of course it's a loser's battle because the pain is never gone. Psychiatrists call this an attempt at "belated mastery." That's a form of prison: we incarcerate ourselves, in a way, with our own sensibilities, and the poem is a kind of release, a kind of parole we earn.

Actually it has to do with ways of feeling about oneself which go along with the poetic sensibility. I have another essay in *The Triggering Town* called "Statements of Faith" about how poetic theories, so many of them, seem to revolve around the basic premise that the self is inadequate and will not do. This way of feeling about oneself as not being adequate is a kind of imprisonment, and then you write the poem. Each act of the imagination becomes a form of self-acceptance, which is finally a release. Of course what I'm talking about is something I don't know much about. Nor does anyone else. It's sheer speculation. But I would say I'm close, because when you look at theories of poetry like Keats's, or Valéry's, or Auden's, or Yeats's, or Eliot's—right down at the root there's always the attitude that there must be somebody else doing it because I'm not worthy, the self given isn't adequate to the job. What that means is that it's necessary to feel this way in order to write, and the impulse to write is so strong you'll do anything to serve it. Everything, finally, goes into the service of the impulse to write, and that is a mysterious business.

Q.   What happens after the release from prison? In "Statements of Faith" you talk about Eliot and Roethke: "I was distrustful . . . when late in their careers they announced they were happy. But they were being honest. . . . Poem after poem the self grows more worthy of the mask, the mask comes closer to fitting the face. After enough poems, you are nearly the one you want to be, and the one you want to be closely resembles you." If so, how did they start poems?

A.   I was very skeptical at the time, but now I realize what they were talking about: that they had written so many poems that they were very close to self-acceptance. I think they meant they no longer felt it necessary to commit a wholesale rejection of self in order to write. It may never have been necessary in the first place, but it seemed like it. Poets do it all the time, but maybe you come to find out after thirty, forty years of writing that goddamn it, I don't have to do this at all to write a poem. That would be a way of being happy and still going on, still writing.

Q.   Is that true for you?

A.   I hope so. I'm not quite sure yet. There's some kind of need involved in the impulse to write, and it apparently never stops. It seems to be dependent on self-rejection when you're young. Yet the impulse is so strong that finally, when it's all over and you've transcended that feeling, you find you're still writing. Psychiatrists will admit that it's one area of the mind that nobody knows a damn thing about—creativity.

Q.   You say in "Letter to Levertov" "I want my life inside to go on long as I do." Is that the same idea?

A.   Yes. It does go on. Somehow, without going through all these convulsions and narcissistic attitudes about the self, your inner life goes on anyway. You're just not so tortured by it. As you get older, it's a matter of running out of people you'd like to be. Bing Crosby died; at one time I wanted to be like Bing Crosby. Those you want to be die, and you realize on the whole scale of values, hell I'm not so bad. I can be me. I can't be all bad because a marvelous woman married me five years ago.

Q.   It seems to me that your recent poems don't begin from the same isolated position as your early work.

A.   I know. I always assumed I was a hermetic poet and how I ended up so public is beyond me. (Laughter) I really don't know how it happened, though I can take a few guesses. I do like people; I have a childish desire for a certain amount of attention, and I think the entertainer in me won out. At one time I thought just the sound of words themselves would be interesting enough. I've always had that in me. But finally it became a bigger thing, that is to say I've tended to open up more in the poems. It's a side of my nature that won out. I'm just guessing now. I was sure I was Eugenio Montale, but I don't seem to be in that league anymore.

Q.   I wonder about the difficulty of losing that isolation. I saw a poem last year in *Graham House Review*, "Changes at Meridian," in which you say "what nags is loss of loss."

A.   Yes, that's right. What nags is loss of loss. Stafford believes that poems are celebrations of loss. That's interesting. I'm coming to the point where I'm losing the sense of having lost things. (Of course, one nice thing about America is that you're always losing. They're always tearing down something you love and putting something uglier in its place. So I don't think we'll run out of losses.) Actually, what I suppose I'm losing is a kind of sentimentality about older places. Meridian is a lake about thirty miles out of Seattle. The old man in the poem is my grandfather—he used to take me fishing there. Even though I grew up in the Pacific Northwest, my first fishing was Midwest fishing because my grandfather was from the Midwest and always fished for bluegills and crappies and perch. I modeled the old man on him, although he didn't say "keep your line in the water"—that's something I tell fishermen. What nags is loss of loss . . . yes, I remember writing that, a fear that if I run out of losses I can't redeem my world with poems and may stop writing.

Q.   Do you want to comment on the letter poems as a group?

A.   No, I'm a little disappointed in them. I made a mistake in that book which I didn't realize I was making. When the first letter poems were published in *The American Poetry Review,* they were enormously popular. I got some fan mail and I forced some poems to fill out the book. I didn't realize I was doing that at the time, but I think I wrote several letter poems when I had no impulse to write. This is unforgiveable for someone who has written as long as I have. I won't make that mistake again. But some of the letter poems, I think, work pretty well.

Q.   I like "Letter to Levertov" very much: you get close enough to identify with the laborers "stained by the perpetual dust from loading flour or coal" but are still able to criticize the "mean near-insanity of being and being deprived."

A.   Thank you. Yes, I think that's probably the best of the bunch. That poem seemed to generate a lot, enabled me to talk about certain things that have been on my mind that I wasn't able to handle in more conventional form. I imagine I couldn't have done that in a lyric. That was a lucky stroke, that "Levertov" poem. I was taking some risks in that book. Actually I prefer the dream poems. What I like about them is that they're written exactly the way dreams happen: we dream one thing then without any transition we dream another. Dreams are wild like that.

Q.   You've been in psychoanalysis. Could you analyze these dreams if I asked?

A.   (Laughter) Yes, I could analyze them. I think they're written for psychiatrists.

Q.   "In Your Big Dream" seems to touch on what we've been talking about. The hero hides in a ruined church from an army, then follows a river to the sea, walks the streets of a deserted city, calls himself the chief of police, then begins waving his hair in surrender. It ends:

> Bison stampede the plain. You climb a mountain
> leading seven men who look like you. They depend
> on you for their safety. You climb higher
> and higher until you are alone under a sun
> gone pale in altitude. You climb above birds
> and clouds. You are home in this atmosphere.

How did we get here?

A.   Does the person float in that dream?

Q.   Yes.

A.   Have you ever had the dream where you could set a broad jump record because you could jump about a foot off the ground and go for a long, long way? I always thought that those were men's dreams, but I found out not so long ago that women have them too: you can defy gravity, suspend yourself in the air. That dream may be a way of transcending feelings about yourself. There is always a kind of wish fulfillment that goes on: you would like—at least in your dream—to transcend momentarily all these other inadequate selves. You feel good and all of a sudden you're up in the clouds.

Q.   Did you stop writing during the years you were working at Boeing?

A.   Oh, no. Some nights I would get going on poems and stay up all night, then go to work. The poems were coming very slowly those days. I'm a self-disciplined poet. I studied under Roethke and he insisted on that, and after I got out of school I had to do it myself. The best way for me to write is to put myself under some pretty strict disciplines, and finally technique becomes a matter of second-nature. "Changes at Meridian" is more the way I should be writing. It's a system that generates poems for me.

Q.   You went to Italy a few years ago and recently spent a year in Scotland. Were you searching for poems? Is travel a system that generates poems?

A.   That's a very intelligent question. I was in Italy in World War II. I was there again in 1963 and 1964 and started *Good Luck in Cracked Italian*. When I got the Rockefeller Grant in 1967, yes, I deliberately went back to Italy to get enough poems to finish the book. Absolutely. I was there running down poems. At this time my marriage had broken up, and I had to go back and live in the village where my wife and I had lived. I thought these Southern Italians would be very sentimental about the fact we had broken up, but all they did was question me at great length about the process of divorce—which they didn't have in Italy at that time. (Laughter) And in the Scotland case, yes, I wanted to try and do a good book of poems with a foreign setting as a base. I'd been disappointed with the Italian book and wanted to take one more whack at it. This time I was going to go to a country where my language—more or less—was going on around me. I told the Guggenheim Foundation that if they gave me the money I was going to go live on the Isle of Skye. So far it's been working. I've been getting the poems.

Q.   Is there any difference between a poem that possesses you and one you systematically search out?

A.   One funny thing about writing a poem is that the passion that goes into the writing may not be there at the time you're writing. That is to say, the passion that goes into the poem may have preceded it by years, may be there at the very moment you're writing and sometimes—oddly enough—occurs after the poem is over. There's no correlation between the emotion that goes into the poem—no temporal connection—and the time you write the poem. Things don't happen that neatly. It's a mysterious thing. I depend on instinct to ferret out those initiating subjects which are going to result in poems from those things which would be nice to write a poem about but which have no real poem in them.

Q.   In "Statements of Faith" you say that "Certain feelings can lead to certain stances in the poem. If the feelings are strong enough the stances may be overstances, or poses." Is stance also a way of initiating poems?

A.   When I talk about stance I'm talking about becoming the kind of person necessary to use the language you're using. In "Leda and the Swan" Yeats would have had to be an uncompromising person to write that first line: "A sudden blow: the great wings beating still." You see, he would have had to be there instantly on stage in the middle of the act because he starts the poem not with Zeus getting an erection but in the middle of the rape. That's a stance: there's a kind of person you have to be to start a poem. Usually I find if I start out too loudly, that if I go back and take a softer beginning I'm sometimes able to get the poem where I wasn't able to with the other opening. At one time I continually took the more dramatic stance, like in "Degrees of Gray in Phillipsburg":

> You might come here Sunday on a whim.
> Say your life broke down. The last good kiss
> you had was years ago. You walk these streets
> laid out by the insane, past hotels
> that didn't last, bars that did, the tortured try
> of local drivers to accelerate their lives.

Just opening it all up. But now I tend to start more gently and I find my language loosening up, a little more air between the words.

Q. Were there stages to that progression? "Degrees of Gray in Philipsburg," for example, seems the best try at that voice.

A. Yes, the Philipsburg poem was actually the culmination of a kind of writing. It was the poem I had been trying to write for twenty years. Of course, these things aren't neat and you don't realize that at the time you write the poem. You try to keep writing that way, but eventually that was the best of all those poems, "West Marginal Way," "Duwamish." Everything just fell into place one day, all within four hours, from five in the morning until nine. I had been in Philipsburg only three hours the day before, and that was the only time I'd been there.

Q. That's amazing.

A. Yes, very fast. But now I'm more apt to be thoughtful at the beginning of a poem. I like the beginning of my new Bing Crosby poem: "We are what we hear." Or there are other openings—"Now I'm dead, load what's left on the wagon"—which take, perhaps a little more gentle stance.

Q. Some of your poems take that tough opening then change in the middle.

A. Yes, that's right: Humphrey Bogart going in and Leslie Howard coming out, which is typical of me. I've always wanted to be a tough guy and I never was, of course. The opening stanza of "The Lady in Kicking Horse Reservoir" is almost an ideal example:

> Not my hands but green across you now.
> Green tons hold you down, and ten bass curve
> teasing in your hair. Summer slime
> will pile deep on your breast. Four months of ice
> will keep you firm. I hope each spring
> to find you tangled in those pads
> pulled not quite loose by the spillway pour,
> stars in dead reflection off your teeth.

Really vengeful, nasty, but then about three stanzas later, the guy is saying "Sorry. Sorry. Sorry." Oddly enough, I've written a poem called "Museum of Cruel Days" which appeared in *The New Yorker* a few months ago and which Howard Moss thought was a tough poem. Although I wasn't trying, maybe now that I'm not so tough, I'm tougher.

Q.   Some of your autobiography appeared in William Heyen's *American Poets in 1976.* Does prose also demand a stance?

A.   I would have said no to that a few years ago, but now I think it does. It's perhaps just as unconscious as in the best poems you write. I find the reason I didn't write prose at all for a long time is that I assumed it was different than poetry. But the rules are almost the same: keep it moving, don't dwell, don't repeat, keep presenting. A poet who writes prose has a first tendency to luxuriate.

Q.   Do you see any difference between autobiography and a lyric poem?

A.   Now there's a question! Perhaps one difference is that in autobiography your writing is inclusive, that is to say, you write everything you believed happened as though it had some central purpose. In a poem, you tend, at times, to deliberately create things. You tell lies to create possibilities for things to say. I know that when I do the autobiography what I'm saying is not true because memory always modifies things. Auden says when we look in the mirror we never see ourselves because we always compose our face into the face we want to see, before we look. I believe that memory does that too: it creates the situation into one where you fit in, one way or another. So, it's always a kind of lie, but not a deliberate lie. In a poem, you'll fictionalize something just to see where the possibilities in the language take you.

Q.   Do pronouns set up possibilities in the language? Why, for example, did you decide to do your dream poems in second person: "You run and run. You cannot leave the town"?

A.   I've never been able to answer that adequately. It too has to do with stance. There's some kind of psychology involved in the person—first, second, third—you write in. You write differently when you use one or the other. I would use one because that would be what I had to do to write the poem, but I don't know why.

Q.   You don't use third person as much anymore, do you? This is from "Back of Gino's Place":

He was right to come. Light
in this place cannot kill the lines
of the charred boat, the rusted net,
the log-boom beached and slanted
waiting for a tide. Not when a need to die
here, just to be an unobtrusive ghost,
takes from mud and wood the color of the day.

A.   I remember that. I know I would fall into one person or another at any one time. For a long time I was using "you" poem after poem. The psychology of the person enables you to talk; when you say "you," you're able to say certain things that you aren't able to say when you use "I," and vice versa. Now I'm back to using "I" a little more.

Q.   I'd like to return to the poem we started our talk with. In "Letter to Birch" you write about a railroad spur along a swamp which "ignites some old feeling of self inside." How important are landscapes to you? How many landscapes can a person own?

A.   That's a fascinating question—and obviously I can't answer it. When I went to Scotland it was already there for me. It's panoramic and open—there aren't many trees—so it's a lot like Montana. But it's also a lot like Seattle. It has the same ferns—we call them ferns in Seattle, they call them bracken in Scotland—it has gorse, it has Scots Broom which grows everywhere. It has alder trees which you find in abundance around Seattle; hazel nut trees, or filberts, which we have around Seattle. It has a constant wind from the west and southwest as does Seattle. So I had the best of both landscapes. I had Seattle's weather and limited forms of Seattle's vegetation, but also the openness and panorama of Montana. No, I don't know how many but I would say this: I've never run out of them. If I was a religious person I would be an earth-worshipper.

Q.   I wonder if foreign landscapes are also a way of achieving the alienation—or isolation—you seem to need to write?

A.   Yes, somewhat. But you might note that I always pick foreign settings that are out of the way. For example, in Italy I lived in the relatively remote South, and in Great Britain I chose the western isles of Scotland. Even when I lived in London, in 1968, I usually went out of town for my poems, western Ireland or Cornwall. I don't know if isolation is the point, or alienation. I think it goes back to my childhood, growing up in the Pacific Northwest and feeling that I was near the edge of civilization, almost out of it. Nearly all of "civilized" America lay to the east. To the west, soon one found the void. For some reason I find being on the edge or border of the civilized world compatible with writing. I can't involve myself in the center of things and write my best. If I could I would. I like feeling just barely a part of civilization when I write; I mean that actually or geographically more than psychically perhaps. I like to feel I'm living where finding one more friend is difficult and therefore very important. Soon we will run out of people. Maybe a poem will locate one more friend or even one more self before the ocean opens forever to nothing.

An Interview with John Barth

Conducted by Charlie Reilly

This interview, held in Baltimore in the fall of 1979, is perhaps the longest one Barth has given since the publication of *Letters*, his first novel in thirteen years and his first book in seven. Taking a long look at the complexities and achievements of contemporary writing including Barth's own works, the discussion focuses on *Letters;* but because that novel includes characters from all of Barth's previous novels and most of his stories, and because Barth studies and thinks about serious literature when he is not writing it, we made a number of stops along the way. One was in eighteenth-century England, another in nineteenth-century France, a third in our own boisterous sixties.

Barth also had much to say about his recently completed essay, "The Literature of Replenishment," the long awaited follow-up to his controversial "Literature of Exhaustion." The latter had appeared in *The Atlantic* in 1967 and engendered vigorous discussion among critics and authors alike. Barth's purpose seemed innocent enough. "The simple burden of my essay," he recalled later, "was that the forms and modes of art live in human history and are therefore subject to used-upness, at least in the minds of significant numbers of artists in particular times and places" (*R*, p. 71). But certain phrases were imperfectly interpreted and, far from recognizing the essay as a celebration of new developments in fiction, many readers concluded that Barth was heralding the demise at least of fiction and perhaps of all literature as well.

With the completion of *Letters*, and with some galleys-to-hardback time on his hands, Barth composed a second essay, the optimistic tone of which is suggested by its title, "The Literature of

Replenishment." What the article isn't concerned with is fence-mending with literateurs whose feathers were ruffled by "Exhaustion." Rather, the new essay comprises a second, and perhaps final, attempt by Barth to speculate about the complexities of modern literature, and an attempt to describe the remarkable new directions that it has taken and continues to take.

The interview concludes with comments about a work in progress and an idea in storage. The former is, of all things, a play aimed at the television medium and keyed to Barth's story about a spermatazoa in progress (the one making a "Night Sea Journey"). The idea involves Barth's hope to create a special kind of literary "image" in a future novel.

Q.   *Letters*, your most recent book, was an ambitious undertaking, a brave book to attempt.

A.   I'll agree it was risky and, at the risk of seeming immodest, I'll happily say I'm very pleased with it. I think our shared pleasure won't be universal, though. I've seen some of the early reviews and, as I suspected, they're mixed. Some people feel the way I do about the novel; some sure don't. It's a book that is somewhat vulnerable, I think, because of its length and because of some of the chances I took.

Q.   I thought about that as I read it. In fact, I'll be interested to see some of the angry responses and guess whether the reviewer had read the entire book.

A.   (laughing) And I thought writers were the only ones who had such suspicions! You know, the only type of review that gets me upset is one in which the reviewer gets the names wrong. It doesn't necessarily mean he hasn't read the book, but you would think if he was going to take the trouble to kick a character around, he could at least figure out what the character's name was.

Q.   It's been seven years since your last book, thirteen since your last novel, and *Letters* surely reflects a lot of work and thought. In fact, given the nature of your earlier works and theories, it seems almost a summa. I suppose all recent books are precious to their authors, but does *Letters* seem special to you?

A.   It's special in a sense anyone who reads through to the end will probably pick up on. For years I had been interested in experimenting with the ways the human voice could be adapted to forms of written literature. I worked with tapes for a while, spent a lot of time trying to orchestrate tales within the oral tradition, and finally came up with the "series" of short fictions that appeared in *Lost in the Funhouse* [1969]. When I completed that project, I found myself enormously interested in a different aspect of the narrative tradition. I decided to return to the eighteenth century—it wasn't my first visit—to examine the beginnings of the novel in English; my hope was to discover something I could orchestrate to my own purposes. At the time, I knew I wanted to move away from short fiction. I knew I wanted to write a special type of novel, one as far removed from contemporary norms as I could make it. In a sense, I guess I was honoring André Gide's dictum. When Gide finished a project, he used to make it a point to walk to what he called the farthest corner of his imagination before beginning a new one. So I decided to return to the earliest form of English fiction, the epistolary novel, and out of that came *Letters*. Because it grew into what impresses me as a substantial work, because it took so many years and pages, because it represents an honest attempt to work with and within the form of the novel, yes, it is special.

There is something else special about it, as far as I'm concerned. As I started digging into eighteenth-century fiction, I was struck by the almost uncannily modern sense that the inventors of the English novel had about what they were up to. That is, although they were spinning yarns, fabricating, entertaining, they never lost sight of the documentary nature of what they were doing. After the dust had settled on the theories of chaps like Marshall McLuhan in the sixties, what we all came away with, whether we agreed with them or not, was a livelier sense of the differentiations between the various media and the sense in which print is really print. In other words, a reader of nineteenth-century continental fiction is not really dealing with Anna Karenina or Emma Bovary; he is dealing with a sentence on a page. When I was re-reading Richardson, Fielding, Smollet and the rest, I was impressed with that spookily "modern" awareness they had that each novel was a document. They manifestly were aware that a novel wasn't life itself. It was an imitation, a convention for imitating life and, especially in their case, a convention for imitating life's documents. Well, this aspect of early epistolary fiction, an aspect I hadn't paid much attention to before, made my own work with *Letters* all the more exciting.

Q.   I think you caught the spirit of those novels. In fact, I recall delighting in what impressed me as echoes of Fielding's *Joseph Andrews* as I progressed through *Letters.*

A.   Good, good. You know, one of my earliest notions was that if one followed the modernist road back far enough, he'd find Lawrence Sterne living at the end of it. I've felt for some time that his *Tristram Shandy* has been a kind of godfather to the modern formalist novel. But for all my awareness of *Shandy*, I had never really contemplated the way even earlier works, such as Richardson's *Pamela* and the rest, should be associated with that same line of thought. What Richardson says in effect is: "I'm not so much creating a reality called 'Pamela' as I am imitating Pamela's documents, her letters." So, I thought it a challenge to keep with the notions and strategies of the old-time epistolary novel and, concurrently, deal with something like the here and now. I had been working with classical antiquity for quite a while, and I decided I wanted to work with something closer to the present—or at least the very recent past. Also, I wanted to return in some way to the "Old Turf," the Maryland Tidewater country. I even wanted, God help me, to deal with something like contemporary problems among contemporary people—people whom I wished to be believable. Whether I succeded in the last respect is not for me to say.

Q.   I'll say it. I think your Lady Amherst is wonderful. She seems as vivid a creation as anything Fielding came up with; I almost feel I could bump into her on the street tomorrow.

A.   Well, I hope so. She certainly is a whole-cloth character, isn't she?

Q.   There are a few comments in the novel which anyone who has followed your fiction and literary theorizing is going to wonder about. Two of them are given to the character in *Letters* whom you call "The Author." Now, I wouldn't presume to identify "The Author" with you, but . . .

A.   He's certainly an authorial chap like me.

Q.   Right. At the beginning, he describes himself as "a fictionalist who . . . had long since turned his professional back on literary realism in favor of the fabulous irreal, and only in this latest enterprise had projected, not without misgiving, a détente with the realistic tradition. It is as if Reality, a mistress too long ignored, must now settle scores with her errant lover." Later "The Author" concedes that during his long and Barth-like career, he has "changed cities and literary principles, made up other stories, learned with mixed feelings more about the world and Yours Truly." And at the end Ambrose Mensch, a refugee from *Lost in the Funhouse*, says that, although he is a "last-ditch, provincial Modernist," he has become infatuated with the "Great Tradition" and wants "hopefully, perhaps vainly, to get her one final time with child." Given all this, have you changed or modified or watched grow the theory you advanced in your famous 1967 essay, "The Literature of Exhaustion"? I'm referring to your suggestion that "it may well be that the novel's time as a major art form is up, just as the 'times' of classical tragedy, grand opera or the sonnet sequence came to be."

A.   Ah, "The Literature of Exhaustion." Now, I never personally believed, or wrote, that the novel's time was up—although the prospect that it might be never bothered me either. Although genres seem to be born, then peter out, then die, the novel's death, if it ever occurs, would not signal the end of narrative literature or story telling. Indeed, with *Letters* . . . let me digress a little. One of the things that I, a man who by temperament is more of an orchestrator than anything else, found beguiling in my researches was the fact that the epistolary novel, the form that established the novel as the most popular form in literature, was also the first novelistic form to die. So, given the fact that I was not only a novelist but a novelist who had muttered about the possibilities of novelistic exhaustion, I regarded it as part of my literary function to administer a kind of artificial resuscitation to this apparently exhausted form.

Now, to get back to the question. I haven't really changed my mind as much as I've decided to clarify what I regard as a common misunderstanding about my "infamous" essay, "The Literature of Exhaustion." What was unfortunate about that essay was that I never meant to imply—as many readers, one of them Jorge Luis Borges, concluded—that I thought fiction had all been done with, that there was not much more for us latecomers to do except parody our predecessors. That wasn't, and isn't, my thought—although I don't consider it all that "unthinkable." On the contrary, I can readily imagine how a serious but stalled writer might flirt with such a conclusion on a given day. Even better, I've learned that over

2,000 years ago a scribe named Khakheperresenb was so distressed about the accomplishments and scope of the then extant writers that he complained into his papyrus: "Would I had phrases that are not known, utterances that are strange, in new languages that had not been used." And so forth. I've made this observation before: Khakheperresenb's complaint sounds as if it had been wrenched from the pages of Donald Barthelme's *Snow White*. There are a couple of points to be made here. My own experiments with the oral and epistolary traditions should indicate that I consider the novel far from dead. And I never said the novel was dead in the first place.

Q.   In the "Literature of Exhaustion," you seem more to specu-late and theorize than to pronounce. In any case, the essay certainly set a lot of us thinking.

A.   It was a time that invited thinking. I wrote the essay in 1967 in Buffalo, in the middle of a very apocalyptic time in the history of our republic. It was a time when both the "Peace Bridge" in particu-lar and Canada in general were again serving as escape hatches for Americans—a time when people could be forgiven for wondering whether a lot of institutions were falling apart. I was teaching at the State University of New York then, and though I enjoyed many happy years there, in the late sixties the campus seemed beseiged by riot police and saturated with tear gas. Not only that, in the middle of it all there seemed to be this voice booming down from Toronto, Marshall McLuhan's, assuring us that print, along with everything else, was kaput. So in that environment, I wrote "The Literature of Exhaustion." I don't pretend that at the time I believed either the country or its literature had entered a Doomsday situation. But there certainly was plenty of apocalypse floating around in the breezes of Buffalo, and it impressed me. I hope the essay conveyed the thought that there were significant numbers of people who shared a conviction that an apocalypse of some kind was in the offing. And I feel that a work, an essay, done in that spirit and at such a time, was worthy of consideration.

Obviously, the world didn't end. But as I review what I said then and what has occurred in subsequent years, I feel there was a good deal of validity to my remarks. I can see more clearly now that what I was really trying to speak to were some feelings of my own, feelings that were explicitly developed later by other writers. I believe that what I was talking about was the coming to birth of—it's hard to find a phrase—a "postmodern fiction." What I was trying to get at, I guess, was the thought that we tend to think of modern fiction in a disorganized manner, and when one combines the word "modern" with the word "fiction," he no longer has a very useful term. In a sense I can see at least three waves of "modern" fiction writers: Joyce, Proust, Kafka et al.; Borges, Nabokov, Beckett and company; writers my age and younger. I think that Borges, Nabokov, Beckett and company share an unspoken conviction with a great many of the rest of us who, though younger, cut our apprentice teeth on those older "High Modernists." We share a feeling that the aesthetics of "capital 'M' Modernism"—which to my mind was certainly in the mainstream of western aesthetics in the first half of this century—really *belong* to that half of the century. And the trick is not to pretend that wonderful phenomenon hadn't happened, but to realize at the same time that the adversary energy which fueled the modernist movement in literature, music, and art has no doubt done its job or run its course. One of the things that Viet Nam and the politicizing of the universities can teach us is that those great authors like Joyce and Proust, authors who were idols when I was a graduate student, were not simply brilliant artists. They were literary aristocrats as well. Let's face it: their stuff is difficult to read; not an awful lot of it is immediately accessible or delightful. And certainly their work has exacerbated the divisions between popular art on the one hand and "elitist" art on the other. It's a lamentable, perfectly understandable, perhaps inevitable split.

So I am coming more and more to feel that among the—I doubt if there is any way to phrase this without infuriating someone—the truly-modern, or perhaps recent-modern writers, one finds essentially three groups. First, there are the ones who in essence are really carrying forward the programs of the modernists—some of the French structuralists spring to mind here. Second, there are the antimodernists, the ones who regard the whole modernist phenomenon as a literary aberration and are glad to see it done with. You know, the let's-get-back-to-good-old-fashioned-nineteenth-century-story-telling crew. Finally there are those of us—and if I'm not in their number I hope soon to get there—who believe that "neither of the above" positions is ideologically correct. My hope for postmodernism, or whatever you wish to call it, is that it will embody a kind of literature which can find a way to transcend that quarrel between the cultural aristocrats and the pop novelists. You might even say, the quarrel between irrealism and realism. I don't know whether such a body of literature can be written. Every novelist aspires to be a Dickens or a Mark Twain or a Cervantes, a writer who seems able to produce substantive works and at the same time earn a degree of popular acceptance. Perhaps that was easier to do in earlier centuries. Or, perhaps those authors were so extravagantly gifted that their achievements can't even be approximated. I don't know. I hope not.

Q.   An admirable quality about *Letters* is your control of the plot. No matter how frequent your warnings to the reader to "Beware of the Narrator," I invariably find myself ignoring the narrator and getting engrossed in the plot. Fortunately for the reader, you certainly succeeded in pulling everything together at the end.

A.   It's interesting to hear you say that because the response of a reader to the type of long and complex work I occasionally produce has always interested me. In fact, most people read novels for entertainment and delight, not because they wish to command the novel or interview the writer, and most novels are read only once. There is the occasional work that becomes a kind of sacred document, one which is read time and again, but most works have to get their point and pleasures across at a first reading. Now this has led me to a sort of operating principle about the degree of complexity a writer can hazard. The principle is: as long as one works hard to keep his work interesting and literate, he needn't become unduly worried about whether the reader will command all the complexities of the novel. An analogy I like to make involves music. Good, serious music—say, good jazz or a classical piece—can be terribly complex and still be well received. But such compositions had better be ravishing the first time through. If so, the listener will become enthused and curious and will return to the piece again and again. He will examine the score and will see that a hell of a lot is going on that he didn't catch the first time through.

Q.   I can see you did worry about the reader. You reminded him or her, in other words, about what has happened earlier and who a particularly obscure character is.

A.   There has to be a certain amount of discretion about the degree to which an author should remind; and yes, an author has an obligation to be both cautious and merciful. I would extend that principle to the business, which is conspicuous in *Letters*, of recycling characters from earlier fictions. The practice isn't original to me, of course. Homer did it first and no doubt best and, as I recall, Mark Twain began his masterpiece by having his narrator say, "You don't know about me, without you have read a book by the name of 'The Adventures of Tom Sawyer'"—which has proved ironic since so many more of us have read *Huckleberry Finn* than *Tom Sawyer*. What Twain and Homer have in common, though, is a confidence that their readers had in fact read their earlier work. But Faulkner couldn't have made that assumption, and I can't. At the time Faulkner began resurrecting and recycling his characters through the whole body of his fiction, he was not a famous author; in fact, it was unlikely that bloody anybody had read his works. I'm in a similar boat. I have no business assuming my readers have pored over my previous works, so the rule in my house is that it's okay to bring back or refer to past characters if you don't presume for even one sentence that even one reader has so much as heard of any of them. The corollary to the rule is that everything the reader needs to know must be right there in the text at hand. That was my intention, at any rate; I hope I was successful.

Q.   I think you were. I think people like me who have read your other works would watch you in that respect, since you had promised the reader at the beginning of *Letters* that you weren't going to presume prior knowledge. To me, you honored that promise.

A.   Again, I hope that's so. I don't want to gild myself with a comparison to Faulkner but, in fairness to the man, a reader doesn't have to know that Quentin Compson had done such and such in a previous story to enjoy and respond to a new work. If you happen to know it, and I guess the same is true for my *Letters*, there is an added dimension, a certain resonance, that may make matters a bit more fun. But it isn't necessary. Sounds like the *Jaws-II* theory of literature, doesn't it?

Q.   When John Updike reintroduced the cast of *Rabbit, Run* in *Rabbit Redux*, he was worried about visiting the same scene too often. Did you have similar reservations?

A.   Of course; and it should have made me uneasy if for no other reason than the fact that the recycling of characters is a sure sign that the author is past forty. At the same time, I am sure different authors do it for different reasons. I think I know what John's reasons were for being interested in resurrecting "Rabbit." To me it seemed a way of Updike's measuring his own progress through his imagination. John Updike once said to my students here at Johns Hopkins that his earlier works were, in a sense, "skins" one sheds on his snakelike way down the road. Normally, he said, you don't wish to return to pick up those skins and examine them, but for special purposes you may want to. Updike surely wished to measure his own progress and to record the extraordinary ways in which the world had changed since his earlier work.

But my *Letters* had a different origin. In my case, the novel began with a growing feeling about what the theme was to be. I became increasingly aware that the book's true subject, stated simply, would be Reenactment, or Recycling, or Revolution—the last in a metaphorical sense rather than a political sense. And, of course, if one looks about to see, as I do, how many readings or aspects of a story can be made to reflect the main concerns of the story—if one endeavors to see that everything reflects everything else—then one of the things you might think of recycling along the way is recurrences in history: repetitions, echoes, reverberations, second cycles of human lives. In that context, taking another look at one's own imaginative past, resurrecting old characters, seemed highly appropriate. For the same reason, my interest in the War of 1812 did not derive so much from a historical novelist's interest in past events as from the fact that, when it was going on, the war was frequently referred to as the "Second American Revolution." One thinks immediately of Marx's famous observation that important events in history tend to occur twice: the first time as tragedy, the second time as farce. In short, what I'm trying to say is that I looked around for a "history" to fit the theme, rather than a theme to coincide with the history. Some authors do bring characters back in a way that resembles a company using a trademark. Kurt Vonnegut makes wonderful use of Kilgore Trout in this sense; it's almost a signature. But with *Letters* this was not the case.

Q.   Given the fact that you often write about writers writing, I suppose it would be inevitable that some of the characters written about resurface.

A.   Let's put it this way: if it's not inevitable, it's not inappropriate either. I mentioned the word "orchestrator" a while ago. I'm a frustrated musician, someone whose ambition was originally to be not a composer or writer but an orchestrator. I once was a drummer in a jazz band, but even then I was far more interested in becoming an arranger than a performer or a composer. In that context, I would not be distressed if someone were to describe my work as being, in part, a reorchestrating of old conventions and old melodies. In this sense I'm frequently tempted to, well, reconstruct an old story—something to the effect of "Let's run it through again, but in another key."

Q.   Anyone reading *Letters* would surely be struck by the proliferation of characters and the complications in the plot. Although you were careful to provide organizing "clues" throughout the text, and although you did pull all of the strings together at the end, it does raise the question of how the author of such a complex book feels about his reader. Did you worry about your reader's inclination to "drop out" along the way? Or is it simply a matter of you alone with your muse and pencil, and let the reader take care of himself or herself?

A.   Oh no, I always worry about my readers' interests and feelings—moreso, I think, as I get older and perhaps wiser. Probably if I were a little more attuned to the lines of thought of our modernist masters, I would take a more disdainful, more Olympian attitude in responding to that question. But I find myself lately putting some respectful distances between those masters and myself, and one of those distances involves myself and my readers. When I'm asked whom I write for or who my reader is, I no longer regard that as a dopey question—although I probably did when I was in my twenties and thirties. To respond to your question, a writer, if he's lucky, will be aware of that delicate point where he had better not tax the reader's patience too much. Just as a juggler has to control the number of tenpins in the air or an acrobatic team has to monitor the number of performers on the wire, an author has to avoid introducing that final complication which will bring his reader to a point where he or she says, "That's just one avatar too many." But, of course, no two readers are alike. There will no doubt be many people for whom three turns of the screw might be too many, and others who would enjoy a fourth or fifth turn.

Q.   As a writer, though, you have some safety valve or whistle, even if it's unconscious, that warns you when you might be going too far?

A.   Sure. I recall Joyce and smile when he responded that his ideal reader would be one whom he could expect to do nothing other than devote the rest of his life to the study of *Ulysses* and *Finnegans Wake.* I'd settle for a good deal less.

Q.   John Barth only wants a reader willing to keep turning pages for a few hours?

A.   Turning pages, I fervently hope, with enjoyment. If the *Letters* novel isn't put together like a Swiss watch, it is at least a respectable Switzerland cuckoo clock where all the cogs and pendulums actually do engage. Like my other works it's not the sort of novel that has to be studied like a Nabokovian production. I think, for example, that it's the kind of novel where if one is charmed by Lady Amherst and not so charmed by A. B. Cook, one could more or less skim through the Cook passages. You might not get precisely the same assemblage, but I think you would emerge with a sound sense of what is going on in the overall novel.

Q.   Speaking of Nabokov and *Letters*, Nabokov's *Pale Fire* contains elaborate instructions about how its oddly-packaged contents should be read: the madman-narrator insists his "commentary" should be read at least twice before the real narrative is considered. Granted you're neither insane nor a Nabokovian creation, you have produced a stunningly complex narrative. How should the reader read it? Should he or she follow each of your seven letter writers seriatim, or simply turn one page after the other?

A.   It's a complex problem and I don't want to be coy. I could say there are various ways of reconciling a bank statement—you can take the checks by numerical order, or by date cashed, or by the order in which they presented themselves to the computer. I daresay the best way to read *Letters* is by beginning with page one, and proceeding to page two, and continuing to the last page. But you're right; it's not that simple. There are letters responding to other letters that the reader hasn't seen yet, and that occurs because I'm convinced there is a nice dramatic effect achieved by departing from chronological order. On the other hand, I don't think much is lost if the reader devises his own method and sticks to it. If you think about it, you might see there's a kind of metaphor for the plot—a metaphor of waves crashing ashore on a tidal beach. The plot surges up to a given point, then seems to recede a little, then crashes back upon the beach.

Q. Probably any reader of *Letters* winds up wondering where on earth the inspiration for this swirl of characters and centuries came from: Were you first thinking about writing a novel concerning Lady Amherst, or did you have a sequel to *The Sot-Weed Factor* in mind? Or did you have a form in mind from the start? Or have I succeeded in making simple things complicated?

A. No, that's simple enough to answer. Granted any plans for a novel change in incubation, my early thoughts were far more concerned with form and structure than with anything else. My original plan was to write a novel, as I've said, of documents, and I decided early on the novel would be composed of letters. I've also been enamored with the frame tale, the tale within a tale, and so my initial plan was to compose an epistolary novel which employed the frame-tale device. Also, I wanted to write about second cycles, about reenactments, and I hoped the novel would include texts within texts—as opposed to tales with tales, which is a convention that I prefer to keep more or less at arm's length. So once I realized I needed several letter writers, I found myself with another, a ventriloquistic task: that of devising separate and believable voices.

Q. Your narratives are remarkable in that respect. Was it difficult to achieve such diversity, or can an old pro just shrug off the business of representing a middle-aged British lady, an old Maryland lawyer, a spaced-out starlet and a computer-oriented madman?

A. Put it this way: I now know why the epistolary novel died early; it's beastly difficult to write. What the epistolary novelist must do is divest himself of a number of artifices such as, oh, extended dialogues. You can't use such things when you're working with the letters since real letter writers don't bother with them. The strategy of the eighteenth-century novelists was to cheat—to slap in dialogues extended far beyond all plausibility and hope no one noticed. Another problem with the epistolary form is that you don't have a chance to establish an "authorial" voice as you do in most third-person narratives and all first-person narratives—a voice that will carry the novel. In the case of my epistolary novel, I had to establish six separate voices, six writing styles. To answer your question: yes, it was difficult.

Now, to get back to what I think was the first question: my wish was to use a variety of voices. That raised the question of "Whose voices?" which in turn made me ask myself whether I should reintroduce voices from previous fictions. As often happens when a good idea presents itself to me, my immediate response was "Of course not." But finally I decided it would be okay to reintroduce those "old friends" as long as I honored a couple of rules. The first, and I've already mentioned it, was that I should presume no prior knowledge on the reader's part. The second was at least as important. I feel that an important part of being a writer involves one's commitment to keep raising the high-jump bar with each new effort, and giving each new effort as much energy, grace, commitment, and brio as possible. With *Letters* I felt that the complicated business of maintaining six narratives, along with a seventh authorial voice that serves as commentator and clearinghouse, was the most challenging task I had undertaken. And I can honestly say I gave the novel as much energy and dedication as anything else I've written.

Q.   What you're saying, then, is that it was only after you decided about form and structure that you really considered a plot. One of my questions—a question prompted by my admiration for and delight in Lady Amherst—*was* going to be, did you have her in mind at first for a novel of her own and then decide to add the other narrators?

A.   Well, she was the first character invented. But, no, the form came first.

Q.   She's such a vivid character; was she modeled upon a real person?

A.   I'm tempted to make my contribution to a venerable, mendacious tradition, but I won't. The eighteenth-century epistolary novelists loved to tease you with the possibility that a character was carefully modeled on a real person. They kept it up in the nineteenth century too—you're supposed to nod shrewdly and say, "Aha, *Goethe* . . .*Werther!*" and whatever. I suppose from this date it all seems a bit ham-handed, but all of those works were conceived as *romans à clef* and their authors seemed convinced that if their works were sufficiently realistic, by God, they were *real*. So, I decided the challenge for a person writing in my century was to invent a character who bore no resemblance to anyone I'd ever met in my life, although I'd be delighted to run across someone like Lady Amherst. I came up with a middle-aged British gentlewoman who had been a lover or intimate of a number of "big gun" novelists earlier in the century and who was currently marooned in some tenth-rate American college. Despite the unusual nature of the fiction I was putting her into, I wanted to make her as believable as possible. The other characters, to me at least, are clearly ancillary, complementary, supplementary; her voice is the sustaining one. It's not the first time I've told a story in a woman's voice—there was my "Dunyazadiad," for example—but, by George, it certainly was an occasion when I worked hard on and worried a good deal about a narrator's voice.

Q. Letters spans centuries and focuses upon modern times—toward the end a reference is even made to 1978—but every letter is dated 1969. Surely you weren't writing a political allegory, but it does strike me that 1969 was an extraordinary and turbulent year.

A. To be honest, I would have to concede that 1968 was even more extraordinary and turbulent; it's the one that is most commonly considered the "Big Bang" year. There were assassinations and, well, I referred to most of it in the novel. But even if 1968 was the cultural watershed year in that decade, 1969 wraps up the decade. I suppose what we enjoy calling "the sixties" didn't end until 1972 or 1973, but I did have a certain *fin de décade* feeling as I was writing the novel, and the year served my purposes well. Already by 1969, the Vietnam war had turned its corner. Although the domestic explosions would continue for a couple of years, there was a genuine feeling that a lot of the uproar was winding down. And there was the happy detail that, although in 1969 no one had really begun to talk about our Bicentennial, the Bicentennial was in the wings and that event would occur precisely seven years down the road. I'm referring here to the fact that *Letters* abounds in sevens: seven chapters, seven narrators, etc.

Q. So that sad period of the sixties did have an effect upon you?

A. Indeed it did, and I confess that *Letters* was to be my Bicentennial book. I consoled myself with the thought that the revolution didn't end until 1783, and I gave myself until 1983 to finish this one. But, thank God for symmetry and sanity, it is coming out a neat decade after the date of the letters. I like the idea that it is coming out at the end of this decade. It's a happy coincidence and serves as some consolation that I couldn't have had it ready for 1976.

Q. Anyone thinking of the sixties can't help but note that in *Letters* you locate some action in two commune-like locales: Jerome

Bray's drug and goat community and Jacob Horner's Remobilization Farm. When I think of the lifestyles within the communes and of the frightening treatment accorded some of the women—Jeanine, Merope, and Marsha seem ravaged by drugs and metaphorically and literally raped—I wonder if you were making a comment about that aspect of the sixties. Were you commenting about, say, the violent and ugly forms that some of the glorious revolutions assumed?

A.   What was the word you used about the women?

Q.   "Raped, metaphorically and literally."

A.   That's a complex question and I'd like to give it a fair answer. Certainly most of the women up there spend a lot of time stoned out of their heads. And, you're right, a couple of them fare badly, don't they? But it seems to me that an equivalent number of men are violently dealt with, or at least dealt with in a spectacularly unpleasant manner.

Q.   The question took a direction I hadn't intended. What I meant to ask was, do the passages suggest you felt strongly that a number of disturbing and wrong turns had been taken in, let's say metaphorically, "1969"?

A.   Disturbing turns, for sure; I wouldn't say wrong ones. I'm not at all comfortable about describing *Letters* as a commentary upon the counterculture of that period. The counterculture is there in the novel, but it's there because it figured in everyone's life at that time. I don't know how you could write a book set in 1969 and fail to acknowledge what went on.

Q.   I guess you were especially confronted with it up in Buffalo?

A.   Perhaps it was as intense everywhere, but it's hard to imagine that it could have had a significantly greater presence than in Buffalo. There was a constant flow of refugees across the border: draft resisters, deserters, conscientious objectors, I suppose some malcontents as well. I'm afraid that, while I'm certainly not a nonpolitical animal, I'm not very political either, and during the time when there was so much turmoil on the campus at Buffalo, I was more of a deeply sympathetic spectator than a participant. So, the counterculture and the protests are in the novel, but I don't feel they're at the center of it. As I said, it's a difficult question. I wouldn't be surprised to learn that any true commune dweller or activist, or anyone deeply committed to the—what? validity, nobility?—of the psychedelic experience would find my portraits caricatures. To some extent, they are meant to be caricatures.

I guess I was worried about the suggestion I was giving short shrift to the women in the novel. I'll grant that Jeanine ends poorly, but I feel I portrayed her as sympathetically as I could. And the degradation and debasement of Lady Amherst, whom I admire enormously, does not occur as a result of any submissiveness on her part. I hope I have conveyed the idea that she has a large measure of British pluck and is constantly astounded about what *she permits* herself to get involved in. This has nothing to do with feminism or anything else; it's just the way some people's fates work themselves out. Lady Amherst does have ignominious times, I confess, but there are a number of other characters in the novel who suffer catastrophes of their own. It's odd, but there is an awful impulse one has at the end of a long project to sort of blow away a healthy portion of the cast of characters.

Q.   One thing a reader of *Letters* or *Sot-Weed Factor* can't help but notice is your extraordinary familiarity with history. I'm not simply referring to dates and events, though there are scads of both, but to the use of vocabulary and prose rhythms as well. Is this the result of an enormous amount of research, or have you always been a closet historian?

A.   "Research" is too presumptuous a term; let's say "homework" instead. I'm not an authority on American history in any of its aspects, nor do I pretend to have researched Tidewater Maryland history with any thoroughness. In this sense a novelist like me can be contrasted with an iceberg: nine-tenths of what I know is right there in the novel. That knowledge is picked up by inglorious— though, I hope, diligent—homework, and most of it is forgotten by the next book. You mentioned *The Sot-Weed Factor*; I have to admit I'd be hard-pressed to pass a quiz on the distinctions between what I looked up and made up in that novel. With *Letters*, I have every confidence that anyone who has an authoritative knowledge of Napoleonic history, the War of 1812, or those other convulsions of the nineteenth century will find some howlers in my pages. If so, my only defense, feeble though it may be, is they're howlers which escaped a reasonably attentive eye. It's my opinion that a novelist can become what can good-naturedly be called an "authority" on any subject if he's willing to spend a couple of honest weeks in the library, and if he's sensible enough to confine his pontifications to a chapter or so.

My aim is verisimilitude. I have no delusions about becoming an authoritative spokesman about a given historical era. On the other hand, it is part of the writer's sport to do this kind of thing somewhat rigorously. I surely don't wish to embarrass myself or insult a reader's intelligence. I hasten to add that I had the benefit of some superb fact-finders and copy readers; my wife, to whom I dedicated the book, is the foremost of them. You asked me earlier about whether I imagined an ideal reader. Well, I've been fortunate to find an ideal, and relentless, reader in Shelly. She has a tenacious memory and her recollection of details is breathtaking. If I hang a rifle on the wall in chapter one and forget to fire it 700 pages later, she'll pick it up at once. It's such a blessing. It's as if you're in love with a wonderful and beautiful woman who sobbingly confesses one day that she's spectacularly wealthy. So when an audience asks for whom I'm writing, I finally know the answer. There's nothing sentimental about it either.

Q.   You may disagree with this response, but I'd like to ask you about the way you ended *Letters*. I wasn't angry or saddened by the final portion of the novel, but I was rocked by what impressed me as both literal and psychological violence. The only thing I can compare it to is my horror at Rennie's death at the close of *The End of the Road*—although medically-attuned folks insist you made it obvious she would never have survived the abortion. So many things go badly at the end of *Letters*. A reader should be prepared to put up with Todd Andrews' rehearsing his *Floating Opera* suicide promises again. But, whatever Jacob Horner's sins, he is treated hideously by "Saint Joe"; Jeanine's problems are heart-breaking; Marsha and Merope seem to be addicts; the "damaged child" Angela is at least impregnated, perhaps raped, by Bray; Jane Mack seems widowed again, A. B. Cook VI may well have been obliterated. It really had an impact upon me—especially since I think these victims were quite believable and I really became involved with them. The catastrophes seemed appropriate and presaged but they hit hard. My question— an overly long question, I'm afraid—is, am I over-responding? Did I miss some kind of put-on?

A.   You didn't miss a thing. In fact, my earnest hope is that even the more fantastic characters—such as Bray, who might be a large insect of some kind—elicit a certain amount of sympathy by the novel's close. Fireworks play a role in *Letters*—it ends with explosions and references to the bombardment of Fort McHenry, and one could fairly draw an analogy to the extent that the characters in the novel are subjected to a similar bombardment at the end. The people start blowing up; it's no longer pyrotechnics but an actual massacre. Now this didn't come about, I hope, because I'm a violent or sadistic person. Rather, all my intuitions as a writer told me *Letters* was a novel in which the lives of some characters would end happily—or, better, would end in a mockery of a happy ending. But for the most part the lives of a number of characters had to end in violence and death, or in the likelihood of violence and death. Surely that's the way the decade ended; it's the way most historical periods seem to end. History *is* a bloody business, after all. As one character observes, the twentieth century may be turning out to be a disaster, but the nineteenth and eighteenth centuries were horrors too. And the other centuries hardly compare favorably.

Q.   You brought it off well; although the final carnage was alarming, it still seemed appropriate.

A.   You know, I should hasten to add, or Shelly will kill me, that it is not a foregone conclusion that Todd Andrews dies. Nor is it a foregone conclusion that he doesn't die.

Q.   You do leave Todd up in the air, don't you? He doesn't have the last page but his last letter is the most "recently" dated, and, accordingly, no one has a chance to tell whether he followed through on his suicidal plans. Also, there's a chance that A. B. Cook may not have been "lost at bay." And even though Lady Amherst is settling down with her hard-won husband, there is a splendid chance that the child she is carrying is Bray's. I wonder why you ended with so much ambiguity?

A.   Well, okay, it does end on an ambiguous note. But I don't think it's a clouded note since the terms of the ambiguity are quite clear, and I hope very much it doesn't end on an equivocating note. To answer: I think that dramaturgy is my strong suit and, in my role as teacher, I think it's the aspect of writing in which I can best serve an apprentice. Usually, dramaturgy is the last thing a talented writer learns, by the way. Usually a flair for language and a gift for observation are the first signs of talent that a teacher encounters. But dramaturgy, that business of creating a "whole action" in the

Aristotelian sense, the awareness that literary works really do have a beginning, middle, and end, is what a writer learns last. Indeed the ability or disinclination to come to terms with dramaturgy sometimes sorts out fiction writers from the people whose gifts essentially lie with the lyric. So because I regard dramaturgy as my strong suit, you can imagine I gave considerable thought and attention to the ending of *Letters*—even, I should say especially, in the very early stages of planning. I knew from the start I would be working with six separate voices and an authorial voice, and I quickly decided how I wanted to bring the threads together and end each narrative. One of the pleasures of composing a huge argyle-sock-of-a novel is the joy one feels in tying up all the threads. I hope, and believe, none of them was overlooked in *Letters*. You know, whenever I'm asked about the way I end a long work of fiction, I have to recall E. M. Forster's observation that if it weren't for funerals and weddings, God knows how novelists would get through their last chapters. In *Letters* I think I wound up with a sufficient number of funerals and weddings to satisfy Forster, and I feel the conclusions were appropriate.

I am one of a number of authors who believe that certain types of characters or types of suspense and narrative qualities demand appropriate denouements—conclusions that grow logically out of the plot and provide the reader with a challenging ending without causing him to make concessions to the writer's needs. Writers with that conviction must always be on guard against the temptation to fall back upon the escape hatches of what I call shaggy-dog dramaturgy: techniques like shuffling a problem around in the text until it gets lost, or contriving a happy ending designed to please as many people as possible. I think a danger I faced at the end of *Letters* was plotting myself into a corner. I think that in at least portions of the plot I was in a situation wherein if I had made it absolutely clear that a person did or didn't die, I would have stumbled. Rightly or wrongly, I felt it critical that the reader remain in doubt, for example, about whether that tower Todd Andrews is last seen holed up in blows up or not. I wasn't going to blow it up; I wasn't going to be the one to push the detonator at that point. And if my instincts were correct, as I hope they were, that is exactly and the only way to solve the dramaturgical problem without lowering some god down on wires.

Q.   You've done so much in your fiction and have done so in a way that is not repetitive. You've referred to your first two works as "twins" of sorts. Subsequently in *Sot-Weed Factor* you wrote an "eighteenth-century novel," in *Giles Goat-Boy* a computerized epic, in *Lost in the Funhouse* a "series" reflecting the various forms narration can take, and in *Chimera* a triptych of novellas about the creative process. Now you've re-created the epistolary novel and, in the process, resurrected some characters from earlier works . . .

A.   Let me anticipate: no, I have no intention of ever bringing any of those characters back again. Of course, I heard Kurt Vonnegut say that in *Slapstick* and then saw him wonderfully re-create Kilgore Trout in *Jailbird.*

Q.   That was the second half of the question. The first half was, where on earth are you headed next?

A.   I've never been lucky enough, the way some of my author friends are, to have two or three projects in the works at a given time. In fact, I find myself incapable of thinking about a new project until I'm immersed in the tedious but wonderful business of galley-proofing and ushering a just-finished book into print. The reason, I guess, is that although it *feels* like writing to proofread and whatever, it really isn't. You get the sensation of being creatively busy but in fact you're not composing, so half your mind is cleared to speculate about a new work. In every case, I've always moved to my next work in that out-of-the-corner-of-my-eye thinking that occurs when I'm making my contributions to the printing process.

Now, at this moment I know exactly what I want to do next and I don't mind talking about it to an extent. In a sense this is a remarkable moment in that I have two works in mind. On one hand, I've made a number of preliminary notes for a novel. I want it to be a short one and I've identified a number of prerequisites about form and whatever. But at the same time something has happened which has interrupted my work on the novel. A short time ago, I became a grandfather for the first time and, during the nine months of my daughter's pregnancy, it worked out that I was giving a reading about once a month. The readings were enjoyable and, no doubt because I was thinking about my future grandchild, I began to include in them a story I wrote for *Lost in the Funhouse*, one which was told from the point of view of an exhausted spermatazoa, swimming "upstream" and wondering what it was all about.

Q.   "Night Sea Journey"?

A.   Exactly. By the time my daughter gave birth, at any rate, I found myself appending a one-liner to the effect that, "Someday I want to write the egg's reply." Well, one of these days we authors are going to learn to be more cautious about our whims. By the time I had returned from a tour of some German universities with Jack Hawkes and Bill Gass, I discovered that my notes for the new novel had been pushed aside and the only thing I wanted to write about was that "egg." I had devised a plot and, remarkably for me, it gave every sign of becoming a television play. I have no idea where and how such a play could be produced. I've never written a play before; I've never written for the films or television; certainly dialogue is not my strong suit. But suddenly I find myself in the happy position of working with, in a way I hardly remember for a good many years, a story that wants to write itself. I can hardly wait!

In fact, when we finish this conversation—although I'm a "morning" writer by nature—I want very much to go back and play with my "egg" again. It's in the process of turning into two eggs, in fact. It's one of those serendipitous coincidences, but my wife and I just moved into a house on the eastern shore of Maryland. It's situated on the banks of a river, and the river forks at a certain point and divides into two equal and fairly large branches. I've looked at it on a map, and as I looked I was struck by the thought that it looks like nothing so much as two fallopian tubes conjoining in a uterus. And there I sit working on a plot where I have two eggs coming down, about to encounter a spermatazoa. I love the story! God help you, I feel as though I want to hold you here the way Coleridge's [Ancient] Mariner did and tell you my story—while all the time you're fidgeting to push on to the feasts of Philadelphia.

Q.   I'll sit here all night.

A.   Well, who knows? Whether or not the story comes out the way I've dreamt it, the idea has absolutely taken hold of me. And my next novel is going to have to wait until the story is finished.

Q.   That paves the way to a good last question: whatever the complexities of literary exhaustion, you haven't given up on fiction?

A.   Oh no, by no means. I'm a novelist and, although I've written short stories I'm proud of, I'm not a short-story writer. I definitely plan to write more novels, although I have no plans to produce another long one. I think three impositions upon the civilized mind along the lines of *Giles Goat-Boy*, *The Sot-Weed Factor*, and *Letters* should be sufficient for any writer's career. But I love short novels and I love novellas, and I do have a special ambition which I don't mind owning up to—because it won't break my heart if I never fulfill it. There are images in fiction that haunt my imagination, so much so that I even keep a little list of them. Foremost among them are: Odysseus trying to get home; Scheherazade telling her stories; Don Quixote riding with Sancho across LaMancha; and Huckleberry Finn floating down that river. I would love one day, without aspiring to include myself in that biggest of leagues, to come up with a similar image, one that was as much larger than the book in which it appeared as those images are larger than the stories in which they appear.

I love language, and I really believe that Huck's language, Huck's voice, is as much a substance in that novel as the image of Huck and Jim drifting down the Mississippi. But an old poet and a former teacher of mine here at Johns Hopkins once warned me: no actual book could possibly live up to the magnitude of that image of Don Quixote and Sancho as it works on our imaginations, all of us, even before we read the book. I think that's an accurate remark about *Don Quixote*. There are certain images that have mythopoetic voltage, that really are larger than the text, however magnificent the text might be. Gregor Samsa's cockroach is one of those images; Moby Dick is another. Leslie Fiedler talks about this sort or thing—although I suppose you could say that's his "bag"—but what we're all addressing is a tapping of some kind of mythic well that is larger than actual sentences. I don't agree with Fiedler when he suggests that what's really important in literature is what you remember when you've forgotten all the words. But, to say it more accurately, and certainly he said it this way too, an index of the mythic element in fiction may be what you remember when you've forgotten all the words. It's also that aspect of the story that could be most easily translated into another medium without loss. This sounds like heresy, but such an image could lend itself to the creation of a movie, or a T V show, or an opera. So who knows? It happened to Dickens once; one of his images got translated into sets of cheap china. The china isn't Dickens, of course, but it is a sort of mythic or mythopoetic element of Dickens which will never get lost in translation.

An Interview with Nadine Gordimer

Conducted by Stephen Gray

This interview took place on the mellow afternoon of 8 April 1980, during the South African autumn, at Nadine Gordimer's home of many years in Parktown, a lush, old residential suburb of Johannesburg. The setting is familiar to many South African writers, for, although Gordimer avoids coverage of her very private life, her house is always open to those blacks and whites who have a little magazine to launch, a new manuscript to prepare for print, a practitioner's problem to solve. Gordimer is the *doyenne* of South African English letters. Her concern has always been that the literature should flourish despite the climate of repression that has created a daily struggle with censorship, bannings of books and people, police intervention, and financial hardships.

For three decades, now, her firm support of the notion of freedom of expression in literature, a notion alien to the apartheid society, has been an inspirational touchstone to many. Although to her countrymen at large she might seem a remote figure—an intellectual stylist who has accumulated an international reputation, one who brings back home the big prizes no South African has won before—to the few peers she has within the country of her birth, she is reliably at the center of the tender and beleaguered literary scene, on call, ready with a strategy or a statement.

A slight and elegant person, a grandmother at 57, Gordimer has in recent years had her inscrutable privacy invaded by the publicity following her joint winning of the Booker Prize for *The Conservationist* (1974) and the promotional hype attendant on the appearance of her *Burger's Daughter* in 1979. After a promotional tour for Jonathan Cape and for Viking—she appeared even on the *Tonight Show*—she was off again, this time to Belgium, to receive an honorary doctorate at Leuven (Louvain), alongside El Salvador's Archbishop Romero, assassinated shortly thereafter. Awarded an honorary doctorate in South Africa, she had refused it as a gesture of nonacceptance of the segregated nature of the university in question. Her growing success has caused far more public appearances than one imagines she would like to make.

With her new collection of short stories (*A Soldier's Embrace*, 1980), the first since her *Selected Stories* (1975), in preparation in London, she was, during the week of this interview, once again fighting another round of the old, protracted, and gruesome battle with the South African controllers of publications. This time it was the fate of the imported copies of *Burger's Daughter*, which had precipitated the publication of her pamphlet, *What Happened to Burger's Daughter, or How South African Censorship Works*—a semi-clandestinely published collection that describes in full the bureaucratic labyrinth of checks that had had *Burger's Daughter* embargoed, banned from sale within the Republic, and—curiously—unbanned, from within, as *"bona fide* literature."

Since the novel describes among other things the inner workings of the revolution in South Africa, the dynamics of subversion on the part of liberation groups, Gordimer was fortunate: many works, particularly and predictably by black writers, not necessarily as frontal in their approaches to such contentious and, in fact, illegal matters, are neither sprung nor cleared. Currently all her work is available in her own country.

But compulsory involvement with the crisis situation of all other South African writers in a restricting situation like this has been Gordimer's platform at home for an unendurably long time—and her answer has consistently been a refusal to collaborate with, or participate in, the controls that drastically reshape the flow of information and opinion about literature and politics between the outside world and South Africa.

Yet, and this came out in the hours we talked, the everyday urgency of having to make a stand proves wearying, eroding. I had asked her if she would talk, for once, about herself—if she would drop, for once, the role of defender and champion, and let her attitudes to her own work be the subject. With that conceded, we began, almost with relief, to discuss what in other societies is a writer's privilege, taken for granted—his or her own right to a private world of ideas—but which, in the context of the society around us, felt like a rare luxury.

Q.   With the publication in 1974 of *The Conservationist,* and now with *Burger's Daughter,* it seems that your novels are showing a marked turning inward. Do you feel you have entered a new phase?

A.   I don't see it as definitively as that; I don't see a break. I see it as part of learning your craft, entering a new phase with every book.

Q.   What is your aesthetic motivation for this increasing exploration of the internal landscapes of character?

A.   Insofar as it's aesthetic, it has to do with finding the right means to express what I am discovering. Perhaps it's got more to do with the degree to which we conceal ourselves here. It's part of living in South Africa, having these incredible layers of concealment, and I suppose I've become more and more conscious of them in relation to other people, and even to myself. I've always said, and I still feel, that style is something that is dictated by the subject; it comes about through looking for the right way to deal with a particular subject, or an aspect of a subject. This inner-directed style comes about from the feeling that what we say and do—well, it's always only half of what we mean, but in South Africa it's less than half. And this constant shifting of foothold is both in terms of our society—in terms of relations to other people around you—and in terms of your own self-respect and your own self-esteem. I want to convey this constant shifting along, on very uncertain and uneven ground.

Q.   Both these novels use an alternating method of narration, between an exterior, impersonalized narrator and an interior monologue, juxtaposed. Is your intention to strip off exteriors more effectively by this means?

A.   It's to get increasingly at what is really there. I suppose it comes about through finding that if you are drilling straight ahead, so to speak, you are constantly slipping and glancing off what is in the person, off the true center of their motivation and the conglomeration of circumstances and inherited attitudes that make up the inner personality. I think the method is almost spelled out and becomes part of the actual book at the beginning of *Burger's Daughter,* where Rosa says to herself, in a natural kind of way, because she doubts what she is, what is it that they saw when they saw me standing outside the prison? That sums up the method that I've come to use. In order to grasp a subject, you need to use all the means at your disposal: the inner narrative, the outer, the reflection on an individual from other people, even the different possibilities of language, the syntax itself, which take hold of different parts of reality. So in the beginning of *Burger's Daughter* the high-toned, brave-sounding political prose of the faithful—all the clichés strung together, the set of half-truths along with the truths that go there—is contrasted with the very personal, allusive style of the old interior monologue.

Q.   Do you feel that this method is ultimately more liberating for your reader in South Africa, given our contemporary situation?

A.   Yes, I think so. It should be. That's what one is trying for.

Q.   Do you take the South African reader much into account?

A.   Well, I hope this doesn't sound patronizing, but no. The South African public, normally speaking, doesn't read much modern fiction, never mind contemporary fiction that breaks with the mode of direct narrative. In *The Conservationist* I completely ignored the difficulties of the reader. I've had some complaints. But people who have difficulty with a book like that one of mine have probably never read Faulkner, nor Virginia Woolf, never mind the *nouvelle vague.* I'm a little bit embarrassed by their difficulty. But the fact is that I made a tremendous effort to let the context spring its meaning upon the reader—I wasn't lazy or self-indulgent, I think. The success or failure of the book is the degree to which I have succeeded in doing that. But I felt in that book, writing about somebody, Mehring, who so lacked self-knowledge—not through lack of intelligence, but out of fear—it was absolutely necessary to let him reveal himself, through the gaps, through the slightest allusions. In *Burger's Daughter* there are two things going—Rosa's conscious analysis, her reasoning approach to her life and to this country, and then there is my exploration as a writer of what she doesn't know even when she *thinks* she's finding out.

Q.   The method is very similar in both novels, yet the characters are poles apart. How do you relate them to their society?

A.   The same method, but it's being used *on* Mehring in *The Conservationist,* whereas for Rosa it's being used much more subjectively. Mehring is hidden in a different way from the way that Rosa is hidden, in terms of the South African scene. And it's quite a shock even for me to think of it—Rosa Burgers and Mehrings are probably living within a few miles of one another. Right, there are tremendous differences between individuals in other parts of the world, particularly economic differences, but this instance is, somehow, particularly striking to me. Mehring is living a consciously restricted life, and he's doing it successfully so far as he's concerned. What this is doing to him, he really doesn't see. There's a glimmering of it only when his son comes to visit him. The terms of his relationship to society, I think, are worked out in his conversation with the woman with whom he has a love affair. From my point of view, that is the most successful part of the book, in achieving what I wanted to do; in the two people they are, in the pretenses that both of them have, I think very much comes out and conveys itself to the reader, even if the reader does not know the surrounding factual circumstances of their lives and doesn't understand every reference that is there. But in the case of somebody like Rosa—she belongs to a segment of society whose prime motivation is their relationship to society; it's the touchstone of their lives. So that, I suppose, sums up how I see it: that you can't opt out altogether. You are either running away from your inevitable place, or you are taking it on. By place I don't mean a predetermined place; your place depends on the role you take in society. But the fact is that you *have* a role; there's no such thing as an ivory tower—that's a place in itself. You are consciously or unconsciously creating a position in your society.

Q.   The common theme is the pursuit of happiness for the individual in conflict with his or her duties to society. Is this more densely true of *The Conservationist* and *Burger's Daughter* than of your previous works?

A.   It's densely and deeply true of these two, and if I've moved in a certain direction in the second half of the seventies, it has been in this direction. But I don't think that you can draw any moral about the happiness or unhappiness of the individual life. It would be very nice to say that if you live only for yourself, you're miserable. But I'm afraid it's not true. That's one of the truths that I've tried to air in *The Conservationist*. You can live Mehring's way, and probably get more fun, more immediate satisfaction out of life on many levels, than living the kind of life the Burger family did. Then again, it depends on what being alive means to you.

Q.   Do you consciously rely on common givens between yourself and your readers?

A.   There are givens that are understood only in South Africa, that perhaps people in England and America simply don't understand. But it's happened to me again and again, since I've traveled after my books have been written and have talked to people or perhaps been interviewed, that these blanks obviously do exist. But this is something that happens *after the event,* after the book has been written, and I could put my head on a block—I'm not lying to you when I say that I never think about them when I'm writing. Perhaps it's because in my own life, and in my own experiences, I feel that I'm living proof of the patronage and falsity of deciding that there is a reader who will understand this or that, a specific being to whom you are speaking, and a reader who will understand or will not. If I look back at my childhood and early adolescence, and remember what I was reading—without any preconceived notions of what I *ought* to be reading as an intelligent girl—then I can see that you simply never know what will light a spark of understanding in a reader who has never thought along that line before. To me that is what writing is about. So, the business of in-jokes, never mind in-inferences—if they come up naturally among my characters, then they are there. But it's not something that I would seek consciously. I think I've only done it once, and that's at the end of *Conservationist,* where the body that has been buried and "comes back" refers to Mayibuye, the black political slogan that means "Come back Africa"—back after the years of internal exile and white domination. It's the only beautiful, poetically valid slogan I've ever heard. That I put in, really, for myself, hoping perhaps that somebody would take note of my affirmation; as far as I know, nobody has . . .

Q.   In reviews of *Burger's Daughter,* when you are compared to any other writers, it is quite frequently to the Russian novelists of the nineteenth century. Do you feel that parallel is there? Were they and are you both writing about pre-revolutionary societies?

A.   Yes, there is a basic similarity of historical stages. Because of this, overseas reviewers sometimes recognize things that people over here very often miss. For example, we are in a revolutionary stage; we are in that stage *now.* A revolution doesn't happen overnight. The Russian Revolution started in 1905, and it went on through the century. And if you look at the pattern, our revolution is happening; our revolution started a long time ago, at least in the sixties, if not the fifties, and we go from phase to phase inexorably. I'm not talking about revolution in classic Marxist terms, obviously; when black majority rule comes, it will not necessarily be the dictatorship of the proletariat . . . it may be black capitalism, though I doubt it.

Q. In *Burger's Daughter* Rosa's consciousness dawns with the Sharpeville Massacre and the novel really closes with the riots of Soweto in 1976. Her life is drastically bracketed by these events. Is the novel a historical critique of this period, then?

A. I think it is a historical critique. But you must remember that Soweto overtook me while writing that book. This is what I think is so interesting about writing—how closely connected you are, not in a journalistic way, but inescapably connected with events.

Q. So the events weren't part of your structuring from the very beginning?

A. No, but Rosa would have come back to South Africa; that was inevitable. There would have been a different ending, though, without the Soweto riots. But that shows how there is a logical pattern to what is happening here. And when Rosa begins to talk to her father, at the end—I paraphrase—"You knew what the children have discovered, you knew that it would come from the people, as Lenin predicted." Well, here it came, indeed, not from the fathers of the people but from their children. Which is also, of course, a kind of reversal of what has happened to her; it's a turning over of predestination. She struggles against what she inherited from the father, embraces and struggles; and here you have a generation that turns the tables and takes the initiative.

Q. Do you regard your work as extremely personal?

A. Well, there is always this constant interplay of factors in a writer's life. This is what often distresses me, or very often distresses me, when I have an interview in America or in England—because the interest there tends often to be only in my life vis à vis the apartheid society in which I live. The other side—what happens to you as an individual, as a woman, as a writer—nobody is very interested in that. And I think that this kind of journalistic approach is tremendously one-sided, because the one couldn't be without the others.

Q.   You've said elsewhere that Africa needs an "articulated consciousness" and that it's the novelist's job to provide it. Do you stick with that?

A.   Yes, and I think that is what changes all the time in my own writing. My own consciousness has changed. I can certainly see that if I look at my early work. And, no doubt, if I keep my wits about me for a few more years, it'll keep on changing.

Q.   Reaction to your work here is severely polarized between awards of the highest literary honors and reliable official execration, bannings, embargoes, and so on. How do you handle this invariably bizarre reception?

A.   Well, I suppose I've never really thought about it, because I suppose I know it is going to happen. I have been protected all my life, and still am—after all this time and all these books and this middle age of mine—by such a fascination with what I'm trying to do, while I'm writing it, that I honestly don't think till afterwards, and sometimes in quite personal ways, of the consequences. I'm reckless when I write, and I always have the feeling that, oh well, it doesn't really matter, I'm *going* to do it. It's got to be done completely, or not at all.

Q.   But when the book's out, published, then embargoed, next thing wins some prize, it's banned, it's unbanned—do you just take it? I know that as a public spokesperson you are powerfully against this censorship process. But I mean, how are you personally affected? Water off a duck's back?

A.   Yes, because if you look at what happens to writers here, there's nothing unusual, really, about what happens to me.

Q.   Has this recurring humiliation worn you down over the years?

A.   No; but it depresses me. There's always this feeling about the book's life here, where it is so important to me. It's a platitude, but it's true; here you are among your own people, and you want to be read by them, and there's this grey area, this fog, that you struggle through to reach them. Indeed, you can't struggle through it, because there's nothing you can do—what *can* you do?—sell the damn thing on the street-corner? And be arrested for doing so?

Q. What has your general attitude to your work become in the seventies?

A. Well, speaking for myself as a woman and a citizen, I've become in the seventies much more radical in my outlook. This doesn't mean to say that I have suddenly taken on a new faith; I haven't. My way of coming to certain convictions, and accepting my convictions, is with eyes open; I can't do it any other way—I haven't in me that element of faith; it's missing. I mean "radical" in both senses. Politically I've become socialist in my general outlook, philosophically speaking, despite the fact that these are the years where one has seen the greatest failures of socialist experiments. But still, it's not in my nature to be totally cynical. I think that to be alive is an expression of belief in something, of an unkillable element in human advancement. I don't believe in perfection; I believe in limited goals, Camus' limited goals. So I'm ready to accept a tremendous element of failure that can't be eliminated, that one's never going to see the millenium—it probably doesn't exist. But this doesn't mean that one can live saying, right, let chaos come. I will still, in my life and in my work, seek for some principle of transcendental order, which implies progression in human terms. I still believe in that. But I would also say that the only thing that I'm one hundred percent sure of—and I have been since before I could formulate what was wrong with our life here, with this country—I just know that any form of racism is wrong. I don't see how one can see both sides of this ugly question; there aren't two sides—there are people who have the right to be human. That's the only thing I can say that I'm sure of. Nothing else.

An Interview with Joyce Carol Oates

Conducted by Leif Sjöberg*

Q.   Among all the poetry readings at the 92nd Street "Y" that I have attended, yours was the only one in which the writer held the manuscript up to the audience so that they could see its length. You wanted to "give warning," as you said, and to prepare your listeners "for the length of the poem" and the need for "concentration" for the duration of the poem. It was as if you established an agreement with your listeners about this particular poem, and when it was read we all relaxed, and you talked a little about it, quite informally. Have you done this at other readings, too?

A.   I make it a practice to suggest to the audience the relative length of a poem. This *is* important, but we take it for granted when we read the printed page, since we absorb the length unconsciously. Of course, my audience at the "Y" was too large for the necessary sort of intimacy. At smaller gatherings, or when meeting with university students, I make certain that they can see the size of the poem, so to speak.

Q.   In one piece that you read, "Leave-taking," there seemed to be a strong personal element. What was your central purpose in that poem?

A.   I had wanted to give voice to the uncanny, and rather beautiful, "presence of absence" we sometimes experience when we see the

---

* This interview, which originally appeared in the Stockholm magazine *Artes,* began at Princeton, where Joyce Carol Oates is a professor in the Writing division of the English Department. It was conducted over a period of several weeks in 1980, and continued through letters and telephone conversations.

familiar world emptied of ourselves. So many people have commented on this poem in which the house, emptied of furniture, belongings, and its tenants, has a future and a past, but no present! I was very pleased with the number of personal responses from listeners.

Q.   Did I miss something you said in that context about existential matters: doubting one's existence at certain moments, or the like?

A.   We *believe* we exist in terms of other people, our surroundings, our activities, or our environment. If these are altered or denied us — what then? Is there a personality that is, to quote Dickinson, a "zero at the bone?" Or is personality nearly all cultural — external trappings? These are questions some of my poems address themselves to.

Q.   At this same reading, you mentioned that you had extracted a large portion of a one-thousand page novel manuscript and made prose poems of it. How can that be done without getting the genres all mixed up?

A.   My new long novel is a series of interlocking tales, many of them mountain legends, fairy tales, and fabricated history. A typical mountain legend would lend itself easily to the narrative poem structure. The novel itself consists, in part, of prose poem sections. I chose deliberately to bring together the lyric, the epic, and the dramatic in a single experimental form.

Q.   What do you want to achieve with your poetry?

A.   I hope to achieve with my poetry whatever I hope to achieve with my fiction.

Q.   And that is?

A.   It is a kind of homage or worship, very difficult to explain.

Q.   Is inventiveness enough in poetry/art? How important is the corollary, observation, or "discovery," as Stevens put it?

A.   I am not a didactic person and cannot feel comfortable prescribing any general rules for poetry. I tend to feel that the practice of poetry is all — the theorizing is often a feeble attempt to justify the practice. I think that, if Stevens could have written as powerfully as Whitman, along Whitman's lines, no doubt he would have. But he could not — so his aesthetic theories differ. The same is true for Eliot, who often teaches cultural prejudices in the guise of poetry.

Remember that poetry is a great, great art — an enormous art — it can accommodate a great multitude of individuals!

Q.   O. K. Let's hear what you think of some of them. "The time for Beauty is over," said Pound, and continued, "Mankind may return to it but it has no use for it at present. The more Art develops the more scientific it will be, just as science will become artistic." Do you think we are likely to get more poems closer to science and the methods it employs?

A.   I believe that the science most humanists reject is bad science, devoid of human subtlety and imagination. Though I have not the training to appreciate it, I feel fairly certain that higher mathematics and physics can be as beautiful as poetry. Perhaps the inevitable tragedy of our complex civilization is that we must be specialists in our fields — and our fields have become increasingly difficult, so that communication is nearly impossible.

Q.   To return to Pound: he must have been of two minds in his views on "learned" poetry, on the one hand, and pure emotional poetry, on the other, since in "A Retrospect" he suggests that "Only emotion endures," and feels it is better to recall those particularly beautiful lines that ring in a person's head rather than locating them and accounting for their source and meaning, as scholars tend to do. What are some of the lines of poetry that have been especially haunting, meaningful, or beautiful to you?

A.   Many lines of poetry! — many indeed. Lines from Whitman, Yeats, Frost, Lawrence, Stevens ("Sunday Morning"), Eliot (*Four Quartets* above all), Keats . . . and, of course, Shakespeare, Donne, Wordsworth, Chaucer. For brevity, there is no one quite so uncanny as Emily Dickinson:

> After great pain, a formal feeling comes —
> The Nerves sit ceremonious, like Tombs —
> The stiff Heart questions was it He, that bore,
> And Yesterday, or Centuries before?
>
>   . . .
>
> This is the Hour of Lead —
> Remembered, if outlived,
> As Freezing persons, recollect the Snow —
> First — Chill — then Stupor — then the letting go —

Q.   What about Pound?

A.   I am quite ambivalent about Pound. Much of his poetry, it seems to me, is shrill and indefensible – as poetry and as wisdom.

Q.   I sense that you are not too keen on influences?

A.   As a student and teacher of English and American literature I have read literally thousands of poems, by both the classic poets and relatively unknown poets. No doubt there have been innumerable influences, but they are diffuse.

Most American poets have been influenced by Walt Whitman, our most "American" poet, and, to a lesser extent, Emily Dickinson. But I think Dickinson is so unique a voice that it is almost impossible to be influenced by her. Many of us writing now have been influenced – perhaps far in the past – by William Carlos Williams, who is, of course, related to Whitman, too.

Q.   I recall a poem you dedicated to the short story writer Flannery O'Connor; is there a connection there?

A.   My dedication in that instance indicates a thematic concern rather than any indebtedness to her writing. I was interested in O'Connor's apocalyptic imagination and what I take to be an excessive puritanism in her – a punitive inclination which I do not share.

Q.   Do you have a convenient definition of poetry?

A.   Poetry is a rite involving language – at its very highest a sacred rite in that it transcends the personality of the poet and communicates its vision, whether explicitly or by indirection, to others. Many poets speak of the almost impersonal nature of their art when it is most pure and inspired.

Q.   I would like to ask what poem satisfies you the most among your own works?

A.   Always the most recent work; that is, a long poem in *The Atlantic* called "The Present Tense."

Q.   If I am not mistaken, you have published nine major novels, ten collections of short stories, five collections of poetry, two books of essays, plays, and anthologies, and at present you are at work on a major novel while teaching. Creativity seems to be your proper element, but the rest of us do not create a great deal, or at least not much of permanent value. Do you feel that you are unusually prolific?

A.   I believe I have a reputation for writing a great deal only because the older, healthy tradition of the writer as an extremely hard-working and persistent craftsman is no longer fashionable. It appears that I am somewhat unusual, but measured against Balzac, Dickens, Henry James, Edith Wharton, Dostoevski, and many others, among the serious writers, I am certainly not unusual. I find solace in their example and would place myself—I hope not immodestly, but one must have ideals—in their tradition.

Q.   Do you write every day?

A.   Yes, usually for many hours. I write and write and write, and rewrite, and even if I retain only a single page from a full day's work, it *is* a single page, and these pages add up. As a result I have acquired the reputation over the years of being prolific when in fact I am measured against people who simply don't work as hard or as long.

Q.   Do you find this unfair?

A.   That goes without saying, but I have learned to be amused rather than hurt or antagonized by certain charges. I take with absolute seriousness Flaubert's claim that "we must love one another in our art as the mystics love one another in God"—and so my dedication to literature springs from a conviction that it is a "mystical" affirmation or our common human bond.

Writing and, of course, reading are quite simply, for me, the most transcendent of experiences. Even ostensibly violent or despairing literature, like Beckett's, for instance, or much of Faulkner's, I interpret in James Joyce's words as underscoring the eternal affirmation of the human spirit. I am somewhat embarrassed to be speaking in such terms, but those are my beliefs. That I am so passionately committed is probably evidenced by my presumed proliferousness! But even so mandarin a writer as Nabokov—whom I admire, but with qualifications—manages to be prolific, when his total oeuvre is examined.

Q.   Coming back to the question of your own creativity. Is there a compulsive element in all this activity . . . ?

A.   I assure you, there is very little that is compulsive about my life, either in my writing or otherwise. I believe that the creative impulse is natural in all human beings, and that it is particularly powerful in children unless it is suppressed. Consequently, one is behaving normally and instinctively and healthily when one is creating—literature, art, music, or whatever. An excellent cook is also creative! I am disturbed that a natural human inclination should, by some Freudian turn of phrase, be considered compulsive—perhaps even pathological. To me this is a complete misreading of the human enterprise. One should also enjoy one's work, and look forward to it daily.

Surprisingly enough, over the years I have come to be more and more certain of these beliefs. I am possibly more dedicated to teaching now than I was in my early twenties, and the same is true about my feelings toward literature. In the past twenty years I have seen my ideals affirmed rather than eroded. Of course I have difficult days with my writing, but in general all that I have just said is true for every hour of my life.

Q.   Swedish literature is, of course, far from lacking in violence, but it has tended to emphasize sex rather than violence, while American literature—and TV—tend to be more violent. What is your rationale for employing the theme of violence so often in your books?

A.   I don't accept charges that I am unduly violent in my writing. Most of my novels and stories are explorations of the contemporary world interpreted in a realist mode, from what might be called a tragic and humanistic viewpoint. Tragedy always upholds the human spirit because it is an exploration of human nature in terms of its strengths. One simply cannot know strengths unless suffering, misfortune, and violence are explored quite frankly by the writer.

Q.   In the case of Balzac, who was so enormously productive, there was a plan, which, as you know, later became *La Comédie humaine*. Since your books all seem to deal with American social unrest, are you following a specific plan in your own writing?

A.   I certainly do have a general plan for my writing. But I am not accustomed to making statements about my writing, since this seems like self-advertisement. I would prefer to allow the books to stand on their own—even at the risk of being misinterpreted from time to time. Though I am ambitious about my writing I am not ambitious about my career in terms of recognition. Some understanding and sympathetic readers are the most I dare hope for.

Q.   You can't leave the question half answered like that . . .

A.   Since approximately 1965 I have set myself the task, in both novels and short stories, of exploring contemporary society on many levels. My focus has been a close examination of the sources of power. The political and economic milieu; professions like medicine, the law, and most recently education and religion; and, to some extent, the predicament of the young and of women—all these have fascinated me.

Q.   What is your position on women's liberation?

A.   I am very sympathetic with most of the aims of feminism, but cannot write feminist literature because it is too narrow, too limited. I am equally sympathetic with male characters as with female, which has been a source of irritation to some feminist critics. . . . An unfortunate situation, but one which I cannot help.

Q.   In his book *The Progress of the Human Mind* Condorcet gives an outline of history that ends on a hopeful note: that equality of men, equality of nations, and also "the real improvement of men" would some day come about. Since 1794 when his essay appeared, we have seen small wars, large wars, world wars, despotism, totalitarianism, natural disasters, the Holocaust, failures of all kinds. How do you assess the chances for "improvement" of the human condition?

A.   First I must state my position about all forms of creativity, including my own: these acts are gratuitous offerings and bring something—a vision, an argument, an illumination of a certain corner of the world, a style, a music, an aspect of personality—into the world which did not previously exist. The creative act is an *acte gratuite*. It withdraws nothing from the world—not the intellectual world, not the material world. At its base it is a spontaneous birth, usually presented to the world as an offering or gift. Consequently the creative act and its product are an end in themselves, complete. Like a bird's song—on a much higher structural level. The artist is forever being called upon in the United States to justify himself or herself: and in a way that for instance the manufacturer of toothpaste, automobiles, cigarettes, every sort of material goods is not.

My feeling about art in every form is that, first, it is primarily a natural, spontaneous, inevitable motion of the soul, unique in our species; and, second, that it becomes transformed as it is directed toward a certain social, moral or religious context—at which point it generally acquires its "moral" dimension.

I am responding, of course, to your questions *only* in the spirit of the second category. My persistent and fundamental belief is that art is an expression of the human soul and need not ever, in any circumstances, justify its existence.

Q.   And the "human condition" . . .

A.   It has been greatly—enormously—in fact miraculously improved. One simply cannot look at the civilized world as it exists today, in 1980, and compare it to an abstract Platonic condition of perfection. Improvement exists in nearly every sphere of life, particularly domestic and social life, in civilized nations of the West, and elsewhere. One must go slowly, of course, and prudently, always with an awareness that Utopia is a myth, but if one considers the conditions of workers, for instance, in both the United States and Europe—not simply wages and work-hours, but working conditions, benefits, pensions—the progress within a few decades has been astonishing. I speak as the child of a working class family.

Q.   Where did your family come from?

A.   My maternal grandparents emigrated from Budapest in the early years of the twentieth century. Working and living conditions were extremely difficult at that time, as one might imagine.

In another sphere, that of women's rights, immense progress has been made. It is simply too easy to cast one's eye about to find faults, set-backs, "imperfections." They will always exist, our world is not Utopia. I could speak at great length on this subject, because I feel strongly about it.

Q.   How do you relate to the "past?"

A.   There is nothing more absurd than to hear someone, often an intellectual, speak romantically of the past: the nineteenth century, in which children of eight or nine toiled in sweat-shops; the medieval period, in which mad religious struggles killed so many people; even antiquity, when the Greeks, a refined people, held onto their slaves and denied citizenship to women! Only someone without a realistic historical perspective can believe sincerely that "the past" is superior to the present.

Q.   What do you think the arts can do to improve or develop people?

A.   It was said by W. B. Yeats that "tragedy breaks down the dykes between people." This is true, and it is true for comedy as well. As soon as one opens a book, by an American, a Japanese, a South African, a Hungarian, one is in the consciousness of another. The psychological and emotional act of reading has yet to be fully explored or understood. In no other art is this really possible. For instance, I have taught classes of as many as 130 students, working with them on novels like Mishima's *Confession of a Mask,* which in many ways is a difficult novel for North American students to understand. Within a few days the students' sympathy and interest are remarkable. Or consider the work of Anzia Yezierska, a Jewish writer of the 1920s and 30s, now little known, whose novels about immigrant life on the Lower East Side did so much to bridge the gap between her people and Americans. Abraham Lincoln, meeting Harriet Beecher Stowe, commented that *here* was the person who had brought about the Civil War, hence the freeing of the slaves.

Q.   Auden used to say that none of his poems had saved the life of a single Jew during the Hitler era . . .

A.   That may be, but in recent times one might think of Solzhenitsyn. One can hardly measure the effect his books have had upon the world, politically as well as emotionally. It would be possible for me to name many writers who have had a considerable impact upon their culture, in both private and public ways. Dickens, for instance, Dostoevski. And Yeats, whose effect upon Irish nationalists was great.

Q.   What can your own books do in that direction? Or, what would you want them to do?

A.   Evidently my books are taught in university classes in various parts of the world. I can't be certain, however, *how* they are taught . . . or even how accurately they are translated. At a recent conference of Soviet and U. S. writers it was explained to me that my books were read in the Soviet Union, apparently with sympathy. I am surprised to learn that a group of short stories sold quite well in Hungary.

But, of course, I would be very modest about claiming that my books might "improve" humanity. The writer hopes to reach out to a reader . . . to a single reader at a time. The proper object of the writer's hope is not a crowd but an individual. Beyond that it is vainglorious to speculate. Writers who might be accused of being extremely self-absorbed, like Flaubert, for example, often create works of art that are devastating in their power to arouse sympathy in others.

Q.   Take someone like Joyce . . .

A.   Yes, it is rarely commented upon that his *Ulysses* is a masterpiece of empathy, for Leopold Bloom, the lonely Jew, who is at once a Dubliner and a member of the human species: an extraordinary creation for a writer whose reputation is generally considered elitist.

Q.   Are your books used in courses in departments other than the English department?

A.   At least in the United States; in sociology, for instance, or psychology, and then I am a bit apprehensive. For though the writer naturally hopes that various kinds of insights and information might be gleaned from his/her work, she/he does create a work of art primarily, which must obey its own internal laws of structure and aesthetic resonance. But I never write to lure the reader, or to "entertain," in the light sense of the word.

Q.   Why not?

A.   There are quite enough entertainments, especially in America, at the present time.

Q.   But to diminish, mitigate or lessen problems?

A.   Never! And never to solve problems by authorial fiat. My personal experience—both as a reader and a teacher of literature—is that difficult and troubling works of art, *King Lear,* for instance, are far more beneficial than happy works. One learns so much from Thomas Mann, Dostoevski, Kafka, Melville, and other great writers precisely because they refused to soften their vision of humanity. Yet, even including Kafka, they are by no means negative. I have written an essay on Kafka's mysticism, in particular his relationship to Taoism. He is a much misunderstood writer!

Q.   Like many of his contemporaries, Condorcet hoped that science would explain human behavior. What hopes do you have for science in this respect?

A.   Once again, outlawing the very concept of Utopia or perfection, I must say that science and its subsequent technology has done immeasurable good for mankind. Science is, of course, of two kinds, theoretic and practical. In the first category we might very well place great philosophical thinkers, for instance, who have helped mankind think its way through superstitions and other forms of ignorance. Great scientists, like Einstein, are usually mystics, guided by impulses (perhaps laws?) of creativity they cannot understand. I am convinced that the great scientists, like the great artists, are expressions of the evolutionary motion of a species.

Q.   What would you say the novel has done which science has failed to do?

A.   The novel, like all forms of art, is an expression of a subjectivity which might then be translated into the *universal,* while science deals only with the universal or the representative. One of the little-understood responsibilities of the artist is to bear witness — in almost a religious sense — to certain things. The experience of the concentration camps . . . the experience of suffering, the humiliation of any form of persecution. Ralph Ellison's novel *Invisible Man* is a brilliant portrayal of the experience of one black man in America — one cannot read it without being deeply moved. . . . The experience of being a woman in a patriarchal culture. . . . Any form of subjectivity that resonates with universal power complements the function of science, the objective discipline.

Q.   The gap seems to be widening between serious literature and light literature. Serious, intellectual literature requires more and more commentaries, it appears, for fewer and fewer readers. Is there, in your opinion, a risk that literature is becoming too intellectual?

A.   No. I cannot agree that the gap is widening between serious literature and light literature! Our great age of modernism, in English, at least, is past. Though we read Joyce and, to a lesser extent, Pound, though we admire Henry James immensely, most of us who are serious about our writing have no interest in the high modernist position. One can point confidently to a writer of genius who has never been a self-consciously coy artist, and who has written books — at least one of them a masterpiece — that can be read by nearly anyone: Saul Bellow.

Q.   What other writers are readily accessible?

A.   Bernard Malamud. John Updike. Iris Murdoch. John Fowles, and many others.

Q.   How about poetry?

A.   We are, perhaps temporarily, in a period in American poetry in which difficulty, obscurantism, and private allusions are applauded by the critics, sometimes with justification — for a highly self-conscious writer, like Yeats himself, can also be an extraordinarily good writer. Certainly there are extremely obscure experimental writers — but their influence on the culture is quite minimal. Some of them are friends of mine — and so I can appreciate the sincerity of their art. It is their art; they haven't much choice about its degree of difficulty. Since I prefer Saul Bellow's writing to that of his experimental contemporaries, and since his books have been translated widely, and have made an impact, I can't feel pessimistic about this problem. Garcia Marquez's *One Hundred Years of Solitude* is another recent phenomenon: a lengthy, difficult, rather quirky novel in Spanish that has sold more than *Don Quixote*! Offhand I would say that in the U. S. the gap was far more serious in the nineteenth century. One can scarcely believe how our American masterpieces were ignored in favor of utterly insipid, improbable "novels" which became fantastic best sellers and are now completely forgotten. For a serious American writer — especially for a woman writer — this is by far the best era in which to live.

Q.   How would you define your concept of beauty? And why is there so much sordidness in your books?

A.   Beauty is a cultural ideal, often a cultural prejudice. In the abstract it really cannot exist, for even Einsteinian standards of "Spinozan calm" have meaning only within the human imagination.

In my more recent stories there is probably less that is disturbing or violent since I have become far more concerned with the tragic within the human spirit. In *Son of the Morning,* the most extreme violence is that which occurs when the divine and the human intersect — and this is a subjective, interior experience, difficult to explain in ordinary language.

It should perhaps be re-emphasized that literature — particularly dramatic literature — focuses upon the moment in lives at which conflicts erupt. Think of Ibsen, Strindberg, Chekhov, and of course Shakespeare! Consequently it seems to concern itself with conflict; but this is not, strictly speaking, true. It concerns itself with the momentum of lives, the accumulating fears, tensions, lies, and illusions that then erupt on stage within a two- or three-hour duration.

So very economic and condensed an art always appears to be more violent, or sordid, than in fact it is.

Q.   Obviously it would be boring if there were too much sameness, if we were all alike, like polished grains of rice. The unusual, the unpredictable, that which is different, should command our interest. But why are so many of your most important characters on the boundaries of sanity?

A.   Sanity, too, is a cultural prejudice, especially in nations that insist upon conformity in public affairs, like the United States. Many of the most imaginative and original thinkers — from Mozart to Newton to Einstein to Emily Dickinson — can be too casually dismissed by "normal" people as eccentrics. I agree with recent criticism of the psychiatric profession that focuses upon narrow and outmoded standards of normality and sanity against which people are presumably measured. Can Oedipus, King Lear, Ivan Karamazov, and Faulkner's doomed heroes be casually categorized as mad? On the contrary, it has always seemed to me, even as a much younger woman — as a high school student, in fact — that insane behavior of many kinds was the norm in our society.

Q.   Would you give an example of what you have in mind?

A.   As children of eleven and twelve we were forced to participate in "atomic bomb" drills and told "Better dead than red!" — the idea being that the United States and Soviet Russia might blow up the world within a few years, and that this probably would have to happen since neither could tolerate the other's existence. Other aspects of collective madness, many of them frankly absurd, impressed upon me the fact that the individual who thinks for himself or herself, critically and unsentimentally, would probably be branded as eccentric or even crazy in such a society. I do not exactly accept the statement that many of my most important characters are on the boundaries of sanity: it seems to me that these people extend the boundaries — that they are not to be measured by the usual conformist standards.

Q.   In the event critics would venture to state that you tend to repeat yourself, how would you reply?

A.   I am not really aware of repetition within my work. Each novel is a stylistic and structural experiment, from my point of view. Of course, all writers repeat themes, one way or another . . . Proust,

Joyce, Faulkner, Bellow, certainly Kafka, Beckett, and others — but it is to be hoped that a new angle of vision, or a newer depth, makes the work innovative. Since I have written more than 300 short stories, for instance, it is perhaps unavoidable that some themes might be repeated; but from my personal point of view each project is new, and addresses itself to new problems and explorations. I am currently much interested in the drama, for instance, which forces a new perspective, and is very stimulating indeed.

Q.   Do you think you have learned more from books or people? I refer particularly to books by others, but perhaps also to your own books, or writing them.

A.   But one cannot distinguish between books and people! An excellent study of Mozart, for instance, leads us deeply into Mozart; a novel by Faulkner leads us into an aspect of human nature we have perhaps not yet encountered; poetry by one's friends and close colleagues reveals an angle of vision, and often a depth, or soul, not available in ordinary social discourse. No novelist scorns or undervalues reality, of course, for this is the very life-blood of our art: close observation of people, places, customs, beliefs, practices.

    The writer also learns immensely from his own writing — for each work of art, particularly the lengthy ones, demands an immersion in thinking and experience that would not ordinarily be one's own; and of course the discipline in creating such long works is very strict and very rewarding. D. H. Lawrence believed that the novel was, among other things, an arena for the testing of the author's ideas — those which were weak would be revealed as weak, and those which were strong would triumph. This is perhaps not always the case, for there are powerful works of art whose "ideas" sometimes seem questionable but which satisfy as aesthetic accomplishment none the less.

Q.   Whom did you have in mind?

A.   Beckett, whose extreme nihilism puzzles me . . .

Q.   This may be a ticklish question, but how do you rate some of your contemporaries?

A.   I would not rate them, since it is offensive to my principles to "rate" human beings, especially in such very subjective terms.

    But Faulkner is clearly the most significant writer. Hemingway is second. Others should not be rated along the same scale at all; they cannot be spoken of in the same context as Faulkner and Hemingway. I can't evaluate Dreiser and Sinclair Lewis, for example, as "artists," only as writers who have contributed important commentaries on social life in America. Dreiser's curious elephantine "mysticism" — in *Sister Carrie,* for example, when he speaks of an inevitable evolution, a "progress" in history — is intellectually indefensible. Lewis, though a good satirist, lacks subtlety and a sense of the depth of human experience.

Q.   Among the older American authors Eudora Welty and Katherine Anne Porter are supposed to belong to your favorites?

A.   Eudora Welty is a favorite of nearly everyone! A very fine, wise writer, less ambitious than the other authors we just mentioned, of course; but within the range of her intention she is completely successful. Of non-American women writers Isak Dinesen is much-admired.

Q.   What are your standards in determining what is important in literature?

A.   Standards of greatness must encompass depth of vision; a breadth of actual work; a concern for various levels of human society; a sympathy with many different kinds of people; an awareness of and concern with history, or at least contemporary history; a sense of the interlocking forces of politics, religion, economics, and the mores of the society; concern with aesthetics; perhaps even experimentation in forms and language; and above all a "visionary" sense — the writer is not simply writing for his own sake, but to speak to others as forcefully as possible.

Q.   It seems obvious especially in your later works that Jung is of importance to you. What books of his have you read and what have you got out of them?

A.   I am a voracious reader, and Jung is one of innumerable writers and thinkers I have read. Since I cannot accept his theories on the "male" and "female" archetypes I am not a "Jungian" — but I find his exploration of the Unconscious extremely intriguing. He is quite different from Freud, who imagines the unconscious as an adversary to consciousness. Jung understands that the wellsprings of life — creativity above all — reside in the Unconscious and its functions.

In Jung one confronts a bold, original, and "poetic" imagination, valuable for the questions it raises as much as for the answers it hopes to provide. I would set Jung beside Nietzsche; both men are brilliant, and brilliantly provocative. One need not *believe* in their theories in order to learn from them.

Q.   To what extent do you study influences with your writing students?

A.   It is dangerous to place too much emphasis upon influences; this is a critical method of the past decade, as you know, exemplified by the Yale critic Harold Bloom, which has recently been subjected to wide and quite convincing rejection. Most novelists and poets are probably most powerfully influenced by their early surroundings: they wish to capture universal truths in the form of particular, even local types, and give life to the larger element of the human psyche by way of familiar images.

Q.   You have indicated that it is the restless who interest you as a novelist, "for only out of restlessness can higher personalities emerge, just as, in a social context, it is only out of occasional surprises and upheavals that new ways of life can emerge." In what way can we expect that this point of view will be employed in your future novels?

A.   My next novel, which is my most ambitious and also longest to date, is a complex parable of American aspirations and tragic shortcomings.

Q.   Have you already decided on a title?

A.   It is called *Bellefleur* and is imagined in the symbolist mode, though its concerns are very historical. It covers a period of time from approximately the American War of Independence until the present day, though time is treated symbolically. The elder members of the powerful Bellefleur family are destroyed but, one by one, their children—who may represent a younger or at any rate more selfless and idealistic America—escape their influence, and achieve their independence apart from the family's authority.

Q.   That sounds like both tragedy and comedy.

A.   It is. It is a tragedy in that many people are destroyed, in both a spiritual and literal sense, and a comedy in the higher sense that the instinct for survival and self-determination is celebrated. It was a considerable challenge for me, as the author, to imagine a conclusion that was both tragic and comic simultaneously . . . *Bellefleur* is, as I said, quite long, and filled with many characters and stories, all of them centering upon the American dream in both its daylight and nightmare aspects.

Q.   Isn't there a certain risk that a work that mixes tragedy and comedy will be misinterpreted?

A.   Sure. It has happened before. One of my longest books, *The Assassins,* was misunderstood by more than one critic. But if the new book is viewed as a poetic analysis of America, its meanings should not be elusive.

Q.   Some of your short stories, such as "The Lady with the Pet Dog" and "Metamorphosis," are related to the work of familiar writers. Is this technique a lower form of creativity, not entirely original?

A.   Postmodern writing often gains a secondary meaning by its juxtaposition to other works of literature or art. The stories stand on their own and were, of course, published on their own, but they are meant to have an allusive quality. Contrast is, of course, gained – but also a curious and ironic sympathy. The great writers were once young and unknown and struggling merely to be published; their works were not pronounced "great" for many years. I think the similarities between us all are far stronger than one might commonly realize.

Q.   What are your feelings about experimentation? I would assume that a master stops experimenting at a certain point.

A.   All serious writers are interested in experimentation. It is a means by which they honor their craft.

Q.   Are there critical assumptions from which your stories operate?

A.   The short story is the form in which I have worked most with experimentation. Virtually each story is an attempt to do something different – consequently it is extremely difficult for me to speak of my short stories in general terms. They proceed from a basis of psychological realism; however, often they take place in an individual's mind. I have become more and more interested in recent years in developing stories that are really miniature novellas: stories that deal with a person's entire life, greatly condensed and focused.

An example would be "Daisy" in the 1978 volume *Night-Side,* which deals in a surrealist manner with some of the issues involved in the relationship between sanity and insanity—the story is based very informally on James Joyce's relationship with his schizophrenic daughter Lucia. Another story from the same volume, "A Theory of Knowledge," is a poetic attempt to dramatize the contradictions inherent in philosophizing—in abstracting from the world of sense experience and personal history: this story is very informally based on the later life of the famous American philosopher Charles Sanders Peirce. Of course it is entirely fiction.

Q.   Are there any of your stories in which escape or humor, rather than interpretation or revelation, dominates?

A.   I have written a number of satiric stories set in a fictitious university, gathered in the collection *The Hungry Ghosts.* These are serious stories, too, but their structure, pace, and characterizations mark them as deliberately light or humorous reading.

Q.   Which is your favorite of your stories?

A.   A very difficult question to answer. "Queen of the Night," which appeared in a special limited edition (Lord John Press, 1979), is one of my favorites. I am extremely fond of "Daisy," too, and "Stalking" and "The Dead" from *Marriages and Infidelities*; and "In the Region of Ice," "Where Are You Going, Where Have You Been?" and "How I Contemplated the World from the Detroit House of Correction . . ." from *The Wheel of Love.* "Famine Country" and "The Widows" (which I recently expanded into a play) from *Night-Side* are additional favorites.

A final comment on discursive conversations: as Nietzsche warns, "Talking much about oneself may be a way of hiding oneself." The most reliable introduction to any writer is simply the books.

An Interview with Margaret Atwood

Conducted by Betsy Draine

On a warm afternoon in April 1981, Margaret Atwood greeted a mixed group of University of Wisconsin undergraduates, graduate students, and faculty—all gathered for a question-answer session with the Canadian writer. Like most other Americans, these questioners were more knowledgeable about Ms. Atwood's novels than about her poetry.

The American fame of Margaret Atwood began in 1972 with the publication of *Surfacing,* a stunning novel with a style as blunt and cruel as the topics it addressed: abortion, abandonment, death, pollution, numbness. Subsequent novels—*Lady Oracle* (1976), *Life Before Man* (1980), and *Bodily Harm* (1982)—confirmed Ms. Atwood's reputation as an accomplished storyteller and stylist. Her narrative voice is direct but disturbing—decidedly flat, modulated slightly by shifts into sarcasm. She makes this voice express a stance toward life: defensive, measured, ironic, determined to suppress any forceful emotion. Resentment, disappointment, yearning—each is always there, but in hiding.

The tone of emotions "in exile" dominates her poetry, as well:

> I said, in exile
> survival
> is the first necessity.
>
> After that (I say this
> tentatively)
> we might begin
>
> Survive what? you said.
>
> In the weak light you looked
> over your shoulder. You said.
>
> Nobody ever survives.

In this last section of the poem "Roominghouse, winter," from *The Animals in That Country* (1968), Atwood announces themes that run through her poetry, her fiction, and, by her own diagnosis, through Canadian literature as a whole: the necessity of survival, yet its inadequacy; the desire for a goal that survival might serve, yet the recognition—or the fear—of its absence. Atwood named her 1972 critical survey of Canadian literature *Survival,* and there she acutely notes the potential grimness of the survival theme. What good is survival, if one cannot share with someone a conviction of the meaning of continued existence? The poems of *The Journals of Susanna Moodie* (1970) confront this question directly, since the volume is based on journals of a nineteenth-century woman who pioneered in the Canadian "bush." In her seven other volumes of poetry—as in this one—the theme of survival is translated to the metaphoric level. As Atwood herself notes, today's writer tends to focus not on obstacles to physical survival but on "obstacles to what we may call spiritual survival, to life as anything more than a minimally human being." This is an apt description of Atwood's own poetic "matter" —from the early poems of *The Circle Game,* which won the prestigious Governor General's Award in 1966, to her latest volume, *True Stories.*

The first half of the interview is based on questions by students, the second half on my follow-up questions. Many of the students sought reassurance that their own personal histories, working methods, or literary theories would be conducive to good writing. Ms. Atwood startled the young writers with responses that refused comfort. She challenged the assumptions behind their questions and demonstrated in her answers that independence of mind which she often explicitly recommended.

Q.   Can you tell us a little about your education?

A.   I luckily did not have to go to school full time until I was in grade eight, and I think that was probably a good thing. After that I went to high school, and then I went to Honors English at University of Toronto. That course does not exist anymore, but it was a very intensive course which began with Middle English and ended with T. S. Eliot, roughly. It was English literature—not much American and not a great deal of modern. I then went to Radcliffe, for graduate school in English, specializing in Victorian; it turned into Harvard the next year, so then I went to Harvard. And about all I can tell you about that is that it was a lot preferable to being a waitress as a way to write and that they wouldn't let women into the Lamont Library, which is where they kept the modern poetry, so I didn't read any modern American poetry while I was there. I did, however, study Puritan literature and the Romantics, and I could read all the modern Canadian poetry I wanted to, because it wasn't in with the "real" poetry—it was in with the folklore. Stuck underneath werewolves and vampires they had "Canadiana"—it wasn't just poetry, it was everything, including fashion magazines, but that's where it was. So it was easily accessible to me, whereas other modern poetry wasn't.

I don't think that was necessarily the important part of my education, however. Important parts of your education occur in extra-curricular activities. For example, it was very constructive to learn how to build treeforts and to pick up items of information such as that if you build a tunnel in the sand it's dangerous to crawl through it, because it may fall in on top of you. Those are the kinds of things that you really need to know if you are going to be a writer. Let me put it this way: A young student came to me who had been through a program of theology, so she was very heavily cerebral. She said she wanted to be a writer and showed me something she had written. I said, "What are the people wearing?" and she said, "I don't care." I said, "Unless you care, you're not going to be a writer." You don't have to put all that stuff in the story—what they had for breakfast, what kind of socks they have on, but you have to know it, and not only that, you have to care enough about such details to pay attention to them. Paper dolls are useful in that respect.

Q.   Have you always written?

A.   According to one of my aunts, whose word I do not necessarily take, I announced when I was five that I was going to be a writer, but I think that was probably in the same spirit that I announced a number of other things that I was going to be. I did write at that age, and I wrote books. I made the book first, and then I wrote in it until it was full. That gives you a sense of the book as an object in itself.

At that time I wrote poetry, novels, all of which remain unfinished, and comic books, and plays, and then I stopped at about the age of eight. I had a "dark period" between the age of eight and the age of sixteen. When I was sixteen, I decided to write again, and I decided that it was much more interesting than anything else I was being led to believe I could do—though it was not in the guidance book. What was in the guidance textbook for girls was public school teacher, secretary, airline hostess, nurse, and home economist. That was 1955, roughly.

Q. What was the influence that your parents had on you, either negatively or positively?

A. My parents gave me an excellent set of genes. That's about the best thing your parents can do for you. My parents are both very smart. They had three weird children, which they probably don't know entirely what to make of, but we're all quite smart, no matter what our other differences may be. And my parents were readers, so there were a lot of books around the house. They were "readers *to.*" They read stories to children, so I got read to as a young child, and I quickly felt that there were certain things that I wanted to read, namely comic papers, that no one was willing to read to me, namely them. So I learned to read in order to read the funny papers. That's a disheartening story, no doubt.

Q. What is the strongest motivation for your writing?

A. At the moment? Getting it finished.

Q. Isn't there something that you draw from your own experience that you find recurrent in your writing?

A. Writing is not necessarily autobiographical. I know this is heresy in some quarters, but I look at it this way: Once upon a time it was the view—I'm sure this is obsolete by now—that women were so lacking in powers of invention, also so subjective and emotional and, indeed, hysterical, that they could do nothing but record their own experiences. So, criticism of women's writing leaned heavily on biographical interpretations. I just hate that kind of criticism.

You ask me what I draw from my own experience. Well, what is your "own experience"? To me your "own experience" is any experience that is real to you. It can be something you read in the newspapers. It can be a story one of your friends tells you. It doesn't necessarily have to have happened to *you.* I think a lot of people do have things happen to them that are not real to them at all. So it's what is *real* to you, not what has "happened" to you, that counts in writing, and what is real to you partly depends on how well you can write it—

whether you can make it real. Writing, to me, is not necessarily an outpouring of your soul or telling about your life, but making something real for the reader.

A writer's "real experience" includes the act of writing, just as for a piano player the "real experience" is all those hours of practicing you put in and how you feel about the piano, not necessarily who you're in love with or any of that stuff—rather, how you feel about the art you're practicing.

Q. When you finally decided that writing was going to be your vocation, what kind of schedule did you follow?

A. There's a difference between a vocation and a profession. A vocation is a calling—something you are called to. A profession is something that you practice. "Many are called, but few are chosen." In the States, I think, about 10 percent of the novel writers actually make a living out of their novel writing. The others have the vocation, but they can only partly have the profession, because they have to spend the rest of their time making money in order to keep themselves in their habit. They are word junkies. They've got to pay for their fix. I chose university teaching because there was a long summer vacation, and also because you could fake it. (Waitressing you can't fake; you've got to get the food on the table.)

At the time, 1956, there was no chance of anybody being able to have a profession of writing in Canada. Nobody did. Arthur Hailey, I think, was revving up at the time. He moved to the States. Somebody who wanted to have a profession had to go elsewhere. So, if I wanted to remain in Canada, I had to have another profession. However, now, since 1972, I have been a professional writer, by which I mean that I don't do anything else. Writing is my profession as well as my vocation. Before 1972, things were spotty. I would write prose in summer, during vacations, and I could only write poetry during winters, because I had a job or I had to pretend I was a graduate student, things like that. Now I work from about 10 to about 4:30 every day if I can. I also have a family. Having a child is about like having a job, in that it's quite demanding. It takes up certain blocks of your time, which you have to plan for.

Q. Do you feel that you approach the act of writing from a different position, being a woman—that the act of writing, the syntax, the language, everything is conditioned by your experience as a woman?

A. This is a very complicated question. First of all, I don't know what it is like to be a man, so I have no control group. Second, I once taught a course in which we tried to determine the answer to this question by analyzing the styles of various writers. We did have a control group—we had male writers. We chose ten of each, and we read them. What we concluded was that, although the subject matter was different, the approach to language, the approach to style, was usually determined by the period in which the person was writing. There was a period approach to style, and it was not influenced by the sex of the writer. That's what we felt. We, then, just to liven things up, did two other things. We wrote to ten women and ten male writers and asked them whether they felt that criticism of their work had been influenced by the fact that they were male or female. The answers we got back broke down fairly neatly. Eight of the women said yes, and nine of the men said no. The women who said yes wrote long letters on the subject. All of the men wrote very short replies— postcards, pretty much. We then, to see whether this was paranoia or realistic evaluation on the part of the women, assigned different organs of criticism, like a newspaper or magazine, to each student, and they went to the back files and picked out reviews of the men and women and tried to determine whether the women were correct. We found that yes, they were correct, but not to the extent that they said. In other words, the women writers felt that it was even worse than we found that it was. But this was a sort of hazy experimental method. I think that with a computer you could probably do it much better.

So, I would say that your approach to style probably has nothing to do with gender, but how people will perceive your style probably does. Social scientists have done experiments in college classes in this regard. They've taken a composition and put a woman's name on it and fed it to everyone in the class and said, "What do you think of that?" The student replied: "hazy and wishy-washy, lacking in energy, pastel"—echoing Sir Anthony Quiller-Couch's turn-of-the-century essay on masculine and feminine style. Then they put a man's name on the composition and sent it around to a different class, and the students said "super and well-voiced, good show, energetic," and gave it an A. The results of that experiment coincided with my own conclusions. I don't think that an artistic talent is sexually determined. I think that the subjects people choose often are, and choice of subject will tend to dictate a vocabulary, of course. But as for broad distinctions of male and female style—Barbara Tuchman writing about the 2nd World War is not going to be of a different species, stylistically, than a male historian writing about the same war.

Q. Certain writers have placed a great deal of importance on evolving a female relationship to the language—almost on an ideological level.

A. I am aware of that kind of thinking and those kinds of experiments, and if it makes people feel better to think that they're doing that, it's fine with me. However, I feel that if you are a writer you have a loyalty to your art that transcends your loyalty to any sexual or other ideology. What you believe ideologically is going to get into your writing whether you like it or not, if you truly believe it. But if you turn out a piece of crap that is ideologically worthy, you have to make a choice between publishing or not publishing it. God give us the grace to recognize when we are writing pieces of crap, because otherwise you are not a writer—you're a propagandist of some kind.

That's not to say that the ideas of your time are not important, or that you shouldn't have political beliefs—I think you should. However, if you happen to be a Republican and a writer, do you write a national anthem in praise of Ronald Reagan that is crummy? No, you do not. Do you write an ode to womanhood that happens to be not a very good ode? Let us hope that you do not.

Then I know what comes next: what about the standards by which such things are evaluated? I refer you to Annette Kolodny, who is a good friend of mine, who wrote an excellent article on that very subject. Yes, the standards have been biased. Yes, men do overlook women's writing, and on and on into the night. It's all true. However, if you are a writer, your loyalty is to your own art, primarily. Otherwise, you are not a writer. If you want to feel you are evolving a female style, that's dandy—I think that's just fine. I'd like to see the results. I'd like to see how they differ from experiments done in language by male writers. I'd like to see if one can run it through a computer and say this is a different thing from male writing. It's very hard when you are using the same language. If a different language were invented, then it would be very easy.

Q. But there are obviously ways in which style fuses with content. You were talking about content as being related to gender.

A.   It is only once in a while that style and content fuse, by the way. Ideally they do, but the rest of the time they don't.

Let me put it this way. I was against Arthur Quiller Couch's essay to begin with—the positing of a masculine and feminine style, the application of words like "pastel" to something called feminine style. I was equally against the application of words like "energetic" to something called masculine style—and I'm still against it, no matter in what guise it comes.

I think one of the highest virtues of a writer, male or female, is an imagination that can attempt to transcend. I said that I didn't know what it felt like to be a male writer; however, it is also true that I have written several stories and one novel in which one of the characters that we see from the inside is a man. And male writers have done that with women, with what success you may yourself judge. They are generally held to have done pretty well sometimes. I think I'm against water-tight compartments. I'm against ghettoization of anybody, including women and including men, and I'm against that kind of determinism that says because you are *this,* thou shalt be *so* —you know, because you have a womb, your style has to have a hole in the middle of it. I'm against it when men say it, and I'm against it when women say it, too.

I don't think writers should let themselves be dictated to by any group as to what it is proper for them to be writing about—or how it is proper for them to write. You know, no matter how worthy the cause, you cannot be told what to write.

Q.   On the subject of artistic control—can you talk about your experiences with publishing houses and with editing? Have you been forced by editors to make any changes?

A.   Publishing houses: my first novel was universally rejected by them all. They said it was too gloomy. This was 1963. The editor of the house considering it took me out to lunch. He was an ex-military man, a colonel, I do believe. He asked if I could change the ending, because everybody found it too gloomy. I said I could not. The ending, by the way, involved the heroine and hero on the roof and the heroine deciding whether or not to push the hero off, and in 1963 this was considered quite strange. So he asked if I would change it, and I said no—and he leaned across the table and patted my hand and said,

"Is there anything we can do?" Making the autobiographical assumption. So that's my first story.

My second story concerns my poetry. I submitted about a volume a year, all of which got rejected for about six or seven years. It was just as well they did—they weren't very good. Finally a volume was accepted by the only poetry publisher in the country. It had, however, three people on the editorial board, and only two of them had read my book when they accepted it. The third read it and rejected it. After that, my next book of poetry—*The Circle Game*—did get accepted. It did get published, and it was with a small press—not much else around in our day. My first novel got rejected completely. My second one got accepted and then the publisher lost the manuscript, which delayed publication for two years until feminism hit, causing everyone to say it was a feminist book—but I had in fact written it in 1965. All on my own, I might add.

Q.   Was this *The Edible Woman?*

A.   Yes. What else can I tell you? *Surfacing* went from Atlantic Monthly Press to Simon and Schuster because the people at Atlantic Monthly Press thought I should take out all the characters except one. It is true that Simon and Schuster is a larger publisher, but the other truth is that they liked the book. Let us not leave out such considerations.

Q.   For someone you like, how much revision would you do?

A.   I do a great deal of revision, but I do it before I give it to the publisher.

Q.   Based on going through it yourself—or friends, or editors?

A.   Mostly myself. I have a couple of people whom I think of as the general reader, by which I do not mean the general person, because the general person is someone who does not read books at all. The general reader is the person who likes to read but is not a writer or an editor or a poet or a teacher—just a general reader. I have one of them who is a lawyer, and another who is a social psychologist, and they are just book junkies. They like to read. So I give them the manuscript and say, "Did it keep you moving? How long did it take you to read it?" Then I have some other people who are somewhat more professional—they may be other writers. Then there's myself and my agent, and after that there's the publisher. In Canada the position of editor is much more lowly than it is in the States. It's usually just a copy-editor, and I have a good one who says things like, "You've got the traffic going the wrong way around the traffic circle"—which has always been a problem of mine. All they can give you is opinions and suggestions, and if you don't happen to agree with them—well, you're the writer.

Q. Do you always know how a book is going to end when you begin it?

A. No, I never do. I never know how a book is going to end when I begin it. If I knew how it was going to end, I probably would not continue on. You remember, I said I had written six and a half novels. The half was one I'd thought I'd be very clever with and have it all plotted out on filing cards before I started, and you know what that did to writing the book? First of all, it made it very long, but secondly, I already knew the plot, so it was like walking through, going through the motions. It was "writing down" rather than "writing."

Q. Reading—or re-reading—*Life Before Man,* one feels that you are constantly preparing for exactly the ending that is there. For example, the metaphor of evolution that you use throughout the book seems to establish an expectation of progressive development—for all the characters, and perhaps for their society. Is that how you planned it?

A. Evolution does not necessarily mean progress toward something better. Darwinists often assume that the end result of evolution is going to be good. Anybody who actually thinks about the origin of that metaphor will realize that it is not necessarily so. We all would like to have a little hope, a light at the end of the tunnel, and I think that's necessary for people to go on. But if you're asking me whether I meant to suggest that progress is necessary, that it is fated, that the human will will triumph, that the species will go on to greater and better things, my answer is no. I don't necessarily think that. If I thought that, I'd just sit back and relax. That's like believing that everybody is going to heaven. It means you don't have to do a whole lot about it now. I don't think that it is fated. The future is really an open field.

Q.   Were you using this notion of the open field of evolution as a structural device as you plotted *Life Before Man?* One of the things that is so striking about the novel is the absence of a normal, discernible plot line. Instead of a plot *line* (analogous, perhaps, to an evolutionary line presumed to lead to a goal of development), you seem to have an open plot field (analogous to the notion of the open field of the future, which you just mentioned).

A.   Actually, I wanted to have a structure in which the points of view were triangularly balanced. In other words, you could not be on the side of Nate without thinking that the women were doing him dirt and not understanding him. You could not be on the side of Elizabeth without thinking that the others were being grossly inconsiderate, to say the least. My aim was to present all those points of view with equal weight and fairness, so that in the end the reader cannot, except through personal preference alone, choose one over the other.

Q.   Why did you want to do that?

A.   Often one does things for silly reasons. I was very tired of people making autobiographical constructions about my novels, all of which until that time had been first-person-singular novels. And I just got really tired of answering those questions: Are you the person in *Surfacing*? Are your parents dead? Did your father drown? Have you ever been anorexic? Have you ever been crazy? All those autobiographical questions. I wanted to write a book in which one of the characters was male, so that the autobiographical construction absolutely could not be made, and a book in which the two female characters were very different from each other—and then let them figure it out from there. So that is the silly part of the motivation. The other part, which is not so silly, is partly like "Why did you climb Mt. Everest?" Well, because it was there. I wanted to do it because I hadn't done that before, which is always a good reason. I wanted to see if I *could*.

I also had not written any novels that were main-line realism before. The others all had some weird element. *Surfacing* had that freak-out scene, which structurally makes it a ghost story, and *Lady Oracle* had all kinds of fantasy in it. And *Edible Woman* had one of those transposed fantasies at the end. I wanted to write a book in which there were no elements of supernatural intervention or total grotesquerie. I wanted it to be a fairly ordinary, limited scenario—a fairly ordinary, limited space. In fact, the entire novel takes place within about three square miles of downtown Toronto. Nobody goes out and nobody comes in. They all stay right there. The only person that goes out is Chris, who is dead. Everybody else stays there, and even the dead ones go down rather than out anywhere else.

Q. At the end of *Life Before Man,* I can follow what has happened to Nate and Lesje, but I have some trouble evaluating Elizabeth.

A. Elizabeth is the easiest one. Let's go back to the first China scene. In the first China scene, she was in the bathtub, as I recall, hearing voices coming through the pipes, and she was trying to get a fix on this exhibit that was going to go on, and she was reading the catalog of these paintings and it was making absolutely no sense to her whatsoever; and it was all about "Confucius was mean to women," and it has nothing to say to her.

She's somebody who has been very involved in immediate family problems—her immediate family of the past, especially the relationship with Auntie Muriel, who has really determined her own behavior to a great extent. She absolutely hates, loves, and detests her Aunt— which gives her a lot of her energy. Her hatred drives her on. And her desire for control, her desire to have power because she was powerless as a child. (The good thing about her is that she doesn't do it to her own children. So the link is broken there.) The next thing that happens to her is that Nate gets out from under her. She's not going to have power over him anymore, although she tries to keep as much of a grip as possible. The next thing that happens is that Auntie Muriel dies. With Auntie Muriel gone, her motivation—the hatred that has been driving her on—is suddenly taken away from her. She does have that deathbed scene with Auntie Muriel in which she manages something that to her is a colossal gesture. Instead of grabbing the chance that she now has to tell the dying Auntie Muriel exactly what she thinks of her, she makes a gesture of compassion. Then Auntie Muriel dies.

Auntie Muriel gets buried, and Elizabeth is left without anything to push against. She has a great feeling of evaporation. That is when she faints. At that period, she can either give in to the suicidal feelings she has had all along or try to make a commitment to something outside herself. Auntie Muriel has really been part of her. That was a thing that she was locked into. She does two things. She reconnects with her children, who have felt her becoming really quite disconnected from them during the course of the book. She reconnects with them in the last scene. She's thinking about going home and getting them dinner. She is moved by the Chinese exhibit, which shows people working together—shows people in groups. She knows that it's propaganda, and that's why the next to the last line in the book is "China does not exist." The next line is "Nevertheless she longs to be there."

So what you get in her is a movement from a completely enclosed, solipsistic self which interprets and manipulates everything in terms of herself to two movements outwards. In fact, each of the characters makes a movement outwards. Lesje, by getting pregnant, even though it's for awful reasons. Nate, by getting involved in one of his mother's things, even though it is his mother's thing and even though it isn't very involved. Elizabeth, by reconnecting with her children and realizing that there is something outside herself—that there is a world out there but not everything is something that relates personally to her or something that she can control. There might instead be something that she can participate in without controlling.

Q.   What are you working on now?

A.   At this very moment, I am finishing a novel called *Bodily Harm,* as in "assault causing . . . ." In Canada, I've just published a volume of poems called *True Stories.*

Q.   Do you intend to continue the balance between writing novels and writing poetry that you seem recently to have had. First you started out writing more poetry and now it seems that you alternate between genres.

A.   Actually I started out writing both, but it took me longer to get the prose published. As I say, they rejected my first novel. I wrote the next immediately afterwards, and the publisher lost the manuscript. Looking at the pub dates, you might think that I was first a poet, but if you go back and look at when the things were actually written, you can see that I was writing poetry and fiction all at once.

Q.   This versatility comes up again in the variety of tones that you strike in your writing. It's so striking to read your novels and to see that although themes and motifs clearly run through them all, each one is extremely different from the others in tone. One thinks of the zany comedy of *Lady Oracle* and the dead seriousness of *Surfacing.*

A. I could not write one *Surfacing* after another—it would be too much of a strain on the brain. And I certainly could not write *Surfacing,* followed by a volume of poetry (which is not comic, usually), followed by another heavy book like that. So for me it's a question of pacing in my life as a writer.

A lot of people seem to think that a serious or lofty tone is better because it's more difficult to achieve, but this is not so. In fact, to write a comedy is often much more difficult than to write a piece that has doom and gloom in it.

Q. Why is that? Is it a question of wit?

A. No, it's a question of timing. I don't know whether you saw *La Cage au Folles.* Well, it was beautifully done. The reason it was beautifully done was that the timing was just impeccable. Now, we can go off and see a Sam Peckinpah movie and see somebody being beaten to death, and that would have an impact, whether it was well done or not, because the image is a shocking one. To make a beautiful, light, airy thing that works the way *La Cage au Folles* does is a much more difficult thing to do well. In fact, it took me three years to write *Lady Oracle* and only six months to write *Surfacing.* And it was a more difficult book to write because there were more people in it, more events, more ornaments, more intricacy. *Life Before Man* was an easy book to write. It only took me about eight months. That's not necessarily indicative of anything. The one I'm working on now is somewhat more difficult. I can't say if it's because it is comedy or tragedy, because it has some of both.

Somebody has put a finger on what they think I write. And it is not called comedy—in fact, I called *Edible Woman* an anti-comedy when I wrote it. I called *Surfacing* a ghost story. I called *Lady Oracle* an anti-gothic romance. *Life Before Man* I think of as my answer to *Middlemarch,* a more realistic fiction. The one I'm writing now is an anti-thriller.

Q. And when you say anti, you certainly don't mean it doesn't have any components of the genre.

A. No, I mean that it has the components and then pulls them inside out, as you would a glove. For example, a comedy would end in a marriage. Well, my anti-comedy, *Edible Woman,* does end with a marriage, but it's the wrong one. This is where you occasionally miss education in your readers. I don't know what people who haven't read *Wuthering Heights* make of *Lady Oracle.*

As for what form or genre I write in—someone said that what I really am writing is Menippean satire, and you may do with that what you will, because Menippean satire can include elements of just about any form.

People aren't sure what to do with my books. The ones who stood on their hands over *Surfacing* were absolutely floored by *Lady Oracle.* They weren't expecting me to write that, and they didn't know what to do with it. It was too frothy for them, and indeed what was I up to? There have been some quite good pieces on *Lady Oracle,* however—about heroine-ism versus feminism, and about the fact that the main character is a traditional heroine rather than a feminist. That's quite accurate.

Q. Perhaps that is precisely what astonished many readers. *Surfacing,* after all, has been a favorite book of feminist reading groups, since it was first published.

A. A little bit later than that, actually. At the time it came out, according to the publisher, the primary readership was male, because they thought it was going to be about woods and fishing. Women stayed away from it for the same reason. The publisher virtually advertised it as the woman's answer to *Deliverance,* not realizing what the implications of that indeed were. Only later did it acquire its feminist readership.

Q. The debates I remember among feminists tended not to be about the aesthetic qualities of the book.

A. No, they were about whether or not it endorsed abortion, that kind of thing. You cannot determine the predilections of your readers, nor can you anticipate them. You have to do what you are doing the best way that you can and then pretty much forget about it, because you can't influence it after that. If you make a clock, you can't determine who buys the clock, and if you work in a bakery, you can't determine who eats the cake.

I know that I am not writing to everybody. I assume an intelligent reader. I assume that my reader is going to be up to any little tricks I may pull. I assume that my reader has a sense of humor, which is not always the case. I assume all kinds of things about the reader that won't necessarily be true. Otherwise I would be writing down to people, and I have no interest in that. So I think that the reader takes his or her chance.

What you are obliged to is your art, and once you start betraying your notions of that in favor of anybody, some critic or somebody you assume is reading your work, you betray yourself as a writer. The readers really have to take care of themselves. And they do—it's obvious that they do.